CA Proficiency 1
Taxation 1 (RoI)
2021–2022

CHARTERED
ACCOUNTANTS
IRELAND

Published in 2021 by
Chartered Accountants Ireland
Chartered Accountants House
47–49 Pearse Street
Dublin 2

ISBN 978-1-913975-07-4

Typeset by Deanta Global Publishing Services
Printed and bound by CPI Group (UK) Ltd, Croydon, CR0 4YY

MIX
Paper from
responsible sources
FSC
www.fsc.org   FSC® C013604

Contents

PART TWO   CORPORATION TAX

PART THREE   CAPITAL GAINS TAX

PART FOUR   VALUE-ADDED TAX

Chartered Accountants Ireland's *Code of Ethics*

Chartered Accountants Ireland's *Code of Ethics* applies to all aspects of a Chartered Accountant's professional life, including dealing with income tax issues, corporation tax issues, capital gains tax issues, capital acquisitions tax issues and stamp duty issues. The *Code of Ethics* outlines the principles that should guide a Chartered Accountant, namely:

- Integrity
- Objectivity
- Professional Competence and Due Care
- Confidentiality
- Professional Behaviour

As a Chartered Accountant, you will have to ensure that your dealings with the tax aspects of your professional life are in compliance with these fundamental principles. Set out in **Appendix 3** is further information regarding these principles and their importance in guiding you on how to deal with issues which may arise throughout your professional life, including giving tax advice and preparing tax computations.

Overview of Tax System

1.1   Introduction

The main taxes levied in Ireland may be classified as **taxes on income**, **taxes on transactions** and **taxes on capital**.

The main taxes on **income** are income tax and corporation tax. The main taxes on **transactions** include value-added tax, customs and excise duties, stamp duty, capital gains tax and capital acquisitions tax. The main tax on **capital** is local property tax.

A further distinction is also made between **direct taxes, indirect taxes** and **social contributions**.

Direct taxes are typically taxes on earned income or wealth, e.g. income tax, corporation tax, capital gains tax, capital acquisitions tax and local property tax.

Indirect taxes are typically taxes or levies on transactions or production, e.g. VAT, stamp duty, customs and excise duties and carbon tax.

Social contributions are levies that are paid into social security funds or schemes.

1.2   Legislation

Income tax, corporation tax and capital gains tax law is based on legislation contained mainly in the **Taxes Consolidation Act 1997 (TCA 1997)** and the annual **Finance Acts**. Certain tax rules relating to the legislation are set out in regulations or Statutory Instruments that are issued by the Revenue Commissioners under powers conferred by the foregoing legislation.

Relevant tax case law and tax practice also play an important role in putting tax legislation into effect. Decisions from the **Court of Justice of the European Union (CJEU)** (also commonly referred to as the European Court of Justice (ECJ)) and **EU Directives** are also influential. Under EU state aid rules, EU consent is also required where tax measures support an industry sector or region.

1.3 The Revenue Commissioners, the Tax Appeals Commission and the Collector-General

Responsibility for the care and management of the Irish tax system rests with the Office of the Revenue Commissioners. This is a division within the Department of Finance and overall control rests with the Minister for Finance.

- The board of the **Revenue Commissioners** consists of three Commissioners, one of whom is chair, appointed by An Taoiseach.
- **Inspectors of Taxes** are appointed by the Revenue Commissioners and are deployed throughout the country in five separate divisions. The inspectors are responsible for the efficient operation of, and compliance with, the Irish tax system.
- The **Collector-General** is appointed by the Revenue Commissioners and is responsible for the efficient collection of taxes, including the pursuance of unpaid taxes.
- The Appeal Commissioners of the **Tax Appeals Commission** are appointed by the Minister for Finance and adjudicate between Revenue and taxpayers on matters of disagreement.

1.3.1 Revenue Divisions

As noted above, there are five main Revenue divisions:

- **Large Corporates Division (LCD)**, dealing with the largest companies and managed through sectoral branches.
- **High Wealth Individuals Division**, dealing with high-wealth individuals, pensions and tax avoidance issues.
- **Medium Enterprises Division**, dealing with a tier of large businesses and wealthy/high-income individuals that fall below the thresholds for the LCD and the High Wealth Individuals Division.
- **Business Division**, dealing with the majority of business taxpayers.
- **Personal Division**, dealing with all personal or non-trading taxpayers as well as not-for-profit organisations.

There are also a number of other divisions within Revenue as follows:

- Investigations and Prosecutions Division
- Revenue Legislation Services, comprising the Business Taxes Policy and Legislation Division, the Indirect Taxes Policy and Legislation Division, the International Tax Division, and the Personal Taxes Policy and Legislation Division
- Planning Division
- Corporate Services and Accountant General's Division
- Customs Division
- Revenue Solicitors Division
- Information, Communications Technology and Logistics Division
- Collector-General's Division.

1.3.2 Tax Appeals Commission

Where assessments to tax cannot be finalised due to a dispute between Revenue and the taxpayer, or where a taxpayer disagrees with a Revenue decision, an appeal can be made directly to the Tax Appeals Commission (TAC), which has the sole responsibility for accepting or refusing the appeal. Under the Finance (Tax

Appeals) Act 2015, all appeal hearings are held in public unless a party seeks a direction from the Commission that a hearing, or part thereof, is held *in camera*.

Decisions of the Appeal Commissioners are final and conclusive. However, an appeal to the High Court is possible in situations where either party considers that the Appeal Commissioners erred in its determinations on a **point of law** only.

1.4 Residence and Domicile

Residence and domicile are key criteria where liability to Irish income tax is concerned.

Residence is specifically defined depending on the number of days a person spends in Ireland in a particular year. A person who is not resident in a particular year can still be liable to income tax as an "ordinary resident", which relates to an individual's pattern of residence over a number of tax years.

Domicile is a legal term underlying the concept of the **permanent** home and is generally the country of nationality and where one resides permanently. A person can only ever have **one domicile** at any one time.

Put simply, persons who are:

- **resident and domiciled** in Ireland are liable to Irish income tax on their worldwide income;
- **resident in Ireland but not domiciled** are only liable to income tax on their Irish income and any worldwide income that is remitted into Ireland;
- **domiciled but not resident** in Ireland are not liable to income tax in Ireland, but may be subject to the Domicile Levy.

1.5 Tax Evasion, Tax Planning and Tax Avoidance

Tax **evasion** is the deliberate and illegal practice of not paying taxes by not reporting income/profits, claiming expenses not legally incurred or allowed, or by not paying taxes owed.

Tax **planning** is where a taxpayer organises their affairs in a tax-efficient manner so as to reduce their tax liability. For example, a taxpayer may decide to lodge money in an Ireland State Savings certificate or bond as operated by the National Treasury Management Agency (NTMA), rather than with a commercial bank, to avoid paying tax on the interest received. These schemes, and other tax incentive schemes such as the Employment and Investment Incentive scheme (EII), are legitimate tax planning options open to all investors.

Tax avoidance is often viewed as a grey area because it is regularly confused with tax planning. Tax avoidance is the use of loopholes within tax legislation to reduce the taxpayer's tax liability. Revenue defines tax avoidance as the claiming of tax reliefs and allowances in a manner not intended (by the Government when setting tax law) to be claimed in order to gain a tax advantage, or to re-label or re-characterise a transaction undertaken **primarily** to claim a tax advantage and not primarily for business reasons. Revenue takes a stringent approach to tackling such avoidance schemes, including:

- a **mandatory disclosure** regime that obliges promoters and users of "disclosable transactions" to notify Revenue of certain aspects of these transactions;
- the **General Anti-Avoidance Rule (GAAR)** set out in section 811C TCA 1997, which is intended to limit or defeat the effects of transactions that are entered into to reduce, avoid or defer a tax liability but which has little or no commercial reality; and
- specific anti-avoidance rules (SAARs) as set out in Schedule 33 TCA 1997.

Where a scheme falls foul of a section 811C GAAR or a Schedule 33 SAAR and is successfully challenged by Revenue, the taxpayer may be liable to interest and penalties or up to a 30% tax avoidance surcharge.

Appendix 4 discusses the issues of tax planning, tax avoidance and tax evasion in more detail.

1.6 The Government's Taxation Objectives

In designing the Irish taxation system, the government's main consideration is to raise money for public services, in an efficient and equitable manner, and to do this in a way that causes least harm to economic activity. Efficient refers to the amount of tax revenue raised by the government in relation to the cost, to taxpayers and the government, of collecting it. The tax system requires taxpayers to pay taxes to the government, which affect the behaviour of consumers and suppliers/producers. It also places an administrative burden on taxpayers. An efficient tax system imposes minimum negative effects on behaviour and a smaller administrative burden on taxpayers. An equitable tax system is one where the burden of taxation is greater on those who earn the greatest amounts.

The policies of the government in power will affect the tax system in place. Every year the government passes the Finance Act(s), amending relevant tax legislation to implement its policy initiatives.

The government levies taxes for three main reasons:

1. economic,
2. social, and
3. environmental.

1.6.1 Economic Reasons

The taxation system requires taxpayers to pay taxes to the government and the government, in turn, uses this money to run the country. For example, the money collected in taxes will be used to fund the public sector, education and health.

The government also uses taxation to encourage or discourage certain types of activity or behaviour. For example, tax-free savings accounts (i.e. National Solidarity Bonds and NTMA Savings Certificates and Bonds) and income tax relief for paying money into a pension scheme are provided to incentivise individuals to save.

To discourage unwanted or undesirable activities, taxes can be increased, e.g. increasing the duty on tobacco products and alcohol discourages their use and the use of the 'sugar tax' to encourage reduced consumption of sugary drinks.

1.6.2 Social Reasons

Taxation policies can have the impact of redistributing income and wealth from the rich to the poor in society. Different taxes have different social impacts. For example, direct taxes (e.g. income tax and capital gains tax) are taxes on earned income or wealth. The more income an individual has, the higher their tax liability.

Indirect taxes (e.g. VAT) tax the consumer and so have the same impact on everybody, regardless of their income. The government may, for example, decide to reduce the standard rate of VAT or to zero-rate certain goods to encourage individuals to spend on certain products or services.

1.6.3 Environmental Reasons

Taxation can also be used to further the government's environmental policies. For example, the government reduces the level of capital allowances available on cars with higher levels of CO_2 emissions; it offers a tax incentive in the form of accelerated capital allowances for businesses that invest in energy-efficient equipment; and it provides for an exemption from employee benefit-in-kind on the provision of an electric car. The carbon tax and the levy on plastic bags also form part of the environmental agenda.

Part One

Income Tax and Local Property Tax

2

Introduction to the Computation of Income Tax

Learning Objectives

After studying this chapter you will understand:

- how different types of taxpayer are identified;
- how different types of income are classified;
- the general terms and definitions used when computing income tax;
- the tax bands and rates for 2021;
- an overview of the taxation of married couples and civil partners;
- the difference between tax credits and tax reliefs; and
- the steps involved in calculating income tax.

Chartered Accountants Ireland's *Code of Ethics* applies to all aspects of a Chartered Accountant's professional life, including dealing with income tax issues. As outlined at the beginning of this book, further information regarding the principles in the *Code of Ethics* is set out in **Appendix 3**.

Students should also be aware of the issues around tax planning, tax avoidance and tax evasion, which are discussed in **Appendix 4**.

2.1 Introduction

Irish income tax is generally assessed on the **worldwide income of Irish resident** persons. Non-residents are, in general, liable only to the extent that they have income arising in Ireland. A non-resident company is liable to **income tax on Irish source income** if it is not trading in the State through a branch or an agency.

2.2 Classes of Taxpayer

Income tax is assessed on the following persons (the term "person" for tax purposes includes individuals, corporate bodies and trusts):

1. Individuals, be they single, widowed, married or a civil partner.
2. Individuals in partnerships.
3. Trusts.
4. Non-resident companies are liable to income tax on certain types of income.

Income tax is levied on income applicable to the above classes of taxpayer. It may be assessed by **direct self-assessment** (i.e. the profits of a sole trader) or by **deduction at source** from an individual's income (i.e. employees under the PAYE system).

2.3 Classification of Income

In order to compute or calculate the amount of income tax payable by an individual, a number of stages need to be followed. The first, and probably most important, stage is the classification of income according to its **source**, as defined by the Schedules in the Taxes Consolidation Act 1997 (TCA 1997). This stage is crucial because different rules apply to the taxation of the income, and the applicability of reliefs and deductions against it, depending on the income classification.

Under the schedule system as defined by sections 18–20 TCA 1997, the various sources of an individual's income are classified as follows:

Schedule D

- **Cases I & II** Trading income and income from vocations and professions.
- **Case III** Investment Income and Income from foreign employments and possessions, provided they have not suffered Irish standard rate income tax at source.
- **Case IV** Republic of Ireland deposit interest that has suffered deposit interest retention tax (DIRT).
  Income not taxed under Schedules E or F or under any other Case of Schedule D; and income received under deduction of Irish income tax at the 20% standard rate.
- **Case V** Rents and income from property in the Republic of Ireland.

Schedule E
Income derived from employments, directorships and pensions arising in Ireland.

Schedule F
Income derived from dividends and other distributions paid by Irish resident companies.

Once income is classified according to source, a separate computation of the taxable profits/income under each schedule is calculated.

2.4 General Terminology and Definitions

The following are some **general** terms and definitions that are used when discussing income tax.

Income tax year The tax year is a **calendar** year. For example, the 2021 tax year is the year from 1 January 2021 to 31 December 2021.

Year of assessment Income tax is charged for a **year** of assessment.

Basis of assessment Income is assessable to income tax on a **current year basis** (i.e. income earned in 2021 is assessable to tax in the 2021 tax year).

Self-assessment Individuals must file a return of income for each tax year not later than 31 October in the year following the income tax year.

Where returns are filed and taxes paid **electronically** through the Revenue Online Service (ROS), the deadline is extended by up to two weeks. For 2020 income tax returns, the extended date to 'pay and file' is **17 November 2021**. Since 1 January 2015, all newly registered or re-registered individuals for income tax must file their tax returns electronically.

Tax-adjusted profits   Net Schedule D, Case I and Case II profits as per the taxpayer's accounts, less any adjustments required for tax purposes.

Total income/Net statutory income   Total income from all sources as computed in accordance with the provisions of the TCA 1997 and reduced by charges on income, such as covenant payments, etc.

Taxable income   Total income less allowances, reliefs and deductions at the marginal rate.

Tax allowances   Allowances given by way of reduction of taxable income.

Tax credits   Reliefs given as a deduction from tax payable and not by way of a deduction from income.

Tax reliefs and deductions   Reliefs that vary on expenditure and given by way of a deduction from income.

Standard rate of tax   The lower rate of income tax, currently 20% for 2021.

Marginal/higher rate of tax   The higher rate of tax, currently 40% for 2021.

2.5   Income Tax Rates and Bands for 2021

Income tax is calculated by reference to ranges of taxable income (referred to as **tax bands**) with a corresponding rate of tax. The applicable tax bands are dependent on the taxpayer's status as a single person, a widowed/one-parent family, a married spouse or a civil partner.

Tax Rate	Tax Year 2021 Taxable Income			
	Single/ Widowed/Surviving Civil Partner	One-parent Family	Married Couple/Civil Partnership – One Income	Married Couple/Civil Partnership – Two Incomes
20%	€35,300	€39,300	€44,300	€70,600*
40%	Balance	Balance	Balance	Balance

*Transferable between spouses/civil partners up to a maximum of €44,300 for any one spouse/civil partner.

2.6   Tax Treatment of Married Couples and Civil Partners

2.6.1   Overview

A married couple means any couple, **same-sex or heterosexual**, who marry in accordance with the provisions of the Marriage Acts. Any references in the **Tax Acts** to a man, married man or husband can be construed as including a reference to a woman, married woman or wife.

The Civil Partnership and Certain Rights and Obligations of Cohabitants Act provided for a civil partnership registration scheme for **same-sex** couples and conferred a range of rights, obligations and protections **consequent on registration**. It also set out the manner in which civil partnerships may be dissolved and with what conditions. Additionally, it set out a redress scheme for long-term opposite sex and same-sex cohabiting couples who are not married or registered in a civil partnership.

Following the commencement of the Marriage Act 2015 on 16 November 2015, which legislated for same-sex marriage, a couple can no longer register a civil partnership. Couples in a civil partnership prior to this date can apply to marry or remain as they are. Once a couple marry, their civil partnership is automatically dissolved.

On the registration of a civil partnership, civil partners are treated **in the same way** as spouses under tax law. This does not give opposite-sex cohabiting couples or same-sex cohabiting couples the same tax treatment as married couples or civil partners. **Cohabiting couples are treated as single persons under tax law.**

2.6.2 Assessment to Tax of Married Couples and Civil Partners

Married couples and civil partners can be assessed for tax in three different ways, as follows:

- **Joint Assessment**, where all income is taxed as if it were the income of one of the spouses/civil partners, but with higher tax bands at the standard rate of tax.
- **Single Assessment**, where each spouse/civil partner is assessed to tax as if they were not married or in a civil partnership, with no transferability of unutilised credits or tax bands.
- **Separate Assessment**, where a married couple/civil partners, who are assessable on a joint assessment basis, can claim for separate assessment of their joint tax liability.

In **Chapter 9** we will look in detail at the tax treatment of married couples/civil partners under each type of assessment. At this stage it is enough to be aware that they can be assessed (taxed) differently.

2.7 Tax Credits and Tax Relief

Tax credits and reliefs are deductions given against an individual's tax liability, either as a **credit** against their income tax liability (tax credit) or as a **deduction** against taxable income.

Tax credits are given at the standard rate of tax – currently 20% – and are generally **non-refundable**, that is, the credits cannot reduce the tax due below zero, nor can they reduce any tax payable on charges on income (e.g. covenants). Tax reliefs given as deductions against taxable income are generally at the marginal rate (currently 40%). Taxes already paid on income, such as PAYE or dividend withholding tax (DWT), are given as **refundable** tax credits and can reduce the tax due to below zero, prompting a refund of tax paid.

2.7.1 Personal Tax Credits

Personal tax credits are credits to which an individual is entitled depending on their personal circumstances. The amount of the qualifying credit is the same for each individual and is given at the standard rate of 20%. In other words, every €1,000 of a personal tax allowance is equivalent to a **tax credit** of €200.

Personal tax credits include the single person's tax credit and the employee tax credit. A more detailed consideration of all the tax credits available in 2021 is given in **Chapter 8**.

2.7.2 Tax Reliefs

Tax reliefs differ from tax credits in that the amounts **vary** depending on the expenditure involved. Some reliefs, for example medical expenses relief, are granted at the standard rate of tax (20%) and are given as a **credit** against the income tax liability. Other reliefs, for example nursing home expenses, are given as a **deduction** against taxable income and are effectively available at the marginal rate (40%).

2.8 Pay Related Social Insurance and Universal Social Charge

Pay Related Social Insurance (PRSI) and Universal Social Charge (USC) are deductions collected by Revenue based on income levels and personal circumstances. Both PRSI and USC are calculated separately to income tax and no credits or allowances are available against PRSI and USC liabilities.

2.8.1 Pay Related Social Insurance

Employees and self-employed individuals who are aged between 16 and 66 pay PRSI contributions. These contributions are collected by the Collector-General and paid into the national Social Insurance Fund from which social insurance payments are paid. PRSI is also payable by the employers of those in "insurable employment", which is a term used to describe employment that is liable for social insurance contributions.

PRSI is payable on most sources of income (e.g. salaries, trading profits, dividends, etc.), but it is not charged on social welfare payments, such as illness or maternity benefits, etc. **Chapter 10** deals with PRSI contribution classes and rates in more detail.

2.8.2 Universal Social Charge

Universal Social Charge (USC) is an additional tax on income introduced in 2011. USC is payable if an individual's income is more than €13,000 (2021) per annum. It then becomes payable on **all** of the individual's income. It is payable by all ages, although some reduction in rates is available to those aged over 70 and/or in receipt of medical cards.

USC does not apply to social welfare payments and certain other income, for example, deposit interest subject to deposit interest retention tax (DIRT). **Chapter 10** deals with USC rates and thresholds in more detail.

2.9   Income Tax Computation

Income tax is calculated on taxable income, and the tax due is then reduced by personal tax credits and refundable tax credits, resulting in net tax due or net tax refundable.

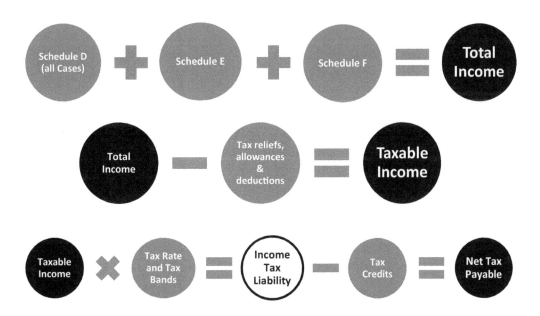

- **Gross income** is income from all sources (i.e. Schedules D, E and F) net of relevant deductions.
- **Total income** or **net statutory income** is gross income reduced by charges on income (e.g. covenant payments, qualifying interest, etc.).
- **Taxable income** is total income/net statutory income reduced by personal reliefs at the marginal rate.
- **Income tax liability** is the tax calculated on the taxable income (by reference to the marital status of the taxpayer); the tax so calculated is then reduced by non-refundable tax credits, i.e. personal tax credits such as single personal tax credit, employee tax credit, etc., and other credits allowed at the standard rate such as medical expenses.
- **Net tax payable** is the income tax liability reduced by refundable tax credits, i.e. tax already paid such as PAYE and DWT, and increased by income tax deducted from payments made (e.g. covenants).

2.9.1 Simple Income Tax Computation Layout

The computation of income tax is laid out as follows:

Income Tax Computation of _____ **for 2021**

	€	€
Taxable income		X
TAX PAYABLE: €35,300 @ 20% (single person)	X	
Balance @ 40%	X	
Gross income tax liability		X
Deduct: Non-refundable tax credits		(X)
Net tax payable		X

Example 2.1

John is single and his trading income for 2021 was €46,000. His tax credits were €3,300. Compute his income tax liability for 2021.

Income Tax Computation of John for 2021

	€	€
Taxable income		46,000
TAX PAYABLE: €35,300 @ 20%	7,060	
Balance (single person) €10,700 @ 40%	4,280	
Gross income tax liability		11,340
Deduct: Non-refundable tax credits		(3,300)
Net tax payable		8,040

Example 2.2
Martin and Mary are married and jointly assessed for 2021. Martin's trading income is €17,000 and Mary's employment income is €48,000. Their tax credits are €6,600. Compute their income tax liability for 2021.

Income Tax Computation of Martin and Mary for 2021

		Martin	Mary	Total
		€	€	€
Taxable income		17,000	48,000	65,000
TAX PAYABLE:	Mary – first €44,300 @ 20%		8,860	8,860
(married persons)	Martin – total €17,000 @ 20%	3,400		3,400
	Mary – balance €3,700 @ 40%		1,480	1,480
Gross income tax liability		3,400	10,340	13,740
Deduct: Non-refundable tax credits				(6,600)
Net tax payable				7,140

Questions

Review Questions
(See Suggested Solutions to Review Questions at the end of this textbook.)

Question 2.1

Pat's employment income for 2021 is €15,000 and he is married to Una, whose employment income is €47,000. They are jointly assessed and their non-refundable tax credits are €6,600.

Requirement
Compute their income tax liability for 2021.

Question 2.2

Paul and Jason are civil partners and jointly assessed for 2021. Paul's trading income is €47,000 and Jason's trading income is €41,000. Their non-refundable tax credits are €6,600.

Requirement
Compute their income tax liability for 2021.

Question 2.3

Seán earned €82,000 in 2021 and is married to Norah, who is a home carer with no income. Their non-refundable tax credits are €6,550.

Requirement
Compute their income tax liability for 2021.

Schedule D, Cases I & II – Trading Income

3.1 Introduction

Income tax is charged on profits or gains arising from any **trade** (Case I) or from any **profession** or **vocation** (Case II). The tax treatment and computational rules for Cases I and II are practically identical and are therefore considered together.

Persons chargeable to tax under Case I would include shopkeepers, manufacturers, farmers, etc., while the charge to tax under Case II would extend to self-employed individuals carrying on professions or vocations (whether as single individuals or in partnership), such as doctors, solicitors, architects, accountants, dramatists, and jockeys.

3.1.1 Definitions of "Profession", "Trade" and "Vocation"

Profession

The term "profession" is not defined in TCA 1997 and accordingly one must therefore look at decided tax cases to help clarify the term. The following considerations are relevant in determining whether or not a profession exists.

1. Is the taxpayer a member of a professional body?
2. Does the professional body:

(a) limit admittance to membership to persons who have successfully completed examinations and/ or undergone a period of specified training?

(b) prescribe a code of ethics, breach of which may incur disciplinary measures against the member?

3. Does the occupation require mainly intellectual skill?

4. Is the relationship with clients in the nature of contracts **for** services, rather than contracts **of** service (e.g. employments)?

Examples of individuals regarded as carrying on a profession would include teachers, doctors, opticians, actors and journalists.

Vocation

In decided tax cases, the word "vocation" has been compared with a "calling". Decided tax cases have held that bookmakers, dramatists and jockeys are vocations.

Trade

Section 3 TCA 1997 defines "trade" as including "every trade, manufacture, adventure or concern in the nature of trade". The question of whether or not a trade is carried on is a **question of fact** rather than a point of law. The courts have held this definition to include profits or gains arising from trading in the normal sense of the word but also from **isolated** transactions and activities. Profits from farming and from dealing in development land are assessable under Case I.

3.1.2 "Badges of Trade"

Guidance as to what constitutes "trading" is available from case law and from a set of rules drawn up in 1955 by the **UK Royal Commission on the Taxation of Profits and Income**. These rules, known as the **"Badges of Trade"**, have been approved by the Irish courts. The six "Badges of Trade" listed by the Commission are as follows.

1. **The Subject Matter of the Realisation**

   The general rule here is that property that does not give its owner an income or personal enjoyment merely by virtue of its ownership, is more likely to have been acquired with the object of a trading transaction than property that does, e.g. the principal private residence of an individual is more likely to have been bought for the purposes of his and his family's personal enjoyment rather than for the purposes of a trading transaction.

2. **Length of the Period of Ownership**

   As a general rule, property acquired for a trading or dealing purpose is realised within a short time after acquisition. However, there may be many exceptions to this rule.

3. **Frequency or Number of Similar Transactions by the Same Person**

   If the individual completed a number of transactions involving the same sort of property in succession over a period of years, or there have been several such realisations at about the same date, a presumption arises that there has been a dealing in respect of each, i.e. that they were trading transactions.

4. **Supplementary Work on or in Connection with the Property Realised**

   If the property is improved or developed in any way during the ownership so as to bring it into a more marketable condition, or if any special marketing efforts are made to find or attract purchasers, such as the opening of a sales office or a large-scale advertising campaign, then this would provide some evidence of trading. Where there is an organised effort to obtain profit, there is likely to be a source of taxable income. However, if nothing at all is done, the suggestion would tend to go the other way.

5. **The Circumstances Giving Rise to the Realisation of the Property**

There may be some explanation, such as a sudden emergency or opportunity calling for the realisation of cash, which may eliminate the suggestion that any plan of dealing prompted the original purchase, i.e. in the case of "an unsolicited offer that cannot be refused".

6. **Motive for the Transaction**

Motive is extremely important in all cases. There are cases in which the purpose of the transaction is clearly discernible. Circumstances surrounding the particular transaction may indicate the motive of the seller and this may, in fact, overrule the seller's own evidence.

It is important to appreciate, however, that the 'whole picture' must be taken into account, so that the weight given to the various factors may vary according to the circumstances. Furthermore, it is important to recognise that any given factor may be present to a greater or lesser degree, and that the absence (or presence) of any single factor is unlikely to be conclusive in its own right.

There are a number of significant tax cases that consider this matter.

- The **profit motive** was considered in the UK case of *Erichsen v. Last* (1881) when the judge defined trading as "where a person habitually does and contracts to do a thing capable of producing a profit, and for the purpose of producing a profit, he carries on a trade or business". The motive to earn a profit rather than the existence of profit is the key criterion.
- The matter of supplementary work was considered in the UK case of *Martin v. Lowry* (1927) where the judges referred to the "mantle of trading" which the merchant donned as a result of the elaborate selling organisation he employed to sell his aeroplane linen to the public.
- Lord Sands in the UK case of *Rutledge v. CIR* (1929) considered the subject matter of the realisation, which in this case was a consignment of toilet paper that he considered must be bought for resale and so be "an adventure in the nature of the trade" under the terms of the relevant legislation.
- The case of *Jenkinson (HMIT) v. Freedland* (1961) brought a note of sobriety to the badges as the judge reminded us, "the facts of each case must be considered not merely the motive of acquisition, and conclusion arrived at" but that "the true position is that all facts in each case must be considered".

3.2 Basis of Assessment

The income assessable under Cases I and II is normally based on **the accounting period of 12 months ending during the year of assessment**, e.g. profits earned by a trader for the year end 30 June 2021 are assessed in the tax year 2021. There are, however, special provisions when a trade or profession **commences** or **ceases** business, or changes its accounting date.

3.2.1 Commencement Years

The date on which a trade commences is a question of fact. The *Birmingham & District Cattle By-Products v. Inland Revenue* (1919) case established some tests that are still used to determine when a trade actually commences. These are summarised in the table below.

Activity	Trading commenced?
1. The date when premises are acquired	NO
2. The date when staff are hired	NO
3. The date when supplier contracts are signed	NO
4. The date when raw materials/stock are received	YES

First Year

The basis of assessment for the first tax year is the **profit from the date of commencement to the end of the tax year**. If the accounts of the individual do not coincide with this period, then the assessable profit is arrived at by **time apportionment**.

The first year of assessment is always the tax year during which the trade or profession commenced.

Example 3.1

Mr Jones commenced to trade as a builder on 1 July 2020 and prepared accounts for 18 months to 31 December 2021.

In this case, Mr Jones will be assessed under Case I as a builder for the first year of assessment, i.e. 2020, on the basis of the profits from 1 July 2020 to 31 December 2020. These will be arrived at by time-apportioning the 18 months results to 31 December 2021, i.e. the amount assessed for 2020 will be 6/18ths of the total profits for the period.

Second Year

1. If there is a 12-month accounting period ending in the second tax year and it is the only accounting period ending in that year, assess the taxable profits of that 12-month accounting period.

Example 3.2

Donna commences to trade on 1 June 2020. Accounts are prepared annually to 31 May. Taxable profits for year ended 31 May 2021 = €24,000.

Tax Year		Period	Calculation	Taxable Profit
2020	(1st year)	01/06/2020–31/12/2020	€24,000 × 7/12ths	€14,000
2021	(2nd year)	01/06/2020–31/05/2021	€24,000 × 12/12ths	€24,000

---

2. If there is an accounting period **other than one of 12 months** ending in the second tax year and it is the only accounting period ending in that tax year and the trade had commenced not less than 12 months before that date, assess the taxable profits of the year ending on that date.

Example 3.3

Lisa commences to trade on 1 May 2020. Accounts are prepared for the 17 months ending 30 September 2021. Taxable profits for the 17 months ending 30 September 2021 = €68,000.

Accounts are prepared yearly to 30 September thereafter.

Tax Year		Period	Calculation	Taxable Profit
2020	(1st year)	01/05/2020–31/12/2020	€68,000 × 8/17ths	€32,000
2021	(2nd year)	01/10/2020–30/09/2021	€68,000 × 12/17ths	€48,000

---

3. If there are **two or more accounting periods** ending in the second tax year, and the trade commenced not less than 12 months before the later date, assess the taxable profits of the year ending on the **later** date. (You may add two or more accounting periods to make up the 12 months.)

Example 3.4
Rose commences to trade on 1 July 2020. Accounts are prepared for the 10 months ending 30 April 2021.
Taxable profits for the 10 months ending 30 April 2021 = €10,000.

Accounts are prepared for the 8 months ending 31 December 2021.
Taxable profits for 8 months ending 31 December 2021 = €6,000.

Tax Year		Period	Calculation	Taxable Profit
2020	(1st year)	01/07/2020–31/12/2020	€10,000 × 6/10ths	€6,000
2021	(2nd year)	01/01/2021–31/12/2021	€10,000 × 4/10ths +	
			€6,000 × 8/8ths	€10,000

---

4.   In any other case, assess the actual profits for the tax year, i.e. 1 January to 31 December.

Example 3.5
David commences to trade on 1 November 2020. Accounts are prepared for the 8 months ending 30 June 2021.
Taxable profits for 8 months ending 30 June 2021 = €32,000.

Accounts are prepared for the year ending 30 June 2022.
Taxable profits for year ending 30 June 2022 = €46,000.

While there is an accounting period ending in the second tax year, 2021, David did not commence to trade
at least 12 months before this date. Accordingly, for the second tax year, David is taxed on the actual profits
arising in that tax year.

Tax Year		Period	Calculation	Taxable Profit
2020	(1st year)	01/11/2020–31/12/2020	€32,000 × 2/8ths	€8,000
2021	(2nd year)	01/01/2021–31/12/2021	€32,000 x 6/8ths +	
			€46,000 × 6/12ths	€47,000

Third Year
The basis of assessment for the third year of assessment is **the accounting period of 12 months ending
during the tax year**, i.e. if 2021 was the third year of assessment for a sole trader and a set of accounts
were prepared for the 12 months to 30 September 2021, then these accounts would form the basis for tax
year 2021 (subject to the option discussed below).

Option
If the actual profits of the **second** tax year (i.e. profits for the year 1 January to 31 December) are less than
the profits assessed under the rules outlined above, then the difference can be deducted from the taxable
profits of the third year.

Example 3.6
Date of commencement 1 July 2019.

	Profit
Accounts for 12 months to 30 June 2020	€52,000
Accounts for 12 months to 30 June 2021	€48,000
Accounts for 12 months to 30 June 2022	€30,000
Computation:	
First Year of Assessment 2019	
Profit period 01/07/2019 to 31/12/2019, i.e. €52,000 × 6/12ths	€26,000
	continued overleaf

Second Year of Assessment 2020		
12-month accounting period ending 30 June 2020		€52,000
Third Year of Assessment 2021		
12-month accounting period (basis period) ending 30 June 2021		€48,000
Assessable profits:		
Amount assessed in second year (2020)	€52,000	
Less: actual profits for the second year (€52,000 × 6/12ths) + (€48,000 × 6/12ths)	€50,000	
Excess		(€2,000)
Final assessment 2020: €48,000 – €2,000		€46,000

Fourth and Subsequent Years

The basis period for any particular year of assessment will normally be the accounting period of 12 months ending during the tax year. The taxpayer has no options for these years.

3.2.2 Cessation Years

The date on which a trade ceases is when all its trading stock has been sold or when it ceases to manufacture (although it continues to purchase products to resell). This is demonstrated by the case of *Gordon and Blair Ltd v. Inland Revenue* (1962), where a brewery was held to have ceased the trade of manufacturing beer and commenced the trade of selling beer.

Final Year

The final year of assessment is based on the profits from the beginning of the tax year to the date of cessation, i.e. if the taxpayer ceases on 31 August 2021, the last year of assessment will be 2021, so the 2021 assessment will be based on the actual profits from 1 January 2021 to 31 August 2021. Accounting period profits are time-apportioned where necessary.

Penultimate (second last) Year

The profits assessable for this year are those of an accounting period of 12 months ending during the year of assessment. However, the assessment for the penultimate year must be revised to the actual amount of profits (i.e. profits for the year 1 January to 31 December) for that year if this yields a higher figure.

Where an assessment has to be revised and an additional tax liability arises, the obligation is on the taxpayer to include it in the self-assessed tax return in the year in which the cessation occurred.

Example 3.7

J. Jones, who traded as a butcher for many years, retired on 30 June 2021. The results for the last few years of trading were as follows:

Year ended 30/09/2019	Profit	€36,000
Year ended 30/09/2020	Profit	€48,000
9 months to 30/06/2021	Profit	€45,000

Computation:

Final Tax Year 2021

Basis of assessment: 01/01/2021–30/06/2021

€45,000 × 6/9ths	€30,000

continued overleaf

Penultimate Year 2020

Original assessment based on profits year ended 30/09/2020 — €48,000

Revise to Actual if Actual Profits > €48,000:

Actual profits 2020 (01/01/2020–31/12/2020):

€48,000 × 9/12ths + €45,000 × 3/9ths — €51,000

3.2.3 Change in Accounting Date

Where there is a change to the accounting date of an **ongoing** trade or profession in a particular tax year, the basis of assessment for that tax year is a **12-month period** ending on the **new accounting date**. If there are more than one set of accounts ending in a particular tax year, the basis of assessment for that tax year is a 12-month period ending on the **later** of the accounting dates.

Revision of Previous Year

Where there is a change to the accounting date, the assessment for the previous tax year must be reviewed and if the profits of a corresponding period ending in the previous tax year are higher, the profits assessed for the previous tax year are revised upwards.

Example 3.8

Julie Birch has been trading for a number of years to a year-end of 31 May. In 2021 Julie changed her accounting year-end to correspond with the financial year, i.e. 31 December. Her results are as follows:

	Profit
Accounts for 12 months to 31 May 2020	€22,000
Accounts for 12 months to 31 May 2021	€38,000
Accounts for 7 months to 31 December 2021	€30,000

Computation:	**Final Assessment**
Year of Assessment 2021	
Profit period 01/01/2021–31/12/2021,	
i.e. €38,000 × 5/12ths + €30,000 × 7/7ths	€45,833
Previous Year of Assessment 2020	
12-month accounting period ending 31/05/2020	€22,000
Revise to new accounting period 01/01/2020–31/12/2020:	
i.e. €22,000 × 5/12ths + €38,000 × 7/12ths	€31,333
Additional assessment 2020	€9,333

Note that the tax due on the revised 2020 assessment must be paid on or before the due date for the 2021 assessment, i.e. 31 October 2022.

3.2.4 Short-lived Businesses

Where a trade or profession is set up and discontinued within three tax years and the profits on which the individual is assessed for the three tax years exceed the actual profits arising in the same period, the individual may elect to have the profits of the second last year of trading reduced to the actual profits arising. By electing to reduce taxable profits for the second last year to actual, the individual is taxable on actual profits for all three years. An election for this treatment must be made before the specified return date for the year of cessation.

Example 3.9

M. Ryan commenced trading on 1 July 2019 and ceased trading on 31 March 2021. The Case I profits for these years were as follows:

Year ended 30 June 2020	€65,000
9 months ended 31 March 2021	€30,000

Computation:

First Year of Assessment 2019

Profit period 01/07/2019–31/12/2019

i.e. €65,000 × 6/12ths	<u>€32,500</u>

Second Year of Assessment 2020

12-month accounting period ending 30/06/2020	€65,000

Last Year 2021

Actual 01/01/2021–31/03/2021

€30,000 × 3/9ths	€10,000

Second Year Excess:

Amount assessed in second year (2020)	€65,000	
Less: actual profits for 2020		
(€65,000 × 6/12ths) + (€30,000 × 6/9ths)	<u>€52,500</u>	
Excess		<u>(€12,500)</u>
Final assessment 2021: €10,000 – €12,500		<u>€NIL</u>

In the absence of any relief in this case, the individual would be taxed on profits of €107,500 for the three tax years, whereas actual profits arising in the three years were only €95,000. If the individual elects to be taxed on actual profits arising in the second year, i.e. 2019, he would be assessed as follows:

2019: Actual as above	€32,500
2020: Elect for actual: €65,000 × 6/12ths + €30,000 × 6/9ths	€52,500
2021: Actual (with no second year excess as second year taxed on actual) €30,000 × 3/9ths	<u>€10,000</u>
Profits assessed for three years	<u>€95,000</u>

3.2.5 Post-cessation Receipts

Income received after a trade has ceased (e.g. bad debts recovered) is assessed under Schedule D Case IV (net of any post-cessation expenses). Unused capital allowances from the ceased trade may be offset against the income. The Case I/II cessation assessments are not adjusted.

3.2.6 Revenue Concession in Death Cases

A trade or a profession is treated as being **permanently discontinued** on the death of the person carrying on the trade, even if their personal representative or successors continue the trade after their death. Accordingly, the death of a person will normally trigger the **Case I and II cessation provisions** as outlined above. However, Revenue will, by concession, allow a trade to be treated as a **continuing** one where the trade is continued on by the **deceased's spouse or civil partner**. In such a case, provided the deceased's spouse or civil partner elects for such treatment, the cessation provisions are not applied to the deceased and the commencement provisions are not applied to the deceased's spouse or civil partner. If the election is made for the year in which the trader dies, Case I profits for the year of death are apportioned between them on a time basis.

Before making the election outlined above, the liabilities of the deceased and the surviving spouse or civil partner should be calculated on the basis that the trade is a continuing one and also on the basis of the cessation and commencement provisions being applied to see which basis will result in the lower tax liability.

3.3 Computation of Taxable Income

3.3.1 Overview

A taxpayer carrying on a trade or profession will prepare accounts based on commercial and accounting principles to arrive at their net profit for a particular year. However, the net profit per the accounts **is not the taxable profit**, as TCA 1997 has its own set of rules for determining the taxable profit of a person carrying on a trade or profession. Accordingly, the net profit per an individual's accounts will inevitably need **adjustment** to arrive at "**tax-adjusted**" profits for income tax purposes.

3.3.2 Allowable and Disallowable Items

There are two fundamental principles in deciding whether an item is properly included in a profit and loss account when calculating a Case I or Case II adjusted profit or loss:

1. The distinction between capital and revenue. If an item is of a **capital** nature, it must be **disallowed** in computing profits for income tax purposes.
2. Even if an item is of a **revenue** nature, it **may still** be specifically disallowed by statute as a deduction in computing trading profits.

3.3.3 Capital Receipts versus Revenue Receipts

Capital receipts and capital expenditure (including profits and losses) are **not assessable** under income tax as they are usually assessable under **capital gains tax**.

When deciding for tax purposes whether a receipt is capital or revenue, the following general rules apply:

- a **capital receipt** is the proceeds from the sale of fixed assets, i.e. assets that form part of the permanent structure of a business, and so not liable to income tax;
- a **revenue receipt** is the proceeds from the sale of circulating assets, i.e. assets acquired in the ordinary course of a trade and sold.

There are five basic principles:

1. Payments for the sale of the **assets** of a business are *prima facie* **capital** receipts.
2. Payments received for the destruction of the recipient's **profit-making apparatus** are receipts of a **capital** nature.
3. Payments in lieu of **trading receipts** are of a **revenue** nature.
4. Payments made in return for the imposition of substantial restrictions on the **activities** of a trader are of a **capital** nature.
5. Payments of a **recurrent** nature are **more likely** to be treated as **revenue** receipts.

Income/Gains Not Taxable Under Cases I and II
The following income is not taxable under Cases I and II, Schedule D:

- **Profits on sale of fixed assets** Profits or gains on the disposal of fixed assets or investments are **exempt** from income tax.
- **Grants** Employment grants paid by the IDA, Enterprise Ireland or SOLAS are exempt from income tax. Capital grants on fixed assets (e.g. IDA grants) are also exempt from income tax.
- **Investment income** Includes:
  - Irish dividends – taxable under Schedule F (see **Chapter 6**).
  - UK dividends – taxable under Case III, Schedule D (see **Chapter 6**).
  - Deposit interest received – taxable under Case IV, Schedule D (see **Chapter 6**).
- **Interest on tax overpaid** Interest received on tax overpaid is exempt from income tax (see **Chapter 12, Section 12.7**).
- **Rental income** Rental income is taxable under Case V, Schedule D (see **Chapter 7**).

3.3.4 Capital Expenditure versus Revenue Expenditure

Capital expenditure is **not** a deductible expense when calculating net trading profits for income tax. Where capital expenditure or capital losses (e.g. loss on sale of fixed assets) have been deducted in computing accounts profits, they will be **disallowed** when computing profits for tax purposes. However, certain allowances for wasting capital assets may be deducted after tax-adjusted Case I profits have been ascertained, i.e. **capital allowances**.

Note the judicial statement of Lord Cave in the case of *British Insulated and Helsby Cables v. Atherton* (1926), which is frequently used by the courts to assist them in resolving the problem of whether expenditure is of a revenue nature, and therefore allowable, or of a capital nature, and therefore disallowed:

> "When an expenditure is made, not only once and for all, but with a view to bringing into existence an asset or an advantage **for the enduring benefit of a trade** ... there is very good reason (in the absence of special circumstances leading to an opposite conclusion) for treating such an expenditure as properly attributed not to revenue but to capital."

3.3.5 Allowable and Disallowable Case I and Case II Deductions

Disallowable Deductions

The main statutory provision disallowing expenditure is section 81 TCA 1997, which contains specific provisions disallowing various types of expenditure, the most important of which are:

- Expenditure not **wholly and exclusively** laid out for the purposes of the trade. (This is the general deductibility test applied for Case I and Case II purposes.)
- Maintenance of the parties and their families, and private or domestic expenditure.
- Rent of any dwelling house **not used** for the trade.
- Any sum expended **over and above** repairs to the premises, implements, utensils or articles employed for the purposes of the trade or profession.
- Any loss not connected with the trade or profession.
- Any capital withdrawn from, or employed as, capital in the trade or profession; or any capital employed in improvements to premises occupied by the trade or profession.
- Debts, other than bad debts, or a **specific** estimation of doubtful debts.
- Any annuity or other annual payment (other than interest) payable out of the profits or gains.
- Any royalty or other sum paid in respect of the use of a patent.

- Any consideration given for goods or services, or to an employee or director of a company that consists, directly or indirectly, of shares in the company or a connected company, or a right to receive such shares.
- Any sum paid or payable under any agreement with a connected person, resident outside of the State, as compensation for an adjustment to the profits of the connected person. Transfer pricing adjustments can only be obtained under double taxation agreements or through EU Convention mechanisms.

Expenses Commonly Disallowed
The following expenses are disallowed:

1. **Expenses or losses of a capital nature:**
   - Depreciation
   - Loss on sale of fixed assets
   - Improvements to premises
   - Purchase of fixed assets.

   Note that capital allowances may be claimed on certain assets (see **Chapter 4**).

2. **Applications or allocations of profit:**
   - Income tax
   - Transfers to a general reserve
   - Drawings.

3. **Payments from which tax is deducted:**
   - Royalties.

4. **Expenses not wholly and exclusively laid out for the purposes of the business:**
   - Private element of certain expenses
   - Rental expenses (but are allowable against Case V rents)
   - Charitable and political donations and subscriptions
   - Life assurance premiums on the life of the taxpayer or their spouse
   - Fines and penalties.

In regard to general provisions, provisions made **in accordance with FRS 102** *The Financial Reporting Standard applicable in the UK and Republic of Ireland* and **IAS 37** *Provisions, Contingent Liabilities and Contingent Assets*, **are allowed** for tax purposes **but only if** the following conditions are satisfied:
- the trader has a present obligation to incur the expenditure as a result of a past action;
- the amount of the provision required can be determined with a reasonable degree of accuracy; **and**
- the expenditure in respect of which the provision is made would be an allowable deduction in arriving at profits, e.g. a provision for capital expenditure would not be allowable.

Treatment of Certain Specific Items

(a) Interest Interest on money borrowed is deductible if it is trade-related. This is the case even if the money is borrowed to buy capital assets, providing they are for the purposes of the trade.

(b) Bad debts:
- Bad debts written off – are **allowable** against taxable profits
- Bad debts recovered – are **taxable**, i.e. subject to income tax

▨ Increase in a **specific** provision for bad debts – **allowable**
▨ Decrease in a **specific** provision for bad debts – **taxable**
▨ Increase in a **general** provision for bad debts – **not allowable**
▨ Decrease in a **general** provision for bad debts – **not taxable**.

(c) **Premiums on short leases** If the taxpayer carries on a trade or profession in a premises leased for a period of less than 50 years, a proportion of any premium paid on the lease is allowable in computing the profits of a trade or profession.

The amount allowable on the premium paid is calculated by

$$\text{Premium} \times \frac{51 - \text{Duration of the lease}}{50}$$

spread over the life of the lease.

Example 3.10
On 1 June 2021, James agrees to rent a premises from Mr White for 25 years, at a rent of €2,000 per month, subject to a premium of €20,000.

Allowable premium:

$$€20,000 \times \frac{51 - 25}{50} = €10,400$$

2021:

Allowable premium (€10,400 × 1/25th × 7/12ths)	€243
Rent paid (€2,000 × 7)	€14,000

2022:

Allowable premium (€10,400 × 1/25th)	€416
Rent paid (€2,000 × 12)	€24,000

(d) **Entertainment expenses** General entertainment expenses incurred are **completely disallowed**. Expenditure on **staff** entertainment is allowable, provided its provision is not incidental to the provision of entertainment to third parties.

(e) **Legal expenses** With regard to legal expenses:
▨ Debt recovery – allowable
▨ Acquisition of assets – not allowable
▨ Renewal of short lease – allowable
▨ Product liability claims and employee actions – allowable.

(f) **Repairs** Replacement/redecoration repairs not involving material improvements are allowable. Expenditure on improvements/extensions, new assets, etc. is not allowable.

As a general rule, expenditure incurred on **repairs** to buildings is deductible as a normal Case I or Case II expense. The concept of repair is that it **brings an item back to its original condition**. In this connection, the following particular points are critical:
(i) The expenditure must have **actually** been incurred. For instance, provisions for work to be done in the future are not allowable, as clearly the expenditure has not been incurred (unless the conditions outlined in relation to general provisions at (5) above are satisfied).

(ii) The term "repairs" does **not include** improvements and alterations to premises. In this connection, it is not possible to claim a revenue deduction for the portion of the improvements or alterations which would represent the cost of repairs that could otherwise have been carried out.

(iii) The replacement of a capital asset or the "entirety" will not be treated as a repair. This would cover, for instance, the reconstruction of a trader's premises.

The test to be applied is really whether or not the repair entails the **renewal** of a **component part** of the entirety. If it does, it will be regarded as a repair. On the other hand, if it is regarded as the **renewal of an entirety**, it will be treated as a capital expenditure.

A separate identifiable portion of a building or structure may be regarded as an **entirety** in its own right and, accordingly, its replacement would be disallowed. A practical test is whether or not they are of **sufficient size and importance** to be regarded as an entirety. Examples of entireties from case law include the following:

- a large chimney situated apart from other factory buildings;
- a ring in an auction mart;
- a stand in a football ground;
- a barrier which protects a factory against the overflow from an adjoining canal.

It appears that it is necessary to show that the item that has been replaced is **ancillary** to the complete building. In practice, the accounting treatment adopted and the total cost involved may be important factors.

In *Odeon Associated Theatres Limited v. Jones* (1971) it was held that the expenditure on **repairs to a newly acquired asset** may be deductible provided at least that:

- the cost is properly charged to a revenue account in accordance with the correct principles of commercial accountancy; **and**
- the repairs are not improvements; **and**
- the expenditure is not incurred to make the asset **commercially viable** on its acquisition; **and**
- the purchase price was not **substantially** less than it would have been if it had been in a proper state of repair at the time of purchase.

(g) Leased motor vehicles In the case of a leased vehicle, where the list price exceeds the limit prescribed, a proportion of the lease hire charges are disallowed by reference to the CO_2 emissions of the cars. The CO_2 categorisations and allowances are as follows:

Vehicle Category	CO_2 Emissions (CO_2 g/km)	Leasing Charges Restriction
A/B/C	0g/km up to and including 155g/km	Lease hire charge $\times \dfrac{\text{(List price} - \text{Relevant limit)}}{\text{List price}}$
D/E	156g/km up to and including 190g/km	Lease hire charge $\times \dfrac{\text{(List price} - \text{(Relevant limit} \times 50\%))}{\text{List price}}$
F/G	191g/km and upwards	Lease hire charge disallowed

The relevant limit is €24,000 for the period 2007–2021.

Example 3.11

Joe, who is self-employed and prepares annual accounts to 30 September, leased a car on 20 July 2021, when its retail price was €25,000. Lease charges of €6,000 are included in Joe's accounts for year end 30 September 2021. Joe has agreed with the Inspector of Taxes that one-third of the usage is private. Joe's car falls into Category D.

Lease charges	€6,000
Less: Private element 1/3rd	(€2,000)
Business element	€4,000

Disallowed lease payment:

$$€4,000 \times \frac{(€25,000) - (€24,000 \times 50\%)}{€25,000} \qquad = \qquad €2,080$$

2021:

Lease charge disallowed (€2,000 + €2,080)	€4,080

(h) Interest on late payment of tax Interest on late payment of any tax (including VAT, PAYE, etc.) is not allowed in computing tax-adjusted profits.

(i) Patent fees Fees incurred in obtaining, for the purposes of a trade, the grant of a patent or the extension of the term of a patent are allowable.

(j) Redundancy payments Statutory redundancy payments are specifically allowable. Amounts in excess of statutory entitlements are unlikely to be deductible where a cessation of trade has taken place but would be allowed if the trade continued.

(k) Renewal or registration of trademarks Expenses on renewal or registration of trademarks are specifically allowable.

(l) Capital payments for 'know-how' Payments of a capital nature to acquire technical or other information for the purpose of the trade are specifically allowable as a Case I expense. There are two exceptions to this rule:
- No deduction is allowed where the know-how is acquired as part of the acquisition of the **whole or part** of another business.
- No deduction is allowed where the purchase of the know-how is from a **connected** party, unless the acquiring company exploits it in the course of a trade.

(m) Expenditure on scientific research The full amount of any non-capital expenditure on scientific research is allowable as a deduction in computing the profits of a trade. In addition, sums paid to establishments, approved by the Minister for Finance, to carry on scientific research, and sums paid to Irish universities to enable them to carry on scientific research, are also deductible. This rule applies **whether or not** the payments are **related** to the existing trade currently being carried on.

(n) Accountancy/taxation fees Normal accounting, auditing and taxation compliance costs are allowable. Special costs associated with Appeal Hearings are likely to be disallowed following the decision of *Allen v. Farquharson Brothers (1932)*, where the costs of employing solicitors and counsel in connection with an appeal against income tax assessments were disallowed.

(o) Pre-trading expenses Under section 82 TCA 1997, an allowance **may** be claimed in respect of pre-trading expenses in the case of a trade or profession **provided** that the expenses:
- were incurred for the purpose of the trade or profession; **and**
- were incurred within three years of commencement; **and**
- are not otherwise allowable in computing profits.

Where an allowance is granted for pre-trading expenses, it is treated as if the expenditure were incurred **on the date** on which the trade or profession **commenced**.

Examples of qualifying pre-trading expenses include accountancy fees, market research, feasibility studies, salaries, advertising, preparing business plans and rent.

These pre-trading expenses are deductible against the income of the trade. If the expenses exceed the income and there is a loss, this loss cannot be offset against other income but can only be carried forward against future income of the same trade.

(p) Long-term unemployed JobsPlus Incentive is a scheme administered by the Department of Social Protection to encourage and reward employers who offer employment opportunities to the long-term unemployed.

Two levels of payment are available:

1. a payment of **€7,500** paid over **two** years to an employer for each person recruited, over 25 years of age and under 50 years of age, who has been unemployed for **more than 12 months** (four months for jobseekers aged under 25 years), or persons with refugee status or those in receipt of one-parent family payment; **and**
2. **€10,000** paid over two years to an employer for each person recruited, under 50 years of age, who has been unemployed for **36 months** in the previous 42 months, and jobseekers over 50 years of age who have been unemployed for at least **12 months** in the previous 18 months.

In order to qualify an employer must offer full-time employment of at least **30 hours per week**, spanning at least four days per week, to eligible recruits, i.e. that employee must be on the payroll and subject to tax, PRSI and USC. The income received by the employer under this scheme is not taxable and a deduction for gross wages paid in respect of these employees is allowed in the normal way (see www.welfare.ie).

(q) Key person insurance Key person insurance is insurance taken out by an employer in his/her own favour against the death, sickness or injury of an employee (i.e. the 'key man') whose services are **vital** to the success of the employer's business.

In general, premiums paid under policies insuring against loss of profits consequent on certain contingencies **are deductible** for tax purposes in the period in which they are paid. Correspondingly, all **sums received** by an employer under such policies are treated as **trading receipts** in the period in which they are received. Key-man insurance policies qualify for this treatment where the following conditions are satisfied:
- the sole relationship is that of employer and employee;
- the employee does not have a substantial proprietary interest in the business;
- the insurance is intended to meet loss of profit resulting from the loss of the services of the employee, as distinct from the loss of goodwill or other capital loss; **and**
- in the case of insurance against death, the policy is a short-term insurance providing only for a sum to be paid, in the event of the death of the insured, within a specified number of years. Short-term generally means five years but, in practice, if all other conditions are satisfied and the policy cannot extend beyond the employee's likely period of service with the business, i.e. not beyond the term of contract or beyond retirement age, then a longer term policy will qualify.

3.3.6 *Taxation Treatment Different from Accounting Treatment*

Finance Leases

Assets leased under finance leases may be included as fixed assets in accounts, and interest and depreciation for such assets included in the profit and loss account.

For tax purposes, capital allowances **may not** be claimed in respect of such assets. Instead, a deduction is given for **gross lease payments** made, i.e. interest plus capital. The adjustments to be made to the accounts profit for finance lease assets are as follows:

- add back interest and depreciation charged in respect of finance lease assets; **and**
- give a deduction for gross lease payments (interest and capital) made.

Pension Contributions

Ordinary annual contributions by an employer to a **Revenue-approved** pension scheme for the benefit of employees are **allowable** for tax purposes in the year in which they are **paid**. Thus, any **accruals** in respect of ordinary annual pension contributions due that have been included in arriving at accounts profit will have to be disallowed.

If an employer makes a **special contribution** to a Revenue-approved pension scheme and the total amount of the special contributions made in the year **does not exceed** the **total ordinary annual contributions** paid in the year, relief is given for the special contributions in the year in which they are paid. If, however, the total amount of the special contributions paid **exceeds** the total ordinary annual contributions paid, relief for the special contributions made is **spread forward** over a number of years subject to a maximum of five years. The number of years over which relief is given is calculated by dividing the total special contributions paid by the total ordinary contributions paid. If the factor produced by this calculation is between one and two, relief is given over two years; otherwise, the factor is rounded to the nearest whole number.

Example 3.12
An employer makes the following pension contributions in 2021:

Ordinary annual contribution (OAC)	€10,000
Special contribution (SC)	€27,000

As the SC made **exceeds** the OAC, relief for the SC will be **spread forward**. The **number of years** over which relief is given is calculated as follows:

$$\frac{\text{Special contribution}}{\text{Ordinary annual contribution}} = \frac{€27,000}{€10,000} = 2.7 \text{ rounded up to } 3$$

Relief for the SC will be given over **three years**. In the first two years, the amount of relief given will **equal the amount of the OAC**, with the balance of the relief given in the third year. Accordingly, relief for the SC of €27,000 made in 2021 will be given as follows:

Tax Year	Relief Given
2021	€10,000
2022	€10,000
2023	€7,000

Ordinary Annual Contribution less than €6,350

If the amount of the OAC is less than €6,350, in calculating when relief for a SC is due, the amount of the OAC may be assumed to be €6,350.

Example 3.13
An employer makes the following pension contributions in 2021:

Ordinary annual contribution (OAC)   €5,000
Special contribution (SC)   €8,000

As the OAC is less than €6,350, for the purposes of the calculation the OAC is taken to be €6,350.

$$\frac{\text{Special contribution}}{\text{Ordinary annual contribution}} = \frac{€8,000}{€6,350} = 1.26$$

As 1.26 is between one and two, relief is given over two years as follows:

Tax Year	Relief Given
2021	€6,350
2022	€1,650

3.3.7   Computation of Tax-adjusted Profits

In order to arrive at 'tax-adjusted' Case I and Case II trading profits, the following procedure should be adopted.

Step 1:   Start with the **net profit/loss** per the profit and loss account.

Step 2:   Add this to any expenses charged in the accounts that are **not allowable deductions** for income tax purposes, e.g. depreciation

Step 3:   Add any trading **income that has not been credited** in arriving at the net profit per the accounts.

Step 4:   Deduct any expenses which **have not been charged** in the accounts and which the TCA 1997 allows to be deducted

Step 5:   Deduct receipts that are of a **capital nature** and those that are chargeable under **another Schedule or Case**, e.g. deposit interest, profit on sale of motor vehicle, etc.

Example 3.14
Mr Bailey has operated a sports goods shop for 10 years. The profit and loss account for this business for the year ended 31 December 2021 is as follows:

Profit and Loss Account for the year ended 31 December 2021

Notes	€	€
Sales		313,759
Less: Cost of sales		(226,854)
Gross profit		86,905
Add:		
Deposit interest received	1,300	
Profit on sale of equipment	580	1,880
		88,785

continued overleaf

Less: Expenses

Wages and PRSI	1	45,000	
Rates	2	2,200	
Insurance	3	8,100	
Light and heat	2	850	
Telephone	4	970	
Repairs	5	3,400	
Motor and travel expenses	6	5,440	
General expenses	7	4,575	
Loan interest	2	9,000	
Bank interest and charges		3,260	
Depreciation		4,450	(87,245)
Net profit for the year			1,540

Notes

1. Included in wages are:

	€
Salary to self	20,000
Salary to wife	2,000
Own PRSI	800
Bonus to staff	2,500

2. In March 2016, Mr Bailey purchased, for €100,000, the shop premises in which the business had been carried on for the previous three years. Since 2016, the top floor, which is a self-contained flat, has been occupied free of charge by Mr Bailey's elderly father, who takes no part in the business. 20% of the rates, property insurance, light and heat relate to the flat, which represents 10% of the value of the whole property.

   The loan interest relates to interest paid on a loan taken out for the purchase of the premises.

3. Analysis of insurance charge

	€
Shopkeepers' all-in policy	1,400
Retirement annuity premiums for self	3,000
Permanent health insurance for self	2,400
Motor car insurance	800
Property insurance	500
	8,100

4. Telephone/home expenses

   Telephone costs include Mr Bailey's home telephone and 25% of the total charge is for personal use. Mrs Bailey carries out most of her bookkeeping duties at home and a special deduction of €156 is to be allowed for costs incurred in carrying out these duties at home. This item has not been reflected in the profit and loss account.

5. Included in the repairs charge are:

	€
Purchase of display stand	500
Repairs to shop front	600
Plumbing repairs	800

6. Analysis of motor and travel expenses

   Included in the motor and travel expenses is the cost of a trip to London to a sport goods' wholesale exhibition. Mr Bailey attended the exhibition on two days and then spent a further five days visiting friends and relatives. Details of the expenses are as follows:

continued overleaf

	€
Air fare	140
Hotel bill (for seven days)	400
Entertaining overseas exhibitor	100
	640

The remainder of the expenses relate to Mr Bailey's motor car, which had a market value of €25,000 when first leased on 1 March 2019. It is a Category C emissions car.

	€
Lease of car	2,880
Running expenses	1,920
	4,800

His annual travel (in km) was made up of:

Personal	9,600
Business	19,200
Home to business	3,200
Total	32,000

7. Analysis of general expenses

	€
Covenant to church (net)	405
Donation to church building fund (includes full-page advertisement in magazine – €200)	1,000
Subscriptions to trade association	350
Accountancy fee	1,100
Branded sponsorship of 'open day' at local golf club	900
Entertainment – customers	520
Entertainment – staff Christmas party	300
	4,575

Computation of Case I Tax-adjusted Profits for the year ended 31 December 2021

	Notes	€	€
Net profit per accounts			1,540
Add Back:			
Depreciation		4,450	
Wages and PRSI	1	20,800	
Rates (20%)		440	
Insurance	2	5,500	
Light and heat (20%)		170	
Loan interest (10%)		900	
Telephone (25%)		242	
Repairs	3	500	
Motor and travel expenses	4	2,949	
General expenses	5	1,725	37,676
			39,216
Deduct:			
Deposit interest		1,300	
Profit on sale of equipment		580	
Mrs Bailey business telephone		156	(2,036)
Adjusted Case I Profits			**37,180**

continued overleaf

Notes

1. **Wages and PRSI**

	€
Salary to self	20,000
Own PRSI	800
Disallowed, as these are drawings	20,800

2. **Insurance**

Retirement annuity premiums for self	€3,000
Permanent health insurance for self	€2,400
Property insurance (20%)	€100
Disallowed	€5,500

The restriction in respect of the motor car insurance is included in Note 4.

3. **Repairs**

Display stand is capital expenditure – disallow

4. **Motor and travel expenses**

		€
Leasing charges		2,880
Running expenses		1,920
Motor car insurance		800
Cost per accounts		5,600
Total travel	32,000 km	
Less: Personal mileage	(9,600 km)	
Home to business	(3,200 km)	
Business	19,200 km (60%)	

DISALLOW:

	€
Private element car:	
€5,600 × 40% =	2,240

Lease restriction car*:

$$€2,880 × 60\% = €1,728 × \frac{(25,000 - 24,000)}{25,000}$$ 69

*As the car is a Category C emissions car, no further restriction applies.

Air fare and hotel bill (none allowable because of duality of purpose**)	540
Business entertainment	100
Motor and travel disallowed*	2,949

**The strict position is that because the expenditure was not incurred "wholly and exclusively" for the purpose of the trade, none of the expenditure is allowable. In practice, however, it would normally be acceptable to claim a deduction for a proportion of the total expenditure equal to the business element, e.g. 2/7ths.

5. **General Expenses**

	€
Covenant to church	405
Donation to church building fund (excluding magazine advertisement)	800
Entertainment – customers	520
	1,725

The sponsorship of the 'open day' at the local golf club is allowable as advertising.

3.4 Partnerships

3.4.1 Introduction

The 1890 Partnership Act defines partnership as "the relationship which exists between persons carrying on a business in common, with a view of profit". For the purposes of determining tax-assessable profits, a partnership is regarded as a single unit.

The "**precedent partner**" arranges for the firm's tax computation to be prepared and submitted to the partnership's Inspector of Taxes. This partner is resident in the State, and

- is the first named partner in the partnership agreement, or
- if there is no agreement, the first named partner in the partnership name, e.g. Smith in Smith, Jones & Company.

If no partner is resident in the State, the agent or manager of the partnership who is resident in the State is deemed to be the precedent partner.

Anti-avoidance
Section 1008 TCA 1997 states that the tax-adjusted profits of a partnership **must**, for tax purposes, be apportioned **fully** between the partners each year, with these profits being taxable at each partner's marginal tax rate. This section was introduced to counter the practice of not apportioning tax-adjusted profits between partners (for tax purposes), as any amounts not apportioned were chargeable to tax at the standard rate only on the precedent partner.

3.4.2 Basis of Assessment

For the purposes of tax assessment, each partner's share of the total profits is treated as **personal** to that partner, as if they arose from a **separate trade or profession**.

As a consequence, commencement and cessation rules apply to each partner individually when they enter/leave the partnership. For taxation purposes a partnership continues no matter how many partners are admitted or leave, provided there are **at least two partners at all times**, one of whom was a partner immediately prior to the admission of a new partner.

A partnership **ceases** to exist when:

- the business ceases, or
- only one partner remains (i.e. sole trader), or
- a completely different set of partners takes over from the old partners.

Sole Trader to Partnership
When an individual who previously operated as a sole trader commences business in partnership with one or more others, then the individual is deemed to have ceased their old trade (and the cessation provisions above will also apply) and a new trade is deemed to commence from the date of commencement of the partnership.

3.4.3 Computation of Taxable Income

Apportionment of Tax-adjusted Profits
The partnership firm will prepare an annual profit and loss account, which will be the basis of a tax-adjusted profits computation. Case I and Case II rules regarding allowable and disallowable expenses are applied in arriving at the firm's tax-adjusted profits figure. However, the following items are deemed to be an **apportionment of profit** and are not allowable deductions in arriving at the tax-adjusted profits.

1. **Interest on capital** Interest on capital is a distribution of profit and is, accordingly, a disallowable expense in computing the partnership firm's profits or losses for a period. Interest on capital must, however, be carefully distinguished from interest paid by the partnership in respect of a loan made to the partnership by an individual partner. Such interest, provided the funds borrowed had been used for the partnership business, would be an allowable Case II deduction.
2. **Salaries** Salaries paid to a partner are treated in the same manner as drawings taken out of a business by a sole trader, i.e. they are disallowed for Case II computation purposes.
3. **Rent paid to a partner** If a partner beneficially owns the premises from which the partnership is operated and lets the premises on an arm's length basis to the partnership, then the rent will be allowed as a deduction in computing the partnership profits and the landlord partner will be assessed personally under Case V on the rental income.

The tax-adjusted profits of the partnership are divided among the partners in accordance with:

- the specific terms of the partnership agreement regarding **guaranteed salaries and interest on capital**; and
- the **profit-sharing ratio** that existed during the accounting period.

Example 3.15
Smith and Jones are in partnership as engineers for many years, sharing profits 60:40. The profit and loss account for the business for the year ended 30 April 2021, after allowing for salaries and interest on capital payable to the partners under the partnership agreement, is as follows:

Profit and Loss Account for the year ended 30 April 2021

	€	€
Gross fees		200,000
Less:		
Overheads	50,000	
Salaries paid to partners (Note 1)	41,000	
Interest paid on partners' capital accounts (Note 2)	13,000	
Rent paid to Smith for partnership premises	35,000	
Entertainment expenses	15,000	154,000
Net profit for the year		46,000

Notes

1. Salaries

	€
Smith	18,000
Jones	23,000
	41,000

2. Interest paid on capital accounts

	€
Smith	7,000
Jones	6,000
	13,000

continued overleaf

Computation of Case II Taxable Profits 2021		
	€	€
Net profit per accounts		46,000
Add Back:		
Salaries paid to partners	41,000	
Interest paid on partners' capital accounts	13,000	
Disallowed entertainment expenses	15,000	69,000
Assessable profit 2021		**115,000**
Apportionment of Assessable Profit	*Total €*	*Smith €*	*Jones €*
Salaries	41,000	18,000	23,000
Interest paid on capital accounts	13,000	6,000	7,000
Balance (apportioned 60:40)	61,000	36,600	24,400
Case II taxable profits 2021	**115,000**	**60,600**	**54,400**

Questions

Review Questions
(See Suggested Solutions to Review Questions at the end of this textbook.)

Question 3.1

Ms Lola commenced trading on 1 June 2020 and makes up accounts to 31 May. Her trading results are as follows:

	€
01/06/2020–31/05/2021	48,000
01/06/2021–31/05/2022	39,000
01/06/2022–31/05/2023	37,200

Requirement
Compute Ms Lola's Case I assessable profits for the first four years.

Question 3.2

Mr Charlie commenced trading on 1 May 2020 and makes up accounts to 31 October. His trading results are as follows:

	€
01/05/2020–31/10/2020	44,800
01/11/2020–31/10/2021	54,400
01/11/2021–31/10/2022	53,600

Requirement
Compute Mr Charlie's Case I assessable profits for the first three years.

Question 3.3

Jim commenced practice as a solicitor on 1 May 2020. Tax-adjusted profits for the opening years were as follows:

	€
1 May 2020–30 April 2021	48,000
Year ended 30 April 2022	60,000
Year ended 30 April 2023	9,600

Requirement

Compute Jim's Case II assessable profits for the first four tax years.

Question 3.4

Donna Ross resigned from her job at AIB to sell children's clothing full-time on eBay. She provided you with the following information:

Pay slip showing gross pay from 1 January to cessation on 30 April 2021 of €20,300, with PAYE deducted of €3,850.

She tells you that she has traded on eBay part-time for a "few" years. She sold only household items or sale bargains picked up while shopping. She estimates that her sales were €5,000 in 2019 and her costs were minimal since the items sold were "lying about the house". She used the family computer and packed the product in her garage. In 2020 she spotted a market opportunity when she bought a job lot of designer children's clothes for €10,000 and sold them on eBay individually for €20,000 in just one month! This prompted her to quit her job and start trading from 1 May 2021. Her tax-adjusted profit for the year ended 30 April 2022 was €179,400.

Donna is a 32-year-old single parent.

Requirement

Compute the income tax payable by Donna for 2021 and 2022 assuming personal tax credits of €4,950 for 2021 and €4,950 for 2022.

Advise Donna, with reasons, if her eBay activity for 2019 and 2020 is taxable as trading income.

Question 3.5

Ms Dora ceases trading on 31 December 2021. She made up her accounts annually to 31 May. Her trading results were as follows:

	€
Year ended 31/05/2019	64,000
Year ended 31/05/2020	72,000
Year ended 31/05/2021	9,600
Period ended 31/12/2021	12,000

Requirement

Compute Ms Dora's Case I assessable profits for the last three years.

Question 3.6

Mr Diego ceases trading on 31 May 2021. He made up his accounts annually to 31 July. His trading results were as follows:

	€
Year ended 31/07/2019	32,000
Year ended 31/07/2020	60,000
Period ended 31/05/2021	40,000

Requirement

Compute Mr Diego's Case I assessable profits for his last three tax years.

Question 3.7

Alex, a single man, traded for many years as a butcher. He retired on 30 September 2021 and started work for Fagan Organic Lamb as a salesman. His tax-adjusted profits for the periods to the date of cessation were as follows:

	€
Year ended 30/09/2020	24,000
Year ended 30/09/2021	240,000

His Employment Detail Summary for 2021 showed gross pay of €15,000 and PAYE paid of €3,410.

Requirement

Compute the income tax payable by Alex for 2021, assuming tax credits were €3,300, and advise if any changes are needed in other years.

Question 3.8

J. Cog retired on 30 September 2021 from his newsagent's business after trading for 40 years. His profits for the immediate years prior to cessation were:

	€
Year ended 31 October 2018	40,000
Year ended 31 October 2019	65,000
Year ended 31 October 2020	64,000
11 months to 30 September 2021	24,000

Requirement

Calculate J. Cog's assessable profits for the last four years of assessment.

Question 3.9

Alex and Bill have traded as partners sharing equally for many years. They prepare accounts each year to 30 September. On 1 October 2017 a new partner, Colin, is brought in. From that date profits are shared as follows: Alex 40%; Bill 40%; and Colin 20%.

Tax-adjusted trading profits were as follows:

	€
Year ended 30/09/2017	20,000
Year ended 30/09/2018	25,000
Year ended 30/09/2019	30,000
Year ended 30/09/2020	30,000
Year ended 30/09/2021	35,000

On 30 September 2019, Alex left the partnership and from that date Bill and Colin have shared profits and losses equally.

Requirement

Calculate the assessable profits for Alex, Bill and Colin for the years 2017–2021 inclusive.

Question 3.10

June, Mary and Karen had been carrying on a business for many years, sharing profits in the ratio 40:30:30. Karen retired on 30 June 2018 and was replaced by Jill. The profit-sharing ratio remained unchanged.

Louise was admitted to the partnership on 1 July 2020, from which date profits and losses were shared equally by all the partners. The partnership ceased to trade on 31 December 2021, when the business was transferred to a limited company.

The tax-adjusted profits of the partnership were as follows:

	€
Year ended 30 June 2017	40,000
Year ended 30 June 2018	60,000
Year ended 30 June 2019	54,000
Year ended 30 June 2020	50,000
Year ended 30 June 2021	36,000
Six months ended 31 December 2021	20,000

Requirement

Calculate the assessable profits for the years 2018–2021 for all the partners.

Question 3.11

Joseph Murphy is a trader. He prepares accounts annually to 31 December. His profit and loss account for the year ended 31 December 2021 was as follows:

	Notes	€		€
Salaries	1	61,864	Gross profit	112,500
Travelling expenses	2	17,512	Discounts received	7,349
Commissions		7,236	Dividends from Irish Co.	2,813
Interest on late payment of VAT		1,121	Interest on National Loan Stock	2,250
Interest on late payment of PAYE		1,238	Deposit interest	170
Depreciation		13,793	Profit on sale of fixed assets	5,063
Bank interest		4,008		
Subscriptions	3	1,225		
Repairs	4	6,480		
Bad debts	5	2,475		
Legal fees	6	1,069		
Accountancy fees		2,250		
Net profit		9,874		
		130,145		130,145

Notes:

1. Salaries include a salary to Mr Murphy of €7,500 and a salary paid to his wife of €5,000 for her work as secretary.
2. Travelling expenses include €1,000 for a holiday trip by Mr and Mrs Murphy.

3. Subscriptions

	€
Political party	75
Local football club	50
Traders association	500
Trade papers	200
Old Folks' Home	150
Sports club	250
	1,225

4. Repairs account

	€
Opening provision for repairs	855
Expenditure during period	2,335
New extension to office	3,000
Closing provision for repairs	2,000
Profit and loss account charge	6,480

The closing repairs provision represents a general provision for expenditure not yet incurred.

5. Bad debts account

	€
Opening provision – general	(5,100)
Bad debts recovered	(2,675)
Bad debts written off	2,275
Closing provision – general	7,975
Profit and loss account charge	2,475

6. Legal fees

	€
Bad debts recovery	60
Sale of freehold	1,009
	1,069

Requirement

Compute Joseph Murphy's Case I taxable profits for 2021.

Question 3.12

Andy Reilly operates a consultancy business providing technical advice. He has carried on the business for many years and makes up annual accounts to 31 December. His profit and loss account for the year to 31 December 2021 is set out below:

	€	€
Fees charged		178,000
Less: Direct costs:		
Technical salaries and employment expenses	64,000	
Stationery and printing	4,000	
Repairs to equipment	980	
Professional indemnity insurance	370	
Motor vehicle expenses (Note 1)	6,250	
Depreciation – equipment	2,500	
– motor vehicles	3,000	(81,100)
		96,900
Deduct overheads:		
Rent, rates and property insurance	11,000	
Repairs to premises (Note 2)	6,500	
Lighting and heating	1,100	
Office salaries	7,200	
Telephone and postage	400	
Advertising	800	
Entertaining (Note 5)	3,900	
Bad debts (Note 3)	550	
Defalcations (Note 4)	6,000	
Successful claim by client not covered by insurance	2,500	
Andy Reilly's drawings	20,000	
Depreciation – office equipment and fittings	900	(60,850)
Net profit before taxation		36,050

Notes:

1. €4,000 of the total motor vehicle expenses relate to Andy Reilly's car; 40% of Andy's total travel in his car is on business. The other motor expenses relate to sales representatives' cars, all of which cost €19,000.
2. Repairs to premises include the charge for constructing two additional garages adjoining the firm's buildings for the sales representatives' cars. This amounted to €3,150.
3. The bad debts charge includes a credit for the recovery of a specific debt amounting to €350 and the creation of a general bad debt reserve amounting to €275.

4.   The defalcations were traced to staff and were not covered by insurance.
5.   The charge for entertainment comprises the following:

	€
Private holiday for Andy Reilly (June 2021)	1,200
Tickets for Andy Reilly and his friend to All Ireland football final	300
Staff Christmas party	1,200
Business meals with customers	1,200
	3,900

Requirement
Compute Andy Reilly's Case I tax-adjusted profit for 2021.

Question 3.13

Tony set up business as a car dealer/garage proprietor on 1 October 2020. His first accounts were made up for the 15-month period ended 31 December 2021 and subsequently to 31 December each year. The first two sets of accounts show the following results:

		15 months to 31/12/2021	Year ended 31/12/2022
		€	€
Sales: cars		250,000	200,000
Sales: workshop		100,000	90,000
		350,000	290,000
Direct costs			
Cost of cars sold		211,500	168,300
Salesman's salary and commission		15,000	13,000
Workshop labour and parts		62,500	66,000
		289,000	247,300
Gross profit		61,000	42,700
General and administrative costs			
Accountancy		1,500	1,250
Advertising		900	1,100
Bad debts	(Note 1)	2,500	400
Depreciation		3,000	2,400
Drawings		15,000	12,000
Entertaining	(Note 2)	1,500	700
Insurance		5,000	4,000
Interest	(Note 3)	18,000	14,000
Legal fees	(Note 4)	400	600

continued overleaf

Light and heat		2,250	1,800
Office staff salaries		10,600	8,500
Postage, telephone and stationery		1,500	1,200
Sundries	(Note 5)	1,250	650
Travel expenses	(Note 6)	<u>1,950</u>	<u>1,500</u>
		65,350	50,100
Net loss		(4,350)	(7,400)

Notes:

		15 months to 31/12/2021	Year ended 31/12/2022
		€	€
1.	**Bad debts**		
	General provision	2,500	–
	Bad debt written off	–	2,900
	General provision no longer required	–	(2,500)
		2,500	400
2.	**Entertaining**		
	Hospitality for representatives of car manufacturer during negotiations for supply of cars	800	–
	Entertaining customers	700	700
		1,500	700
3.	**Interest**		
	Interest on loan from car manufacturer to buy stock	9,500	7,000
	Interest on bank loan to establish business	8,500	7,000
		18,000	14,000
4.	**Legal fees**		
	Advice on supply agreement with car manufacturer	250	200
	Recovery of outstanding debts	–	200
	Defending customer claim re: faulty car	150	200
		400	600
5.	**Sundries**		
	Security	500	300
	Drinks at staff Christmas party	150	150
	Subscription to trade association	200	200
	Political donation	100	–
	Charitable donation (eligible charity)	50	–
	Interest on late payment of VAT	250	–
		1,250	650

6. **Travel expenses**

These expenses contain no disallowable element.

Requirement

(a) Compute the Schedule D, Case I profit for the 15 months ended 31 December 2021 and the year ended 31 December 2022.

(b) Calculate Tony's Case I taxable profits for 2021.

Question 3.14

John Smith commenced trading on 1 May 2021. The profit and loss account from 1 May 2021 to 30 April 2022 shows the following information:

	Notes	€	€
Sales		201,230	
Less: cost of sales		(140,560)	
		60,670	
Interest received	1	390	
Gross profit			61,060
Less: expenses:			
Wages	2	23,500	
Motor expenses	3	1,860	
Depreciation		1,250	
Rent and rates		12,800	
Leasing charges	4	4,300	
Repairs	5	3,900	
Telephone		800	
Bank interest and charges		3,800	
Sundry expenses	6	3,400	
Insurance	7	2,630	58,240
Net profit for the year			**2,820**

Notes:

1. Interest received – NTMA Savings Certificates of €390
2. Included in wages charges are:

	€
Wages to Mrs Smith (wife), as bookkeeper	1,800
Wages to self	5,200
Accrued bonus for sales assistants	500
Own PRSI	200

3. Motor expenses relate solely to Mr Smith's own motoring and include a €100 fine for careless driving. 60% of total travel by car is for business purposes. Motor insurance has been included under the insurance charge.

4. Analysis of leasing charges (all operating leases)

	€
Lease of till	300
Lease of shelving	1,200
Lease of Mr Smith's car	<u>2,800</u>
	<u>4,300</u>

The motor car had a market value of €25,000 when first leased on 1 May 2021. It has an emissions rating of Category D.

5. Repairs

	€
Painting outside of shop	1,000
Repairing shop front damaged in accident	1,300
Insurance claim re above accident	(900)
Extension to shop	1,500
General provision for repairs	<u>1,000</u>
	<u>3,900</u>

6. Sundry expenses

	€
Trade subscriptions	250
Interest on the late payment of income tax	120
Donation to church	260
Expenses for son at university	710
Christmas party for staff	560
Accountancy	<u>1,500</u>
	<u>3,400</u>

7. Insurance

	€
Business "all-in" policy	270
Motor car	300
Retirement annuity premiums – single	500
Retirement annuity premiums – annual	600
Life assurance	460
Key-man life assurance on salesman	<u>500</u>
	<u>2,630</u>

Requirement

Compute John Smith's adjusted trading profits for income tax purposes for the year ended 30 April 2022.

Question 3.15

Polly Styrene has been in business for many years manufacturing shoes and she makes up her accounts to 31 December each year. Her profit and loss account for the year ended 31 December 2021 was as follows:

	Notes	€	€
Gross profit			145,000
Less:			
Wages and salaries	1	90,000	
Light, heat and telephone	2	6,000	
Postage and stationery		500	
Repairs and renewals	3	5,000	
Legal and professional fees	4	3,000	
Bad debts	5	2,000	
Travel and entertainment	6	2,500	
Bank interest	7	3,500	
Insurance		3,000	
Freight		4,000	
Sundries	8	3,500	
			123,000
Net profit			**22,000**

Notes:

1. Wages and salaries includes €8,000 for Polly Styrene.
2. Light, heat and telephone includes €1,500 for light, heat and telephone at the residence of Polly Styrene. One-sixth is business related.
3. Repairs and renewals

Painting and decorating	1,600
Extension to shops	1,400
Provision for future repairs	2,000

4. Legal and professional fees

Debt collection	1,200
Accountancy	1,500
Surveyor's fees re: abortive purchase of premises	300

5. Bad debts

Trade debts written off	2,800
Bad debt recovered	(200)
Decrease in general reserve	(600)

6. Travel and entertainment

Car expenses*	1,500
Christmas drinks for employees	400
Entertaining customers	600

* The car cost €32,000 and was bought in 2016. Private use is one-third.

7. Bank interest

Bank interest	1,500
Lease interest	2,000

Polly leased plant and equipment through ABC Commercial Finance under a three-year finance lease. The total repayments (capital and interest) for the year were €18,600.

8. Sundries

Advertising	1,551
Trade protection association	100
Political party subscription	1,000
Parking fines	49
Rubbish disposal	300
Donation to St Luke's Institute of Cancer Research	500

Requirement

Calculate the Schedule D, Case I taxable adjusted profit for 2021.

Question 3.16

Jack and John are in partnership as accountants for many years. The profit and loss account for the year ended 30 April 2021 was as follows:

		€	€
Gross fees			200,000
Less:	Overheads	100,000	
	Jack's salary	20,000	
	John's salary	21,000	
	Jack's interest on capital	6,000	
	John's interest on capital	7,000	(154,000)
	Profit for the year		**46,000**

Disallowable expenses included in general overheads amount to €26,000.

The profit-sharing ratio (after salaries and interest on capital) for the year ended 30 April 2021 was 50:50.

Requirement

Prepare the Case II computation and allocate the profits to the partners.

Capital Allowances and Cases I & II Loss Relief

4.1 Capital Allowances: Plant and Machinery

4.1.1 Introduction

Income tax is a tax solely on income and, consequently, capital expenditure is not deductible for income tax purposes. This means that, when arriving at the tax-adjusted trading profits of a business, depreciation for accounting purposes is specifically disallowed and is **added back** to the net profit/(loss). This, therefore, may deny a business a tax deduction for the depreciation or amortisation of capital expenditure used in the generation of taxable income. To offset this, businesses can claim a capital allowances deduction for the **net cost** of certain capital assets employed for the purposes of the business.

4.1.2 Meaning of "Plant"

The basic test applied is to determine whether the specific capital asset in question is **functional** to the operation of the business, as distinct from representing the **setting** in which the business is carried out.

There is no statutory definition of plant and machinery for the purposes of capital allowances. Accordingly, one must have recourse to case law to determine various tests which must be satisfied if an item of expenditure is to qualify as "plant" for the purposes of capital allowances. The question of whether an item is plant is a **matter of fact**, which will be decided according to the circumstances of each particular case. The question of whether an item is **machinery** can, in certain circumstances, be an easier test to satisfy as it is usually an **either/or** test. However, where there is any doubt, as for plant, the question is a **matter of fact** that will be decided by the circumstances of **each** case.

The most quoted definition of the word "plant" arose under a case, *Yarmouth v. France* (1887), in connection with the Employer's Liability Act 1880, in which Lord Justice Lynley said:

> "There is no definition of plant in the Act, but in its ordinary sense, it includes whatever apparatus is used by a businessman for carrying on his business – not his stock-in-trade, which he buys or makes for sale but all goods and chattels, fixed or moveable, live or dead, which he keeps for permanent employment in the business."

To determine whether an item would qualify as plant, relevant case law has indicated that the following tests are applied:

- Is the item functional or merely a setting in which the business is carried on?
- Is the expenditure incurred directly on the provision of plant and not, for instance, on the provision of finance which is used to acquire plant?
- Does the expenditure replace an item previously regarded as plant?
- Is the expenditure related to an entire unit or is it merely expenditure on part of a larger, non-functional unit?

As the practice in relation to plant has resulted mainly from a study of case law, brief details of some of the more important cases on the subject are outlined below.

Jarrold v. **Good (1962)**
It was held in this case that purpose-built movable partitioning, although forming part of the setting of the business, was an essential part of the equipment necessary for the operation of the business and should be regarded as plant.

CIR v. Barclay, Curle & Co. **Ltd (1969)**
This case, concerning expenditure on a dry dock, was heard by the House of Lords in 1969. The main facts of the case were as follows.

Shipbuilders constructed a dry dock that acted like a hydraulic chamber in which a volume of water, variable at will, could be used to lower a ship so that it could be exposed for inspection and repair, and to raise it again to high-tide level. The taxpayer contended that the dock was a single and indivisible entity, performing the function of a large hydraulic lift-cum-vice, and that the expenditure was machinery and plant. The House of Lords found in favour of the taxpayer.

This decision stressed the functional test as opposed to the setting test.

Schofield (HMIT) v. R & H Hall (1974)
In this case the company claimed capital allowances on the construction of two silos used to take grain from ships and to dispense it to customers. It was held that the function of the silos was an essential part of the overall trade activity in that they held grain in a position from which it could be conveniently discharged in varying amounts. Accordingly, they found that the silos were plant and qualified for wear and tear allowances.

An important aspect of the case was the **detailed description of the plant** given by the company by way of documentation and evidence.

S. O'Culachain (Inspector of Taxes) v. McMullan Brothers **(1995)**

In this case, it was claimed that forecourt canopies at petrol filling stations constituted plant for capital allowances purposes on the grounds that the canopies were essential to provide advertising, brand image and attractive surroundings, and therefore created an ambience and had a function in carrying on the business.

The Revenue Commissioners argued that the canopies provided no more than shelter from the rain and wind and played no part in the trade of selling petrol.

It was held that the canopies performed a function in the actual **carrying out** of the trade and therefore qualified for capital allowances as an item of plant.

Hampton (HMIT) v. Fortes Autogrill **Ltd (1979)**

It was held that a false ceiling is not plant on the basis that it simply provided a covering that was not functional to the actual carrying on of the catering business by the taxpayer.

4.1.3   Wear and Tear Allowance

Plant and Machinery

This is an annual allowance for the wear and tear of plant and machinery (new or second-hand) in use for the purpose of a trade, profession or employment at the end of an accounting period.

The qualifying asset must be **owned** by the taxpayer and **in use**, wholly and exclusively for the purposes of the taxpayer's trade, profession or employment, **at the end** of the relevant basis period for the year of assessment. (The basis period is the accounts year from which the tax year is calculated.)

The allowance is calculated on the **cost price** of the plant **less** any grants received. The **wear and tear rate is 12.5%** on expenditure incurred from 4 December 2002 on a straight-line basis.

The wear and tear allowance is an **annual** allowance. The only circumstance in which a full 12.5% will not be granted is where the **basis period** for the particular tax year, for which the allowance is being claimed, **is less than 12 months**.

This would only occur in the **year of commencement** of trade. (The year of cessation of trade may also be less than 12 months, but no annual allowance would be due for that year as the asset would not be in use at the end of the basis period.)

It is important to emphasise that it is the **length of the basis period** that determines whether or not a full annual allowance is available and **not the period from the date of purchase** of an asset to the end of the particular basis period.

In the year of acquisition, a full year's wear and tear allowance is granted (provided the basis period is at least 12 months long).

In the year of disposal or cessation of use, no wear and tear allowance is granted, as the asset is not in use at the end of the basis period.

The **tax written down value** (TWDV) of an asset is the cost price (as allowable for tax purposes) less any capital allowance (e.g. wear and tear allowance or industrial building allowance) already claimed in previous years.

Example 4.1

	Plant & Machinery @ 12.5%	Vehicles @ 12.5%	Total
	€	€	€
Opening qualifying cost of assets purchased on 1 Jan 2017	50,000	0	50,000
Add:			
Additions at qualifying cost 2021	25,000	20,000	45,000
Deduct:			
Disposals at qualifying cost 2021	(7,000)	0	(7,000)
Cost of assets qualifying for wear and tear allowance (A)	**68,000**	**20,000**	**88,000**
Opening TWDV at 1 Jan 2021	**25,000**	0	25,000
Add:			
Additions at qualifying cost during the basis period, i.e. y/e 30/09/2021	25,000	20,000	45,000
Deduct:			
TWDV of assets sold during the basis period, i.e. y/e 30/09/2021	(3,500)	0	(3,500)
	46,500	20,000	66,500
Wear and tear for 2021 (Line A × qualifying rate)	(8,500)	(2,500)	(11,000)
TWDV @ 31/12/2021	**38,000**	**17,500**	**55,500**

Motor Vehicles

The wear and tear rate for motor vehicles, other than those used in a taxi or car-hire business, is 12.5%, straight-line, on expenditure incurred from 4 December 2002.

For income tax basis periods ending on or after 1 January 2007, the allowable cost of new and second-hand cars (for wear and tear allowance purposes) is restricted to a **maximum limit of €24,000** (specified limit). Note that this specified limit of €24,000 is available for wear and tear allowance even where the actual cost of the car is lower.

Section 380L TCA 1997 introduced certain additional restrictions on capital allowances available on cars, which are based on CO_2 emissions levels, for vehicles bought on or after 1 July 2008.

There are three categories:

1. Category A/B/C Vehicles   0–155g/km
2. Category D/E Vehicles   156–190g/km
3. Category F/G Vehicles   191g/km and upwards

Vehicle Category	Capital Allowances Available
A, B and C	Use the specified amount regardless of cost.
D and E	Two steps to calculate limit:
	1. Take the lower of the specified limit or cost.
	2. Limit is 50% of the above amount.
F and G	No allowance available.

No restrictions apply to:

- commercial vehicles, e.g. lorries, vans, etc;
- cars used for the purposes of a taxi business;
- cars used for the purpose of a car-hire business.

The wear and tear allowance for cars used in a **taxi or car hire** business is **40%** on a **reducing balance** basis. The "specified amount", i.e. the maximum cost limit of €24,000, does not apply to such cars.

Where a business asset is partly used for private purposes, the wear and tear allowance is calculated as normal and is then reduced by the private element. However, the full annual allowance is deducted when arriving at the tax written down value (TWDV) at the end of each tax year.

Example 4.2

Joe, who is self-employed and prepares annual accounts to 31 December, purchased a new car on 1 August 2021 at a cost of €35,000 (emissions Category D). His annual travel is 32,000 kilometres, of which 8,000 are private. Joe's sales director, Sarah, also has a company car, which was purchased on 30 September 2018 (emissions Category C) for €22,000. Sarah's travel is 56,000 kilometres, of which 44,800 are business related.

Wear and Tear Calculation		Sarah's Car	Joe's Car
Motor Vehicles @ 12.5%	**Notes**	€	€
TWDV 01/01/2018		–	
Additions y/e 31/12/2018	1	24,000	
Wear and tear allowance 2018		(3,000)	
TWDV 31/12/2018		21,000	
Wear and tear allowance 2019		(3,000)	
TWDV 31/12/2019		18,000	
Wear and tear allowance 2020		(3,000)	
TWDV 31/12/2020		15,000	
Additions 2021	2		12,000
Wear and tear allowance 2021		(3,000)	*(1,500)
TWDV 31/12/2021		12,000	10,500

Notes:

1. Sarah's car cost is the specified limit of €24,000 for 2018. As Sarah is an employee, there is no private motoring restriction.
2. Joe's car is restricted to 50% of €24,000 for 2020 as a Category D car.

*The wear and tear allowance on Joe's car will be further restricted to the business use only, i.e.

$$1,500 \times \frac{(32,000-8,000)}{32,000} = 1,125$$

4.1.4 Accelerated Capital Allowances for Energy-efficient Equipment

Accelerated capital allowances are available for **approved energy-efficient equipment**, including electric and alternative fuel vehicles. The entire allowance can be claimed in the first year in which the equipment is purchased and in use by the taxpayer.

Qualifying Equipment

The energy-efficient equipment must be new, must meet certain energy-efficient criteria and must fall within one of the 10 classes of technology specified below (Schedule 4A TCA 1997). A minimum amount of expenditure must be incurred on providing the equipment and this varies with the particular category to which the product belongs. The equipment must be included on the **Triple E Product Register** maintained by the Sustainable Energy Authority of Ireland (SEAI).

Class of Technology	Minimum Amount
Electric Motors and Drives	€1,000
Lighting	€3,000
Building Energy Management Systems	€5,000
Information and Communications Technology (ICT)	€1,000
Heating and Electricity Provision	€1,000
Process and Heating, Ventilation and Air-conditioning (HVAC) Control Systems	€1,000
Electric and Alternative Fuel Vehicles	€1,000
Refrigeration and Cooling Systems	€1,000
Electro-mechanical Systems	€1,000
Catering and Hospitality Equipment	€1,000

Electric and Alternative Fuel Vehicles
The accelerated allowance is based on the **lower** of the actual cost of the vehicle **or** the specified amount of €24,000. The taxpayer may opt for the accelerated allowance scheme or the emissions-based scheme of allowances. The allowances available under the emissions scheme are 12.5% over a period of eight years up to a "specified amount" of €24,000 **regardless** of the actual cost of the car.

4.1.5   Balancing Allowances and Charges

Profits and losses on the disposal of fixed assets are **not included** in the tax-adjusted profits of a business. In order to adequately capture these profits and losses, the capital allowances systems use balancing charges and balancing allowances to reflect any profit or loss on the disposal of an asset.

A **balancing allowance arises when the sales proceeds of an asset are less than its tax written down value (loss on disposal).**

A **balancing charge arises when the sales proceeds of an asset are greater than its tax written down value (profit on disposal).**

Note that the "tax" profit or loss will not be the same as the profit or loss on disposal in the accounts, due to the differing rates and rules between depreciation and tax capital allowances.

Balancing allowances and charges may arise when one of the following occurs:

▓ The trade or profession ceases, therefore the assets are no longer "in use".
▓ An asset, on which wear and tear allowances were claimed, is sold/scrapped.
▓ An asset permanently ceases to be used for the purposes of the trade, profession or employment.

In computing the balancing allowance/charge, market value is imposed where the sales proceeds are **not** at arm's length or there are no sale proceeds (e.g. takeover/gift of a business asset for personal use).

Limitation of Balancing Charges
A balancing charge is limited as follows:

▓ it **cannot exceed** the aggregate of the wear and tear allowances **already claimed** on the asset; and
▓ in respect of plant and machinery, it will not arise where the **disposal proceeds are less than €2,000**. However, this does not apply if the disposal is to a connected person.

Example 4.3
Damien Jones is self-employed and prepares annual accounts to 30 June. Damien disposed of the following assets:

	Counting Machine	Binding Machine	Printer
Date of disposal	23/01/2021	10/06/2021	28/04/2021
Proceeds	€6,250	€220	€1,750
Original cost	€5,000	€900	€4,000
TWDV 01/01/2021	€4,000	€425	€1,250

Balancing Allowance/Charge Calculation

	€	€	€
TWDV 01/01/2021	4,000	425	1,250
Less:			
Sale proceeds	(6,250)	(220)	(1,750)
Balancing allowance/(charge)	(2,250)	205	(500)
Restricted to:			
Balancing allowance/(charge)	*(1,000)	205	**NIL

*The balancing charge on the counting machine is restricted to the amount of wear and tear allowances already claimed (cost €5,000, less WDV €4,000 = €1,000).

**No balancing charge will apply in respect of the printer as the sales proceeds are less than €2,000 and the disposal is not to a connected person.

Year-end 30 June 2020 formed the last basis period (i.e. 2020) for which wear and tear allowances were claimed. The assets were disposed in y/e 30 June 2021, which is the basis period for 2021. No wear and tear allowance is claimable in the year of disposal.

Replacement Option

If plant and machinery (including motor vehicles) is replaced with **similar** equipment, any balancing charge arising on the old equipment may be **deferred**. If such a claim is made, the cost of the new equipment is **reduced by the balancing charge** deferred. This claim is referred to as the "replacement option". This option may only be claimed to avoid a balancing charge if a similar item replaces the item of plant sold.

Example 4.4
Damien Jones sold printing equipment and a balancing charge of €1,000 arose. He bought replacement equipment on 10 January 2021 for €6,000. This equipment was in turn sold on 29 March 2022 for €6,050.

	Printing Equipment
Balancing Allowance/Charge Calculation	€
2021:	
Cost of new printing equipment	6,000
Less:	
Balancing charge on original asset	(1,000)
Qualifying cost of replacement asset for capital allowances	5,000
Wear and tear allowance 2021 @ 12.5%	(625)
TWDV 31/12/2021	4,375

continued overleaf

2022:	
TWDV 01/01/2022	4,375
Less:	
Sales proceeds	(6,050)
Balancing charge	(1,675)
Restricted to:	
Actual allowances granted (including deferred balancing charge): €625 + €1,000	(1,625)

Motor Cars

As the qualifying cost of a motor car for wear and tear allowance is capped at **€24,000**, any balancing allowance/charge on disposal must also be restricted in the same proportion as the **original restriction** to the actual cost of the vehicle. The deemed sales proceeds are calculated as follows:

$$\text{Total sales proceeds} \times \frac{\text{Restricted value of car}}{\text{Original cost of car}}$$

Where there is private use, any balancing allowance/charge is further restricted to the proportion of business use.

Example 4.5

Damien Jones purchased a new car on 15 January 2019 for €25,000 (emissions Category A). He sold the car on 15 April 2021 for €15,500. Business usage was agreed at 75%. Damien prepares accounts to 30 June each year.

	Motor Vehicle 12.5%	Allowable 75%
Wear and Tear Allowance	€	€
TWDV 01/01/2019	–	
Additions y/e 30/6/2019 (restricted to €24,000)	24,000	
Wear and tear allowance 2019	(3,000)	(2,250)
TWDV 31/12/2019	21,000	
Wear and tear allowance 2020	(3,000)	(2,250)
TWDV 31/12/2020	18,000	
Disposal:		
WDV 01/01/2021	18,000	
Deemed proceeds: €15,500 × 24,000/25,000	(14,880)	
Balancing allowance	(3,120)	
Restricted to business use of 75%		(2,340)

4.1.6 Treatment of Capital Grants, Hire Purchase, Lessors, Lessees and VAT

Capital Grants

Where capital grants are received/receivable, the qualifying cost is the **net cost**, i.e. total cost minus the grant receivable.

Hire Purchase

For hire purchase situations, a full wear and tear allowance is allowed in respect of the first tax year in the basis period for which the asset is put into use and every year thereafter, subject to the qualifying conditions continuing to be met.

For the purposes of computing the wear and tear allowance, the qualifying cost is limited to the cost of the asset **exclusive** of the hire purchase charges, i.e. interest. The interest charge is allowable against taxable profits.

The timing of the actual hire purchase instalments is not relevant provided the agreement is executed during the relevant basis period.

Treatment of Lessors

A person who **leases** plant or equipment to other individuals carrying on qualifying trades or professions will be entitled to a wear and tear allowance in respect of the cost of the plant and equipment leased, provided it can be shown that the **lessor** bears the burden of wear and tear.

Treatment of Lessees

Section 299 TCA 1997 states that, where plant and machinery is leased to a person (lessee) who is carrying on a trade and the **lessee** bears the burden of wear and tear, then the lessee is **deemed** to have incurred the capital expenditure on the assets and is therefore entitled to claim capital allowances on the assets. The lessee was also able to claim a deduction for the full lease payments payable to the lessor which, in some cases, allowed a double deduction for the cost of the asset.

Section 299 TCA 1997 also ensures that an entitlement to capital allowances only exists where:

1. a joint election is made by both lessor and lessee, **and**
2. the lessor has made a claim under section 80A TCA 1997 to be taxed on the income of the lease in accordance with its accounts, **and**
3. the amount of the lease payments deducted by the lessee does not exceed the amount included by the lessor as income in their accounts, **and**
4. in computing his profits, the lessee is not entitled to deduct an amount equivalent to the cost of the asset to the lessor.

The lessee is not entitled to a deduction for both the "capital" element of the lease payments **and** capital allowances on the equipment, but will get a deduction against taxable profits for the interest.

Qualifying Cost and VAT

The qualifying cost of plant and equipment for wear and tear purposes is the **actual expenditure incurred** on the plant or equipment **exclusive** of VAT, where the VAT amount is recoverable. If, however, the business is not VAT-registered or if the VAT is irrecoverable, then the VAT element of the purchase price obviously represents a cost and the **total cost, including VAT**, would be allowable.

4.1.7 Unutilised Capital Allowances

Where the capital allowance claim for a particular year of assessment exceeds the assessable profits from the trade or profession concerned, the excess may be used in the following two ways:

- the excess capital allowances may be **carried forward** indefinitely against assessable profits in future years from the **same** trade or profession until such time as they have been utilised; or
- the capital allowances may be used to **create** or **augment** a **loss claim** that can be used to reduce the individual's total income liable to income tax in that year.

It should be noted that there is **no right** to carry forward unutilised capital allowances in the case of an **employment**. This is probably not important in practice, as it is difficult to envisage a situation where Schedule E income of an employee would be insufficient to offset any capital allowance claim made.

4.2 Capital Allowances: Industrial Buildings

4.2.1 Introduction

Capital allowances are available in respect of expenditure incurred on **certain types** of building. Such buildings are referred to as "industrial buildings". **If a building is not an industrial building, then no capital allowances are available**.

4.2.2 Meaning of "Industrial Buildings"

Unlike the term "plant", section 268 TCA 1997 contains a clear definition of what is meant by an "industrial building". It is defined as a **building or structure in use**:

- as a mill, factory, dock, mineral-analysis laboratory or airport;
- for growing fruit, vegetables or other produce in the course of a trade of market gardening;
- for the intensive production of cattle, sheep, pigs, poultry or eggs in the course of a trade **other than a farming trade**;
- as a hotel, including holiday camps, guesthouses, hostels or caravan/camping sites;
- as a private nursing home;
- as a convalescent, mental health, or palliative care facility.

Dwelling houses, retail shops, showrooms or offices are specifically **excluded** from the definitions of "industrial buildings".

Allowable Expenditure

The **site cost** is specifically disallowed for the purposes of industrial buildings allowances. However, expenditure incurred on the **development** of such a site would be allowable. This would include the cost of preparing, cutting, tunnelling, levelling land and the installation of services on the site.

In relation to the items excluded above, TCA 1997 provides an **exception** if the following conditions can be satisfied:

1. the retail shop, showroom, etc. must be physically **part of a larger structure** which qualifies, **and**
2. the cost of expenditure on such retail shops, showrooms, etc. must **not exceed 10%** of the total expenditure on the building or structure, inclusive of any grant-aided expenditure, but **exclusive** of the site cost.

It should be noted that the exclusion for offices refers to **administrative offices**, and would **not include**, for instance, **a drawing office**, as under case law it is held to be an industrial building, as it is used for **purposes ancillary to the industrial operations** carried out in the rest of the factory.

Example 4.6

	€
Site cost	5,000
Cost of factory portion of building	55,000
Cost of administrative offices portion of building and factory shop	5,000

The €55,000 expenditure on the factory portion of the building qualifies for a 20% government capital grant.

The appropriate fraction to work out the 10% test is as follows:

$$\frac{\text{Cost of administrative offices}}{\text{Total cost of factory and offices exclusive of site cost}} = \frac{5,000}{60,000} = 8.33\%$$

In this case, therefore, the administrative offices and shop will qualify in full for industrial buildings annual allowance. If, however, the computation worked out at, say, 12%, no part of the expenditure on the offices and shop would qualify.

4.2.3 Industrial Buildings Annual Allowance

To qualify for industrial buildings annual allowance (IBAA), the building or structure must be **in use** on the **last day of the chargeable period** (basis period in the case of income tax) for the purpose of a **qualifying trade**.

Industrial buildings annual allowance rate is normally **4% per year**. This is on a **straight-line** rate and is calculated as a **percentage of the qualifying cost** of the industrial building (exclusive of grants).

Annual allowance is also known as **writing down allowance**.

4.2.4 "Tax Life" of Industrial Buildings

The "tax life" of an industrial building is an important and unusual feature of industrial buildings allowances. Generally, the **length of the tax life** is determined by the **rate of annual allowance applicable** to the industrial building in question. The following table summarises the annual allowance rates.

Type of Expenditure	Writing Down Allowance Rate	Time Limit on Balancing Charge "Tax Life"
Factories, mills and dock	4%	25 years
Buildings for growing fruit and vegetables by market gardener	10%	10 years
Production of cattle, sheep, pigs, poultry and eggs by non-farmer	10%	10 years
Hotels, guesthouses, holiday hostels and caravan/camping sites	4%	25 years
Nursing homes	15%	15/20 years
Convalescent, mental health and palliative care facilities	15%	15 years

Treatment of Property-based Capital Allowances

Section 409 TCA 1997 states that passive investors will not be able to claim accelerated industrial buildings allowances beyond the original tax life of the scheme where the tax life ends after 1 January 2015. If the tax life ended before 1 January 2015, the passive investor cannot carry forward any unused allowances.

A **5% property relief surcharge** under section 531AAE TCA 1997 applies to investors (both passive and active) with gross income of €100,000 or more. The surcharge is collected as an additional Universal Social Charge (USC) of 5% on the amount of income sheltered by property reliefs in a given year. (See **Section 10.3** for more detail on the USC.)

4.2.5 Balancing Allowances and Charges

If the building is sold, and the "**tax life**" of the relevant qualifying expenditure has **elapsed**, then the vendor **does not** suffer a **balancing charge** and the purchaser is **not entitled** to capital allowances in respect of that expenditure (see exception below).

If, on the other hand, any industrial building is sold **before** its tax life has elapsed, the vendor must compute a balancing allowance/charge in the normal way, and the purchaser is **entitled to annual allowances** in respect of all or part of the cost of the building or structure. The allowances available to the purchaser of a second-hand industrial building are only available provided it is **used** as an industrial building. If this condition is satisfied, the annual allowance, based on the **lower** of the price paid for the second-hand building and the original cost of the building, is granted. The annual allowance available is spread **equally** (i.e. on a straight-line basis) over the **balance of the tax life** of the building.

No balancing allowance arises on the sale of an industrial building where the vendor and the purchaser are connected to each other.

4.2.6   Qualifying Cost, Foreign Properties and Lessors

Qualifying Cost

The qualifying cost for the purposes of the IBAA depends on whether or not the vendor is a builder.

If the **vendor is a builder**, the qualifying cost for allowance purposes is equal to:

$$\text{Total Purchase Price} \times \frac{\text{Construction Expenditure}}{\text{Site Cost} + \text{Construction Expenditure}}$$

If the vendor is a **non-builder**, the qualifying cost is deemed to be the **lower of**:

■ the actual construction expenditure, or
■ the net price paid (calculated using the above formula).

The purpose of these rules is to prevent allowances being claimed on any element of the profit or gain made by an investor on the sale.

Foreign Properties

Expenditure incurred on industrial buildings situated outside the State does not qualify for any allowances.

Lessors

The landlord will qualify for industrial buildings allowance where the lessee is carrying on a qualifying trade in the building.

The allowance can also be claimed if the building is leased to the Industrial Development Authority (IDA Ireland), the Shannon Free Airport Development Company (SFADCo) or Údarás na Gaeltachta, which in turn sub-lease the building to a tenant who carries on a qualifying trade.

4.2.7   Unutilised Industrial Buildings Allowance

Where an industrial building is used for the purpose of a qualifying trade, industrial buildings annual allowance (IBAA) is available as a deduction against the tax-adjusted profits of the trade. Any excess can be carried forward against profits in future years.

Lessors

Lessors of industrial buildings can set their IBAA against all rental income in the year. Where the amount of the capital allowances exceed the rental income, the excess can be offset against other income, subject to a **maximum offset of €31,750**. The further excess can be carried forward against future rental profits in priority to Case V losses brought forward. Allowances carried forward from an earlier year are first deducted against Case V income, before allowances for the current year are deducted.

Industrial buildings annual allowance on hotels in excess of rental income **cannot** be offset against non-rental income, **except** where the expenditure was incurred **prior** to 3 December 1997.

Acquisition from a Company

Where an individual lessor acquires an industrial building from a company, the excess of the capital allowances over the rental income of that building may only be carried forward against future rental income of **that** building, i.e. the excess may **not be offset** against rental income from **other** properties or against any other income.

Example 4.7

Jack Brown acquired a second-hand industrial building on 1 December 2018. He is entitled to annual capital allowances of €70,000 in respect of this property and in 2021 received rental income of €20,000 from the property. Jack had other rental income of €10,000 and non-rental income of €50,000 for 2021.

Tax Computation 2021	€	€
A. Property acquired from an individual		
Case V income	30,000	
Less: capital allowances	(70,000)	
Excess capital allowances	(40,000)	
Restricted to: maximum offset		(31,750)
Non-rental income		50,000
Taxable income 2021		**18,250**
Capital allowances carried forward against rental income		
Excess allowances	40,000	
Less: utilised against non-trading income	(31,750)	
Allowances carried forward	8,250	
B. Property is a hotel and acquired from an individual		
Case V income	30,000	
Less: capital allowances	(70,000)	
Restricted to: total Case V income		(30,000)
Net Case V income		–
Non-rental income		50,000
Taxable income 2021		**50,000**
Capital allowances carried forward against all rental income		
Capital allowances	70,000	
Less: utilised 2021	(30,000)	
Allowances carried forward	40,000	
C. Property acquired from a company		
Case V income	30,000	
Less: capital allowances	(70,000)	
Restricted to: amount of rent from new building		(20,000)
Net Case V income		10,000
Non-rental income		50,000
Taxable income 2021		**60,000**
Capital allowances carried forward against rental income from new building only		
Capital allowances	70,000	
Less: utilised 2021	(20,000)	
Allowances carried forward	50,000	

4.3 Cases II & III Loss Relief

4.3.1   Introduction

Section 381 TCA 1997 provides relief for a loss sustained, in a trade, profession, employment or farming, by way of deduction from **any other income** chargeable to tax in that year. The loss is deducted from **gross income** before deduction of charges on income or personal allowances/reliefs.

Any loss not relieved under section 381 can be **carried forward** and set-off against the profits of the **same** trade or profession in subsequent years (section 382 relief). The loss must be set-off against the **first** subsequent year's trading profits, and so on. Losses may be carried forward indefinitely provided the trade that incurred the loss **continues** to be carried on.

Terminal loss relief can be claimed in respect of a loss incurred in the **final** year of a trade or profession. This loss can be **carried back** against profits from the same trade or profession for the last **three years** of assessment preceding that year in which the cessation occurs.

4.3.2 "Legal Basis" and "Conventional Basis"

The strict legal interpretation of section 381 relief indicates that it is the **actual** loss for a particular tax year that may be relieved ("legal basis"). In practice, however, relief will be granted against the total income of the taxpayer for the **year of assessment** in which the accounting period ends ("conventional basis"), e.g. a section 381 claim for a €10,000 loss for the accounts year ended 30 September 2021 is available for 2021. Note, however, the following **exceptions** where the **legal basis** is applied:

- In the first, second and third year of a **commencing** business.
- For any year of assessment immediately **following** a year of assessment where section 381 relief was allowed on the legal basis.
- Where the claimant formally **claims** the legal basis.
- In the year of **cessation** of a business, any relief under section 381 is allowed in respect of the loss applicable to the period from the beginning of the tax year to the date of cessation. For example, if the business ceases on 30 June 2021, the loss period is 1 January 2021 to 30 June 2021, therefore section 381 claim can be made for 2021.

4.3.3 Effect of Capital Allowances

Capital allowances for a year of assessment may be used to create or augment a loss, provided that such allowances are **first** set-off against any **balancing charge** arising in the year of assessment to which they relate, which are not covered by capital allowances forward.

Example 4.8
Mary White has been in business for many years and prepares annual accounts to 30 June. Her details are as follows:

	€
Tax-adjusted profit for the y/e 30 June 2021	9,000
Capital allowances 2021:	
– Wear and tear allowance	7,000
– Balancing allowances	500
– Balancing charge	3,000
Unutilised capital allowances forward from 2020	9,600
Section 381 Claim 2021	
Tax-adjusted Case I profit y/e 30/06/2021	9,000
Deduct: Capital allowances forward (€9,600; limited to actual profit)	(9,000)
Net Case I	**Nil**
Balancing charge 2021	3,000
Deduct: Balance of capital allowances forward (€9,600 – €9,000)	(600)
Net balancing charge	2,400
Deduct: Wear and tear allowance 2021	(7,000)
Balancing allowances 2021	(500)
Section 381 loss (available to reduce total income for 2021)	**(5,100)**

4.3.4　Order of Relief

Section 381 loss relief must be claimed in the following order:

1. against the individual's **earned** income, which is of the same class as the type of income that would have arisen from the business in which the loss is sustained had a profit rather than a loss been made;
2. against other income of the individual;
3. against the earned income of the individual's **spouse or civil partner**, which is of the corresponding class; and
4. against other income of the spouse or civil partner.

This is relevant in calculating the allowance for retirement annuities.

4.3.5　Amount of Relief Taken

A section 381 loss must be used up to the **full amount** of the loss available, or the amount of the **gross income** for the year of assessment, whichever is less. A section 381 loss **cannot** be **partially** used so as to leave sufficient income to cover charges and use up tax credits, or to allow the taxpayer to avoid being taxed only at higher rates. (See **Section 4.3.7** for restrictions on relief.)

4.3.6　Section 381 Relief Claim

Any claim for relief under section 381 must be made, in writing, to the Inspector of Taxes not later than two years after the end of the year of assessment in which the loss is incurred. In practice, the claim is normally made as part of filing the income tax return.

　　Section 381 relief is not compulsory and is only applied if a claim is made.

4.3.7　Restriction of Section 381 Relief for Non-active Individuals

Section 381B TCA 1997 limits, but does not prevent, the claiming of loss relief by individuals not engaged in a trade in an "active capacity". This section limits the amount of loss relief that can be claimed by an individual under section 381 to **€31,750** (annualised).

　　"Active capacity" is stipulated, by section 381C TCA 1997, to be more than **10 hours a week** by an individual personally engaged in the day-to-day management or conduct of the activities of the trade or profession. In addition, the activities of the trade or profession must be carried out on a commercial basis (and not as a loss-making exercise). The restriction does not apply to losses arising from:

- farming;
- market gardening;
- a trade consisting of a Lloyd's underwriting business;
- qualifying expenditure for relief for significant buildings and gardens (section 482); or
- capital allowances arising from specified reliefs (including writing down or balancing allowances).

Where an individual carries on two or more trades, the €31,750 limit is an **aggregate** limit between all trades. Any loss not allowable by reference to the new limit will be available to carry forward as a section 382 loss.

Example 4.9
Jack and Jill share profits and losses equally in their catering business. John also works as a hotel manager and devotes approximately eight hours a week to the catering business in which Jill works full-time. Their results for the year ended 2021 were as follows:

Trading loss year ended 31 December 2021 €82,500

	Jack	Jill
Trading loss (apportioned 50:50)	€41,250	€41,250
Average hours per week engaged in business	8	40
Loss relief available under section 381	€31,750	€41,250
Loss carry forward (section 382)	€9,500	€Nil

4.3.8 Section 382 Loss Relief

Method of Relief

Section 382 loss relief is available where a person incurs a loss in any trade or profession and it entitles him to carry it **forward** for set-off against the assessable profits (after deduction of capital allowances) of **the same trade or profession**.

The loss must be used, as far as possible, against the first subsequent year's trading profits, and so on.

Loss relief under section 382 is only available where it has not already been effectively relieved under section 381 or by time apportionment in commencement and change of accounting date situations. Losses may be carried forward indefinitely provided the trade which incurred the loss continues to be carried on.

Limitation on Section 382 Loss Relief

A loss can only be carried forward under section 382 provided it has not already been effectively relieved by any one or more of the following:

▨ section 381 relief; and
▨ relief by way of apportionment or aggregation of profits and losses (as in a "commencement" situation).

Example 4.10
A trader commenced business on 1 February 2021 and makes up accounts to 30 September each year. His results were as follows:

	Profit/(Loss) €
7 months to 30 September 2021	(7,000)
Year to 30 September 2022	7,200
Year to 30 September 2023	6,000

His assessable profits for the first three years of assessment are calculated as follows:

Year of Assessment	Basis Period	Assessment
2021	01/02/2021–31/12/2021	
	(€7,000) + (3/12 × €7,200) = (€5,200)	Nil
2022	Year ended 30/09/2022 = €7,200	
	Less: loss forward = (€5,200) (Note)	2,000
2023	Year ended 30/09/2023:	
	Profits:	6,000

Note: Loss 30/09/2021   (7,000)
     Less: utilised
     2021   (1,800)
     2022   (5,200)   (7,000)
                        (Nil)

4.3.9 Section 382 Loss Relief arising due to a Third-year Adjustment

As you are aware, the profits assessable in the third year of assessment are based on the basis period of 12 months ending during the year of assessment, but this figure can be reduced by:

Profits assessable in the second tax year

Less: actual profits of the second year of assessment.

Where this deduction is greater than the amount of the original profits assessable for the third year, then the excess is treated as if it were a loss forward under section 382.

The claim for this deduction must be in writing and must be included in the self-assessment tax return for the third year of assessment.

Loss relief in respect of the excess **cannot be claimed under section 381**.

Example 4.11

Derek commenced to trade as a furniture manufacturer on 1 July 2021. His results were as follows:

	Profit
	€
Period 1 July 2021–30 June 2022	28,000
Year ended 30 June 2023	7,000
Year ended 30 June 2024	60,000

Computation of Assessable Profits

Year of assessment	Basis period	Amount assessable
		€
2021	01/07/2021–31/12/2021	14,000
	(€28,000 × 6/12)	
2022	y/e 30/06/2022	28,000
2023	y/e 30/06/2023 (Note)	Nil

Note:

Amount assessable for second year, i.e. 2022:	28,000
Less: actual profits for 2022:	
(€28,000 × 6/12) + (€7,000 × 6/12) = €14,000 + €3,500	17,500
Excess	10,500
Final 2022 assessment: €7,000 – €10,500	(3,500) i.e nil

The excess of €3,500 is carried forward under section 382 against future trading profits for 2024 onwards.

Questions

Review Questions

(See Suggested Solutions to Review Questions at the end of this textbook.)

Question 4.1

Regina Briers, a sole trader in business for many years, makes up accounts to 30 April each year. During the year ended 30 April 2021, she bought the following second-hand assets:

		€
10/05/2020	Office equipment	€1,000
20/04/2021	Printer	€3,500

The tax written down value of her other assets at 1 January 2021 was as follows:

Motor vehicle (Cat. D) (purchased 01/12/2020 for €35,000)	€10,500
Plant and machinery (purchased 10/06/2019 for €2,500)	€1,875

Requirement
Prepare the capital allowances schedule for 2021.

Question 4.2

Lillian Hanney has practised as a self-employed dentist for many years and makes up accounts to 30 June each year. During the year ended 30 June 2021, she purchased the following assets:

		€
10/07/2020	Chairs for waiting room	1,000
22/02/2021	X-ray machine	4,100

The details of her other assets are as follows:

Year of Acquisition	Tax Year	Cost €	TWDV at 01/01/2021 €
Bought y/e 30/06/2018	2018	15,000 (12.5%)	9,375
Bought y/e 30/06/2019	2019	9,000 (12.5%)	6,750

Requirement
Prepare the capital allowances schedule for 2021.

Question 4.3

Barney Connor is a self-employed accountant who has been in business for many years and prepares accounts to 30 September each year. During the year ended 30 September 2021, he purchased the following assets:

		€
29/12/2020	Computers	8,000
01/03/2021	Desktop calculator	120
08/06/2021	Desks	1,800
05/08/2021	Printer ink cartridges	750
20/09/2021	Filing cabinets	2,300
		12,970

The filing cabinets were not delivered until 15 October 2021.
Plant and machinery bought during the y/e 30 September 2017 for €10,000 had a TWDV at 1 January 2021 of €5,000.

Requirement
Prepare the capital allowances schedule for 2021.

Question 4.4

A business commenced on 1 October 2021 and its first accounts were prepared to 30 September 2022. Office equipment was purchased on 12 December 2021 at a cost of €1,000 and immediately put into use.

Requirement

Prepare the capital allowances schedule for the tax years for which the first accounts to 30 September 2022 relate.

Question 4.5

Sean's business commenced trading on 1 June 2021 and the first accounts were prepared to 31 May 2022. Machinery was purchased on 8 December 2021 for €10,000 and immediately put into use.

Requirement

Prepare the capital allowances schedule for the tax years for which the first accounts to 31 May 2022 relate.

Question 4.6

Joan O'Reilly is a bookbinder who commenced business as a sole trader on 1 May 2021. In the year ended 30 April 2022, she purchased the following second-hand assets:

		€
21/05/2021	Bookbinding machine	9,000
10/04/2022	Computer	1,700

Requirement

Prepare the capital allowances schedule for the tax years for which the first accounts to 30 April 2022 relate.

Question 4.7

Cormac Molloy is a self-employed farmer who has been in business for many years and prepares accounts to 31 December each year. Here are his motor vehicle details:

Motor car cost 01/08/2021	€21,000	Emissions Category D
Total estimated annual km	20,000 km	
Total estimated private km	5,000 km	(i.e. 75% of total kms is business)

Requirement

Calculate the capital allowances schedule for the car for 2021.

Question 4.8

Joseph Ryan is a shopkeeper who is in business many years and prepares accounts to 30 June each year. On 10 November 2020 he bought a second-hand car for €27,000 (emissions Category C). The private use is one-third.

Requirement

Calculate the capital allowances schedule and tax written down value of the car for 2021.

Question 4.9

Dan Bell is a doctor who prepares his accounts up to 31 December each year. In the year ended 31 December 2021 he purchased a second-hand car for €25,000 on 20 May 2021 and new office equipment for €1,000 on 1 February 2021. (Assume 70% business use for motor car and emissions Category A.)

Dan Bell also sold equipment on 28 January 2021 for €3,500. The tax written down value of the equipment at 1 January 2021 was €7,500 (cost €15,000). Dan has been in practice for many years.

Requirement
Calculate the capital allowances schedule and the tax written down value of the assets for 2021.

Question 4.10

Joe Bracken is a butcher who prepares annual accounts to 30 September. He has traded for many years. His car is used 70% for business purposes. The cost of his second-hand car (purchased in October 2018) was €27,000. He sold his car in January 2021 for €20,000.

Requirement
Calculate the balancing charge or allowance due on the car.

Question 4.11

Fitzroy carries on a manufacturing business in Dublin. He has been in business for many years and prepares annual accounts to 30 April. During the year ended 30 April 2021 the following transactions took place:

1. Second-hand plant costing €17,000 on 1 May 2011 was sold in February 2021 for €2,200. (Tax written down value at 1 January 2021 was nil.)
2. Plant that was acquired new for €25,000 in November 2013 was sold for €1,500 in January 2021. (Tax written down value at 1 January 2021 was nil.) New plant was acquired for €50,000 on 15 April 2021.
3. On 20 December 2019 he purchased second-hand plant costing €10,000. (Tax written down value at 1 January 2021 was €8,750.)
4. Fitzroy has two lorries. One cost €20,000 on 5 January 2021 and the other €26,000 on 1 December 2013. (Tax written down value at 1 January 2021 was nil.)
5. Fitzroy owns a car that he bought on 16 July 2017 for €25,000 (emissions Category C). One-third of his travel relates to business use.

Fitzroy has no other assets in respect of which capital allowances were claimed.

Requirement
Compute maximum capital allowances for 2021 and 2022, assuming no further additions or disposals are made.

Question 4.12

Sarah commenced to trade as a hairdresser on 1 June 2018. She made the following tax-adjusted profits:

12 months ended 31 May 2019	–	€59,000
12 months to 31 May 2020	–	€46,000
12 months to 31 May 2021	–	€120,000
12 months to 31 May 2022	–	€160,000

During the above periods she bought and put the following assets into use:

1 June 2018	–	General equipment €26,000 (second-hand)
1 September 2018	–	Additional hairdryers €800 (second-hand)
10 April 2019	–	Chairs €1,400 (second-hand)
23 April 2019	–	Car (60% business use) €14,000 (new Category A car)

Requirement

Compute assessable profits and associated capital allowances for first four years of assessment.

Question 4.13

Joe Bloggs has operated a newsagent/tobacconist/confectionery shop for many years. He has previously dealt with his own income tax affairs and supplies the following details relating to his business for the year ended 31 December 2021:

	€	€
Gross profit	26,880	
Sale proceeds of old equipment	1,500	
Building society interest received (gross)	<u>210</u>	28,590
Less: Overhead Costs		
Wages to self	5,200	
Motor expenses	1,750	
Light and heat	1,200	
Wages to wife as bookkeeper and assistant	1,500	
Wages to other employees	7,600	
Advertising	270	
Christmas gifts to customers (bottles of whiskey)	300	
Depreciation:		
Motor car	500	
Fixtures and equipment	400	
Rates	800	
Donation to church	105	
Repairs to yard wall	200	
Painting of shop	450	
New cash register (purchased 1 February 2021)	380	
Deposit on new shelving (paid 10 February 2021)	1,000	
New display freezer (purchased 1 March 2021)	600	
Insurance	375	
Insurance on contents of flat	100	
Hire-purchase instalments on new shelving (8 @ €240)	1,920	
Payment to self in lieu of rent	2,000	
Sundry expenses	<u>2,250</u>	
		(28,900)
Loss for year		(310)

Mr Bloggs owns the property which consists of the shop and the flat above the shop where he and his wife live. He estimates that 25% of the heat and light relate to the living accommodation.

The Category A motor car cost €20,000 on 1 January 2016. Mr Bloggs has advised you that business travel accounts for 75% of his annual motoring.

The new shelving costing €5,633, excluding VAT, was purchased under a hire-purchase agreement and you have calculated that interest charges of €376 have arisen before 31 December 2021.

At 1 January 2021, the following were the tax written down values of the equipment and shelving, and the motor car:

	€
Equipment and shelving (cost €2,500 in January 2017 and sold for €1,500 in 2021)	1,250
Motor car	9,000

Requirement

Compute:

(a) Joe Bloggs's taxable Case I income for 2021; and
(b) his capital allowances schedule for 2021.

Question 4.14

Mr Goa, a long-established manufacturer, acquired a new industrial building on 30 April 2017 for €160,000 (including land costing €20,000). On 1 May 2018 he sold the building for €190,000 (land being valued at €25,000) to Mrs Statham, who immediately commenced trading from it at that date, also as a manufacturer. Mr Goa's accounts are made up to 30 June each year. Mrs Statham made up her first set of accounts to 30 April 2019 and thereafter on a yearly basis.

Requirement

Calculate the industrial buildings annual allowances for Mr Goa and Mrs Statham for the years of assessment 2017–2021.

Question 4.15

James built and occupied a factory for the purpose of his trade during the year ended 30 June 2021.

His costs were as follows:	€
Site purchase cost	10,000
Site development costs	5,000
Construction of factory	95,000
Construction of adjoining administrative office	10,000
Construction of adjoining showroom	15,000
Total cost	135,000

Requirement

Compute James's industrial buildings annual allowance for 2021.

Question 4.16

Mr Plant carries on a manufacturing trade in Ireland. He prepares his annual accounts to 31 December. During the year ended 31 December 2021, he incurred the following capital expenditure:

1. He purchased new office furniture and equipment on 30 March 2021 for €10,000. The items involved were brought into use immediately.
2. He purchased a new truck on 30 September 2021 for €25,000 for the purposes of the trade.
3. On 30 November 2021, he placed deposits on two items of machinery:
   (a) €5,000 on a used milling machine for delivery on 31 January 2022; and
   (b) €4,000 on a new pump for delivery on 15 February 2022.
4. He purchased a new car on 1 April 2021 for €26,000, which is emissions Category D. The agreed portion of business usage is 75%. He sold his existing car on the same date for €7,500 in a straight cash deal. The car originally cost €26,000 in December 2016. The allowable cost for wear and tear purposes had been restricted to €24,000.
5. On 15 April 2021 he purchased new machinery for €24,000, which was brought into use immediately. He received a grant of €4,000 on the purchase of the machinery.
6. On 31 July 2021 he purchased a second-hand factory premises for €120,000. The original qualifying cost of the factory premises for capital allowances purposes was €75,000, and the building has a remaining tax life of 15 years. The factory premises were brought into use within three months of the date of purchase.
7. In October 2021 he commenced building an extension to his original factory premises. The expenditure incurred to 31 December 2021 was €60,000 on actual building work and €8,000 on architect's fees. The extension is due to be completed in March 2022. A grant of €10,000 had been received on the expenditure incurred to 31 December 2021.

The situation regarding assets acquired prior to 1 January 2021 is as follows:

	Date of Purchase	Cost €	Tax Written Down Value at 01/01/2021 €
Fixtures and fittings 12.5%	2018	12,000	7,500
Plant and machinery 12.5%	2018	13,500	8,437
Motor car 12.5%	10/12/2016	24,000	9,000
Trucks 12.5%	June 2019	18,750	14,062

Requirement
Compute Mr Plant's capital allowances schedule for 2021.

Question 4.17

Janet has been in business for many years as a manufacturer. She prepares accounts to 31 May each year. During the year ended 31 May 2021, she engaged in an expansion programme. She incurred capital expenditure and received capital sums as follows:

2 June 2020	Sold machinery for €14,000. This machinery had cost €35,000 when purchased. The written down value at the date of sale was nil.
15 June 2020	Purchased new replacement machinery costing €49,000 on which rollover relief was claimed. This machinery qualified for a grant of €10,000.
30 June 2020	Purchased a second-hand industrial building for €220,000. The building had cost the original owner €120,000 to construct in June 2008.
1 August 2020	She sold her office building, which had been located some distance away from the industrial buildings. The office building had cost €20,000 in May 1998. Proceeds received from the sale amounted to €60,000.

31 October 2020	Completed an extension to the industrial building purchased on 30 June.	
	Details of the expenditure are as follows:	€
	Levelling of site	2,000
	Architect's fees	3,000
	Offices	6,000
	Factory	<u>59,000</u>
		<u>70,000</u>
1 November 2020	Purchased two new cars for sales representatives at a cost of €26,000 each, which are emissions Category C. She partly funded the purchases by trading in a car used by one of the sales representatives for €12,500. That car had cost €24,000 when purchased in June 2016 and had a tax written down value of €12,000 at the date of disposal.	
30 May 2021	Purchased a second-hand photocopier at a cost of €2,000. The copier was not put into use until June 2021.	

The situation regarding assets bought prior to 1 June 2020 is as follows:

	Date of Purchase	Cost €	Tax Written Down Value at 01/01/2021 €
Plant and machinery (12.5%)	July 2016	10,000	5,000
Delivery truck (12.5%)	November 2013	17,000	2,125
Motor vehicles (12.5%)	June 2016	24,000	12,000

Requirement
Compute the capital allowances due for the tax year 2021.

Question 4.18

Linda works part-time as a marketing manager for a soft-furnishings company. She also owns and runs, on a commercial basis, a children's clothing business in which she works at least 15 hours a week. Linda's income is as follows:

	€
Trading loss for year ended 30 September 2021	(60,000)
Salary for 2021	80,000

Requirement
Compute Linda's assessable income for 2021.

Question 4.19

Earl Jones works full-time as a programmer with a local software company. He also runs a small mail-order business in his spare time and devotes approximately seven hours a week to the business. His income for the tax year 2021 is as follows:

	€
Trading profit/(loss) y/e 30 June 2021	(40,000)
Salary	55,000
Interest on government securities	25,000

Requirement
Compute Mr Jones' assessable income for 2021.

Question 4.20

Mr Fool, who has traded for many years, has the following profits and capital allowances:

Profit y/e 31/12/2021	€20,000
Capital allowances 2021	(€37,000)

He also had a balancing charge of €10,000 for 2021.

Requirement
What is Mr Fool's taxable income for 2021?

Question 4.21

John has been in business for many years and prepares annual accounts to 30 September. He has a tax-adjusted profit for year ended 30 September 2021 of €9,000. The capital allowances position for 2021 is:

	€
Wear and tear allowance	7,000
Balancing allowances	500
Balancing charge	(3,000)

Unutilised capital allowances forward from 2020 amount to €9,600.

Requirement
Calculate the capital allowances available to John in 2021.

Question 4.22

Jim's only source of income is his travel agency business, which he has carried on for many years. He prepares annual accounts to 30 June. Recent tax-adjusted results are as follows:

	€
Y/e 30/06/2019 tax-adjusted loss	(18,000)
Y/e 30/06/2020 tax-adjusted profit	17,000
Y/e 30/06/2021 tax-adjusted profit	50,000

Requirement

Calculate Jim's assessments for all years, claiming relief in the earliest possible year.

Question 4.23

Basil Bond has the following income:

	Tax Year		
	2019	**2020**	**2021**
	€	€	€
Rents	20,000	30,000	25,000
Irish taxed interest (gross)	1,000	1,200	1,200
Trading profit/(loss) for y/e 30 September in tax year	80,000	(37,000)	45,000

The above sources of income have existed for many years.

Requirement

Calculate the assessable income for 2019–2021 inclusive, claiming optimum relief for losses.

Schedule E – Employment Income

Learning Objectives

After studying this chapter you will understand:

- the different types of employment income assessable under Schedule E;
- the distinction between an employee and a self-employed person;
- the rules regarding the assessment to tax of employment income;
- the rules regarding the assessment and computation of taxable income as regards benefits in kind and commencement payments; and
- the rules regarding the applicability of expenses against employment income.

5.1 Introduction

Employment income is all income derived from employments, directorships and pensions arising in Ireland and is taxed under Schedule E. Employment income is usually (though not always) taxed at source under the Pay As You Earn (PAYE) system and is assessed on the **actual income received** in the year of assessment. Benefits and perquisites provided by an employer to an employee or director are also assessable and taxable under Schedule E.

5.1.1 Income Assessable under Schedule E

The following income is subject to taxation under Schedule E:

- Emoluments from all offices and employments. Examples include: directors' fees, salaries, wages, bonuses and commission paid to employees (see **Section 5.1.2**).
- Private pensions and annuities. Examples include pensions paid to former directors, employees or their dependants.
- Benefits in kind and perquisites. Examples include: benefits derived from the use of a company car; the provision of rent-free accommodation to an employee; holiday vouchers and preferential loans.
- Certain lump-sum payments deriving from an office or employment, either before its commencement or after its cessation. Examples include: inducement payments; non-statutory redundancy payments; round-sum expense allowances; ex-gratia and compensation payments on retirement or dismissal.
- Payments made, or consideration given, under restrictive covenants.
- Income arising to any person as a member of the European Parliament (MEP) is chargeable to tax under Schedule E where the income is payable out of money provided by the Irish State. (Where the

income is payable out of money provided by the budget of the European Union, it is chargeable to tax under Case III Schedule D (section 127A TCA 1997). An MEP's salary is not exempted from tax.
- Treatment of flight crews. Section 127B TCA 1997 provides that any income arising to an individual, whether resident in the State or not, from any employment exercised aboard an aircraft that is operated:
  - in international traffic, and
  - by an enterprise that has its place of effective management in the State, is chargeable to tax under Schedule E.
- Social welfare benefits **taxable** under Schedule E include:
  - State pension (contributory/non-contributory), widow/widower's or surviving civil partner's pension. Includes any amounts in respect of a qualifying adult dependant, but **excluding** any amount in respect of a qualifying child dependant.
  - Illness, Invalidity, Adoptive, Maternity and Paternity benefits.
  - Carer's Allowance and Carer's Benefit.
  - Jobseeker's Benefit (the first €13 per week is not taxable).
  - Covid-19 pandemic payments: Pandemic Unemployment Payment (PUP) and payments made under the Temporary Wages Subsidy Scheme (TWSS).

Social welfare benefits **not taxable** under Schedule E include:

- Jobseeker's Allowance
- Child Benefit
- Domiciliary Care and Disability Allowance including Respite Care Grant
- Family Income Supplement and Household Benefits and Fuel Allowance
- statutory redundancy payments
- Persons in receipt of Jobseeker's Benefit due to "short-time employment" (e.g. where an individual's normal working week is cut to, say, three days). The benefit received for days of unemployment is exempt.

5.1.2   Meaning of "Office" and "Employment"

Offices
The term "office" is not defined in legislation but has been held under tax case law to mean:
"A subsisting permanent, substantive position, which has an existence independent of the person who filled it, and which went on and was filled in succession by successive holders."

Employment
The **distinction** between an **employee** and a **self-employed** person is not set out in tax legislation. In general, case law has determined that an employee is a person who holds a post and who has a **contract of service** with an employer, which basically involves the relationship of master and servant.

A self-employed person will provide services under a **contract for services**. Whether or not a person is an employee or a self-employed person will normally be clear from the facts of the particular case. Sometimes, however, the distinction between an employee and a self-employed person is not entirely clear and, accordingly, the issue has been the subject of a number of cases.

The UK case of *Market Investigations Ltd v. Minister of Social Security* (1969) established a fundamental test which has been quoted in subsequent cases. It established the fundamental test: "Does the person performing the services perform them as a person in business on his own account?"

If the answer is "yes", then the contract is a contract **for** services; if "no", then there is a contract **of** services.

If an individual is found to be performing the services as a person in business on their own account, then this indicates that the individual is self-employed rather than an employee.

The Irish case of *Henry Denny and Sons Ltd T/A Kerry Foods v. Minister for Social Welfare* (1998) follows this test and established three other tests to determine control, integration and economic relations to discover which type of contract existed.

The *Denny* case involved an examination of the employment status of supermarket demonstrators/ merchandisers of food products. The court found that the demonstrators were in fact employees rather than self-employed.

The Employment Status Group devised the following tests to determine employee or self-employed status.

1. **The terms of the contract**

   If, under the terms of the contract under which the person provides his services, he is entitled to holiday pay, sick pay, pension entitlements, company car or other benefits, he is more likely to be an **employee** rather than self-employed. If the contract provides that the person is required to work fixed hours on particular days, then he is more likely to be an employee, although this is not always the case.

2. **The degree of integration of the person into the organisation to which his services are provided**

   The greater the degree of integration into the organisation, the more likely the person is to be regarded as an employee.

3. **Whether the person provides his own helpers**

   If the individual is free to hire others to do the work he has agreed to undertake and he sets the terms under which such persons are employed, this is more indicative of a self-employed person rather than an employee.

4. **Whether the person provides his own equipment**

   If a person provides significant pieces of equipment to carry out the work he has agreed to undertake, this is also indicative of a self-employed person rather than an employee.

5. **The extent of the control exercised over the individual**

   Generally, a self-employed person will have more control over the work he does than an employee in terms of how, when and where it is to be carried out.

6. **The degree of responsibility for investment and management**

   A person who is responsible for running a business, who uses his own capital and is responsible for determining the running and expansion of a business is clearly a self-employed person. This is essentially the test described above, which examines if the person is performing the service as a person in business on his own account.

7. **The degree of financial risk taken**

   An individual who risks his own money by, for example, buying assets and bearing their running costs and paying for overheads and large quantities of materials, is more likely to be self-employed. Financial risk could also take the form of quoting a fixed price for a job, with the consequent risk of bearing the additional costs if the job overruns. However, this will not mean that the worker is self-employed unless there is a real risk of financial loss.

8. **Opportunity to profit from sound management**

   A person whose profit or loss depends on his capacity to reduce overheads and organise his work effectively is likely to be self-employed.

See the *Code of Practice for Determining Employment or Self-Employment Status of Individuals* (February 2019) at **Appendix 2**.

5.2 Basis of Assessment

Section 112 TCA 1997 provides that the statutory basis of assessment for employment income is the **receipts basis**, i.e when the income is received, subject to certain exclusions as outlined below.

5.2.1 Company Directors

The receipts basis of assessment does not apply to income from certain directorships. Proprietary directors, i.e. directors who own or control more than 15% of the share capital of a company, are taxed on the **earnings basis** of assessment, that is, on the amount **actually earned** in the year, **irrespective** of when the income was paid. Other than the first and last year, the remuneration assessable is taken as the amount of director's remuneration charged in the company accounts for a year ending within the tax year. For example, a director's remuneration charged in the company accounts to September 2021 will form the basis of assessment for Schedule E for 2021. The director will be assessed on the amount shown in the company accounts. However, this arrangement does not apply where either there is a change to the accounting period or the accounting period is not for a 12-month period.

5.2.2 Social Welfare Payments

The Department of Social Protection (DSP) holds an exclusion order in respect of taxable payments that it makes under the Social Welfare Acts. As such, all DSP payments are assessed on the earnings basis of assessment. This is to avoid an overpayment of tax where DSP arrears are accumulated and paid in a single tax year.

5.2.3 Death Cases

Salary payments due to a person who dies are deemed to have been made to the deceased person immediately prior to death. This ensures that the income tax liability remains on the deceased person and not on their estate, avoiding the requirement for the estate to register for income tax.

5.2.4 PAYE Exclusion Orders

The receipts basis of assessment does not apply to income in respect of which a PAYE exclusion order has issued. Exclusion orders are generally issued in respect of non-resident employees who are unlikely to have a tax liability in the State.

5.3 Computation of Taxable Schedule E Income

As outlined in **Section 5.1**, income from all offices and employments, pensions, benefits in kind, perquisites and certain lump-sum payments deriving from an office or employment is assessable to income tax under Schedule E in respect of the actual income received in the year of assessment. Note, however, the exclusions outlined in **Section 5.2** where the earnings basis applies.

Typically, Schedule E employment income is assessed and computed, and the resulting income tax, Pay Related Social Insurance (PRSI) and Universal Social Charge (USC) paid over by the employer on behalf of its employee under the PAYE system. However, a PAYE employee who is registered as a **self-assessed person** (see **Chapter 12**) must also complete a **return of income** (Form 11) and return it to Revenue by 31 October in the following tax year.

Form 11 will contain details of all taxable income, including share option gains, taxable lump-sum payments (e.g. commencement, termination or retirement lump sums) and any claims for allowable expenses for the particular tax year.

A pro-forma income tax computation for a self-assessed employee may look as follows:

Self-assessed Employee – Income Tax Computation 2021

			€	€
Schedule E:	Income from employments/offices:			
	– salary/wages/directors' fee/pensions		X	
	– bonus/commissions		X	
	– benefits in kind		X	
	– taxable lump sum		X	
	– share options		X	X
Less:	Allowable expenses		(X)	
	– Employee's contribution to a Revenue-approved superannuation fund		(X)	(X)
Gross income				X
Deduct:	Relief for charges paid during the tax year:			
	– covenants paid		(X)	
	– qualifying interest paid		(X)	(X)
Total income/net statutory income				X
Deduct:	Personal reliefs (i.e. reliefs @ marginal rate)			(X)
Taxable income				X
Tax payable: (single person)				
	€35,300 @ 20%		X	
	Balance @ 40%		X	X
Deduct:	Non-refundable tax credits			(X)
	(i.e. reliefs @ standard rate)			
Income tax liability				X
Deduct:	Refundable tax credits:			
	– tax paid under PAYE in tax year		**(X)**	
	– RTSO paid in tax year		**(X)**	**(X)**
Add back:	Income tax deducted from payments made:			
	– tax deducted from covenants payments			X
Net tax due/refundable				X

5.3.1 Benefits in Kind

Benefits in kind (BIKs) are:

- living or other accommodation;
- entertainment;
- domestic or other services; and
- other benefits or facilities of whatever nature provided by an employer to an employee (or director), and are chargeable to income tax under Schedule E.

Section 120 TCA 1997 includes as a taxable BIK, any benefit provided by a public body to an office-holder or employee, **whether employed directly** by that body or not. The liability to tax also applies in respect of benefits provided by an employer for an employee's or director's spouse, family, servants, dependants or guests. In addition, "perquisites", i.e. remuneration in non-money form which are convertible into money or money's worth, are also chargeable to income tax under Schedule E.

Examples of BIKs are the use of a company car, loans at a preferential rate of interest, or free or subsidised accommodation. Examples of perquisites are medical insurance premiums, payment of club subscriptions and vouchers.

General Rule for Valuing Benefits in Kind

Except where there are **specific statutory valuation rules**, the amount of the taxable benefit ("notional pay") liable to tax, PRSI and USC is:

A. For **benefits in kind**, the higher of:
    1. the cost to the employer of providing the benefit, **or**
    2. the value realisable by the employee for the benefit in money or money's worth, *Less:* any amount made good/refunded to the employer by the employee.
B. For **perquisites**, which are benefits readily converted into cash (e.g. vouchers), the amount assessable is the amount the employee can realise, on conversion, rather than the cost of providing the perquisite.

It is the employer's responsibility to calculate the value of the benefit and collect the tax, PRSI and USC due thereon through the payroll when the benefit is given.

Tax on Benefits in Kind

Benefits received from an employer by an employee whose **total remuneration** (including BIKs) is €1,905 or more in a tax year are taxable. Where the employee is a **director**, the benefits are taxable **regardless** of the level of remuneration. The main points with regard to tax on BIKs are:

- Income tax due on benefits must be collected through the PAYE system on the taxable value of the benefit.
- PRSI, USC and employer PRSI are also due on BIKs and must be collected by the employer through the PAYE system.
- The notional pay liable to tax, PRSI and USC in respect of BIKs must be the **best estimate** that can reasonably be made by the employer at the time the benefit is being provided.
- *Small Benefit Exemption.* A non-cash BIK with a value **not exceeding €500** is not subject to tax, PRSI or USC. However, no more than one benefit given to an employee in a tax year will qualify and, where a benefit **exceeds €500**, the **full value** of the benefit is subject to tax, PRSI and USC under the PAYE system.

Specific Statutory Valuation Rules
Specific statutory valuation rules must be used to determine the taxable value in relation to the following benefits:

1. the transfer of ownership of property;
2. the free use of property without transfer of ownership;
3. the provision of living or other accommodation;
4. the provision of cars, vans and bicycles; and
5. the provision of preferential loans.

1. Transfer of Ownership of Property
Where the employer gives an asset to the employee/director that the employer has previously used, the **market value of the asset at the date it is transferred** to the employee/director is taken to be the BIK.

If, on the other hand, the asset is purchased by the employer and not used before being given to the employee, then the **cost to the employer** will be the BIK.

2. The Free Use of Property without Transfer of Ownership
If an asset of the employer (excluding accommodation) is available for use by the employee personally, the benefit to be assessed on the employee must include the annual value of the use of the asset in addition to any day-to-day outgoings connected with the asset. Where an employer provides an asset (other than premises, land or motor vehicles) for use by an employee, the annual value of the use of the asset is deemed to be **5% of the market value** of the asset at the date the asset was first provided by the employer. If, however, the employer pays an annual rent or hire charge in respect of the asset and the amount paid by the employer exceeds 5% of the market value of the asset, that amount is the taxable benefit.

Example 5.1
On 1 May 2021, an employer acquired an antique dining-room table and chairs for €15,000 for an employee's house. The table and chairs remain in the ownership of the employer.

Tax Year	Calculation	Taxable Benefit
2021	(€15,000 @ 5%) × 8/12ths	€500
2022	€15,000 @ 5%	€750

Where an employer provides an employee with the use of an asset which has been used or depreciated since the employer acquired it, the annual value of the use of the asset is deemed to be 5% of the market value of the asset when first provided to any employee.

Example 5.2
An employer acquired a dining-room table and chairs for €20,000 in 2014, which were used in the employer's premises for entertaining clients. On 1 July 2021, the table and chairs, which were then valued at €12,000, were given to an employee for use in his own home. The table and chairs remain in the ownership of the employer.

Tax Year	Calculation	Taxable Benefit
2021	(€12,000 @ 5%) × 6/12ths	€300
2022	€12,000 @ 5%	€600

---

3. Provision of Living or Other Accommodation

Where accommodation is owned and provided by the employer for use by an employee, the value of the benefit to the employee is the aggregate of:

- the annual value of the premises (including land); and
- any outgoings (excluding the cost of acquisition) incurred by the employer in connection with the provision of the accommodation.

The **annual value** is the annual rent which the employer might reasonably expect to obtain if the property were rented on an arm's length basis, and on the basis that the tenant undertook to pay the usual tenant expenses and the landlord undertook to bear the cost of repairs, insurance and other expenses necessary to maintain the premises in a state to command that rent.

Generally, Revenue will apply a rule of thumb of **8% of the market value** of the accommodation supplied as being the annual letting value. However, where a vouched lower figure is available (e.g. an auctioneer's estimate), this may be used for the annual letting value.

Example 5.3

Harry, who earns €25,000 per annum, is provided with a company apartment by his employer. The apartment originally cost €180,000 and its current market value is €160,000. His employer pays the following expenses in relation to the upkeep of the apartment:

	€
Insurance	600
Housekeeping supplies	1,500
Management charge	900
Heating and light	1,100
	4,100

The BIK assessable on Harry is as follows:

	€
Annual letting value: 8% × €160,000 (market value)	12,800
Add: expenses paid by the employer on behalf of Harry	4,100
Schedule E BIK	16,900

€16,900 is added to Harry's other Schedule E income to arrive at his total tax liability.

If Harry was obliged to contribute, say, €1,500 annually to his employer, in consideration for the accommodation being put at his disposal, this would be deducted from the BIK of €16,900 to give the net benefit assessable on him, i.e. €15,400.

Exemptions

A taxable benefit will **not** arise where an employee (excluding directors) is **required**, by the terms of their employment, to live-in accommodation provided by the employer in part of the employer's business premises so that the employee can properly perform their duties ("better performance" test) and either:

- the accommodation is provided in accordance with a practice which, since before 30 July 1948, has commonly prevailed in trades of the class in question as respects employees of the class in question, **or**
- it is necessary, in the case of trades of the class in question, that employees should reside on the premises.

In practice, it is accepted that the "better performance" test is met where:

- the employee is required to be on call outside normal hours; and
- the employee is in fact frequently called out; **and**
- the accommodation is provided so that the employee may have quick access to the place of employment.

Examples of such employees include: a Garda who has to reside at the station in a country village; chaplains and governors in prisons; managers or night care staff in residential or respite centres; caretakers living on the premises.

4. Provision of Cars and Vans

(a) Company Cars

Where a car is available for the **private** use of an employee, the employee is chargeable to tax, PRSI and USC in respect of that use.

A "car" means any mechanically propelled road vehicle designed, constructed or adapted for the carriage of the driver, or the driver and one or more other persons and **excludes**:

- motor-cycles (i.e. a vehicle with less than four wheels) where the weight does not exceed 410kg;
- company vans; and
- vehicles of a type not commonly used as a private vehicle and unsuitable to be so used.

The value of the benefit (i.e. the use of the car and any running costs paid by the employer) is calculated by reference to the "**cash equivalent**" of the private use of a company car, **less** amounts made good by the employee to the employer.

To arrive at the cash equivalent, the employer must first apply a **business kilometre-related percentage** to the **original market value (OMV)** of the car supplied, as per the table below.

Annual Business Kilometres	Cash Equivalent (% of OMV)
24,000 or less	30%
24,001 to 32,000	24%
32,001 to 40,000	18%
40,001 to 48,000	12%
48,001 and over	6%

Step 1: Calculate the original market value (OMV) of the car

The OMV of the car is the price (including any customs duties, VAT, VRT) the car might reasonably have been expected to fetch, if sold in the State immediately before the date of its first registration.

Generally, the **OMV** is taken to be the **list price** of the vehicle, **including VAT** and **VRT**, at the time of **first registration**. In cases where:

- an exceptionally large discount was obtained (a fleet discount), **or**
- the discount cannot be determined (e.g. car traded-in against a new car), **or**
- the car in question was purchased second-hand,

claims in respect of discounts are limited to the discounts **normally available** on a single retail sale on the open market. Discounts **in excess of 10%** will not normally be accepted unless there is documentary evidence available to support such a discount in respect of a single car sale. It should be emphasised that the **valuation for second-hand cars** is still the **OMV** of the car and **not** the **second-hand cost** of the car.

Step 2: Calculate the cash equivalent using the appropriate percentage, having ascertained the business kilometres for the year

Business kilometres means kilometres incurred by the employee that they are **necessarily obliged to incur in the actual performance of the duties of their employment** (e.g. kilometres travelled in driving to work and returning home are not business kilometres but personal). To calculate the amount of business kilometres, the total kilometres for the year should be reduced by the amount of personal kilometres where this can be established; where the amount of personal kilometres is not available, a minimum of **8,000 private kilometres** should be subtracted. The employer may accept lower levels of private kilometres, but only where the employee can provide documentary evidence in this regard.

Example 5.4

Sarah is provided with a company car from 1 January 2021. The OMV of the car is €25,000. Sarah did a total of 36,800 kilometres for 2021.

Benefit in kind:	€
Total kilometres	36,800
Less: private element	(8,000)
Business kilometres	28,800
Percentage applicable: 24% (24,000–32,000 km)	
BIK (cash equivalent): €25,000 @ 24%	€6,000

Alternative Calculation for Employees with Low Business Kilometres   Employees whose annual business kilometres do not exceed 24,000 kilometres may reduce their cash equivalent by 20% where the following conditions are satisfied:

- the employee works at least 20 hours per week;
- the employee travels at least 8,000 business kilometres per annum;
- the employee spends at least **70%** of his or her working time away from the employer's premises; and
- a logbook detailing the employee's business kilometres, business transacted, business time travelled and date of journey, is kept and certified by the employer as correct.

Example 5.5

Joe drives 16,000 business kilometres per annum. The OMV of the company car is €20,000. The car was first provided in 2019. Joe satisfies all of the conditions above.

Benefit in kind:	€
€20,000 @ 30%	6,000
Less: 20% reduction	(1,200)
BIK	4,800

Step 3: Company car not available for a full year

If the employee is provided with the car for only part of the particular tax year, the business kilometre thresholds and the cash equivalent percentages used should be adjusted by the following fraction:

$$\frac{\text{No. of days in the year the car was available to employee}}{365}$$

Example 5.6
Alison is provided with a car with an OMV of €25,000 for the first time on 1 July 2021. Her business kilometres for the period 1 July to 31 December 2021 (184 days) are 16,320 kilometres.

Fraction adjustment: $\dfrac{184 \text{ days}}{365 \text{ days}} = 0.5041$

Multiplying 0.5041 by the annual business kilometres and its cash equivalent (see above), the revised table becomes:

Annual Business Kilometres	Cash Equivalent (% of OMV) (Category C)
12,098 or less (24,000 × 0.5041)	15.12% (30% × 0.5041)
12,098–16,131 (32,000 × 0.5041)	12.10% (24% × 0.5041)
16,131–20,164 (40,000 × 0.5041)	**9.07% (18% × 0.5041)**
20,164–24,197 (48,000 × 0.5041)	6.05% (12% × 0.5041)
24,197 and over	3.02% (6% × 0.5041)

Benefit in kind: €25,000 @ 9.07% = €2,268

Change of Car   The same calculation will also be used in a year where there is a change of car, as the annual business kilometre thresholds and the cash equivalent percentages must be calculated for each car **separately**.

In practice, it is simpler to **annualise** the employee's business kilometres and use the original table to determine the correct percentage to use. In **Example 5.6**, 16,320 km for 184 days is equivalent to 32,374 km for 365 days (16,320/184 × 365 = 32,374), and so is within 32,000–40,000 business kilometres. Therefore the appropriate percentage is 18%. The employee's taxable benefit for 2021 is therefore: €25,000 × 18% × 184/365 = €2,268.

Step 4: Amounts reimbursed by employee to employer
The cash equivalent is reduced by any amount which the employee reimburses to the employer in respect of any part of the costs of providing or running the car. In order to qualify as a deduction, the costs must be made good **directly by the employee to the employer**, i.e. if Joe pays for his own petrol, there is no deduction, but if Joe's employer pays for the petrol and Joe reimburses his employer, then Joe is entitled to a deduction for the reimbursement.

Where the employee makes a contribution to the employer towards the cost of the car, the amount of the contribution is **deducted** from the cash equivalent in the year in which the contribution is paid. If the contribution **exceeds** the cash equivalent in that year, the excess is carried forward and offset against the cash equivalent the following year.

Example 5.7
Paul's employer provides him with a car with an OMV of €30,000 on 1 July 2021. Paul reimburses his employer €500 towards the cost of the car on 1 August 2021 and agrees to reimburse his employer €500 annually thereafter. Paul travels 19,200 business kilometres annually.

Benefit in kind		€
2021	€30,000 × 30% × 6/12ths	4,500
	Less: amount reimbursed	(500)
	BIK 2021	4,000
2022	€30,000 × 30%	9,000
	Less: amount reimbursed	(500)
	BIK 2022	8,500

Exemption for Electric Cars/Vans An exemption from BIK exists on the provision of an electric car or van (i.e. one that "derives its motion power exclusively from an electric motor"; 'hybrid' vehicles are not eligible) where the car (new or second-hand) is provided during the period 1 January 2018 to 31 December 2022. From 1 January 2019 to 31 December 2022, the exemption applies for electric vehicles with an OMV not exceeding €50,000. Where the OMV is in excess of €50,000, a BIK will apply to the excess over €50,000. Electricity supplied in the workplace to charge electric cars and vans is also exempt from BIK.

(b) Company Vans

Where a van is made available to an employee for private use, the employee is taxable on the cash equivalent of the benefit of the van, reduced by any amount that the employee is required to, and actually, makes good to the employer in respect of the cost of providing or running the van. The "cash equivalent" of the benefit of a van is **5% of its OMV**. The business kilometre-related percentage does not apply to vans. OMV is calculated in the same manner as for cars.

A van means a mechanically propelled road vehicle which:

- is designed or constructed solely or mainly for the carriage of goods or other burden; and
- has a roofed area or areas to the rear of the driver's seat; and
- has no side windows or seating fitted in that roofed area or areas; and
- has a gross vehicle weight not exceeding 3,500 kilograms.

If the employee is provided with the van for part only of the particular tax year, then the cash equivalent is reduced on a *pro rata* basis, i.e. if the van is provided for five months, then only 5/12ths of the cash equivalent is taken.

Exemption from Benefit in Kind The **private use** of the van will be exempt from BIK if:

- the van is necessary for the performance of the duties of the employee's employment;
- the employee is required, by the person who made the van available, to keep the van at their private residence when not in use;
- apart from travel between the employee's private residence and workplace, other private use of the van is prohibited by the employer; **and**
- the employee spends **at least 80%** of their time away from the premises of the employer.

Car and Van Pool Exemption No benefit will be assessed on an employee in respect of a car or van that is in a 'pool' available for employees generally. A car or van will be treated as belonging to a 'pool' where:

- the car or van must have been made available to, and actually used by, **more than one** employee and it is not ordinarily used by any one of the employees to the exclusion of the others; **and**
- any private use of the car or van made by any of the employees is merely incidental to its business use; **and**
- it is not normally kept overnight at the home of any of the employees.

5. Provision of Preferential Loans

A "preferential loan" means a loan made by an employer to an employee, a former or prospective employee or their spouses, in respect of which no interest is paid, or interest is paid at a rate lower than the "specified rate". It does not include any loan made by an employer to an employee in the course of the employer's trade, on an arm's length basis, where normal commercial rates of interest are charged.

The specified rates for tax year 2021 are:

Qualifying home loans	4%
All other loans	13.5%

The difference between the interest actually paid by the preferential borrower during the particular tax year and the amount of interest calculated at the specified rate, and any waiver of interest, is treated as a perquisite chargeable to tax, PRSI and USC under Schedule E.

Example 5.8

Christopher is employed by a bank and has been advanced the following non-mortgage loans:

1. €10,000 interest-free loan
2. €20,000 loan at the rate of 4.5% per annum
3. €30,000 loan at the rate of 14% per annum

Interest due in respect of the €20,000 loan for the year ended 31 December 2020, amounting to €900, was unpaid at 31 December 2020, and was waived by his employer during the tax year 2021.

The amounts treated as perquisites under Schedule E and included as Christopher's income for the tax year 2021 will be as follows:

		€
Loan No. 1	€10,000 × 13.5% deemed interest rate	1,350
Loan No. 2	€20,000 × 9% (13.5% – 4.5%)	1,800
Loan No. 3	Not a preferential loan (rate not less than 13.5%)	Nil
Total		3,150
Interest waived during 2021 by bank		900
Amount assessable as a Schedule E perquisite for 2021		4,050

---

6. Other Benefits

(a) Benefits on Death or Retirement

The expense of providing any pension, lump sum, gratuity or other like benefit to be given on the death or retirement of a director or employee is **exempt**. The exemption is only given to the extent that the provision is for the benefit of the director or employee themselves or for their spouse/civil partner, children or dependants. This exemption would, for instance, cover normal pension and retirement scheme payments, and death-in-service payments, made by the employer on behalf of the employee.

(b) Medical Insurance

The benefit, which is subject to tax, PRSI and USC, is the gross premium, i.e. the amount paid to the insurer **plus** the tax relief at source (TRS) payable by the employer on behalf of the employee. The employee may claim a standard rate tax credit in respect of the gross premium, subject to certain limits (see **Section 8.3.2**). Medical check-ups that an employee is **required** to undergo by their employer, and which are paid for by the employer, are not a taxable benefit. Flu vaccines paid for by the employer and administered by a registered practitioner (doctors, pharmacists, dentists, etc.) are also not a taxable benefit.

Where an employee (or a person connected to an employee) of a health or dental insurer, a tied health insurance agent or a connected party, receives a discount on such an insurance policy, the discount is taxable as a benefit in kind.

(c) **Expense Allowances**

(i) *Round-sum Expense Allowance* In general, a round-sum expense allowance advanced to an employee to be disbursed at the employee's discretion is regarded as taxable Schedule E income (i.e. a perquisite). It is then open to the employee to make a formal claim for a deduction against this income in respect of the actual expenses incurred in the performance of their duties.

(ii) *Employee Motor Expenses* Where an employee uses their **own private car** for business purposes, the employer may reimburse the employee for allowable motor expenses by way of a flat-rate kilometric allowance. If the employee bears all motoring costs and is reimbursed for the business element of motoring costs by the employer at rates which do **not exceed** the **Civil Service rates**, then such costs may be paid **tax-free** by the employer and are not taxable in the hands of the employee. The employer does not have to seek prior approval from Revenue for the tax-free payment of costs in line with Civil Service rates, provided the employer operates a satisfactory system of control over the payment and keeps adequate records.

(iii) *Employee Subsistence Allowances* Where an employee performs their duties of employment while temporarily away from their normal place of work, or while working abroad on a foreign assignment, the employer may reimburse the employee for actual expenses incurred or, alternatively, may pay the employee a flat-rate subsistence allowance to cover costs incurred by the employee. Where the employee pays all subsistence expenses and is reimbursed for these expenses by a flat-rate subsistence allowance, then such an allowance may be paid **tax-free** by the employer and is not taxable in the hands of the employee, provided the allowance paid is **in line** with prevailing **Civil Service subsistence rates** (see **Appendix 1**).

The employer **does not** have to seek prior approval from Revenue for the payment of such tax-free subsistence allowances, provided the employer notifies Revenue that it pays subsistence allowances in accordance with Civil Service rates, and that the employer operates a satisfactory system of control over the payment and keeps adequate records.

Where the employee's job is such that travel is an integral part of the job (e.g. a sales representative), or where the employee carries out much of their duties at the premises of the employer's customers, their "normal place of work" is regarded as the **employer's** business premises.

(iv) *Removal/Relocation Expenses* An employer may make the payment or reimbursement of certain removal/relocation expenses, incurred by an employee in moving house to take up employment, free of tax. The employer must ensure that the following conditions are satisfied:

- the reimbursement to the employee, or payment directly by the employer, must be in respect of removal/relocation expenses actually incurred;
- the expenses must be reasonable in amount;
- the payment of the expenses must be properly controlled; and
- moving house must be necessary in the circumstances.

Expenses that can be reimbursed free of tax are those incurred **directly** as a result of the change of residence and include such items as:

- auctioneer's and solicitor's fees and stamp duty arising from moving house;
- removal of furniture and effects and insurance on items in transit or in storage;
- storage charges and cleaning costs of stored items;
- travelling expenses on removal;
- temporary subsistence allowance while looking for accommodation at the new location;
- rent (vouched) for temporary accommodation for up to three months.

With the exception of any temporary subsistence allowance, all payments must be matched with receipted expenditure. The amount reimbursed or born.e by the employer may not exceed expenditure **actually incurred**. Any reimbursement of the **capital cost** of acquiring or building a house or any **bridging loan interest** or loans to finance such expenditure would be **subject to tax**. The concession applies to relocations within the same organisation and relocations in order to take up a new employment.

(v) *Directors' Travel and Subsistence Expenses* Expenses paid or reimbursed to **executive directors** to attend meetings (including board meetings) are taxable as a BIK.

For **non-executive directors (NEDs)**, travel and subsistence expenses can be paid tax-free when attending company meetings, which must be for the purposes of conducting the business of the company. **Non-resident** NEDs are reimbursed for vouched amounts only (no Civil Service rates). **Irish-resident** NEDs, provided their annual director's pay does not exceed €5,000 per annum, are reimbursed at Civil Service rates only.

(d) Meals and Meal Vouchers
(i) *Canteen Meals* Where free or subsidised meals in staff canteens are provided and **available to all employees**, a taxable benefit **does not** arise. If the facility is not available to all employees, the running costs of the canteen must be apportioned between the employees entitled to use the canteen and taxed as a benefit.
(ii) *Meal Vouchers* Where an employer provides luncheon or meal vouchers to employees, a taxable benefit **does arise** on the **face value** of the vouchers (except for the first 19c per voucher).

(e) Crèche or Childcare Facilities
Where an employer provides free or subsisted childcare, either in-house or externally at an independent facility, a taxable benefit arises.

(f) Sports and Recreational Facilities
(i) *Facilities provided on the employer's premises* Where sports and recreational facilities are made available on the employer's premises and are **available to all employees**, a taxable benefit **does not** arise. If the facilities are not available to all employees, the running costs must be apportioned between the employees entitled to use the facilities and taxed as a benefit.
(ii) *Corporate Membership paid by the employer* Where a corporate membership to sports and recreational facilities is paid by an employer on behalf of an individual employee or specified employees, the amount paid must be apportioned equally among all the employees who are entitled to and indicate an intention to participate in the scheme, and be taxed as a benefit.

(g) Professional Subscriptions
Where an employer pays a subscription to a professional body on behalf of an employee, or reimburses the employee who has paid such a subscription, a taxable benefit arises and must be included in remuneration as a benefit in kind.

However, where the professional subscriptions can be claimed by the employee as a tax deduction under section 114 TCA 1997 as a **"wholly, exclusively and necessarily"** incurred expense of the employee in the performance of their employment duties, Revenue will not seek to have such subscriptions taxed as a BIK where:

- there is a **statutory requirement** for membership of a professional body;
- there is a statutory requirement for a **practising certificate** or licence; **or**
- membership of the professional body is an **indispensable condition** of employment **and** the duties of the employment require the employee to exercise that profession and the employee so exercises such a profession.

For example, where a legal practice employs a solicitor to act in that capacity and the employee cannot practise as a solicitor unless the employee is a member of the Law Society of Ireland, then the annual subscription to the Law Society paid by the employer is not deemed to be a BIK. However, where the solicitor is employed by the legal practice as its human resources manager and it is not an indispensable condition of that employment that the employee is a member of the Law Society (though the employer deems it desirable), payment by the employer of such a subscription is taxable as a BIK.

Where an employer pays two professional subscriptions on behalf of an employee, e.g. subscriptions to an accountancy and a taxation body, only **one** of these subscriptions is deemed wholly, exclusively and necessarily, the other subscription is taxable as a BIK (see Revenue's *Tax and Duty Manual,* Part 05-02-18).

(h) Course or Exam Fees

Where an employer pays, or refunds, an employee for the cost of any course or exam fee, this will not be treated as a taxable benefit if the course undertaken is **relevant to the business** of the employer, where it leads to the acquisition of skills or knowledge which are:

- **necessary** for the duties of the employment; **or**
- **directly related** to increasing the effectiveness of the employee's or director's present or prospective duties in the office or employment.

(i) Examination Awards

Where an employee is given an award for passing an exam or obtaining a qualification, no taxable benefit arises provided:

- the examination/qualification bears some relationship to the employee's duties; **and**
- the award is of an amount that can reasonably be regarded as a reimbursement of the expenses likely to have been incurred in studying for the qualification or sitting the examination.

(j) Staff Discounts

Discounts given by employers on the purchase of goods by an employee are **not** regarded as a taxable benefit if the sum paid by the employee **is equal to or greater than the cost** to the employer of acquiring or manufacturing the goods.

However, where goods are sold **below** the employer's cost, the **difference** between that cost and the price paid **is a taxable benefit**.

(k) eWorking Employees

"eWorking", according to Revenue, is a method of working using information and communication technologies in which the work that is carried out is **independent** of location. This includes working from home on a **full-time** or **part-time** basis. eWorking involves working, for substantial periods, outside the employer's premises, logging onto the employer's computer remotely, sending and receiving e-mail or data remotely and developing ideas, products or services remotely.

Revenue outlined the following practices with regard to eWorking employees:

- Where computers or other ancillary equipment, such as printers, fax machines, etc., are provided by the employer, **primarily for business use**, to enable the employee to work from home, **no taxable benefit** will arise in respect of **incidental** private use.
- No taxable benefit will arise in respect of the provision of a telephone line, mobile phone or broadband for business use.

- No taxable benefit will arise in respect of office furniture or similar equipment provided it is used primarily for business use.
- The employer may make a payment of up to **€3.20 per day tax-free** to an employee to cover additional heating and electricity costs. If actual expenditure incurred by the employee exceeds this amount, the employee may make a claim for a Schedule E tax deduction in respect of the excess.

Note that these arrangements **only apply to eWorking employees**. They do not extend to employees who, in the normal course of employment, sometimes bring work home in the evenings, etc.

(l)   Provision of Computer Equipment, etc.
Where, **for business purposes**, an employer provides an employee with computer equipment, high-speed internet access, a second home telephone or a mobile phone, and the employer bears the cost of installation and use, no taxable benefit will arise where **private use is incidental** to the business use of the item.

(m)   Travel Passes
Where an employer provides an employee with a monthly or annual travel pass for use on bus, train, light railway (e.g. LUAS and DART) and commuter ferries, the pass is not treated as a taxable benefit, provided the pass is issued by an "approved transport provider" as defined by section 118(5A) TCA 1997. Section 118B TCA 1997 provides that an employee may "sacrifice" salary in exchange for the travel pass benefit.

(n)   Car Parking
Car-parking facilities provided by employers for employees are **not treated** as a taxable benefit.

(o)   Employee Security
Costs and expenses incurred by an employer, or incurred by an employee and reimbursed by an employer, in the provision of an asset or service for the improvement of the personal security of the employee, is not treated as a taxable benefit if the necessity for the provision of the security service is due to a "**credible and serious threat**" to the employee's physical security which arises **wholly or mainly** from his employment, e.g. a key-holder in a bank.

An "asset" in this context includes equipment or a structure, but does not include any mode of transport, or a dwelling or grounds attached to a dwelling.

(p)   Staff Entertainment
Staff Christmas parties and special occasion inclusive events or meals are not a taxable benefit where the cost involved is **reasonable**.

(q)   Long-service Awards
A taxable benefit will **not arise** in respect of long-service awards where the following conditions are satisfied:

- the award is made as a testimonial to mark long service of **not less** than 20 years;
- the award takes the form of a tangible article of reasonable cost;
- the cost does **not exceed €50** for **each year of service**; and
- no similar award has been made to the recipient within the previous five years.

This treatment **does not apply** to awards made in cash or in the form of vouchers, bonds, etc. Such awards are fully taxable.

(r) Provision of a Bicycle ("Cycle to Work" scheme)

A taxable benefit will **not arise** in respect of the first €1,250 spent on a bicycle or €1,500 for an electronic bicycle and related safety equipment for an employee for the purpose of travelling to/from work or between jobs where the following conditions are satisfied:

- a claim is made only once every four years (from 1 August 2020);
- an employee may 'sacrifice' salary in exchange for the benefit (but must repay within 12 months).

(s) Company Shares/Share Awards

The benefit accruing to an employee from the receipt of shares and other securities awarded to employees in their employer company, or its parent company, is a **taxable benefit** and must be included in remuneration as a BIK. The benefit is therefore subject to tax, PRSI and USC. **Note that it is not subject to employer PRSI.** Gains or benefits on **share options** are subject to self-assessment and are not taxable under the PAYE system as a BIK.

(t) Company Credit/Charge Cards

Where the card is provided by the employer **exclusively** for business usage, any stamp duty or membership fee paid by the employer is **not** a taxable benefit. Where, however, the card can be used for **private** purchases or payments, any payments **not repaid** by the employee **are** taxable benefits and subject to tax, PRSI and USC.

(u) Provision of Newspapers, Periodicals, etc.

Where an employee is provided with free newspapers, periodicals, etc., which are **generally related** to the employer's business, a taxable benefit does **not** arise.

(v) Exceptional Performance Awards/Staff Suggestion Schemes

Where an employer has schemes in place to reward exceptional performance or staff suggestions, any awards received under such schemes, whether cash or gifts/vouchers, **are** taxable benefits.

(w) Annual Allowance Paid to Reserve Members of An Garda Síochána

The annual allowance in respect of out-of-pocket expenses paid to Reserve Members of An Garda Síochána is exempt from income tax and is not included in the calculation of taxable income.

(x) Expenses Paid to State Examinations Commission Examiners

Travel and subsistence payments (where these do not exceed Civil Service rates – see **Appendix 1**) payable by the State Examinations Commission to any examiner employed by it are exempt from tax.

5.3.2 Commencement and Inducement Payments and Restrictive Covenants

Commencement Payments

Payments received in connection with the commencement of an employment are **taxable**, under Schedule E, as emoluments of the new office or employment where the payment is made under the terms of a contract of service or in consideration of future services to be rendered. However, where it can be shown that the payment is **compensation** for the loss of some right or benefit as a result of taking up the new employment, the payment may not be subject to income tax.

Inducement Payments

An employer may pay a prospective employee a lump sum to induce them to accept an office/other position or as compensation for giving up some valuable right as a result of accepting the position. The question as to whether the payment is taxable under Schedule E as an emolument of the new office/employment has to be decided based on the facts and the true nature of the agreement.

For example, in the UK case of *Glantre Engineering Ltd v. Goodhand (HMIT)* (1983) an inducement fee was paid by a company to a chartered accountant working for an international firm of accountants to enter into the company's services. In the case, it was held that the payment was made to obtain the accountant's services in the future and was therefore taxable under Schedule E.

Payments made **as compensation** for, and as an inducement to, the employee to **give up a personal advantage** before employment is taken up are not taxable under Schedule E.

For example, in *Pritchard v. Arundle* (1972) an allotment of shares was given by a company to persuade a chartered accountant in practice to work for the company. In this case, it was held that the fee was not in the nature of a reward for future services but an inducement to give up an established position and status and therefore not taxable under Schedule E.

In the case of *Jarrold v. Boustead* (1963), inducement payments to rugby union footballers for the permanent loss of their amateur status upon signing on as professional footballers for rugby league were held not to be taxable.

In *Riley v. Coglan* (1967), an amateur player received a signing-on fee upon joining a rugby league club as a professional, a proportionate part of which was refundable if he did not continue to serve the club for the period stipulated in the agreement. The payment was held to be a reward for future services and therefore liable to tax under Schedule E, distinguishing *Jarrold v. Boustead* (1963).

Restrictive Covenants

A restrictive covenant is an agreement between an employer and employee under which the employee, arising out of the **holding of the employment**, gives an undertaking to the employer to restrict their conduct or activities. For example, the employee may undertake not to work in the same sector or in competition with the employer for a period of time after they leave their employment. Payments made or valuable consideration given to an employee, under a restrictive covenant, are deemed to be emoluments from the office or employment and are chargeable to tax **under Schedule E** in the year of assessment in which the payment/consideration is given.

5.3.3 Other Income Exempt from Income Tax

Magdalene Laundries Payments

Ex-gratia payments made on or after 1 August 2013 to beneficiaries under the scheme, administered by the Minister for Justice, Equality and Defence in respect of women who were admitted to, and worked in, Magdalene Laundries, will not be subject to income tax or capital gains tax, nor be treated as a gift or inheritance for the purposes of capital acquisitions tax.

Living Donors

Section 204B TCA 1997 exempts from income tax any compensation payable to a living donor for the donation of a kidney or a lobe of liver for transplantation, under the conditions defined by the Minister for Health.

Compensation Awards made under Employment Law

Section 192A TCA 1997 provides for an exemption from income tax for compensation awards made by a "relevant authority" to an employee or former employee as a result of the employee's rights and entitlements in law having been infringed or breached through, for example, discrimination, harassment or victimisation.

In this instance a "relevant authority" includes the Labour Court, Workplace Relations Commission, Employment Appeals Tribunal, etc., or the Circuit Court and the High Court.

Payments made in respect of remuneration, e.g. salary or holiday pay, arrears of pay, changes in functions or procedures of an employment or the termination of an employment will continue to be taxable in the normal way.

Other Exemptions

Lump-sum payments in the following circumstances are **completely exempt**:

- certain allowances to members of the Defence Forces and under Army Pension Acts;
- statutory redundancy payments; and
- lump-sum payments made to employees under certain company restructuring schemes involving agreed pay restructuring.

5.3.4 Expenses Allowable under Schedule E

In order for an expense to be deductible from an employee's or director's Schedule E income, it must be shown that it was incurred "**wholly, exclusively and necessarily in performing the duties of the office or employment**". The test is extremely difficult to satisfy in practice as:

- the employee or director must be **necessarily** obliged to incur the expense; **and**
- the expense must be wholly, exclusively and necessarily incurred; **and**
- the expense must be incurred in the **actual performance** of the duties.

It will be noted that **all of the above tests** must be satisfied. The difficulty of satisfying the tests is obvious in considering the dicta of judges in deciding cases. For instance, Judge Vaisey said, in the case of *Lomax v. Newton* (1953), that the rules are notoriously rigid now and restricted in their operation. He observed:

> "An expenditure may be necessary for the holder of an office without being necessary to him in the performance of the duties of that office. It may be necessary in the performance of those duties without being exclusively referable to those duties. It may perhaps be both necessarily and exclusively and still not be wholly so referable. The words are indeed stringent and exacting, compliance with each and every one of them is obligatory for the benefit or relief to be claimed successfully."

Restriction of Expense Deduction in Respect of Leased Cars

Where an employee leases a vehicle to carry out the duties of their office or employment, a deduction for the lease expense is restricted. If the list price of a leased vehicle exceeds the **relevant limit** (currently **€24,000**), the amount of lease charges (relating to the business use of the car) are further restricted by reference to the CO_2 emissions of the car, as per the table below.

Vehicle Category	CO$_2$ Emissions (CO$_2$ g/km)	Leasing Charges Restriction
A/B/C	0g/km up to and including 155g/km	Lease hire charge $\times \dfrac{(\text{List Price} - \text{Relevant Limit})}{\text{List Price}}$
D/E	156g/km up to and including 190g/km	Lease hire charge $\times \dfrac{(\text{List Price} - (\text{Relevant Limit} \times 50\%))}{\text{List Price}}$
F/G	191g/km and upwards	Lease hire charge disallowed

Example 5.9

Joe Jones is a salesman and leases a car to carry out his duties under his contract of employment. The Category D car was first leased on 1 January 2019 when its retail price, after cash discount, was €25,000. Joe incurred lease charges of €8,000 in 2021 and 80% of his mileage was related to his employment.

	€
Lease charges	8,000
Less: private element 20%	(1,600)
Business element	6,400

Disallowed lease payment:

Car Category D/E: $\dfrac{€6,400 \times (€25,000 - (€24,000 \times 50\%))}{€25,000}$ 3,328

Disallowed lease payment for Joe Jones:

Private element of lease charges	1,600
Restriction: Category D car	3,328
Total lease payment restriction	4,928

Questions

Review Questions

(See Suggested Solutions to Review Questions at the end of this textbook.)

Question 5.1

Sid Harvey is an employee of General Services Ltd. His gross basic salary for 2021 amounted to €40,000. His employer also gives him €100 every month by way of a round-sum expense allowance to meet incidental outlay. He is not obliged to provide his employer with receipts to account for this expenditure.

Sid is supplied with a company car, which was bought second-hand by General Services Ltd in July 2019 for €15,000. The car is a 2015 model and originally cost €35,000 (after 10% cash discount) when first registered. General Services Ltd pay all the outgoings in respect of the running of the car. However, Sid is required to reimburse the company for private fuel and the cost of insurance. The amount reimbursed by Sid for fuel and insurance during 2021 came to €1,300. In recognition of the fact that he has the car available to him during leisure hours, Sid is also obliged to make a monthly contribution of €100 to his employer. This is deducted from his salary. Sid's total travel by car in the tax year 2021 amounted to 40,000 km, of which 26,400 km were in the course of the performance of his duties. Sid spends approximately 50% of his working time away from the premises of General Services Ltd.

General Services Ltd also provide a free apartment to Sid. The market value of the apartment is estimated at €110,000.

General Services Ltd pay the annual management charge and light and heating costs of the apartment which, for 2021, amounted to €890. The apartment was purchased for €55,000 in 2001.

Sid receives free meals in the staff canteen on the days in which he is located at his head office. The cost of providing these meals to his employer amounted to approximately €300. The staff canteen is available to all staff and all meals are provided free.

On 1 November 2017, General Services Ltd provided Sid with a €1,000 interest-free loan to enable him to go on his annual holidays. On 1 February 2021, the board of directors of General Services Ltd decided to waive repayment of the loan, together with 2021 interest outstanding at that date.

Sid is not married and paid €12,760 tax under PAYE in the tax year 2021.

Requirement
(a) Calculate the amount of benefit in kind included with Sid's gross pay for PAYE purposes for 2021.
(b) Compute Sid's income tax liability for the tax year 2021, clearly showing all workings. His personal tax credits for 2021 are €3,300.

Question 5.2

Terry is reviewing an offer from a new employer, Rich Bank plc, to start on 1 January 2021. In addition to an attractive salary of €70,000, Rich Bank plc has offered to take over his mortgage loan of €125,000, which he used to purchase his first main residence in January 2011. The rate of interest payable on the loan is 2%.

Rich Bank plc has also offered to provide an interest-free loan of €10,000 to pay Terry's affiliation fees at the Posh Golf and Country Club, and to pay annual membership of €3,500 on his behalf.

He will also be provided with a new VW Passat car (CO_2 emissions Category C) with an original market value of €30,000. The bank will pay all expenses. Terry estimates that he will drive 46,400 km in the tax year 2021, of which 10,400 km will be private, which he must reimburse to the bank at a rate of 15c per km.

Terry is married and will earn €75,000 with no benefits if he stays in his current job in 2021. He pays 5% on his mortgage and estimates that his car costs €10,500 per annum. He is not a member of any golf club and has no business mileage in his current job. His wife cares for their two children and does not work outside the home.

Requirement
(a) Calculate the taxable benefits assessable for 2021 from the new job offer. Assume he has tax credits of €6,550.
(b) Prepare income tax computations for both jobs and advise which leaves him better off.

You may ignore tax relief on the mortgage loan for the purposes of this question.

Question 5.3

Philip Stodge is employed as a commercial representative by his employer. Details of his income are as follows:

	2021	2020
	€	€
Gross salary	41,600	28,200
Sales commission	6,000	9,000

The following additional information is available:

1. Tax deducted under PAYE amounted to €5,410 for 2021 and €2,500 for 2020.
2. The sales commission of €6,000 earned during 2021 was paid to him on 1 June 2022 and the commission earned for 2020 was paid in July 2021.
3. He receives a monthly lump sum expense allowance of €100 to meet routine incidental expenses, such as telephone calls, tips, etc. In addition, his employer pays his hotel accommodation costs directly. He is obliged to provide his own car, pay all operating expenses and non-hotel meal costs personally.
4. Philip runs an Audi A4 car, which he first leased on 6 April 2018 for €27,000 on taking up his present employment. His car operating costs were as follows:

	2021	2020
	€	€
Lease charges	5,700	5,700
Car tax	500	480
Car insurance	850	750
Petrol	3,200	2,800
Tyres	–	150
Maintenance	400	230
Crash repairs	1,500	0
	6,450	4,410

He maintains receipts for all his motor expenses and 90% of his total mileage is undertaken in the performance of the duties of his employment. The emissions rating of his car is Category B.

5. In addition to car expenses, Philip wishes to make the following expense claims (vouched with receipts) in his tax return in respect of expenses not reimbursed by his employer:

	2021
	€
Work-related telephone charges	180
Cost of new suit	450
Cost of advanced commercial correspondence course	150
Taxi/train fares while on business	130
	910

6. Philip is married and his wife earned €15,500 (tax deducted under PAYE: €1,450) in 2021.

Requirement

Compute Philip Stodge's tax liability for the tax year 2021, claiming the maximum reliefs available. His personal tax credits are €6,600.

Question 5.4

Frank, a sales representative who is single (tax credits €3,300), received a salary of €50,000 and sales commission of €8,000 from his employer during 2021. To visit his customers, Frank used a car costing €51,000, which he had leased new on 1 July 2019 (emissions Category F). Lease charges paid in the tax year 2021 were €6,600. During the tax year 2021, he incurred the following motor expenses:

	€
Petrol	4,300
Insurance	1,500
Motor tax	1,480
Repairs and service	1,400

Frank travelled 44,800 km in 2021, of which 8,960 km were for private purposes.

Frank's employer has suggested that they enter into a new arrangement whereby the employer would provide Frank with a Category C motor car costing €31,000 and pay all the expenses. In return, Frank would receive his normal salary and two-thirds of his usual commission.

Requirement

(a) Calculate Frank's gross income tax liability (before credit for tax deducted under PAYE) for the tax year 2021.
(b) Recalculate Frank's income tax liability for the tax year 2021, assuming that the new arrangement had been in force during the entire year and that the car was first provided in 2021. Advise Frank which arrangement is financially more advantageous.

Schedule D, Cases III & IV and Schedule F – Savings and Investment Income

6.1 Introduction

While the majority of an individual's taxable income usually falls under the rules governing trading and professional income (Schedule D, Cases I and II) and employment income (Schedule E), other unearned and passive income is classified according to its **source** and taxed accordingly under Schedule D, Cases III and IV, and Schedule F.

6.2 Schedule D, Case III

6.2.1 Income Assessable under Case III

Income tax under Case III is assessed on the following sources of income:

- Interest, annuities and other annual payments, wherever arising, provided it is receivable **without** the **deduction of tax at source** at the standard rate, **nor** does it suffer **deposit interest retention tax (DIRT)**.
- Interest on most government and semi-State securities, where interest is paid **without** deduction of tax.
- Income arising to any person as a **member** of the **European Parliament** (MEP) is chargeable to tax under **Case III** where the income is payable out of money provided by the budget of the European Union. Where the income is payable out of money provided by the Irish State, it is chargeable to tax under Schedule E (section 127A TCA 1997).

Other income assessed under Case III includes:

- interest arising **outside the EU**, which would be deposit interest subject to DIRT if it were payable in Ireland;
- United Kingdom dividends received by Irish resident shareholders;
- income arising from foreign securities and possessions;
- deposit interest from EU financial institutions where the taxpayer has not filed a return and has not paid their tax liability by the filing date of the year in question; and
- all discounts.

Exempt Interest
The following interest is exempt from income tax:

- Interest or bonuses arising to an individual from Savings Certificates, Savings Bonds and National Instalment Savings Schemes with the National Treasury Management Agency (NTMA).
- Interest on savings certificates issued by the Minister for Finance.
- Interest on overpayments of tax.
- Interest paid on certain government securities to persons who are not ordinary resident and/or domiciled in the State.

6.2.2 Basis of Assessment

Income assessed under Case III is the **actual income** arising in the year of assessment.

6.3   Schedule D, Case IV

6.3.1 Income Assessable under Case IV

Case IV was originally a "sweeping up" case to catch any profits or gains not falling under any of the other cases of Schedule D and not charged under any other Schedule. In recent years, however, legislation has tended to use Case IV for charging certain specific items.

Republic of Ireland Bank, Building Society or Credit Union Interest
All interest paid on deposits held with Republic of Ireland banks, building societies or credit unions, **irrespective** of when or how often the interest is paid/credited, is subject to deposit interest retention tax (DIRT). Dividends paid/credited to **share accounts** of credit unions are also subject to DIRT at the current rate of 33% for 2021.

Income Received under Deduction of Income Tax at the Standard Rate
Certain types of income are received under deduction of income tax at the standard rate (20%). Examples include **covenants, patent royalties, interest** paid by a company to an individual and interest payments by one individual to another individual.
   The **gross** amount is assessed and a **refundable tax credit** is given for the income tax deducted at source.

Example 6.1

Monica Green receives €8,000 net each year from her niece, Jane, under a seven-year deed of covenant. Monica is 85 and in excellent health. Her only other income is her DSP pension of €13,432. Her non-refundable tax credits are €3,545. Calculate Monica's income tax liability for 2021.

		€	€
Case IV gross covenant income	€8,000/0.8	10,000	
Schedule E DSP pension		13,432	23,432
Taxed as follows:			
€23,432 @ 20%		4,686	
Deduct: Non-refundable tax credits		(3,545)	
Deduct: Refundable tax credits			
Tax deducted at source from covenant	€10,000 @ 20%	(2,000)	
Income tax refundable		(859)	

Example 6.2

Mary Byrne is a widow, aged 66, who has been incapacitated for a number of years. Her son, Peter, has executed an annual covenant of €5,000 in her favour. Her only other source of income is her pension of €25,000 (tax deducted: €915). Her personal tax credits for 2021 are €2,435 and her employee tax credit is €1,650.

Mary Byrne – Income Tax Computation 2021	€	€
Income:		
Case IV, Schedule D (gross covenant income)	5,000	
Schedule E – pension	25,000	
Total/taxable income		30,000
Tax Calculation:		
€30,000 @ 20%	6,000	
Tax liability		6,000
Deduct: Non-refundable tax credits		
Personal tax credit	2,435	
Employee tax credit	1,650	(4,085)
Deduct: Refundable tax credits		
Tax deducted by Peter on payment of covenant	1,000	
Tax paid under PAYE	915	(1,915)
Income tax due		NIL

6.3.2 Basis of Assessment

The basis of assessment for income falling within Case IV is the actual income arising in the year of assessment, i.e. if Case IV income arises in June 2021 then the income is taxable in 2021.

6.3.3 Deductions Available

Income tax legislation gives no guidance as to what expenses are deductible in computing Case IV profits. However, in practice the general rule is that any expenses incurred in earning the Case IV income will be treated as allowable deductions.

6.3.4 Treatment of Deposit Interest Retention Tax (DIRT)

As previously stated, all interest paid on deposits held with Republic of Ireland banks, building societies or credit unions, **irrespective** of when or how often the interest is paid/credited, is subject to DIRT. If the amount of DIRT deducted is greater than the individual's income tax liability on this interest, **no refund** is due **unless**:

- ▨ the individual (or spouse, if married) is aged 65 or more; **or**
- ▨ the individual (or spouse, if married) is permanently incapacitated during the year of assessment.

The interest received must always be included in an individual's income tax computation. This is because it is income **liable** to tax, even if no further tax charge occurs. It may also be liable to PRSI. Income subjected to DIRT is not liable to the USC.

Relief from Payment of DIRT

Section 267 TCA 1997 provides a relief whereby deposit interest can be paid, **without the deduction of DIRT**, to those aged over 65 whose total income does not exceed the relevant tax exemption limits or to those permanently incapacitated, upon the completion of the relevant declaration form (Forms DE1 and DE2; see www.revenue.ie).

Individuals who qualify for a refund of DIRT paid (being aged over 65 or permanently incapacitated) may apply to Revenue, on a **Form 54**, for a refund of DIRT where their total annual income for the year exceeds, or marginally exceeds, the exemption limit, but their annual tax credits are such that they would be entitled to a full or partial refund of DIRT.

Special Treatment of Income Subject to DIRT

To include income that is subject to DIRT in the income tax computation the following steps must be taken:

Step 1: Gross-up the net interest received by dividing by 0.67 (i.e. 1 minus the 33% rate).

Step 2: Add a new rate band for Case IV interest income @ 33% for the amount of the gross interest.

Step 3: Include the DIRT credit (i.e. 33% of gross interest) as a non-refundable tax credit.

Example 6.3

Joe, who is single, is employed by a local supermarket. His gross salary for the tax year 2021 was €36,000 (tax deducted: €4,040) and he received net interest on his AIB deposit account of €750. This was subject to DIRT at 33%. His tax credits for 2021 are the personal tax credit of €1,650 and the employee tax credit of €1,650.

Income Tax Computation 2021

	€	€
Income:		
Schedule D Case IV:		
AIB (€750 × 100/67)	1,119	
Schedule E	36,000	
Total taxable income		37,119
Tax Calculation:		
€1,119 @ 33%	369	
€35,300 @ 20%	7,060	
€700 @ 40%	280	
€37,119		7,709
Deduct: Non-refundable tax credits:		
Basic personal tax credit	1,650	
Employee tax credit	1,650	
DIRT paid (€1,119 @ 33%)	369	(3,669)
Tax liability		4,040
Deduct: Refundable tax credit – tax paid under PAYE		(4,040)
Net tax payable		NIL

DIRT is not refundable, even where the taxpayer only pays income tax at the standard rate (20%).

Example 6.4

Monica works in the local hair salon and earned a salary of €21,000 gross in 2021 (tax deducted was €900). She received interest of €1,210 (net of DIRT at 33%) from PTSB in 2021. Monica has personal tax credits of €3,300 for 2021.

Income Tax Computation 2021

	€	€	€
Income:			
Schedule E income		21,000	
Schedule D Case IV income:			
PTSB (€1,210 × 100/67)		1,806	
Taxable income			22,806
Tax Calculation:			
€21,000 @ 20%	4,200		
€1,806 @ 33%	596		4,796
Deduct: Non-refundable tax credits:			
Personal tax credit	1,650		
Employee tax credit	1,650		
DIRT paid (€1,806 @ 33%)	596		(3,896)
Tax liability			900
Deduct: Refundable tax credit – tax paid under PAYE			(900)
Net tax payable			**NIL**

Even though Monica has surplus capacity at the 20% rate (€35,300 – €21,000 = €14,300), her Case IV income is liable to tax at 33%.

The computation of Case IV profits is outlined in **Example 6.5** below.

Example 6.5

John and Brigid Murphy had the following income for 2021:

	John	Brigid
	€	€
Salary (gross)	50,000	32,000
Tax deducted under PAYE	(9,640)	(3,100)
Bank ordinary deposit interest (net)	2,336	190
Credit Union interest: share account (net)	295	785
deposit account (net)	176	–

Their non-refundable tax credits are:

Married couple tax credit	€3,300
Employee tax credit: €1,650 × 2	€3,300

continued overleaf

Income Tax Computation 2021		
Income:	€	€
Schedule D Case IV:		
– John Murphy (Note 1)	4,190	
– Brigid Murphy (Note 2)	1,455	5,645
Schedule E		
– John Murphy	50,000	
– Brigid Murphy	32,000	82,000
Total taxable income		**87,645**
Tax Calculation:		
€ 5,645 @ 33%	1,863	
€70,600 @ 20%	14,120	
€11,400 @ 40%	4,560	20,543
€87,645		
Deduct: Non-refundable tax credits:		
Married couple tax credit	3,300	
Employee tax credits	3,300	
DIRT paid (€5,645 @ 33%)	1,863	(8,463)
Tax liability		12,080
Deduct: Refundable tax credits - tax paid under PAYE		
– John Murphy	9,640	
– Brigid Murphy	3,100	(12,740)
Tax refund due		(660)
Notes:		
1. John Murphy: Schedule D, Case IV income		
Bank interest – ordinary deposit account (net)		2,336
Credit Union interest:		
– deposit account (net)		176
– share account (net)		295
Interest net		2,807
Interest gross (€2,807 × 100/67)		**4,190**
2. Brigid Murphy: Schedule D, Case IV income		
Bank interest – ordinary deposit account (net)		190
Credit Union share account (net)		785
Interest net		975
Interest gross (€975 × 100/67)		**1,455**

6.3.5 Case IV Losses

While in practical terms Case IV losses are very rare, where they do occur they may be set against Case IV profits of the **same year** of assessment or, alternatively, of **subsequent years**.

6.4 Schedule F

6.4.1 Income Assessable under Schedule F

Dividends and certain other distributions paid by **Irish-resident** companies to individual shareholders are liable to tax under Schedule F. Dividends received by Irish resident individuals are received after the deduction of **dividend withholding tax (DWT)** of **25%**, effective **1 January 2020**. The recipient can claim an off-set for DWT against their tax liability and, where DWT exceeds their tax liability, the balance will be refunded.

Shares in Lieu of Dividends

If a company issues shares in lieu of dividends, the distribution is **only** considered under **Schedule F** if the distributing company is Irish-resident and quoted (i.e. listed on Euronext Dublin (the Irish Stock Exchange)). If the distributing company is Irish-resident but unquoted, the distribution is taxed under Schedule D, Case IV.

Shares issued in lieu of dividends by an Irish-resident quoted company (i.e. those taxable under Schedule F) are valued, at the date of distribution, by:

- the dividend foregone, minus
- tax of 25% payable on the dividend foregone.

Therefore, the shareholder's Schedule F taxable income is the full amount of the gross dividend foregone, and credit is given for the DWT paid.

The redemption of bonus shares and bonus debentures is also taxable as income under Schedule F.

Exempt Dividend Income

Dividends paid by Irish-resident companies from **profits** arising from **stallion** fees or **stud greyhound** fees, or from the occupation of **woodlands**, managed on a commercial basis with a view to the realisation of profits, are exempt from income tax in the hands of the shareholder. In the case of such dividends they are ignored for income tax purposes but should be disclosed in the income tax return; they are, however, subject to PRSI and USC.

6.4.2 Basis of Assessment

The amount assessable is the amount received **in the tax year** plus DWT, i.e. the gross amount of the distribution. The date on which the dividend is **paid** determines the tax year, irrespective of the accounting year's profit from which the dividend was declared.

6.4.3 Computation of Schedule F Income

The amount assessable on the individual is the amount received in the tax year plus DWT.

Example 6.6

Jane Conway, who is single, received the following Irish dividends from LUX DAC in respect of its accounting year ended 31 March 2021:

Interim dividend (net) paid 30 September 2021	€2,640
Final dividend (net) paid 1 May 2022	€1,360

Jane also had Schedule E income of €33,500 for 2021 (tax deducted €3,400). Her personal tax credit was €1,650 and her employee tax credit was €1,650.

Jane Conway Income Tax Computation 2021	€	€
Schedule E:		
Salary		33,500
Schedule F:		
Net dividend received 2021 (Note)	2,640	
Dividend withholding tax deducted	880	
Gross Schedule F income		3,520
Taxable Income		37,020
Tax:		
€35,300 @ 20%	7,060	
€1,720 @ 40%	688	
€37,020		7,748
Deduct: Non-refundable tax credits:		
Basic personal tax credit	1,650	
Employee tax credit	1,650	(3,300)
Net tax liability		4,448
Deduct: Refundable tax credits		
Tax paid under PAYE	3,400	
Dividend withholding tax	880	(4,280)
Tax payable		168

Note:

Net dividend received €2,640 × 100/75 = gross dividend of €3,520.

The dividend is not apportioned, so the dividend paid on 30 September 2021 is taxable in full in 2021. As the date of the payment of the dividend determines the tax year, the dividend paid on 1 May 2022 is assessable in 2022.

Questions

Review Questions

(See Suggested Solutions to Review Questions at the end of this textbook.)

Question 6.1

Maeve, a 78-year-old widow with no dependent children, is in receipt of the following sources of Irish income:

Dividends received net:	€
Tyson DAC	17,520
Holyfield Manufacturing DAC	2,600
	20,120
Deposit interest received net	
Permanent TSB Bank	6,400
Credit Union interest	1,200
AIB interest	720
	8,320

Maeve is also in receipt of a contributory widow's pension of €12,912.

Requirement
Compute Maeve's 2021 income tax liability. Her personal tax credits are €4,085.

Question 6.2

Anthony and Sandrine Kelly are married and have four children, one of whom is incapacitated. They are both resident and domiciled in Ireland. Details of their income for the tax year 2021 is as follows:

Anthony Kelly:	€
Salary	50,000
Tax deducted under PAYE	(6,340)
AIB ordinary deposit interest (gross) 31/12/2021	130
Credit Union interest (gross) – deposit account	80
Credit Union interest (gross) – share account	100
Sandrine Kelly:	
Salary	28,000
Tax deducted under PAYE	(2,300)
KBC Bank – deposit interest gross	2,000
Independent Newspapers plc (Irish) dividend received net	2,500

Requirement

Calculate their liability to income tax for 2021 on the assumption that a valid election for joint assessment is in force. Their personal tax credits are €9,900.

Question 6.3

David Lee, who is a single person aged 44, works for a travel agency. He lives with his daughter Judy, aged 14, whom he maintains. He had the following income and outgoings in 2021:

	€
Income:	
Salary (gross)	42,000
Ordinary bank interest (net)	500
Interest on government stock (gross)	1,130
Ordinary building society interest (net)	140
Dividend from credit union share account (net)	29
Outgoings:	
PAYE deducted	3,990

Requirement

Calculate David Lee's income tax liability for 2021, stating clearly the amount payable by, or refundable to, him. His personal tax credits are €4,950.

Schedule D, Case V – Property Income

Learning Objectives

After studying this chapter you will understand:

- the income assessable under Case V;
- the special tax treatment of premiums on short leases;
- what expenses are allowable and deductible against letting income; and
- the relief available under Rent-a-Room Relief.

7.1 Introduction

Case V income is income received from the renting of property or lands situated in the **Republic of Ireland** (the State). While the rules for calculating the net rents from property situated abroad are the same as the Case V rules, such income is assessable to tax under Schedule D, Case III.

7.1.1 Income Assessable under Schedule D, Case V

The following income is assessable under Case V:

- Rents in respect of any premises or lands in the State, i.e. offices, shops, factories, land, etc.
- Receipts in respect of an easement (right over land, e.g. a right of way). An easement includes any right in, over or derived from any premises in the State. e.g. payments for the right to erect advertising signs, communication transmitters or for the grant of a right of way.
- The granting of sporting rights, such as fishing and shooting permits.
- Payments made by a tenant for the maintenance or repair of the premises, which are not required by the lease to be carried out by the tenant.
- Certain premiums received for the granting of a lease.
- Service charges for services connected to the occupation of the property.
- Insurance payments covering the non-payment of rent.
- Lettings under conacre.

7.2 Basis of Assessment

Tax is charged under Case V on the income arising during the year of assessment. The rent taken into account is the amount receivable in the tax year **whether or not** it is actually received. However, if the taxpayer claims and proves that the whole or part of a rent was not received due to it being irrecoverable because of:

▪ the default of the person liable, **or**
▪ because the taxpayer waived payment of the rent without consideration and in order to avoid hardship,

then the rent not received is **excluded** from the Case V computation.

A Case V source of income does not commence until **rental income arises**, not when the property is acquired; and it does not **cease** until the property is **disposed** of. There are no other special commencement or cessation rules for Case V income.

7.3 Computation of Taxable Income

As outlined above, income taxable under Case V is Irish rental income **receivable** in the year of assessment. Certain costs associated with the letting are deductible from gross rents (see **Section 7.3.2**) to arrive at the net Case V profit or loss. Case V income from multiple properties is calculated on each property separately, and aggregated as total Case V profits or losses for the year of assessment.

7.3.1 *Premiums on Short Leases*

A premium on a lease is an upfront payment, paid by the tenant, on the creation of a lease. This is often a method used by the property owner to get an upfront lump sum return on, say, a refurbishment or redevelopment of an existing property or an investment in a new property. On leases shorter than 50 years, a portion of the premium is deemed to be income and not a capital receipt.

A "short" lease for the purposes of this section is deemed to be a lease the duration of which is less than **50 years**.

Calculation of Taxable Portion of Premium

Where a landlord receives a premium on the creation of a "short lease" (i.e. the duration of the lease does not exceed 50 years), this will be treated as receiving an amount **by way of rent** (in addition to any actual rent), as computed by the following formula:

$$\text{Premium} \times \frac{51 - \text{Duration of the lease}}{50}$$

Note, the balance of the premium is subject to capital gains tax.

Example 7.1

On 1 June 2021, Mr White rents a premises to Mr Blake for 25 years at a rent of €2,000 per month, subject to a premium of €20,000.

Taxable portion of premium:

$$€20,000 \times \frac{51 - 25}{50} = €10,400$$

Case V assessable 2021:	€
Taxable portion of premium	10,400
Rent receivable (€2,000 × 7)	14,000
Total assessable	**24,400**

Case V assessable 2022:	
Rent receivable (€2,000 × 12)	**24,000**

7.3.2 *Allowable and Disallowable Deductions*

The following amounts may be deducted from the gross rents receivable (section 97 TCA 1997):

- Rent payable on the property (e.g. ground rent).
- Rates payable on the property (e.g. commercial property rates, water rates, refuse, etc.).
- The cost of goods or services which the landlord is obliged to provide and for which he receives no separate consideration (e.g. gas, electricity, waste disposal).
- Cost of repairs, excluding improvements and items treated as capital expenditure.
- Cost of insurance, maintenance and management of the property.
- Loan interest paid on money borrowed for the purchase, improvement or repair of an industrial or commercial property is allowable, but interest charges incurred prior to the first letting are not deductible.
- **100%** of the loan interest accrued in 2021 on money borrowed for the purchase, improvement or repair of a residential property are allowable but, as above, interest charges incurred prior to the first letting are not deductible.

    Where interest accrues on a loan taken out to acquire a residential premises from a spouse, or civil partner, such interest is not deductible. In this context spouse or civil partner does not include a legally separated or divorced spouse, a legally separated civil partner or where the civil partnership has been legally dissolved.

    A deduction for loan interest will not be allowed unless the landlord **registers all tenancies** that exist in relation to that property with the **Residential Tenancies Board (RTB)**, in accordance with the Residential Tenancies Act 2004.
- Accountancy fees incurred in drawing up rental accounts and keeping rental records.
- Mortgage protection and life assurance policy premiums paid.
- Wear and tear allowances may be claimed on the cost of fixtures and fittings for furnished lettings at a rate of **12.5%** per annum on a **straight-line basis**.

Allowable expenses are normally deducted on an **accruals basis** rather than on a paid basis. In order to be deductible, the expense must be incurred **wholly and exclusively** for the purpose of earning the rent and must be **revenue** rather than **capital** in nature.

Disallowable Expenses

Expenses not deductible against Case V income include:

- **Local property tax (LPT)** is not allowable as a deduction against Case V income.
- Expenses incurred in respect of a property **before** the first lease commences in respect of that property (other than legal and advertising expenses). In the case of interest and rent, **no deduction** is allowed for either interest or rent payable in respect of a period before the property is first **occupied** by a lessee. (See exception below for vacant residential property.)
- Expenses incurred **after** the termination of a lease are not deductible. However, expenses incurred **after** the termination of one lease **and before** the commencement of another lease in respect of the property are deductible provided the following three conditions are satisfied:
    1. the expenses would **otherwise** be deductible;
    2. the person who was the lessor of the property **does not occupy** the premises during the period when the property is **not let**; and
    3. the property is let by the **same lessor** at the end of the period.

Pre-letting Expenses in respect of Vacant Residential Property
Section 97A TCA 1997 provides that pre-letting costs of up to **€5,000** incurred in the 12 months before the date of the first residential letting are allowable as a deduction against rental income. This applies only to expenditure on a premises that has been **vacant for at least 12 months** and which is then let as a residential premises between 25 December 2017 and 31 December 2021.

If the person who incurs the expenditure ceases to let the property as a residential premises **within four years** of the first letting, the deduction will be clawed back in the year in which the property ceases to be let as a residential premises. The cessation can be either on sale of the property or change of use from rented residential property.

7.3.3 Rent-a-Room Relief

Where an individual rents out a room (or rooms) in a "qualifying residence" and the gross income received (including sums arising for food, laundry or similar goods and services) **does not exceed €14,000 per annum**, this income will be **exempt** from income tax. It is also not liable to PRSI or USC, but it must be included in an individual's income tax return. In determining whether the limit has been exceeded for the tax year, deductions for expenses and costs incurred in providing the accommodation are not allowed (e.g. additional light and heat costs, food, laundry, etc.). Where the income **exceeds €14,000**, the **entire** amount is taxable.

A "qualifying residence" is a residential premises situated in the State which is occupied by the individual as their sole or main residence during the year of assessment.

Room rentals under this scheme **will not affect**:

- mortgage interest relief available to the individual who qualifies for relief; or
- principal private residence relief for CGT purposes on the disposal of the house.

Where the room or rooms are rented out by more than one individual, the €14,000 limit is divided **between** the individuals.

The relief does apply to shorter-term residential accommodation that is not leisure or business, such as lettings for respite care of incapacitated individuals or accommodation for full- or part-time students (including language students). Although note the exclusion of the relief for "short periods" listed below.

An individual may, if they wish, elect to have any income/losses from this source assessed under the normal rules for rental income (e.g. if there is a rental loss on the room).

Exclusions
The Rent-a-Room exemption will not apply where:

1. the room is rented to a child of the individual or the civil partner of the individual renting the rooms;
2. the individual receiving the rent (or a person connected to them) is an office-holder or employee of the person making the payment (or someone connected to them) (section 216A TCA 1997);
3. the income is from the provision of accommodation to **occasional visitors for short periods**. A "short period" means less than **28 consecutive days**. Use of the room as **guest accommodation** rather than for residential purposes is not permitted, including where such accommodation is provided through online accommodation booking sites (e.g. Airbnb.com).

7.3.4 Case V Losses

Case V losses incurred in a year of assessment can be carried forward **indefinitely** and used against **future** Case V profits. Unutilised Case V losses may **not be set off** against any other type of income. A net profit or loss is computed for each property **separately** for the particular tax year. The profits/losses are then aggregated to arrive at the total profit/loss for the tax year.

Section 384 TCA 1997 provides that Case V capital allowances arising in a year are to be deducted against Case V income arising in that year **in priority** to Case V losses that are brought forward from a prior year.

If a property is let otherwise than on an arm's length basis (known as an 'uneconomic letting') and the rent receivable is insufficient to cover expenses, any loss arising is to be carried forward until the property is re-let on a commercial basis. Tax relief is therefore not available for those losses against rental profits from other properties.

7.3.5   Computation of Case V Taxable Income – Example

Example 7.2

John Black has owned rental properties for several years. You are given the following information about the properties owned during the tax year 2021.

Property A	€
Rent receivable	40,000
Expenditure incurred:	
Insurance (for all of 2021)	1,200
Repairs (incurred December 2021)	400
Interest on loan to acquire the property	36,000

This is a commercial property let for the first time on a 10-year lease, which commenced on 1 April 2021. A premium of €20,000 was payable on commencement of the lease. The property was acquired on 1 January 2021 for €450,000 with a bank loan taken out on the same date.

Property B	€
Rent receivable	9,600
Expenditure incurred:	
Insurance	280
Painting exterior	740
Repairs to door and alarm following burglary	1,250
LPT	225

Property B is a residential property which was let at €800 per month on a two-year lease that commenced on 1 January 2020. The tenant left suddenly in December 2021 leaving rent owing for the month of November and December. Mr Black subsequently found out that the tenant had emigrated to Australia and has written off the rent owing as a bad debt. The property was re-let to another tenant in February 2022.

Property C	€
Rent receivable	6,000
Expenditure incurred:	
Repairs and painting prior to letting	1,850
Insurance	500
Construction of conservatory (May 2021)	12,400
Interest	11,000
LPT	315

Property C is a residential property that has been vacant since 30 June 2020. It was let on a one-year lease from 1 September 2021 at €1,500 a month. The tenancies in properties B and C are registered with the RTB.

continued overleaf

Property D

	€
Rent receivable	30,000
Expenditure incurred:	
Interest	25,000

Mr Black acquired property D from his wife in 2015 for €450,000. Mrs Black had inherited the house from her mother in 2015. Mrs Black used funds from the sale of property D to Mr Black towards the cost of a new house purchased by Mr and Mrs Black as their principal private residence.

John Black – Case V Assessment 2021	Notes	Prop. A €	Prop. B €	Prop. C €	Prop. D €
Rent received/receivable	1	40,000	8,000	6,000	30,000
Income element of premium	2	16,400	0	0	0
Gross rent		56,400	8,000	6,000	30,000
Deduct:					
Pre-letting expenses	6			5,000	
Insurance	3	900	280	167	0
LPT	5		0	0	
Repairs/painting		400	1,990	0	0
Loan interest	4	27,000	0	3,667	0
Total deductions		28,300	2,270	8,834	0
Net profit/(loss)		28,100	5,730	(2,834)	30,000
Total Case V Income Assessable 2021					**60,996**

Notes:

1. *Rent received/receivable – Property B*

	€
Rent receivable	9,600
Less: amount written off as bad debt	(1,600)
Total rent	8,000

2. *Premium – Property A*

Taxable portion of premium: $€20,000 \times \dfrac{51-10}{50} = €16,400$

3. *Insurance*: expenses incurred before first letting are disallowed.

Property A: Insurance allowed	€1,200 × 9/12ths = €900
Property C: Insurance allowed	€500 × 4/12ths = €167

4. Loan interest: expenses incurred before first letting are disallowed.

Property A: Loan interest allowed: €36,000 × 9/12ths = €27,000

Property C: Residential property and registered with the RTB, therefore no interest restriction.

€11,000 × 4/12ths = €3,667

Property D: interest incurred is not allowable, as property was acquired from wife.

5. Local property tax (LPT) is not allowable.
6. Pre-letting expenses in respect of vacant residential property.

Repairs and painting	€1,850
Insurance €500 × 8/12ths	€333
Loan Interest €11,000 × 8/12ths	€7,333
Total pre-letting expenses	€9,516
Restricted to	€5,000

Questions

Review Questions

(See Suggested Solutions to Review Questions at the end of this textbook.)

Question 7.1

Mr O'Reilly owns several properties that he lets. Details of his income from these properties and the letting terms are as follows:

Property A (residential property) Acquired in November 2017 and let on a five-year lease expiring in November 2022 at a monthly rent of €500 payable monthly in advance. The rent due on 1 December 2021 was not received until 10 January 2022. Interest of €5,500 was incurred evenly during the year on a bank loan taken out to acquire the property. The property is registered with the RTB.

Property B (commercial property) Acquired on 1 April 2021 and let for the first time on 1 August 2021 on a 21-year lease at a full annual rent of €12,000 payable monthly in advance. A bank loan was raised to help purchase the property and interest of €1,800 was paid on 30 June 2021 and €3,600 on 31 December 2021 for the period 1 July to 31 December 2021. A premium of €10,000 was also received under the terms of the new lease.

Property C (residential property) Let at a full annual rent of €6,000 under a seven-year lease, which expired on 30 April 2021. The property was vacant until 1 November 2021, when it was let again on a five-year lease at a full rent of €9,000 per annum. The property is registered with the RTB.

Property D (residential property) The property was purchased in 2019 and was vacant until its first letting on 1 May 2021 at a monthly rent of €1,200. Mr. O'Reilly paid €9,250 loan interest on the property in 2021. The property is registered with the RTB.

Mr O'Reilly is responsible for repairs on all properties, except for Property A, in respect of which there is a "tenants repairing" lease.

During the tax year 2021, the following additional expenses were incurred:

Property B

		€
30 April	Dry rot repairs	950
30 June	Window broken by vandals	80
31 December	Storm damage	1,400

Property C

20 May	Blocked drains	90
31 July	Painting	700
31 October	Advertising for tenant	130

Property D

25 January	Replace broken windows	390
9 March	Painting and decorating	1,100
28 March	Cleaning	420
28 September	Roof repairs	160

Requirement

Compute Mr O'Reilly's rental income assessable under Schedule D, Case V for the tax year 2021.

Question 7.2

Sonya, a widow, has recently brought you details of her rental income, which will be needed to prepare schedules supporting her tax return. All properties are commercial, non-residential properties. Relevant information is as follows:

Property 1   Let on a 10-year lease which was granted in December 2015 at an annual rent of €16,000, payable monthly in arrears and subject to review every three years.

Property 2   Let at a rent of €8,000 per annum, payable monthly in advance.

Property 3   Let at a rent of €9,600 per annum, payable monthly in advance. The instalment of rent due on 1 December 2021 was not received until 10 January 2022. This property was first let some years ago.

Property 4   First let on a 15-year lease on 30 June 2021 at a rent of €9,000 per annum, payable quarterly in arrears on 30 September, 31 December, 31 March and 30 June, subject to review every three years.

Property 5   Let on a 15-year lease, expiring in June 2022, at a nominal rent of €10 per month, payable annually in advance on 30 June. The tenant is Sonya's sister.

The expenses (all allowable) paid in 2021 by Sonya for each property were:

	€
Property 1	4,300
Property 2	1,200
Property 3	800
Property 4	NIL
Property 5	900

In addition, mortgage interest of €1,400 gross was paid on a loan to finance the purchase of Property 3. Her property portfolio is entirely commercial.

Requirement

(a) Prepare a schedule summarising Sonya's property income assessable in 2021.
(b) Sonya is contemplating an investment in:
   (i) The National Instalment Savings Scheme
   (ii) government securities.
   Prepare notes briefly summarising the tax effects of each of these investments.

Question 7.3

Liz Darcy wishes to rent two of her spare bedrooms to four students attending the local college from September 2021 under the Rent-a-Room scheme. Each student will pay €450 per month from September to May for lodging, food and laundry. Liz estimates that the costs associated with the provision of the accommodation will be as follows:

	€
Light and heat	1,350
Food	4,150
Cleaning and laundry costs	900
Total costs	6,400
Monthly costs	711

Requirement

Advise Liz on the tax implications of the above lettings for 2021 and 2022. (Assume that the same tax rules apply in both years.)

Tax Credits, Reliefs and Exemptions and Charges on Income

Learning Objectives

After studying this chapter you will understand:

- the main income tax credits available to individual taxpayers;
- the manner of granting tax relief at the standard rate and at the marginal rate;
- expenditures which attract tax relief – medical expenses, fees to third-level institutions, etc.;
- the operation of tax relief at source;
- the concept of charges on income and the granting of tax relief for the payment of charges; and
- special tax incentive-based reliefs and exemptions.

8.1 Introduction

Personal allowances are given as **credits** against **income tax liabilities** instead of **deductions** against **income**. Therefore, every €1,000 of a personal tax allowance is equivalent to a **tax credit** of €200, i.e. the tax allowance at the standard rate of 20%.

However, it must be noted that some reliefs are still given as a **deduction from income** and, therefore, obtain tax relief at the marginal rate, i.e. 40% for 2021.

There are three methods of granting tax relief for reliefs relating to personal status, expenses incurred or source of income:

1. Non-refundable tax credit – related to personal circumstances, e.g. married tax credit or age.
2. Refundable tax credit, e.g. dividend withholding tax.
3. Deduction from income source (e.g. employee pension contributions) **or** deduction from total income (e.g. employment of carer for an incapacitated person).

Non-refundable tax credits **cannot** reduce the tax due **below zero**, **nor** can they **reduce** the tax payable on **charges on income** (e.g. covenants).

Refundable/Non-refundable Tax Credits
Generally, credits for tax withheld from income are refundable (e.g. tax deducted under PAYE; DWT), whereas all other tax credits (e.g. basic personal tax credits, incapacitated child, home-carer, etc.) are not refundable. However, DIRT is repayable in certain circumstances (see **Section 6.3.4**).

8.2 Personal Tax Credits

8.2.1 Introduction

Personal tax credits are credits to which an individual is entitled depending on their personal circumstances, e.g. married, civil partner, single, widowed, employed, etc. The amount of the qualifying credit is the same for each individual.

8.2.2 Chart of Personal Tax Credits

Description	Tax Year 2021 €
Single Person	1,650
Married Couple/Civil Partners	3,300
Widowed Person/Surviving Civil Partner	
– in the year of bereavement	3,300
Widowed Person/Surviving Civil Partner in the years following the year of bereavement:	
– without dependent children	2,190
– with dependent children*	1,650
Single Person Child Carer Credit (additional)	1,650
Widowed Person/Surviving Civil Partner – Parent (additional)	
– First year after bereavement	3,600
– Second year after bereavement	3,150
– Third year after bereavement	2,700
– Fourth year after bereavement	2,250
– Fifth year after bereavement	1,800
Employee (PAYE) Tax Credit	1,650
Earned Income Tax Credit	1,650
Sea-going navy personnel credit	1,270
Fisher Tax Credit (maximum)	1,270
Blind Person	1,650
Both Spouses/Civil Partners Blind	3,300
Age Credit (65 years and over)	
– Single/Widowed Person/Surviving Civil Partner	245
– Married/Civil Partners	490
Incapacitated Child	3,300
Dependent Relative	245
– Income limit	15,740
Home Carer	1,600
– Income limit lower	7,200
– Income limit upper	10,400

* Also entitled to Single Person Child Carer Credit.

8.2.3   Basic Personal Tax Credits

The basic personal tax credits are determined by the marital or civil partnership status of the taxpayer.

Single Tax Credit
This credit is available to individuals who are not married or in a civil partnership, or who are not widowed or a surviving civil partner.

Married/Civil Partners' Tax Credit
This is available for a year of assessment where:

■   a married couple (including married same-sex couples) or civil partners are jointly assessed; or
■   where the couple are living apart and one party, in the year of assessment, is wholly or mainly maintained by the other, and that person is not entitled to deduct any legally enforceable maintenance payments to the other when computing his or her total income for the year of assessment.

Widowed/Surviving Civil Partner Tax Credit
This is available to a widowed person or a surviving civil partner and varies depending on whether there are dependent children and the year of the bereavement.

1.   Widowed Person/Surviving Civil Partner Without Dependent Children
A widowed person/surviving civil partner without a dependent child will get the Widowed Person/ Surviving Civil Partner Tax Credit in the year of bereavement **(2021: €3,300)**.

For subsequent years the person will receive the Widowed Person/Surviving Civil Partner (without dependent children) Tax Credit **(2021: €2,190)**.

2.   Widowed Person/Surviving Civil Partner With Dependent Children
A widowed person/surviving civil partner with a dependent child will get the Widowed Person/Surviving Civil Partner Tax Credit in the year of bereavement **(2021: €3,300)**.

For subsequent years, as long as the person has dependent children, the person will get the Widowed Person/Surviving Civil Partner (with dependent children) Tax Credit **(2021: €1,650) and** the Single Person Child Carer Credit **(2021: €1,650)**.

In addition, there is a Widowed Person/Surviving Civil Partner – **Parent** Tax Credit available for the **first five years** after the year of death as follows:

■   €3,600 in the first year after bereavement
■   €3,150 in the second year after bereavement
■   €2,700 in the third year after bereavement
■   €2,250 in the fourth year after bereavement
■   €1,800 in the fifth year after bereavement.

A widowed person/surviving civil partner with a dependent child who is cohabiting with a partner is **not entitled** to the allowances available for persons with a dependent child, but will qualify for the Widowed/ Surviving Civil Partner (without dependent children) Tax Credit **(2021: €2,190)**.

A "qualifying child" for the purpose of this allowance is a child who:

■   is born in the year of assessment; **or**
■   is a child of the claimant, or a child in the custody of the claimant, who is maintained by the claimant at the claimant's own expense for the whole or part of the year of assessment; **or**

■ is **under 18 years** at the start of the year of assessment; **or**
■ if **over 18 years** at the start of the year of assessment:
  ● is receiving full-time education at an educational establishment or is in full-time training with an employer for a trade or profession, **or**
  ● is permanently incapacitated by reason of mental or physical infirmity and, if he or she has reached 21 years of age, was so incapacitated before reaching that age.

"Child" includes a stepchild, a child whose parents have not married, and an adopted child.

Example 8.1
Mary is a widow since 2016 with one dependent child. She has not remarried and lives alone with her child. What are her non-refundable tax credits (NRTC) for 2021?

	€
Widowed person – with dependent children	1,650
Single Person Child Carer Credit	1,650
Widowed parent 5th year	1,800
Total NRTC 2021	5,100

Single Person Child Carer Credit

The Single Person Child Carer Credit (SPCCC) is a tax credit for single people who are caring, on their own, for a "qualifying child" (see above). The credit is available to the **primary claimant**, i.e. the individual with whom the qualifying child resides for the whole, or greater part, of the year. It is possible for a qualifying primary claimant to **surrender** his or her entitlement to the credit in favour of another qualifying individual, i.e. a **secondary claimant.**

The credit cannot be claimed where any claimant (either primary or secondary) is:

■ jointly assessed for tax, i.e. as a married person or civil partner;
■ married or in a civil partnership (unless separated);
■ cohabiting, **or**
■ a widow/widower/surviving civil partner in the year of bereavement;
■ in the case of a secondary claimant, the qualifying child must live with the claimant for **at least 100 days** in the year (not required to be consecutive).

Only **one** SPCCC is available to **either** the primary claimant **or** the secondary claimant, irrespective of the number of children and the time spent with each parent. The person in receipt of the SPCCC is also entitled to the increased single standard rate tax band of €39,300.

Example 8.2
Jenny is divorced from Colin and is the primary carer of their three children, Sarah, James and Ben. The children spend weekends and some holidays with Colin (more than 100 days in a year). Both Jenny and Colin are single and are not cohabiting. Their non-refundable tax credits for 2021 are as follows:

	Jenny	Colin
Single Tax Credit	€1,650	€1,650
Single Person Child Carer Credit	€1,650	NIL
Standard rate tax band	€39,300	€35,300

continued overleaf

Jenny agrees to surrender her entitlement to SPCCC to Colin. Their non-refundable tax credits for 2021 are:

	Jenny	**Colin**
Single Tax Credit	€1,650	€1,650
Single Person Child Carer Credit	NIL	€1,650
Standard rate tax band	€35,300	€39,300

Where a primary claimant surrenders their entitlement to the tax credit, **two or more** secondary claimants can claim the credit provided they satisfy the requirements above.

Example 8.3
Susan, who is single, has two children, Jack and Patrick, and is a qualifying primary claimant. Jack resides with his father, Seán, for more than 100 days in the year; Patrick resides with his father, Stephen, for more than 100 days in a year. If Susan surrenders her entitlement to SPCCC, both Seán and Stephen can each claim SPCCC provided they satisfy all the other criteria.

	Susan	**Seán**	**Patrick**
Single Tax Credit	€1,650	€1,650	€1,650
Single Person Child Carer Tax Credit	NIL	€1,650	€1,650
Standard rate tax band	€35,300	€39,300	€39,300

If Susan does not surrender her entitlement to SPCCC their credits for 2021 are as follows:

	Susan	**Seán**	**Patrick**
Single Tax Credit	€1,650	€1,650	€1,650
Single Person Child Carer Tax Credit	€1,650	NIL	NIL
Standard rate tax band	€39,300	€35,300	€35,300

Note that a primary claimant is only entitled to **one credit**, regardless of the number of qualifying children residing with him or her, and cannot surrender the credit in respect of one child and retain the credit in respect of other children. Where, however, there is more than one child between the claimants, both parents can make a claim as the primary claimant in respect of one child each, provided the child is not the subject of a claim by any other person and the child satisfied the 100 days habitation requirement.

Example 8.4
Sharon and David are separated and have two children: Lucy, who lives full-time with her mother, and Eoin who lives full-time with David.

Sharon is the primary claimant for Lucy and is entitled to SPCCC and the increased single standard rate tax band, while David is the primary claimant for Eoin so he too is entitled to SPCCC and the increased tax band.

The credit must be claimed in writing by submitting to Revenue either claim form SPCC1 (primary claimant) or SPCC2 (secondary claimant).

8.2.4 Employee Tax Credit

An individual who is in **receipt of emoluments** chargeable under Schedule E and subject to the PAYE system is entitled to this tax credit. In the case of joint assessment and where **each** spouse/civil partner is in employment, the credit is available to each spouse/civil partner.

The employee tax credit **cannot exceed** the individual's Schedule E income at the standard rate of tax, i.e. if the individual's salary for 2021 is €1,000, the employee tax credit would be limited to €200 (€1,000 @ 20%).

An individual may also receive the employee tax credit where they receive income from an employment held **outside the State** and where the income has been subject to a tax deduction system similar to the Irish PAYE system, e.g. an Irish individual, living in Dundalk and working in Newry for a UK employer, receives their salary after deduction of tax under the UK PAYE system. The individual will be entitled to the employee tax credit.

The employee tax credit is **not applicable** to emoluments paid:

- by a company to **proprietary directors**, their spouses/civil partners or children (see below). A "proprietary director" means a director of a company who is the beneficial owner of, or able to control, either directly or indirectly, more than 15% of the ordinary share capital of a company;
- by a person to their spouse, civil partner or child;
- by a partnership to the spouse, civil partner or child of one of the partners.

Children of proprietary directors who are employees in the business will only get the employee tax credit where:

- the child is required to devote, throughout the tax year, substantially the whole of their time to the duties of the employment; **and**
- the child's gross salary from the employment is at least €4,572 (where the work is part-time, this may be apportioned); **and**
- the child is in insurable employment for PRSI; **and**
- the child's salary is paid and taxed under the PAYE system.

Note that proprietary directors and/or their spouses/civil partners or children may be entitled to the **earned income tax credit**.

8.2.5   Earned Income Tax Credit

The earned income tax credit is available to those with earned income who are not entitled to the employee tax credit of €1,650, or can only claim a portion of the employee tax credit. "Earned income" can generally be taken to mean income charged under Cases I and II of Schedule D (i.e. trading or professional income) and income earned under Schedule E that does not attract the employee tax credit (e.g. emoluments of proprietary directors).

The credit for 2021 is the **lower** of either:

- 20% of the earned income; or
- €1,650 (2020: €1,500).

If the individual is also entitled to a portion of the employee tax credit, the **aggregate** of the employee tax credit and earned income tax credit cannot exceed €1,650. Where joint assessment applies, a separate tax credit may be due in respect of each spouse's individual income.

Example 8.5

Joe is a proprietary director of GS Games Ltd and earned €85,000 in 2021. His wife Susan, who took early retirement, has a Schedule E pension of €6,200 and Schedule D Case I income of €12,000. They are jointly assessed. Calculate their tax liability for 2021.

Income	€	€
Joe: Schedule E salary		85,000
Susan: Schedule E pension		6,200
Schedule D Case I		<u>12,000</u>
Taxable income		<u>103,200</u>

Tax Calculation		
€62,500 (€44,300 + €18,200) @ 20%	12,500	
<u>€40,700</u> Balance @ 40%	<u>16,280</u>	28,780
€103,200		
Deduct: Non-refundable tax credits:		
Basic personal tax credit (married)	3,300	
Employee tax credit – Susan restricted to (Schedule E: €6,200 @ 20%)	1,240	
Earned income tax credit – Joe (maximum)	1,650	
Earned income tax credit – Susan (€1,650 – €1,240)	<u>410</u>	<u>(6,600)</u>
Tax liability		**22,180**

8.2.6   Blind Person's Tax Credit

A blind person is entitled to the blind person's tax credit of €1,650 for 2021. An individual does not have to be completely blind to obtain the credit, but a medical certificate showing the degree of blindness is required before the credit will be granted. If a married couple or civil partners are both blind, they are entitled to double the tax credit.

Relief is available if an individual or the individual's spouse/civil partner incurs expenditure on maintaining a guide dog and is a registered owner with the Irish Guide Dog Association. The amount of the additional credit is €825 at the standard rate.

8.2.7   Age Tax Credit

In addition to a basic personal tax credit, an individual may claim the age tax credit of €245 for 2021 where he, or his spouse/civil partner, is at least 65 years of age during the year of assessment. The married couple's/civil partners' age tax credit of €490 for 2021 may be claimed where only one of the couple is aged 65 or more.

8.2.8   Incapacitated Child Tax Credit

Where an individual has a "qualifying child" living with them at any time during the year, they are entitled to an incapacitated child tax credit of €3,300 for 2021 for each qualifying child.

In this context, a "qualifying child" is one who:

- is **under** the age of 18 and is permanently incapacitated by reason of mental or physical infirmity; **or**
- **if over** the age of 18, is permanently incapacitated by reason of mental or physical infirmity from maintaining themself, and was so before they reached 21 years of age, **or** after reaching 21 years, was in full-time education/training with an employer when they became so incapacitated; **and**
- is a child of the claimant or, if not such a child, is in the custody of the claimant, and is maintained by the claimant at the claimant's own expense for the whole or part of the year in question.

"Maintaining" for the purposes of this tax credit means an ability to support oneself by earning an income from working.

"Child" includes a stepchild, an adopted child, a child whose parents have not been married or an informally adopted child or any child of whom a person has custody. The credit is available for **each qualifying** child.

Where two or more persons are entitled to relief in respect of the same child, i.e. where both parents maintain the child jointly, the tax credit is allocated among those persons by reference to the amount which each spends in maintaining the child.

Qualifying Incapacities

The incapacity of the child must be such that it permanently prevents the child from being able, in the long term (i.e. when over 18 years of age), to maintain themself independently. If the incapacity can be corrected or relieved by the use of any treatment, device, medication or therapy (e.g. coeliac disease, diabetes, hearing impairment which can be corrected by a hearing aid, etc.), the child will not be regarded as permanently incapacitated for the purposes of this relief.

Examples of some disabilities regarded as permanently incapacitating include: cystic fibrosis, spina bifida, blindness, deafness, Down's syndrome, spastic paralysis, certain forms of schizophrenia and acute autism.

Note that a person who is entitled to incapacitated child tax credit is not entitled to dependent relative tax credit (see below) in respect of the same child.

8.2.9 Dependent Relative Tax Credit

An individual who proves that they maintain at their own expense a "dependent relative" is entitled to a "dependent relative tax credit". A "dependent relative" is defined as:

- a relative of the claimant or of their spouse/civil partner who is incapacitated by old age or infirmity from maintaining themselves; **or**
- the widowed father or widowed mother of the claimant or the claimant's spouse/civil partner, whether incapacitated or not; **or**
- the son or daughter of the claimant who lives with the claimant and upon whom they are dependent, by reason of old age or infirmity.

If the income of the dependent relative exceeds the specified limit (2021: €15,740), the dependent relative tax credit is not available.

Where two or more persons jointly maintain a dependent relative, the tax credit is allocated between them in proportion to the amount which each spends in maintaining the relative.

8.2.10 Home Carer Tax Credit

This is claimable by a married couple or civil partners who are jointly assessed where one spouse/civil partner (i.e. the home carer) works in the home caring for one or more dependent persons. The tax credit will be granted where:

- the couple are married or civil partners and are **jointly assessed**;
- one or more qualifying persons normally **reside** with the claimant and their spouse/civil partner (or, in the case of an aged or incapacitated person, resides nearby within 2 km); and
- the home carer's **income** is not in **excess of €7,200**. A reduced tax credit applies where the income is between **€7,200 and €10,400**. In calculating total income, no account is taken of the carer's allowance payable by the Department of Social Protection (DSP), but such allowance is a taxable source of income.

A "dependent" person is defined as:

- a child for whom child benefit is payable, i.e. children under 16 and children up to age 18 in full-time education, **or**
- a person aged 65 years or more in the year, **or**
- an individual who is permanently incapacitated by reason of mental or physical infirmity.

Note: a spouse/civil partner cannot be a "dependent" person.

Only **one** tax credit is given **regardless** of the number of dependent persons being cared for.

For 2021, if the home carer has total income of **€7,200** or less, the full tax credit of **€1,600** is given. If the income of the home carer is in excess of €7,200, the tax credit is reduced by **one-half of the excess over the limit**. For example, if the home carer has income of €8,000, a tax credit of €1,200, i.e. €1,600 − ((€8,000 − €7,200) × ½), may be claimed. If, however, a home carer has income of €10,400 or more, no tax credit is due.

Where the income of the home carer exceeds the permitted limit, the credit **will be granted** for that year if the home carer qualified for the credit in the **immediately preceding** tax year. However, in these circumstances the tax credit granted is **restricted to the tax credit** granted in the previous tax year.

Example 8.6

Jim and Katie Bloom are jointly assessed and they have two children under the age of 16 years. Jim has a salary of €47,000 and Katie has investment income of €7,800.

Option One: Claim Increased Standard Rate Tax Band 2021	€	€
Taxable Income:		
Jim	47,000	
Katie	7,800	54,800
Tax Calculation:		
€52,100 @ 20% (Jim max. €44,300 + Katie €7,800)	10,420	
€2,700 @ 40%	1,080	11,500
€54,800		
Deduct: Non-refundable tax credits		
Personal tax credit (married)	3,300	
Employee tax credit (Jim)	1,650	(4,950)
Tax liability		**6,550**

continued overleaf

Option Two: Claim Home Carer Tax Credit 2021	€	€
Taxable Income:		
Jim	47,000	
Katie	7,800	54,800
Tax Calculation:		
€44,300 @ 20% (Jim max. €44,300 only)	8,860	
€10,500 @ 40%	4,200	13,060
€54,800		
Deduct: Non-refundable tax credits		
Personal tax credit (married)	3,300	
Home carer tax credit €1,600 – ((€7,800 – €7,200) × 50%)	1,300	
Employee tax credit (Jim)	1,650	(6,250)
Tax liability		**6,810**

As their tax liability is lower if the increased standard rate tax band is claimed, Jim and Katie should claim this instead of the home carer tax credit

A married couple or civil partners, **where both persons have income**, are entitled to a standard rate tax band of up to €70,600. A married couple or civil partners cannot claim **both** the increased standard rate tax band **and** the home carer tax credit. However, they can claim whichever of the two gives them a lower tax liability.

In practice, when calculating tax credits and the standard rate cut-off point applicable, Revenue will grant whichever option is more beneficial to the taxpayer.

8.3 Tax Reliefs at the Standard Rate

8.3.1 Introduction

These reliefs are available in the same manner as the personal tax credits at **Section 8.2**, but the amounts of the relief **vary** depending on the expenditure involved. These reliefs are granted at the standard rate of tax and are given as a credit against the income tax liability.

8.3.2 Medical Insurance

Relief is available for premiums, paid to an authorised insurer or society, in respect of insurance to provide for the payment of actual medical expenses of the individual, their spouse/civil partner and their dependants. Relief is also available in respect of premiums paid on **dental insurance** policies for non-routine dental treatment.

The relief is granted **"at source"**, i.e. the amount of the gross premium is **reduced** by the **tax credit** available (20%). The medical insurance company **reclaims the 20% tax** from Revenue and the taxpayer **does not** need to make a separate claim for relief.

Section 470 TCA 1997 introduced a limit to the amount of relief that can be claimed. The relief is limited to:

- 20% of the premium paid up to a maximum of **€1,000** per adult, per policy;
- 20% of the premium paid up to a maximum of **€500** per child, per policy.

The definition of a "child" for the purposes of this relief includes an individual, **under the age of 21**, who is entitled to a health insurance contract at a reduced child rate. The maximum credit of €1,000 at the 20%

rate is available for all adults aged 21 years and over, regardless of whether they are in full-time education or whether or not they are paying a child-reduced rate of premium.

Where an employer pays medical insurance premiums for an employee, the employee is treated as if they had received additional salary equal to the gross medical insurance premium payable. In these circumstances, the employer pays the premium to the medical insurer net of the tax credit allowable, and pays the tax deducted (tax relief at source (TRS)) to Revenue. The employee must then claim a tax credit for this tax deducted.

Example 8.7
Monica, aged 25, is an employee of Scalp Ltd and earned €50,000 (tax paid €10,200) in 2021. Scalp Ltd also paid her medical insurance of €1,200 net to VHI.

Income:	€	€
Schedule E salary		50,000
Benefit in kind:		
Medical insurance (net paid to VHI)	1,200	
Tax credit (TRS paid to Revenue) (maximum €1,000 @ 20%)	200	
Medical insurance (gross)		1,400
Taxable income		
Tax Calculation:		51,400
€35,300 @ 20%	7,060	
€16,100 @ 40%	6,440	13,500
€51,400		
Deduct: Non-refundable tax credits:		
Basic personal tax credit	1,650	
Employee tax credit	1,650	(3,300)
Tax liability		10,200
Deduct: Refundable tax credits		
Tax paid under PAYE	10,200	
Medical insurance credit (maximum €1,000 @ 20%)	200	(10,400)
Net tax repayable		(200)

8.3.3 Medical Expenses

Section 469 TCA 1997 provides for relief by way of tax credit at the standard rate (with the exception of nursing home expenses, which may be claimed at the marginal rate – see **Section 8.4.2**), in respect of **un-reimbursed** medical expenses incurred by the individual on their **own behalf**, or **on behalf of others**.

There is no requirement for a defined relationship between the taxpayer and the subject of the tax relief claim.

"Medical expenses" include expenses incurred on:

- Fees to doctors, consultants, physiotherapists, children's speech and language therapists and educational psychologists.
- Maintenance or treatment in a hospital or other location (whether in Ireland or not) where such expenses were **necessarily** incurred on the advice of a medical practitioner.
- Drugs and medicines (including prescription charges), **prescribed by a doctor**, including some medical aids and equipment and specialist food for coeliac and diabetic patients.

- Supply, maintenance or repair of any medical, surgical, dental or nursing appliance used on the advice of a practitioner.
- Transport by ambulance.
- Assistance dogs for blind or disabled individuals, including children with autism. If a person maintains a trained assistance dog, a sum of €825 may be claimed as a health expense at the standard rate.
- Some travel, telephone, electricity or accommodation costs in respect of kidney patients or a child suffering from a life-threatening illness
- Specialised dental treatment (see below).
- Routine maternity care and in-vitro fertilisation.

Section 469 TCA 1997 specifically excludes **cosmetic surgery**, unless such surgery is necessary to ameliorate a physical deformity arising from or directly related to:

- congenital abnormality;
- personal injury; or
- disfiguring disease.

The emphasis on medical expenses relief appears to be relief for **unavoidable** health costs as opposed to those that are **discretionary**.

Where qualifying health care is only available outside Ireland, reasonable travelling and accommodation expenses can also be claimed. In such cases the expenses of one person accompanying the patient may also be allowed where the condition of the patient requires it.

The following **dental treatments** qualify for relief, provided the **dentist** supplies a Form MED2:

- Bridgework.
- Crowns (including post and core buildups made from materials other than gold).
- Tip replacing.
- Veneers/Rembrandt-type etched fillings.
- Endodontics – root canal treatment.
- Orthodontic treatment (including provision of braces).
- Periodontal treatment.
- Surgical extraction of impacted wisdom teeth.

Tax relief is **not available** for **routine dental care**, i.e. the cost of scaling, extraction and filling of teeth, and the provision and repair of artificial teeth and dentures, or for **routine ophthalmic care**, i.e. the cost of sight testing, provision and maintenance of spectacles and contact lenses.

Relief may be claimed, electronically, at the end of the year of assessment by submitting an eForm12 on Revenue's myAccount, if an employee; or by submitting Form 11 through ROS under self-assessment.

Receipts do not have to be submitted to claim relief, but only receipted expenditure can be claimed. Receipts must be retained for a period of six years. A claim for tax relief must be made within four years after the end of the tax year to which the claim relates. To claim relief for the year 2021, for example, you must submit your claim before the end of the year 2025.

8.3.4   Fees Paid for Third-level Education and Training Courses

Third-level Education

Relief is available, under section 473A TCA 1997, for qualifying fees, net of grants, paid in the tax year in respect of an "approved course" to an "approved college" on behalf of the individual or any other person. (There does not need to be a defined relationship between the taxpayer and the subject of the tax relief claim.)

"Approved college" means a college/university in the State, the EU, or in a non-EU Member State which is maintained by public funds. (See Revenue website www.revenue.ie for a full list of colleges.)

An "approved course" is:

- a full-time or part-time undergraduate course that is of at least two academic years' duration; or
- a postgraduate course of at least one year's duration, but not exceeding four years. This course must lead to a postgraduate award based on exam and/or thesis.

Relief is available on qualifying fees per course, per academic year, e.g. if an individual pays qualifying fees for two students attending college in an academic year, they are entitled to relief up to the maximum limit for **each** of these students.

The maximum level of qualifying fees (including the Student Contribution) per academic year is **€7,000** per course, per student. Where fees, in respect of which relief has been claimed, are fully or partly refunded, the taxpayer must notify Revenue within **21 days**.

Relief is **not** available in respect of:

- The **first €3,000** of all fees where **any one** of the students is a **full-time** student.
- The **first €1,500** of all fees where **all** of the students are **part-time**.

Example 8.8

Mary Weary has three children in third-level education in 2021. Details of fees paid for 2021 are as follows:

Student	Student Contribution	Tuition Fees	Total
April (Full-time)	€3,000	Nil	€3,000
Seán (Full-time)	€3,000	€6,000	€9,000
Kate (Part-time)	€1,500	€3,000	€4,500

Tax Relief Available:			
April	€3,000		
Seán (max.)	€7,000		
Kate	€4,500		
Less: disallowed	(€3,000)		
Allowable	€11,500		
Relief @ 20%	€2,300		

Fees Paid in Instalments

Tuition fees are often paid in instalments over two tax years (e.g. in September and January), so relief can be claimed either:

- in the tax year that the academic year commenced; or
- in the tax year in which the instalment was paid.

It is generally more beneficial to claim relief in the year the academic year commenced as the amount disallowed is often greater than the first fee instalment.

Training Courses

Relief is given for tuition fees paid for certain approved training courses, of less than two years' duration, in the areas of **information technology** and **foreign languages**. For 2021, relief applies to fees ranging from €315 to €1,270. The relief is given as an additional tax credit equal to the fees paid, subject to the €1,270 maximum, at the standard rate of tax.

The course must result in the awarding of a certificate of competence, not just a certificate of attendance.

8.4 Tax Reliefs at the Marginal Rate

Tax reliefs at the marginal rate are given as a deduction against taxable income and are thus available against the taxpayer's highest rate of tax (the 'marginal' rate).

8.4.1 Employment of Carer for Incapacitated Person

Where an individual employs a person to take care of a **family member** who is totally incapacitated by reason of old age or physical or mental infirmity, the individual is entitled to a deduction from their **total income** in calculating this taxable income. For 2021, this deduction is the **lesser** of the amount actually borne by the individual in employing the carer and **€75,000**.

Where two or more persons employ the carer, the allowance will be apportioned between them in proportion to the amount borne by each. A separate carer's allowance is available for each totally incapacitated person for whom the individual incurs expense. Carers may be employed on an individual basis or through an agency.

The **incapacitated child tax credit** (see **Section 8.2.8**) and/or the **dependent relative tax credit** (see **Section 8.2.9**) **cannot** be claimed where this carer's allowance is being claimed in respect of the same incapacitated relative.

The deduction for the first year of claim will be limited to the lower of the actual cost incurred or the maximum deduction of €75,000 **apportioned** by reference to the number of months during the year in which the individual was permanently incapacitated.

8.4.2 Nursing Home Expenses

Relief is available for expenses paid to a nursing home for health care, maintenance or treatment. Section 469 TCA 1997 states that the expenses will only qualify if the nursing home provides **24-hour nursing care on-site**. Section 469 also states that, even if the individual has received State support under the **Fair Deal** scheme (NHSSA 2009), any contribution to nursing home fees by the individual over and above the Fair Deal scheme will be allowable at the marginal rate. Nursing home expenses can be claimed in the same manner as medical expenses, i.e. online using myAccount or, if the individual is self-assessed, the tax relief is claimed by completing the 'Health Expenses' section on Form 11 of their income tax return.

8.4.3 Permanent Health Benefit Schemes

Relief is given for premiums payable under Revenue-approved permanent health benefit schemes, which provide for periodic payments to an individual in the event of loss of income in consequence of ill health.

Relief is given by way of **deduction** from the individual's total income but no relief is available against USC or PRSI.

Allowable premiums are **restricted** to a **maximum of 10% of total income**. Total income being income from all sources before deducting reliefs allowable as deductions in calculating taxable income, e.g. allowance for employed person taking care of incapacitated person, etc.

Any **benefits** payable under such schemes are **chargeable to tax** under PAYE.

8.4.4 Pension Contributions

Tax relief is available, at the marginal rate, to those individuals who make pension contributions to:

1. a Revenue-approved occupational pension scheme, i.e. an employee contributing to a company pension scheme;
2. a retirement annuity contract (RAC) or personal retirement savings account (PRSA), i.e. if self-employed or where there is no company scheme; or
3. deducted by way of pension-related deduction (PRD) for public service employees.

The relief is calculated by reference to an individual's age, their remuneration or net relevant earnings and the earnings limit. Relief is limited to the **lower** of:

▦ the pension contribution made; or
▦ the individual's remuneration/net relevant earnings (see definitions below) by the age-related percentage. The remuneration/net relevant earnings are capped at **€115,000**.

The maximum allowable deduction for pension contributions is given in the table below.

Age	% of Remuneration/ Net Relevant Earnings
Under 30 years of age	15%
30–39 years of age	20%
40–49 years of age	25%
50–54 years of age	30%*
55–59 years of age	35%
60 years and over	40%

* The **30% limit** also applies to individuals who are engaged in specified occupations and professions, primarily **sports professionals**, irrespective of age.

The individual's age is taken at any time during the tax year, e.g. if a person is age 30 at any time in the tax year they will qualify for the 20% rate.

Example 8.9
David Jones, aged 48, is employed by BigBank Ltd at an annual salary of €160,000. David makes a 20% personal pension contribution to his pension scheme for 2021. Calculate the maximum pension relief available to David for 2021.

Relief equals the **lower** of:

Contribution made: €160,000 @ 20%	= €32,000 *or*
Earnings cap @ age-related %: €115,000 @ 25%	= €28,750

David is only allowed tax relief of €28,750 on his pension contribution for 2021.

---

1. Employees in Company Pension Schemes

Contributions paid by an employee to a Revenue-approved occupational pension scheme are allowed as a deduction against gross assessable Schedule E remuneration from the employment subject to the restrictions already mentioned for age and the earnings cap. **Remuneration** for this purpose includes fees, bonuses and benefits in kind.

The pension contribution paid is deducted directly from Schedule E income to arrive at the assessable Schedule E income. For example:

	€
Gross salary of employee aged 45	35,000
Deduct: Superannuation paid (>25% of €35,000)	(2,000)
Schedule E income assessable for income tax	33,000

Note, however, that the pension contribution is **not exempted from PRSI and USC** and the gross figure of €35,000 in the above example is the relevant figure for calculating PRSI and USC.

Where the full amount of the premium paid does not qualify for relief due to an insufficiency of remuneration, the amount not qualifying for relief **is carried forward** and treated as a premium paid in the **next** year. Where an employee pays a retirement contribution before 31 October, which is not an ordinary annual contribution, he may elect that the premium should be treated as a premium paid in the **previous tax year**. For example, an individual makes a non-ordinary annual contribution to their company pension scheme on 1 July 2021. The individual may elect to treat the contribution **as if it had been paid** in 2020 and claim relief for the contribution against their 2020 remuneration.

The **earnings cap of €115,000** applies to **all contributions** paid in the year of assessment, **irrespective** of the fact that the contribution relates to the previous year.

Contributions paid by **employers** to occupational pension schemes are not treated as a benefit in kind and can be paid **in addition** to the contribution limits for employee contributions.

2. Contributions to a RAC or a PRSA

Contributions paid to a RAC or a PRSA are also entitled to tax relief and, while the earnings cap of €115,000 is the same as for employees in company pension schemes, the age-related restriction is calculated on net relevant earnings.

"**Relevant earnings**" is defined to mean the following types of income:

■ non-pensionable salaries, wages, fees, benefits, etc. taxable under Schedule E; and
■ Case I and Case II profits from trades or professions (including profits arising to a partner).

"**Net relevant earnings**" is defined to mean the "relevant earnings" assessable for a particular year of assessment **as reduced** by:

■ Loss relief available for the particular year of assessment in respect of losses, which, if they had been profits, would constitute "relevant" income.
■ Relief for capital allowances claimed in respect of the "relevant" source of income for the particular year of assessment.
■ Charges paid (see **Section 8.6**) during the particular year of assessment to the extent that they cannot be set against other non-relevant income (i.e. income under Cases III, IV or V or Schedule F) of the taxpayer. Broadly, this means any earned income that is not already subject to a pension scheme.

Non-relevant income represents any income of the taxpayer for the particular year of assessment **other than** relevant income. For example, a self-employed solicitor would be assessed under Case II on any profits from their practice and this would be regarded as relevant earnings. However, the solicitor may have other sources of income to be assessed, e.g. bank deposit interest, dividend income, rents, etc. and these would **not** be taken into account in computing net relevant earnings, except and to the extent that they are used to offset charges paid during the particular year of assessment.

It is specifically provided that **remuneration from an investment company** is **not included** in computing net relevant earnings.

Example 8.10

Joe Green is a Chartered Accountant, aged 50, who has been in practice for many years. His Case II tax-adjusted profits assessable for 2021 are €37,000. He is entitled to Case II capital allowances of €14,000 for 2021 and he has an allowable Case II loss forward from 2020 of €10,000. His only other income is €1,500 interest from government securities received annually. He pays an allowable covenant to his widowed mother of €2,000 (gross) per annum and he pays €4,000 per annum under a Revenue-approved retirement annuity contract.

Net Relevant Earnings	€	€
Case II (relevant earnings)		37,000
Less:		
Loss relief	(10,000)	
Capital allowances	(14,000)	(24,000)
Reduced by: Charges paid in 2021 to extent not covered by non-relevant income:		
Gross covenant paid	2,000	
Less: non-relevant income (government securities)	(1,500)	(500)
Net relevant earnings (NRE)		**12,500**
Amount of retirement premium paid		4,000
Relief restricted to max. 30% of NRE: €12,500 @ 30%		(3,750)
Unrelieved portion of premium		250

In cases where the full amount of the premium paid does not qualify for relief in a particular year of assessment (as in **Example 8.9**), any **unrelieved portion** of the premium may be **carried forward** to the following and subsequent years and treated as a **premium paid** in those years until such time as relief has been granted. For instance, in the above example Joe did not receive relief in respect of €250 of the total €4,000 premium paid during 2021. He would, therefore, be entitled to treat the €250 unrelieved payment as a premium paid in 2022. It would be added to his annual premium of €4,000 to give a total premium paid of €4,250. Provided this amount was less than 30% of his net relevant earnings for 2022, he would be entitled to a full deduction for the €4,250 in that year.

The relief for qualifying contracts is **normally** based on the amount of the premium paid **in the actual tax year**, i.e. a premium paid on 1 December 2021 would qualify for relief in the taxpayer's computation for 2021.

If a taxpayer pays a qualifying premium after the end of the tax year but **before** the due date for the **filing of their tax return** for that tax year, they may elect for the premium to be deducted in the **earlier** tax year. For example, an individual who is subject to self-assessment must file their 2020 tax return electronically **on or before the relevant 2021 due date** (see **Chapter 12**). Such an individual may elect that a qualifying retirement annuity premium paid in the period 1 January 2021 to the 2021 income tax due date be deducted from their relevant income for 2020.

Contributions paid by **employers** to an employee's PRSA are treated as a **benefit in kind**, although income tax relief is provided, subject to the overall contribution limits for employee contributions. Employer contributions to PRSAs are **not subject to PRSI or USC**.

3.   Public Service Employees Paying the Additional Superannuation Contribution (ASC)

Public and civil servants who are a member of a public service pension scheme, are required to make an ASC contribution of between 10% and 10.5% of their pensionable pay, dependent on their salary levels. From 1 January 2020, public servants with remuneration below €34,500 will not be liable to the ASC. The ASC is an allowable deduction against Schedule E income for tax purposes, but it is not allowable as a deduction against income liable to PRSI or USC.

Contributions to More than One Pension

If an individual has two sources of income (e.g. Schedule E remuneration and Schedule D, Cases I and II profits from self-employment) and is making pension contributions to an occupational pension scheme **and** to a personal pension plan, a single aggregate earnings limit of €115,000 applies. However, the earnings cap is **first applied** to the earnings used to contribute to an occupational pension scheme, which may restrict the individual's capacity to get tax relief on the contributions to a personal pension.

Example 8.11

Debbie Fisher, aged 29, is employed by Star Ltd and is required to make a contribution of 10% of her annual salary (2021: €90,000) to the company pension scheme. She also had Case I trading income of €100,000 for 2021 on which she paid 5% into a PRSA.

Calculate Debbie's pension contributions tax relief for 2021.

Based on Debbie's age, the allowable tax-relievable contributions in respect of her **employment** income is the **lower** of:

Contribution made: €90,000 @ 10%	€9,000 or
Salary @ age-related %: €90,000 @ 15%	€13,500

While Debbie has not fully used her capacity to make tax relievable pension contributions in respect of her employment earnings (i.e. she only paid 10% as opposed to the maximum allowable amount of 15%), she has 'used up' €90,000 of the aggregate earnings cap of €115,000. The tax-relievable amount of her **contributions to her PRSA** is therefore limited as follows:

Contribution made: €100,000 @ 5%	€5,000
Restricted to: (€115,000 – €90,000) @ 15%	€3,750
Total pension contributions tax relief for 2021	€12,750
Maximum available: (earnings cap @ age-related %) €115,000 @ 15%	€17,250

To maximise the potential tax relief available in 2021, Debbie may be in a position to contribute a further 5% (€4,500) of her **employment earnings** to her occupational pension scheme in the form of additional voluntary contributions (AVCs), for which she will get full tax relief.

8.5   Other Reliefs and Exemptions

8.5.1   Introduction

The tax reliefs outlined in **Sections 8.3** and **8.4** are given by a reduction of the tax payable amount at the standard and marginal rates, but other tax reliefs are available by virtue of being exempt from tax (exemptions) or a repayment of tax already paid (relief). Many reliefs and exemptions are introduced for a limited period to support, say, a particular sector or activity and are often amended on a regular basis.

8.5.2   Help to Buy Incentive

The Help to Buy (HTB) incentive is a measure to assist **first-time buyers** to purchase or build a new home. All parties to the purchase or self-build must be first-time buyers (section 477C TCA 1997).

Relief Available

First-time buyers who purchase or self-build a new residential property between **19 July 2016 and 31 December 2021** may be entitled to claim a refund of income tax and DIRT paid over the previous four years, subject to a maximum tax rebate of €20,000. The tax relief available is the **lower** of:

- 5% of the purchase price of a new home or, in the case of self-builds, 5% of the completion value of the property, up to a maximum of €400,000. The maximum relief is €20,000 (€400,000 × 5%); or
- the amount of income tax and DIRT paid in the four years prior to the purchase or self-build. Where there are more than one first-time buyers, the maximum tax relief is €20,000 per property.

Enhanced Relief

For the period **23 July 2020 to 31 December 2021**, applicants will be eligible for increased HTB relief if the first-time buyers:

- sign a contract for the purchase of a new house or apartment; **or**
- in the case of a self-build property, make the first draw down of the mortgage.

The maximum enhanced HTB refund is the lower of:

- €30,000 (up from €20,000) per property; **or**
- 10% (up from 5%) of the purchase price of a new home or, for self-builds, 10% (up from 5%) of the approved valuation of the property, to a maximum of €400,000; **or**
- the amount of income tax and DIRT paid in the four years prior to the purchase or self-build.

Qualifying Properties

In terms of the property the following conditions must be met:

- Properties must be a new build, subject to VAT in Ireland, and purchased or built as the first-time buyer's home.
- Properties that have never been used as a dwelling and are being converted for residential use may qualify, but extensions to an existing residential building do not.
- The purchase value of the property or self-build cannot exceed €500,000 for properties purchased or built on or after **1 January 2017**.
- The purchase value for self-built properties is the approved valuation by the qualifying lender at the time the purchase loan is entered into.
- The building contractor constructing the property must be a Revenue-approved qualifying contractor (see www.revenue.ie).

Conditions of the HTB Incentive

The following conditions must be met to be eligible for the HTB relief:

- First-time buyers must take out a mortgage of at least **70% of the value** of the purchase price or, in the case of a self-build, 70% of the valuation approved by the mortgage provider.
- First-time buyers must have signed a contract to purchase a new-build property or, for a self-build, have drawn down the first tranche of the relevant mortgage, on or after **19 July 2016**.
- The property must be occupied by the first-time buyer or, if there is more than one first-time buyer, by at least one of them, for a period of **five years** from the date the property is habitable. If the property is sold or rented out in this period, clawback provisions will apply.
- First-time buyers can select **all or any** of the previous four tax years for the purposes of calculating the HTB refund. For example, if the purchase or self-build takes place in 2021, the tax years 2017–2020 apply.
- Applicants must be tax-compliant and have an eTax clearance certificate (see **Chapter 14**).

Applying for the Relief

Before applying, applicants must be registered for myAccount or ROS, and have filed a complete Form 12 (PAYE taxpayer) or Form 11 (self-assessed chargeable person) for the tax years selected for refund.

Application for the relief is made online in two stages.

1. Application – where, on successful completion, an application number and summary of maximum relief available is issued.
2. Claim – once the property is completed.

Refunds made under successful claims will be paid as follows:

- Purchasers of a new build on or after 1 January 2017 – the tax refund will be paid to the **qualifying contractor**.
- Self-builds on or after 1 January 2017 – the tax refund will be paid to the **qualifying loan** bank account.

Example 8.12

In November 2021 Joe Brady purchased a new house, constructed by an approved contractor, for €325,000. He paid a deposit of €45,000 and secured a mortgage for the balance. Joe is a first-time buyer. Details of his income tax and DIRT paid for the past five years are as follows:

Year	Tax paid
2017	€1,200 (year Joe finished college)
2018	€6,200
2019	€6,300
2020	€3,500 (laid off for 4 months)
2021	€6,800

As the property was purchased in 2021 the applicable tax years are 2017–2020.

Calculation of HTB relief:

Loan to value: €280,000 to €325,000 = 80%, so the 70% requirement is met.

Tax paid 2017–2020 = €17,200 – no restriction
Relief = **lower** of:

5% of purchase price = €325,000 @ 5%	€16,250 or
Tax paid	€17,200

HTB refund of €16,250 will be refunded to the contractor on completion of the claim.

8.5.3 Stock Relief

Section 666 TCA 1997 allows for a deduction, against the **farming profits** of an individual, of **25%** of the value of any **increase** in trading stock values in a chargeable period. Where the individual is a "young trained farmer" as defined by section 667B TCA 1997, the deduction is available at a rate of **100%** of any increase in stock values for **three** consecutive years.

Qualifying Conditions
- The relief cannot create or increase a loss.
- Any excess capital allowances or losses forward from a period before stock relief was claimed cannot be carried forward once stock relief is claimed.
- The relief must be claimed in writing on or before the return filing date for the chargeable period (i.e. 31 October 2022 for the tax year 2021).
- The revlief applies up to and including the 2021 tax year.
- There is no provision for a claw-back of the relief if the value of the stock reduces in subsequent years.

Example 8.13

John Merryweather is a beef farmer from Co. Meath. His trading profits for 2021 were €60,000 and his stock values were as follows:

	€
Opening stock	20,000
Closing stock	45,000

Stock Relief:	
Case I profits	60,000
Stock relief ((€45,000 – €20,000) @ 25%)	(6,250)
Case I taxable profits	53,750

If Mr Merryweather's Case I profits were €5,000 for 2021, the stock relief would be restricted to that amount with no loss available to carry forward.

Stock Relief:	€
Case I profits	5,000
Stock relief (€25,000 @ 25%) – restricted to	(5,000)
Case I taxable profits	Nil

Example 8.14

As above, but Mr Merryweather has the following losses and capital allowances forward:

	€
Excess capital allowances forward	3,000
Unused losses forward	5,000

In this instance, Mr Merryweather would not claim stock relief as he would lose his entitlement to the excess capital allowances and unused losses forward of €8,000 in total.

8.5.4 Age Exemption

Exemptions from income tax are available to individuals aged 65 years and over with low incomes. Where a qualifying individual's total income does not exceed the following amounts, there is a **total exemption** from income tax.

Marital Status	Income Limit 2021
Single/Widowed/Surviving Civil Partner	€18,000
Married Couple/Civil Partners	€36,000

Increase in Exemption Limits for Qualifying Children

The age exemption limits are **increased** where a claimant proves that a qualifying child (children) has lived with them at any time during the tax year. The income limits are increased for **each** qualifying child as follows:

	Increase for each child
First and second child	€575
Third and subsequent children	€830

Example 8.15

Peter Blake, aged 66, is a self-employed carpenter and is married with four children. His wife, Sheila, aged 42, works full-time in the home and does not have any income. Peter had a total income of €38,000 for 2021.

Calculation of Specified Income Limit	€	€
Income limit – married couple over 65		36,000
Plus: Increase for qualifying children:		
1st and 2nd child (€575 × 2)	1,150	
3rd and 4th child (€830 × 2)	1,660	2,810
Specified income limit		**38,810**
Actual income		38,000
Income tax liability		**NIL**

Marginal Relief

Marginal relief may be available to a couple in a marriage or civil partnership whose total income from all sources is slightly over the exemption limit. Marginal relief will only be granted if it is more beneficial to the claimant than their tax credits. A certificate can issue during the tax year granting the relevant exemption limit and any income earned over the exemption figure is taxed at 40%.

8.5.5   Provision of Childcare Services Exemption

Section 216C TCA 1997 provides for tax relief for income received from the provision of childcare services in the individual's **own home**. The exemption applies where the income in a tax year does **not exceed €15,000** and no more than **three children** (excluding any children who normally reside in the individual's home) at any time are cared for in the individual's own home. No deductions are allowable when calculating the income limit for this relief and notification of the service being provided must be given to the HSE. Where the income exceeds €15,000, the **entire amount** becomes taxable under self-assessment. Where more than one person is providing the service in the same residential premises, the €15,000 limit is split between them.

An individual in receipt of exempt childcare income must be registered for self-assessment and file an annual Return of Income (Form 11) regardless of any other source of income in the year. The exempt income is not liable to USC but is **subject to PRSI**.

Example 8.16

Karen takes care of three pre-school children in her home every morning and is registered with the HSE. Her income and expenses are as follows:

Childcare receipts	€17,000
Less: provision of food/nappies, etc.	(€3,500)
Net childcare income	€13,500

As Karen's gross income from the childcare service is greater than €15,000, she is liable to tax on the full amount of her net income of €13,500.

8.5.6   Rent-a-Room Relief

Where an individual rents out a room (or rooms) in a "qualifying residence" and the gross income received (including sums arising for food, laundry or similar goods and services) **does not exceed €14,000**, this income will be exempt from income tax (section 216A TCA 1997). It is also not liable to PRSI or USC, but it must be **included** in an individual's income tax return. In determining whether the limit has been exceeded for the tax year, no deductions for expenses incurred are made. See **Section 7.3.3** for more detail.

8.5.7 Artists' Exemption

This exemption is available to individuals who are deemed by the Revenue Commissioners to have produced an original and creative "work" that is generally recognised as having cultural or artistic merit (section 195 TCA 1997).

The first **€50,000** per annum of profits or gains earned by writers, composers, visual artists and sculptors from the sale of their work is **exempt from income tax** in Ireland in certain circumstances. Income in excess of €50,000 is subject to income tax at the individual's marginal rate.

A "work" must be original and creative, and fall into one of the following categories:

- a book or other writing
- a play
- a musical composition
- a painting or other like picture
- a sculpture.

Claimants must be individuals and resident, or ordinarily resident and domiciled, in any one or more EU Member States or another EEA State. The artists' exemption only provides an exemption from **income tax**. All exempt income is subject to USC and PRSI at the appropriate annual rates.

Note: this relief is a "specified relief" and may be restricted in the case of certain high-income individuals (see **Section 8.7**).

8.6 Relief for Charges on Income

Charges on income are payments made that are **deductible** from the **gross income** of the taxpayer, to arrive at total income or net statutory income. In order for relief to be claimed, the amount must be **actually paid** during the tax year in question and not simply incurred.

8.6.1 Payments Made Under a Deed of Covenant

A deed of covenant is a legally binding written agreement, made by an individual, to pay an agreed amount to another individual without receiving **any** benefit in return. To be legally effective, it must be properly drawn up, signed, witnessed, sealed and delivered to the individual receiving the payments. Any amount can be paid under a deed of convenant, but only covenants in favour of **certain individuals** qualify for tax relief.

The person who makes the payment is called a **covenantor**. The person who receives the payment is called a **covenantee** or beneficiary.

To qualify for tax relief, a deed must be capable of **exceeding** a period of **six years**. Therefore, the period provided should be for a minimum of **seven years**.

Covenants Allowable for Tax Relief
Unrestricted tax relief is available for covenants payable to the following:

- a permanently incapacitated minor child (i.e. under 18 years) where the covenant is paid by a person **other** than the parent; and
- a permanently incapacitated person.

Tax relief is **restricted** to **5%** of the covenantor's **total income** (gross income minus all other charges) on covenants payable to persons aged 65 years or older.

Example 8.17

Marie Murphy is single and earned €42,000 from her job in 2021. She paid the following covenants during 2021:

- her permanently incapacitated sister Mary received €3,200 (net);
- her 66-year-old widowed mother received €2,400 (net).

Marie's allowable charges for 2021 were:

Incapacitated sister €3,200 (net) × 100/80	= €4,000 gross (no restriction)

Widowed mother: restricted to the **lower** of gross amount paid **or** 5% of gross income less charges:

Amount paid €2,400 (net) × 100/80	= €3,000 gross
Gross income less charges: €42,000 – €4,000 = €38,000 @ 5%	= €1,900
Total allowable covenants: €4,000 + €1,900	**= €5,900**

The covenantor must deduct tax at the **standard rate** from the gross payment (i.e. not the amount that qualifies for tax relief) and **account** for it to Revenue. The covenantor must also give a **Form R185**, detailing the payment and the tax deducted, to the covenantee **each time** a payment is made.

To **claim the tax relief** in the first year, the covenantor must send the original deed of covenant, together with a copy of Form R185, to Revenue. For subsequent years, only a copy of Form R185 needs to be included with the claim for tax relief.

Relief is allowed in the covenantor's income tax computation for the **gross amount paid** and they must pay over to Revenue the income tax that is deducted. In practice, the liability is simply added to the covenantor's tax liability in respect of his income in the tax computation. **Tax credits**, other than credits for tax paid, **cannot reduce the tax due** on the charges; the individual always remains liable to pay the full amount of income tax on any charges.

Example 8.18

Peter Byrne is a single individual and is employed as a marketing manager. He has a salary of €43,000 for the tax year 2021 and paid tax of €6,840 in respect of this salary. Peter has executed an **annual** covenant of €5,000 in favour of his widowed mother, aged 66 and incapacitated, for seven years. His mother's only other source of income is €6,000 per annum.

Peter Byrne – Income Tax Computation 2021

	€	€
Schedule E salary	43,000	
Less: gross amount of covenant paid*	(5,000)	
Total/taxable income		**38,000**
Tax Calculation: (single)		
€35,300 @ 20%	7,060	
€2,700 @ 40%	1,080	8,140
Deduct: Non-refundable tax credits		
Single person tax credit	1,650	
Employee tax credit	1,650	(3,300)
		4,840

continued overleaf

Add: Tax deducted on payment of covenant		
to be returned to Revenue (€5,000 @ 20%)	1,000	
Net tax liability	5,840	
Deduct: Refundable tax credits		
Tax paid under PAYE	(6,840)	
Tax refund due	**(1,000)**	

*If Peter's mother was not incapacitated, the allowable covenant would be restricted to 5% of Peter's income, i.e. €43,000 @ 5% = €2,150. However, the tax deducted and due on payment of the covenant would be based on the actual payment made, not on the amount that qualifies for tax relief.

Mrs Byrne – Income Tax Computation 2021

Income:	€	€
Case IV, Schedule D (gross covenant income)	5,000	
Other income	6,000	
Total/taxable income		11,000
Tax Calculation:		
Tax liability (covered by exemption limit, therefore no liability)		NIL
Less: tax deducted by Peter on payment of covenant		(1,000)
Tax refund due		**(1,000)**

8.6.2 Patent Royalties

Where an individual pays patent royalties in the course of a trade or a business, a deduction is not allowed for the royalties against the profits of the trade. Instead the **royalties** paid in the particular tax year are allowed as a **charge** against taxable income.

8.7 High Income Earner Restriction

Sections 485C–G TCA 1997 provide for limitations in the use of certain tax reliefs and exemptions (known as "specified reliefs") by high-income individuals. The objective is to ensure that individuals who are fully subject to the restriction pay an effective rate of income tax of approximately 30%.

The high income earner restriction (HIER) applies to an individual where **all** of the following apply:

1. the "adjusted income" of an individual for the tax year is equal to or greater than an "income threshold amount" of **€125,000** or less if the individual had 'ring-fenced' income (e.g. deposit interest); **and**
2. the **sum** of specified reliefs that are used by the individual for the tax year is equal to or greater than a relief threshold amount, which is set at **€80,000**; **and**
3. the aggregate of specified reliefs used by an individual for the tax year is greater than **20%** of the individual's adjusted income.

8.7.1 Adjusted Income

Adjusted income is defined as:

$$(T + S) - R$$

where:

    T = the individual's taxable income (as calculated before any restriction);

    S = the aggregate amount of specified reliefs used in the year; and

    R = the amount of the individual's ring-fenced income for the year.

8.7.2 Income Threshold Amount

The income threshold amount is **€125,000** except where the individual has ring-fenced income. Ring-fenced income is income that is normally liable to tax at a specific rate regardless of the amount received or the marginal rate of tax of the individual (e.g. deposit interest liable to DIRT at 33%). In that scenario, the income threshold amount is calculated by using the formula:

$$€125,000 \times \frac{A}{B}$$

where:

    A = the individual's adjusted income for the year, and

    B = the sum of T + S (same meaning as in adjusted income above).

Example 8.19

Ms Moneypenny has the following income/reliefs for 2021:

Case I income	€120,000	
Less: specified reliefs	(€100,000)	**(S)**
Plus: deposit interest (ring-fenced income)	€70,000	**(R)**
Taxable income (after reliefs)	€90,000	**(T)**
Ms Moneypenny's adjusted income = (T + S) – R	€120,000	

Income threshold amount = €125,000 × $\frac{€120,000}{€190,000}$ = €78,947

The HIER applies to Ms Moneypenny as her adjusted income (€120,000) is greater than her income threshold amount (€78,947), and her specified reliefs (€100,000) are greater than the relief threshold amount (€80,000).

8.7.3 Restriction of Relief

The specified reliefs (S) are restricted by recalculating the individual's taxable income using the formula below and taxing the recalculated amount under the normal rules.

$$T + (S - Y)$$

where:

    Y = the greater of:

        ▪   the relief threshold (€80,000), **or**

        ▪   20% of the individual's adjusted income for the year.

Example 8.20
Using **Example 8.2**1 above, Ms Moneypenny's recalculated taxable amount for 2021 is:

Taxable income (after reliefs)			€90,000	**(T)**
Specified reliefs			€100,000	**(S)**
Less: greater of:				
Relief threshold	€80,000	or		
20% Adjusted income (€120,000 @ 20%)	€24,000	=	(€80,000)	**(Y)**
Recalculated taxable amount 2021			**€110,000**	

Ms Moneypenny's taxable income is increased by €20,000 for 2021. This additional amount is carried forward as "excess relief" to 2022 and will be a "specified relief" in 2022 et seq.

Questions

Review Questions
(See Suggested Solutions to Review Questions at the end of this textbook.)

Question 8.1

The Joyces are a married couple, jointly assessed, with two children aged under 16. Mr Joyce is in receipt of employment income, of €46,000, for 2021. Mrs Joyce is a full-time home carer and has no income in 2021.

Requirement
(a) Calculate the Joyces' income tax liability for 2021.
(b) What would their tax position be if Mrs Joyce had income of €10,600 in 2022 (i.e. the following tax year)?

Question 8.2

The Roches are a married couple, jointly assessed, with two children under 16. One spouse has a salary of €46,000 and the other has investment income, i.e. Schedule F, of €8,000 (gross).

Requirement
Calculate their income tax liability for 2021.

Question 8.3

Mr Murray is married with two children, Michael and David. Michael was formally adopted in 2011 and is 12 years old and in receipt of €2,500 per annum from a trust set up by his aunt. David is 14 years of age and is not in receipt of any income.

During 2021 the following medical expenses were paid:

	€
Mr Murray	80
Michael Murray	200
David Murray	210
Sean Ryan	650

Sean Ryan, his friend, was involved in a motor accident and Mr Murray paid €650 for medical treatment for him.

He also pays €1,100 per month towards nursing home care for his elderly mother. The nursing home provides 24-hour nursing care on-site.

Requirement

Compute Mr Murphy's allowable medical expenses for 2021 and advise how tax relief may be obtained.

Question 8.4

Rachel, aged 45, is an active partner in a firm of solicitors. Her tax-adjusted profits assessable for 2021 are €320,000. Capital allowances for 2021 are €10,000. She pays €75,000 per annum under a Revenue-approved retirement annuity contract.

Rachel has executed an annual covenant of €6,000 in favour of her permanently incapacitated brother, James.

Requirement

Calculate Rachel's net relevant earnings and tax allowable pension deduction for 2021.

Question 8.5

Mr Frost is an employee of ABC Ltd. ABC Ltd paid €960 (net) to the VHI for Mr Frost in November 2021. Mr Frost is single and had a salary of €46,000 for 2021.

Requirement

Calculate Mr Frost's income tax liability for 2021.

Question 8.6

June is a widow, aged 56, whose husband died in March 2018. For 2021, she had a salary of €43,000 (tax deducted €1,690) and a Department of Social Protection contributory widow's pension of €10,842. June's employment is non-pensionable. During 2021, June paid a retirement annuity premium of €2,000. June has three children whose circumstances are as follows:

(a) John is 21 years of age. He works part-time and is taking an evening degree course in computer science in UCD. During 2021 he earned €8,000 from his part-time work. Total fees payable in respect of his degree course came to €4,800, of which €3,000 was paid by June and €1,800 by John. June spent €350 on an eye test and new spectacles for John during 2021.
(b) Mary, who has been incapacitated since birth, receives a covenant net of tax at the standard rate of €3,200 per annum from her elderly aunt.
(c) David, who is 19 years of age, studies part-time at Bolton Street College for which June paid fees of €2,300. He has assessable income of €500 gross per annum. David is also incapacitated since birth. June paid €500 in respect of doctors' fees and prescription medicines for David during 2021.

June and her family live in rented accommodation. June paid rent of €12,600 and a net premium to the VHI of €1,400 during 2021 for herself and Mary.

Requirement

Calculate June's income tax liability for 2021.

Question 8.7

John Fitzpatrick became 65 years of age on 1 May 2021. He is widowed for many years with no dependent children and lives alone. He is retired and his only source of income is his pension of €29,400 gross per annum.

During 2021, €2,040 of tax was deducted from his gross pension. He paid VHI €750 during 2021. The amount paid in respect of VHI was net of tax at the standard rate tax. John contributed €300 to an eligible charity during 2021, and paid medical expenses of €590, of which €200 was refunded by VHI.

John has no other source of income or allowances.

Requirement

Compute John Fitzpatrick's income tax liability for 2021 claiming all reliefs due to him.

Question 8.8

Jason and Damien are aged 61 and 66 respectively and are in a civil partnership. Their only income for 2021 was a pension of €35,000 from Jason's previous employer, from which tax of €2,050 was deducted.

Requirement

Calculate Jason and Damien's income tax liability for 2021.

Question 8.9

Bob, aged 55 in 2021, pays retirement annuity premiums to Irish Life annually to provide for a pension on his retirement as his employer does not operate a superannuation scheme.

The amounts of the premiums paid were as follows:

	€
2020	15,000
2021	16,000

Bob's salary for 2020 was €50,980 and for 2021 was €54,480.

He is married and paid a covenant to his permanently incapacitated brother, Mark, of €3,000 in 2020 and in 2021. His only other source of income is deposit interest of €1,160 gross for 2020 and €1,195 gross for 2021.

Requirement

Calculate his retirement annuity relief for the tax year 2020 and 2021.

Question 8.10

Maria's salary for the tax year 2021 is €35,000 (tax deducted €3,700). She has no other income and is single.

She made a seven-year covenant in 2016 to her incapacitated widowed father, Jim (aged 60). The total covenant payments made in the tax year 2021 were €4,000 net. Her father's only other income is rental income of €8,000 per annum.

Requirement

Calculate the 2021 income tax liability of Maria and her father, Jim.

Question 8.11

Robert O'Sullivan, a 36-year-old single man, is employed as an electrician by Midland Electrical Services Ltd. His Employment Detail Summary for 2021 showed gross pay of €84,000 and tax deducted of €14,120.

He made pension contributions of €22,800 in that year directly into his PRSA and he made a covenant payment of €4,500 (gross) to his father Jack, who is 69 and in good health. He also made a covenant payment of €3,200 (net) to his permanently incapacitated brother, Anthony. He receives bank interest of €1,600 (net after DIRT) annually on 31 December each year.

He owns an apartment, which is registered with the RTB and is let. In 2021, rents received were €1,200 per month and he paid mortgage interest on the property of €3,200 and also paid €2,250 for new furniture, a management fee of €3,100 and allowable expenses of €2,600. He had a tax rental loss forward from the previous year of €3,000.

John received a cheque from Independent Newspapers plc of €5,200 (net) in respect of dividends on shares which he owns in this quoted Irish company. He also owns shares in Chemcorp, an unquoted Irish resident pharmaceutical company.

He also paid €45 for a doctor's visit, non-routine dental fees of €800 for his brother Dermot (who lives with him full-time) and €125 for a new pair of reading glasses.

Requirement
Calculate Robert's income tax liability for 2021.

Question 8.12

Jenny McFee is a widow, aged 51, whose husband James died in January 2020. Jenny has three children attending college as follows:

1. Maria is 22 years old and is studying for a Masters in Biochemistry on a full-time basis. Total fees payable by Jenny were €8,500.
2. Maria's twin brother John is studying for a degree in hotel management on a part-time basis and he also works by night in a busy city-centre restaurant. Total fees payable by Jenny were €1,740.
3. The youngest child, Colm (aged 18), commenced a training course of two years' duration to study computer technology and coding. At the successful completion of the course Colm will be awarded a Certificate in Information Systems. Fees payable by Jenny were €1,300.

Jenny works part-time at JZ Ltd, a music distribution company, as company accountant. Jenny earned €55,000 in 2021 (tax paid €5,590) and JZ Ltd paid her VHI premium of €1,540 (net) for 2021. Jenny is in receipt of a small widow's pension of €12,150 (tax deducted €2,550) from James' pension plan.

Jenny also cares for James' elderly mother, Rose (aged 85), who has Alzheimer's and lives with them. She employs a carer to take care of Rose while she is at work at a cost of €12,500 per annum.

Jenny has two students staying in her spare room and they paid her €7,800 for accommodation and meals. She also earned €1,200 deposit interest (net) from KBC Bank in 2021.

Requirement
Calculate Jenny's income tax liability for 2021.

Income Tax Computation – Treatment of Married Couples/Civil Partners

Learning Objectives

After studying this chapter you will understand:

- how single individuals and married couples/civil partners are assessed using single, joint and separate assessments;
- in the case of joint assessment, who is accountable for the income tax due/repayable; and
- the tax consequences of divorce, separation or dissolution of a civil partnership.

9.1 Introduction

As stated in **Section 2.6.1**, a married couple means any same-sex or heterosexual couple who are married in accordance with the provisions of the Marriage Acts. Civil partners are same-sex couples who are registered as civil partners under the Civil Partnership and Certain Rights and Obligations of Cohabitants Act 2010. Following the enactment of the Marriage Act 2015 on 15 November 2015, civil partnership is no longer available in Ireland. This does not affect civil partners registered prior to that date. Cohabiting couples, whether same-sex or heterosexual, are treated as single persons under tax law.

Married couples and civil partners are treated in the same manner under the Taxes Acts and can be taxed under either:

1. joint assessment;
2. single assessment; or
3. separate assessment.

9.2 Joint Assessment

Under joint assessment the income of **each** spouse/civil partner is taxed as if it were the income of the assessable spouse or nominated civil partner. The couple themselves elect which one of them is to be the **assessable spouse** or **nominated civil partner** and the nomination can be done in writing or verbally to Revenue. In the absence of such a nomination, the spouse/civil partner with the highest income becomes the assessable spouse or nominated civil partner.

Joint assessment is automatic, i.e. it is provided in the legislation that a married couple or civil partners will be deemed to have elected for joint assessment **unless**, before the end of the year of assessment, **either** spouse/civil partner writes to Revenue indicating that they would prefer to be assessed as **single** individuals.

Joint assessment is generally only available where both individuals are Irish tax resident, although some exceptions may arise and would be examined on an individual basis. Under joint assessment, the tax credits and standard rate tax band can be allocated between spouses or civil partners in a way that suits their circumstances. For example, where one spouse/civil partner has no taxable income, all transferable tax credits and €9,000 of the standard rate tax band will be given to the other spouse/civil partner. The PAYE tax credit, employment expenses and remaining standard rate band of €26,300 are non-transferable.

The **income bands** chargeable at the standard rate of tax are increased, depending on whether the married couple/civil partners have one or two incomes.

	Tax Year 2021 Taxable Income	
Tax Rate	**Joint Assessment (One Income)**	**Joint Assessment (Two Incomes)**
20%	€44,300	€70,600*
40%	Balance	Balance

* *Transferable between spouses/civil partners up to a maximum of €44,300 for any one spouse/civil partner. The balance of €26,300 is available to the lower-earning spouse only.*

9.3   Single Assessment

If a married couple/civil partners wish to be assessed on the single assessment basis, then either spouse/civil partner must give notice to this effect to Revenue before the end of the year of assessment for which they wish to be assessed as single persons. If such a notice is given for any year of assessment, it will then apply for that year and all future years **unless** withdrawn by the spouse/civil partner who gave the notice of election.

If an election for single assessment is made, then each spouse/civil partner will be assessed to income tax as if they were not married or in a civil partnership, i.e. they are effectively treated as single persons, and tax credits and reliefs are granted accordingly. In such cases, if either spouse/civil partner has tax credits or reliefs in excess of their assessable income, there is **no right to transfer** unutilised credits to the other spouse/civil partner. From a tax point of view, in most cases it will probably be undesirable for married couples/civil partners to elect for single assessment unless each spouse/civil partner is fully utilising their standard rate band and income tax credits and reliefs.

9.4   Separate Assessment

A married couple/civil partners that are assessable on a joint basis may claim for separate assessment of their joint income tax liability. Either spouse/civil partner can make an election for separate assessment not later than 1 April in the year of assessment.

Such an application applies for the year of claim and all subsequent years and may only be withdrawn by the spouse/civil partner who made the application. An election for separate assessment will result in the **same total income tax liability** as if the spouses/civil partners were jointly assessed, with each spouse paying their portion of the total tax liability.

The amount of income tax payable by each spouse/civil partner is calculated by reference to their total income and the proportions of tax credits or reliefs to which they are entitled. Separate assessment **does not diminish** or **increase** the total liability that would have arisen under normal joint assessment.

A couple might opt for separate assessment so that they could each deal with their own tax affairs while not losing out financially.

9.4.1 Calculation of Separate Liabilities

1. Ascertain the gross income assessable for each spouse/civil partner and the overall reliefs and allowances due for the year.
2. Any deductions from total income, e.g. permanent health insurance, are deducted from the income of the person who incurred the expenditure.
3. Each spouse/civil partner is given a standard rate tax band equal to that applicable to a single person, i.e. €35,300. However, to the extent that one spouse/civil partner does not fully utilise the standard rate band, i.e. their income is less than €35,300, the part of the tax band not utilised may be transferred to the other spouse/civil partner, subject to the proviso that the spouse/civil partner with the higher income may not have a standard rate tax band in excess of €44,300.
4. Apportion tax credits as follows:

Basic personal tax credit	}	Half each
Blind person's tax credit	}	Half each
Age tax credit	}	Half each
Incapacitated child tax credit	}	Half each
Employee tax credit	}	Granted to each spouse/civil partner to the extent that each has Schedule E income to utilise the allowance
Earned income tax credit	}	Granted to each spouse/civil partner to the extent that each has earned income (excluding PAYE income)
Medical insurance relief, long-term care policies, college fees, employment of a carer, dependent relative, health insurance, etc.	}	Allowed to the person who bears the expenditure

5. If any tax credits or reliefs are not fully utilised in calculating the tax liability of one of the spouses, then the unutilised balance is available in calculating the other spouse's/civil partner's tax liability.

9.5 Comparison of Treatment under Joint, Single and Separate Assessment

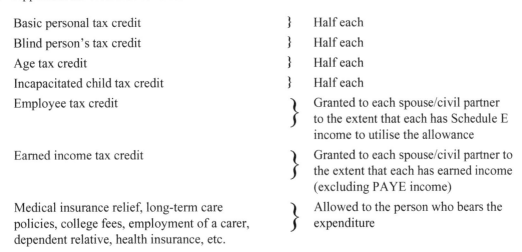

Example 9.1

James Cotter is married to Claire and they have one child who is incapacitated. Their income for 2021 is as follows:

	James	Claire
Salary	€52,000	€27,500
Tax paid under PAYE	€8,790	€550

Income Tax Calculation for 2021 – Joint Assessment

	€	€
Income:		
Schedule E		
– James	52,000	
– Claire	27,500	79,500

continued overleaf

Tax Calculation:

(€44,300 + €26,300) = €70,600 @ 20% (Note 1)	14,120	
(€79,500 – €70,600) = €8,900 @ 40%	<u>3,560</u>	17,680

Deduct: Non-refundable tax credits		
Basic personal tax credit (married)	3,300	
Employee tax credit (Note 2)	3,300	
Incapacitated child credit	<u>3,300</u>	<u>(9,900)</u>
Income tax liability		7,780
Deduct: Refundable tax credits		
Tax paid under PAYE		<u>(9,340)</u>
Tax refund due		<u>(1,560)</u>

Notes:

1. The standard rate band is increased by €26,300, being the lower of the income of the lower-income spouse (Claire €27,500) or €26,300, i.e. to an overall maximum of €70,600 at the standard rate.
2. As both are employed, both spouses are entitled to the employee tax credit.

Income Tax Calculation for 2021 – Single Assessment

		James		Claire
Income:		€		€
Schedule E		<u>52,000</u>		<u>27,500</u>
Tax Calculation:				
	€35,300 @ 20%	7,060	€27,500 @ 20%	5,500
	€16,700 @ 40%	<u>6,680</u>	€0 @ 40%	<u>0</u>
		13,740		5,500
Deduct: Non-refundable tax credits				
Basic personal tax credit	€1,650		€1,650	
Employee tax credit	€1,650		€1,650	
Incapacitated child credit	€1,650	(4,950)	€1,650	(4,950)
Income tax liability		8,790		550
Deduct: Refundable tax credits				
Tax paid under PAYE		<u>(8,790)</u>		<u>(550)</u>
Tax refund due		<u>(NIL)</u>		<u>(NIL)</u>

Income Tax Calculation for 2021 – Separate Assessment

		James		Claire
Income:		€		€
Schedule E		<u>52,000</u>		<u>27,500</u>
Tax Calculation:				
€70,600 – €27,500 =	€43,100 @ 20%	8,620	€27,500 @ 20%	5,500
€52,000 – €43,100 =	€8,900 @ 40%	<u>3,560</u>	€0 @ 40%	<u>0</u>
		12,180		5,500
Deduct: Non-refundable tax credits				
Basic personal tax credit	€1,650		€1,650	

continued overleaf

Employee tax credit	€1,650		€1,650	
Incapacitated child credit	€1,650	(4,950)	€1,650	(4,950)
Income tax liability		7,230		550
Deduct: Refundable tax credits				
Tax paid under PAYE		(8,790)		(550)
Tax refund due		**(1,560)**		**(Nil)**

Comparison of liability under each type of assessment:

	James	Claire	Total
	€	€	€
Tax refundable 2021:			
Joint			**1,560**
Single	NIL	NIL	NIL
Separate	1,560	NIL	1,560

The total amount refundable is the same under joint and separate assessment. Single assessment would result in an extra amount of tax payable of €1,560, which equates to the unutilised portion of Claire's 20% tax band (i.e. €35,300 – €27,500 @ 20%).

9.6 Tax Treatment of Separated Spouses/Civil Partners

The general rule is that separated spouses/civil partners are assessed to income tax as **single individuals**. If there are maintenance payments, the following rules apply:

- **Legally enforceable** maintenance payments are **deductible as a charge** in arriving at the tax liability of the payer and are chargeable to income tax under Case IV of Schedule D in the hands of the receiving spouse/civil partner. **Voluntary** payments (i.e. payments which are not legally enforceable) are **not** taken into account when calculating either spouse's/civil partner's tax.
- Income tax is **not deducted** at source from legally enforceable maintenance payment arrangements by one party to the other party.
- **Legally enforceable** maintenance payments made for the use or **benefit of a child are disregarded** for tax purposes, i.e. the payer does not get a tax deduction for the payment and the child is not assessed on the payment. Only the parent in receipt of the **Single Person Child Carer Credit** (2021: €1,650) can avail of the **one-parent family** tax band (2021: €39,300), even if the child resides with each parent for part of the tax year.

Example 9.2

Mr and Mrs Pearce are separated. Under a legal deed drawn up in 2016, Mr Pearce pays Mrs Pearce €900 per month, of which €500 is specifically for their only child, Stuart, aged eight. Mr Pearce is employed by an insurance company and Mrs Pearce is employed by a local wholesale company. His salary for the tax year 2021 was €59,000 and her salary for the tax year 2021 was €30,000.

The child resides with Mrs Pearce (who is the primary claimant) during the week and with Mr Pearce at weekends and some holidays.

Mr Pearce – Income Tax Liability 2021	€
Income:	
Schedule E	59,000
Less charges:	
Maintenance payments (€400 × 12)	(4,800)
Net income	54,200
Tax Calculation (single person):	
€35,300 @ 20%	7,060
€18,900 @ 40%	7,560
€54,200	14,620
Deduct: Non-refundable tax credits	
Basic personal tax credit	(1,650)
Employee tax credit	(1,650)
Tax liability	**11,320**

Mrs Pearce – Income Tax Liability 2021		€
Income:		
Schedule D, Case IV		4,800
Schedule E		30,000
		34,800
Tax Calculation (single person child carer):	€34,800 @ 20%	6,960
Deduct: Non-refundable tax credits		
Basic personal tax credit		(1,650)
Employee tax credit		(1,650)
Single person child carer credit		(1,650)
Tax liability		**2,010**

Total tax liability: Mr and Mrs Pearce	**13,330**

Example 9.3

Taking **Example 9.2** above, if Mrs Pearce surrenders her entitlement to the single person child carer credit to Mr Pearce, and Stuart resides with him for more than 100 days, the potential tax saving is as follows:

Mr Pearce – Income Tax Liability 2021	€	€
Income:		
Schedule E	59,000	
Less: Maintenance payments (€400 × 12)	(4,800)	
Taxable income		54,200
Tax Calculation (single person child carer):		
€39,300 @ 20%	7,860	
€14,900 @ 40%	5,960	13,820
€54,200		
Deduct: Non-refundable tax credits:		
Basic personal tax credit	1,650	
Employee tax credit	1,650	
Single person child carer credit	1,650	(4,950)
Tax liability		8,870

Mrs Pearce – Income Tax Liability 2021	€	€
Income:		
Case IV, Schedule D	4,800	
Schedule E	30,000	
Taxable income		34,800
Tax Calculation (single person):		
€34,800 @ 20%		6,960
Deduct: Non-refundable tax credits:		
Basic personal tax credit	1,650	
Employee tax credit	1,650	(3,300)
Tax liability		3,660
Total tax liability Mr and Mrs Pearce		12,530

There is a potential overall saving of €800 if Mrs Pearce surrenders the SPCCC to Mr Pearce. The saving will only apply if the parent in receipt of the SPCCC is unable to fully utilise the one-parent family tax band, currently €39,300.

9.6.1 Option for Joint Assessment on Separation, Divorce or Dissolution of Civil Partnership

A separated couple can elect to be treated as a married couple for income tax purposes if:

▪ maintenance payments by one to the other are legally enforceable; and
▪ they are both resident in the State.

If the marriage/civil partnership has not been **dissolved or annulled**, and the couple obtain an Irish divorce/ civil partner dissolution, then the same rules apply for income tax purposes as apply to separated spouses/ civil partners, i.e.:

- they are treated as **single individuals**;
- **legally enforceable maintenance payments** are deducted as a **charge** in arriving at the income tax liability of the payer, and are chargeable to income tax under Schedule D, Case IV for the receiving spouse/civil partner;
- each spouse/civil partner will be entitled to the **single person tax credits** and **rate bands**; and
- only the parent in receipt of the **Single Person Child Carer Credit** (2021: €1,650) can avail of the **one-parent family** tax band (2021: €39,300), even if the child resides with each parent for part of the tax year.

In the case of separation, divorce or dissolution of civil partnership, the couple may elect for **joint assessment** only if:

- both individuals are **resident in Ireland** for tax purposes for the year of assessment;
- **legally enforceable maintenance payments** are made by one spouse/civil partner to the other; and
- **neither has remarried or registered a new civil partnership.**

If this election is made under section 1026 TCA 1997, the following rules apply:

- the payer **cannot deduct maintenance payments** made to the separated or divorced spouse/civil partner in arriving at their total income and the separated or **divorced spouse/civil partner is not assessed** on the maintenance payments;
- the **married person's/civil partner's tax credits** and rate bands are granted; and
- if the separated or divorced spouse/civil partner has income in their own right, apart from maintenance payments received by them, the income tax liability applicable to each spouse's/civil partner's separate income is calculated using the separate assessment procedures.

Example 9.4

Same circumstances as **Example 9.2**, but this time with joint assessment option.

Mrs Pearce – Income Tax Calculation 2021

Income:	€	€
Schedule E		30,000
Tax Calculation:		
€30,000 @ 20%		6,000
Deduct: Non-refundable tax credits:		
Basic personal tax credit	1,650	
Employee tax credit	1,650	(3,300)
Tax liability		**2,700**

Mr Pearce – Income Tax Calculation 2021

Income:	€	€
Schedule E		59,000

Tax Calculation:		
€35,300 @ 20%	7,060	
€5,300 @ 20% (Note)	1,060	
€18,400 @ 40%	7,360	15,480
€59,000		

Deduct: Non-refundable tax credits:		
Basic personal tax credit	1,650	
Employee tax credit	1,650	(3,300)
Tax liability		**12,180**

Total tax liability: Mr and Mrs Pearce		**14,880**

Note: part of standard rate tax band not used by Mrs Pearce = €5,300 (€35,300 – €30,000) can increase the standard rate tax band of Mr Pearce.

In this case, it is more beneficial for Mr and Mrs Pearce not to opt for joint assessment as not only will they lose their single person child carer credit but their combined income taxed at 20% is reduced by €4,000.

Questions

Review Questions
(See Suggested Solutions to Review Questions at the end of this textbook.)

Question 9.1

Patrick and Helen have been married for a number of years. They have the following income and outgoings for the tax year 2021.

	Patrick	Helen
	€	€
Income:		
Salary	10,500	50,000
Benefit in kind	–	2,100
Outgoings:		
Permanent Health Insurance	–	950

Requirement

Compute the income tax liability on the basis that the following options had been claimed for 2021:

(a) joint assessment;
(b) separate assessment;
(c) single assessment.

Question 9.2

Mr and Mrs Thorne separated in 2016. Under the terms of the deed of separation which was drawn up at that time, Mr Thorne pays Mrs Thorne €800 per month, of which €600 is specifically for their two children. The children reside with Mrs Thorne from Monday to Saturday, and with Mr Thorne on Sundays. Joint assessment does not apply.

Mr Thorne's projected salary for the tax year 2021 is €50,000 and Mrs Thorne's projected salary is €35,000.

The terms of the deed are being reviewed at present and Mr Thorne has suggested increasing the maintenance payments to €1,000 per month, on condition that only €100 per month is specifically for their two children, and that the deed is reviewed every year.

Mrs Thorne, who has little knowledge of income tax, has contacted you confirming that she seems satisfied with this, as long as there are no tax disadvantages arising.

Requirement

(a) Calculate Mrs Thorne's income tax liability for the tax year 2021, if:
   (i) the deed is not reviewed;
   (ii) the deed is reviewed with effect from 1 January 2021.
(b) Indicate under which situation she is better off financially and by how much.

Question 9.3

Mr and Mrs Lynch separated on 30 June 2020. Under the terms of the deed of separation drawn up on that date, Mr Lynch pays Mrs Lynch €700 per month, of which €100 is specifically for their only child, Mary, who resides with her mother. The first monthly payment is made on 1 July 2020. He also pays the mortgage on the family home, where Mrs Lynch continues to reside.

Mr Lynch's salary for 2021 was €48,000 and Mrs Lynch's salary was €15,000.

Requirement

Calculate Mr and Mrs Lynch's tax liability for 2021 on the basis that:

(a) Joint assessment was claimed for the year of assessment in accordance with section 1026 TCA 1997.
(b) No election was made under section 1026 TCA 1997.

Pay Related Social Insurance and the Universal Social Charge

Learning Objectives

After studying this chapter you will understand:

- the calculation of Pay Related Social Insurance (PRSI); and
- the rules relating to, and the calculation of liability of, the Universal Social Charge (USC) for employees and the self-employed.

10.1 Introduction

In addition to income tax, two further charges are levied on income earned by an individual:

- Pay Related Social Insurance (PRSI), and
- the Universal Social Charge (USC).

10.1.1 Pay Related Social Insurance

Employers, employees and the self-employed pay social insurance contributions into the national Social Insurance Fund. PRSI contributions paid into the Social Insurance Fund are used to fund social insurance payments made by the Department of Social Protection (DSP).

10.1.2 Universal Social Charge

Universal Social Charge (USC) is an additional tax payable on gross income, including notional pay (i.e. the value of a non-cash benefit such as a benefit in kind), after any relief for certain capital allowances.

10.2 PRSI

PRSI is payable by:

- all employees, whether full-time or part-time, earning €38 or more per week; and
- self-employed workers with an income of €5,000 a year or more

who are aged **over 16 and under 66 years** of age.

The **employers** of such employees are liable to pay employer PRSI contributions on the reckonable earnings of the employee.

10.2.1 Income Liable to PRSI

PRSI is payable on most sources of income, including:

- salaries and pensions;
- any benefits arising out of employee share schemes, such as share option schemes and approved profit-sharing schemes. The net value of share-based remuneration is treated as notional pay for the purposes of calculating **employee PRSI** only. Employer's PRSI is not chargeable;
- benefits in kind (e.g. company cars, vans, etc.) and perquisites (e.g. preferential loans) provided by an employer to an employee;
- tax-adjusted profits of a trade or profession (less capital allowances);
- dividends received;
- rental income;
- investment income, including bank deposit interest.

Employee contributions to occupational pension schemes and other pension arrangements are not allowable deductions from income that is subject to PRSI, i.e. PRSI is charged on income before deduction of pension contributions. The pension-related deduction ("pension levy"), which is charged to earnings in the **public service**, is also not deductible from income that is subject to PRSI.

PRSI is **not** charged on:

- social welfare payments (e.g. illness, maternity benefits or pension payments);
- redundancy payments (although USC is payable on the **taxable** element of a redundancy lump-sum payment), including gratuities and ex-gratia payments paid to employees when they leave employment.

A separated person may claim a refund of PRSI on **enforceable maintenance payments** (see **Section 9.6**) made to the person's spouse. The pay or income for PRSI purposes is reduced by the amount of the maintenance payment and the PRSI recalculated. Any overpayment of PRSI can be claimed, after the year end, from the PRSI Refunds Section of the DSP.

10.2.2 PRSI Contribution Classes

The rate of PRSI payable is determined by the contribution class of the taxpayer. In general, for employees, contribution classes are decided by the **nature** of the employment and the **amount** of the employee's gross 'reckonable earnings' in any week. An employee's 'reckonable earnings' are earnings from an insurable employment and include benefits in kind. Most workers pay PRSI contributions at **Class A** and are covered for all social welfare benefits and pensions. However, employees in private sector employments who earn less than €38 per week (from all employments) and a small number of employees no matter how much they earn are covered for occupational injuries benefits only – **Class J**. Some workers in the public sector do not have cover for all benefits and pensions and pay a modified PRSI contribution – **Classes B, C, D or H**.

Others, such as those who are retired but receiving pensions from their former employment, are recorded under different classes of PRSI – **Classes K or M**. These classes do not give cover for social welfare benefits and pensions.

Self-employed individuals and company directors pay **Class S** contributions and are covered for certain pensions, such as the widow's, widower's or surviving civil partner's (contributory) pension and the State pension (contributory). This class is also covered for Guardian's Payment (contributory), Maternity and Paternity Benefits, Adoptive Benefit and certain treatment benefits, e.g. dental care. Class S does not provide cover for any other schemes or benefits.

The PRSI contribution classes are further divided into **subclasses, 0 and 1**. **A8** is a subclass of **A9**, which is used for community employment participants only. These subclasses represent different bands of weekly earnings and categories of people within each earnings band, as outlined below.

Deciding the Correct PRSI Class

If there is any doubt as to whether PRSI should be paid or which class of PRSI should apply, the Department of Employment Affairs and Social Protection's Scope Section may be asked to decide the issue. Before a decision is made, the employment details are investigated thoroughly by a social welfare inspector.

10.2.3   Rates of PRSI Contribution 2021

Employee contributions and employer contributions are calculated separately and then added together to get "**Total PRSI**".

The rates of contribution for private and public sector employments are given on the government website (https://www.gov.ie/en/publication/b32a18-operational-guidelines-prsi-pay-related-social-insurance-contributio/#prsi-contribution-classes), as shown below.

PRIVATE AND PUBLIC SECTOR EMPLOYMENTS

Class A This covers employees under the age of 66 in industrial, commercial and service-type employment who have reckonable pay of €38 or more per week from all employments as well as Public Servants recruited from 6 April 1995.

Weekly pay is the **employee's money pay plus notional pay** (if applicable).

EE is the rate payable by the employee
ER is the rate payable by the employer

Rates of contribution for 2021

Subclass	Weekly pay band	How much of weekly pay	All income EE	All income ER
AO	€38–€352 inclusive	ALL	Nil	8.8%
AX*	€352.01–€398 inclusive	ALL	4%	8.8%
AL*	€398.01–€424 inclusive	ALL	4%	11.05%
A1	More than €424	ALL	4%	11.05%

* PRSI credit applies.

Employee PRSI Credit

An employee PRSI credit of a maximum of €12 per week is available to Class A employees with gross earnings between €352 and €424 per week. The credit is reduced by one-sixth of gross earnings in excess of €352 per week. The reduced credit is then deducted from the employee PRSI liability calculated at 4% of gross weekly earnings.

Example 10.1
John commenced work in a garden centre and was paid €380 for his first week's work. Calculate the total liability to PRSI.

Gross wages – **Class AX**		€380.00
EE PRSI – **4%**		€15.20
PRSI credit calculation:		
Maximum credit	€12.00	
Less: 1/6th × (€380 – €352.01)	(€4.67)	
Net PRSI credit		(€7.33)
EE PRSI		€7.87
ER PRSI – **8.8%**		€33.44
Total PRSI		€41.31

The rates of contribution for self-employed individuals (Class S) are given on www.gov.ie (as per the link above).

SELF-EMPLOYED

Class S This covers self-employed people, including certain company directors, and certain people with income from investments and rent.

Subclass	Weekly pay band	How much of weekly pay	All income from Self-Employment
S0	Up to €500 inclusive	ALL	4%
S1	More than €500	ALL	4%

Self-employed contributors, with annual self-employed income of over **€5,000** per annum, are liable to PRSI at 4%, subject to a minimum PRSI contribution of **€500 per annum**. Those who have an annual self-employed income in excess of €5,000 but who have **no net liability** and have been told by Revenue that they do not need to file a tax return, pay a reduced flat rate of €300.

10.2.4 Calculation of PRSI for Employees

Employers are obliged to calculate and deduct employee PRSI from the pay of every employee. They are also obliged to calculate and pay employer's PRSI to Revenue, together with tax and USC deducted under the PAYE system (see **Chapter 11**).

PRSI is based on a PRSI contribution week, which is each successive period of seven days starting on 1 January each year. Week 1 is the period from 1 to 7 January inclusive, week 2 from 8 to 14 January, etc. A contribution week at the appropriate class is awarded to an employee for each contribution week, or part thereof, for which the employee was in 'insurable employment'. Contribution weeks are important as they form the basis for calculating eligibility to certain social welfare benefits, such as contributory State pension, Jobseeker's Benefit, etc.

Example 10.2
Julie works in a restaurant and was paid the following amounts for the first three weeks of January 2021. Calculate her and her employer's liability to PRSI.

Week 1: Gross wages	€350
Week 2: Gross wages	€370
Week 3: Gross wages	€420

Week 1:

Gross wages	€350.00	Class A0
EE PRSI – 0%	NIL	
ER PRSI – 8.8%	€30.80	
Total PRSI	€30.80	

Week 2:

Gross wages	€370.00	Class AX
EE PRSI – 4%	€14.80	

PRSI credit calculation:

Maximum credit	€12.00	
Less: 1/6th × (€370 – €352.01)	(€3.00)	
Deduct PRSI credit		(€9.00)
EE PRSI		€5.80
ER PRSI – 8.8%		€32.56
Total PRSI		€38.36

Week 3:

Gross wages	€420.00	Class AL
EE PRSI – 4%	€16.80	

PRSI Credit calculation:

Maximum credit	€12.00	
Less: 1/6th × (€420 – €352.01)	(€11.33)	
Deduct PRSI credit		(€0.67)
EE PRSI		€16.13
ER PRSI – 11.05%		€46.41
Total PRSI		€62.54

Julie's PRSI record for the first weeks of 2021 will looks as follows:

Week No.	Gross Pay PRSI Purposes	PRSI Class	PRSI Employee's Share	Total PRSI
	€		€	€
1	350.00	A0	0.00	30.80
2	370.00	AX	5.80	38.36
3	420.00	AL	16.13	62.54

10.2.5 Calculation of PRSI for the Self-employed

PRSI is charged on the gross income of the taxpayer before pension contributions. Capital allowances and trading losses forward may be deducted.

A taxpayer with annual self-employed income over €5,000 will pay Class S PRSI at the rate of 4% for 2021 on all self-employed income, subject to a minimum payment of €500. Under the self-assessment system (see **Chapter 12**), PRSI, together with income tax and USC due, is payable to Revenue by 31 October in the year following the year of assessment. An individual with self-employed income over €5,000 but with no liability to income tax must pay a minimum PRSI contribution of €300 directly to the DSP.

Example 10.3

John Healy is a married man who owns and operates an equestrian centre in Cork. His accounts for the year ended 31 October 2021 show a tax-adjusted profit of €48,000. He has capital allowances due for 2021 of €7,000. He received net interest of €420 on his Credit Union share account. His wife Mary is employed by the local doctor and her gross salary for 2021 was €32,000. She received net bank deposit interest of €630 in 2021. The Healys are jointly assessed.

Calculate the PRSI payable by the Healys for 2021.

	€	€
Income:		
Schedule D, Case I	48,000	
Less: capital allowances	(7,000)	41,000
Schedule D, Case IV – John - (€420 × 100/67)		627
Schedule D, Case IV – Mary (€630 × 100/67)		940
Schedule E – Mary		32,000
Taxable income		74,567
PRSI payable:		
Mary: Schedule D, Case IV		
€940 @ 4%		38
John:		
Schedule D, Case I (net)	41,000	
Schedule D, Case IV	627	
Total	41,627	
€41,627 @ 4%		1,665
Total PRSI liability		1,703

PRSI was collected from Mary's salary through the PAYE system.

10.3 Universal Social Charge

10.3.1 Income Liable to USC

The Universal Social Charge (USC) is a tax payable on **gross income**, including notional pay, **after** any relief for certain trading losses and capital allowances, but **before** any relief for pension contributions. All individuals are liable to pay USC if their gross income is greater than **€13,000 per annum**.

Note that once the total income exceeds the relevant limit, all the income is subject to USC and not just the excess over the limit.

Persons who are **not domiciled** in Ireland are liable for USC on Irish source income in the same way as they are liable to pay income tax on it.

Directors' fees paid by an Irish company to a non-resident director are also subject to USC.

Income Exempt from USC

The following income is exempt from USC:

- Where an individual's total income for the year does not exceed **€13,000**.
- All Department of Social Protection (DSP) payments, including social welfare payments received from abroad.
- Payments that are made in lieu of DSP payments, such as Community Employment Schemes or Back to Education allowances.
- Income subjected to DIRT.
- Termination payments – USC is only charged on the taxable portion of the payment, for example:
  - statutory redundancy payments – i.e. two weeks' pay per year plus a bonus week, subject to a maximum payment of €600 per week are exempt;
  - ex-gratia redundancy payments in excess of the statutory redundancy amount and after claiming any one of the allowable reliefs.

Special Treatment for Medical Card Holders and Individuals over 70 years

Medical card holders (aged under 70) and individuals over 70 years whose aggregate income for the year is **€60,000 or less** will only pay USC at a maximum rate of 2.0% on income over €12,012 per annum. Note that "aggregate income" excludes payments from Department of Social Protection. A "GP only" card is not considered a full medical card for USC purposes.

Surcharge on Self-employment Income and Bank Bonuses

There is a **surcharge of 3%** on individuals who have income from **self-employment** that **exceeds €100,000** in a year, regardless of age.

A special USC rate of **45%** applies to certain **bank bonuses** paid to employees of **financial institutions** that have received financial support from the State. Performance-related bonus payments paid to employees of Bank of Ireland, AIB, Anglo Irish Bank, EBS and Irish Nationwide Building Society are chargeable to USC at 45% where the cumulative amount of any bonus payments **exceeds €20,000** in a single tax year. Where this threshold is exceeded, the full amount is charged to USC at 45% and not just the excess over €20,000.

10.3.2 Rates and Income Thresholds 2021 – Employees

PERSONS UNDER 70 AND NOT IN RECEIPT OF A MEDICAL CARD			
THRESHOLDS			RATE OF USC
Per Year	Per Month	Per Week	Rate %
Up to €12,012	Up to €1,001	Up to €231	0.5%
From €12,012 to €20,687	From €1,001 to €1,724	From €231 to €398	2.0%
From €20,688 to €70,044	From €1,725 to €5,837	From €399 to €1,347	4.5%
In excess of €70,044	In excess of €5,837	In excess of €1,347	8.0%

PERSONS IN RECEIPT OF A MEDICAL CARD OR OVER 70 YEARS WHERE AGGREGATE INCOME IS €60,000 OR LESS			
THRESHOLDS			RATE OF USC
Per Year	Per Month	Per Week	Rate %
Up to €12,012	Up to €1,001	Up to €231	0.5%
In excess of €12,012	In excess of €1,001	In excess of €231	2.0%

PERSONS IN RECEIPT OF A MEDICAL CARD OR OVER 70 YEARS WHERE AGGREGATE INCOME IS GREATER THAN €60,000			
THRESHOLDS			RATE OF USC
Per Year	Per Month	Per Week	Rate %
Up to €12,012	Up to €1,001	Up to €231	0.5%
From €12,012 to €20,687	From €1,001 to €1,724	From €231 to €398	2.0%
From €20,688 to €70,044	From €1,725 to €5,837	From €399 to €1,347	4.5%
In excess of €70,044	In excess of €5,837	In excess of €1,347	8.0%

10.3.3 Calculation of USC for Employees

Employers are obliged to calculate and deduct USC from the pay of every employee and, together with the tax and PRSI deducted under the PAYE system (see **Chapter 11**), return it to Revenue.

USC is charged on a cumulative basis and, as with PAYE tax credits and rate bands, Revenue will notify employers (on the employer's Revenue Payroll Notification (RPN)) of the USC rates and thresholds to be applied for each employee. USC rates and threshold cut-off points, along with previous USC deducted, will be shown.

The following is an extract from an RPN showing USC rates and cut-off points:

Universal Social Charge (USC)	
USC Status	ORDINARY
USC Rates	
USC Rate 1	0.5%
USC Rate 1 Cut-Off	€231.00
USC Rate 2	2%
USC Rate 2 Cut-Off	€397.83
USC Rate 3	4.5%
USC Rate 3 Cut-Off	€1,347.00
USC Rate 4	8%
USC Rate 4 Cut-Off	€0.00
Pay for USC to date	€0.00
USC deducted to date	€0.00

Example 10.4

Joe works for Big Trees Ltd and earned €650 per week for the first four weeks of January 2021, together with overtime of €225 for Week 4. Joe is paid weekly. Calculate his liability to USC for Weeks 1–4.

		€
USC: Week 1	First €231 @ 0.5%	1.16
	Next €167 @ 2.0%	3.34
	Balance: €650 – (€231 + €167) @ 4.5%	<u>11.34</u>
	Total USC (week 1)	15.84
		€
USC: Week 2	First €462 @ 0.5%	2.31
	Next €334 @ 2.0%	6.67
	Balance: €1,300 – (€462 + €334) @ 4.5%	<u>22.70</u>
	Cumulative USC	31.68
	Less: Cumulative USC from previous week 1	<u>15.84</u>
	Total USC (week 2)	15.84
		€
USC: Week 3	First €693 @ 0.5%	3.47
	Next €500 @ 2.0%	10.01
	Balance: €1,950 – (€693 + €500) @ 4.5%	<u>34.04</u>
	Cumulative USC	47.52
	Less: Cumulative USC from previous week 2	<u>31.68</u>
	Total USC (week 3)	15.84
		€
USC: Week 4	First €924 @ 0.5%	4.62
	Next €667 @ 2.0%	13.35
	Balance: €2,825 – (€924 + €667) @ 4.5%	<u>55.52</u>
	Cumulative USC	73.49
	Less: Cumulative USC from previous week 3	<u>47.52</u>
	Total USC (week 4)	25.97

10.3.4   Rates and Income Thresholds 2021 – Self-employed

The rates and thresholds for the self-employed are the same as those for an employed person, **except** for a **3% USC surcharge** on non-employment income in excess of €100,000.

SELF-ASSESSED PERSONS UNDER 70 AND NOT IN RECEIPT OF A MEDICAL CARD	
THRESHOLD	RATE OF USC
The first €12,012	0.5%
The next €8,675	2.0%
The next €49,357	4.5%
The next €29,956	8.0%
The remainder (> €100,000)	11.0%

SELF-ASSESSED PERSONS IN RECEIPT OF A MEDICAL CARD OR OVER 70 YEARS WHERE AGGREGATE INCOME IS €60,000 OR LESS	
THRESHOLD	RATE OF USC
The first €12,012	0.5%
The next €47,988	2.0%

SELF-ASSESSED PERSONS IN RECEIPT OF A MEDICAL CARD OR OVER 70 YEARS WHERE AGGREGATE INCOME IS GREATER THAN €60,000	
THRESHOLD	RATE OF USC
The first €12,012	0.5%
The next €8,675	2.0%
The next €49,357	4.5%
The next €29,956	8.0%
The remainder (> €100,000)	11.0%

10.3.5 Calculation of USC for the Self-employed

Self-employed individuals will calculate and make a payment of USC along with their preliminary tax payment by 31 October, with any balance payable by 31 October in the following year (see **Section 12.4**).

Example 10.5

Julie Kennedy operates a busy clothing shop, Crazy Dolls, in Tralee. She had the following income and trading results for the year ended 31 December 2021.

	€	€
Tax-adjusted profit Crazy Dolls	53,000	
Capital allowances 2021	6,400	
Deposit interest received (net)	586	
Irish dividends received (net)	920	

Calculate Julie's liability to USC for 2021.

USC Calculation:

Income:		
Schedule D, Case I	53,000	
Less: Capital allowances 2021	(6,400)	46,600
Schedule D, Case IV – not liable to USC		0
Schedule F gross (€920/0.75)		1,227
Income liable to USC		47,827
€12,012 @ 0.5%	60.06	
€8,675 @ 2.0%	173.50	
€27,140 @ 4.5%	1,221.30	
USC due	**1,454.86**	

The surcharge of 3% only applies to non-PAYE income that exceeds €100,000 in a year, even if the total income (PAYE and non-PAYE) exceeds €100,000.

Example 10.6

Jim Cameron is 71 years old and is in receipt of Schedule E income, from his role as managing director of TeeHee Ltd, of €58,000 for 2021. He also has trading income of €107,000 for 2021 from his film distribution business.

USC calculation for 2021:

Gross income for USC:	€	€
Schedule E salary		58,000
Case I Schedule D		107,000
Total income		165,000

USC Calculation:

€12,012 @ 0.5%	60.06
€8,675 @ 2.0%	173.50
€49,357 @ 4.5%	2,221.07
€87,956 @ 8.0%	7,036.48
€7,000 @ 11.0%	770.00
€165,000	10,261.11

If Jim's income was reversed, i.e. his trading income was €58,000 and his employment income was €107,000 his USC liability would be as follows:

USC calculation for 2021:

Gross income for USC:	€	€
Schedule E salary		107,000
Case I Schedule D		58,000
Total income		165,000

USC Calculation:

€12,012 @ 0.5%	60.06
€8,675 @ 2.0%	173.50
€49,357 @ 4.5%	2,221.07
€94,956 @ 8.0% (balance)	7,596.48
€165,000	10,051.11

10.3.6 USC: Surcharge on Use of Property Incentives

Section 531AAE TCA 1997 provides for a **property relief surcharge** on investors (both passive and active) with **gross income** greater than **€100,000**. The surcharge will be collected as **additional** USC of **5%** on the **amount of income sheltered** by the use of certain property- and area-based capital allowances as well as section 23-type reliefs in a given year. The surcharge does not apply to income sheltered by non-property tax reliefs.

Where specified reliefs are restricted under the **high income earner restriction** (see **Chapter 8, Section 8.7**) in any year, that relief can be carried forward to be used in subsequent years, subject to the same restriction applying in that year. Any income in the **subsequent year** that is sheltered by relief of this kind **will not** be subject to the surcharge, on the grounds that it already has been surcharged in an earlier year.

Example 10.7

Joe Long's income and allowances/reliefs for 2021 are as follows:

	€	€
Gross income		210,000
Less: Property reliefs	80,000	
Non-property tax relief	7,000	
		(87,000)
Taxable income		123,000
USC surcharge: Property relief €80,000 @ 5%		**4,000**

Example 10.8

Sheila Short's income and allowances/reliefs for 2021 are as follows:

	€	€
Employment income	90,000	
Rental income (gross) (Note)	12,000	102,000
Less: Case V rental expenses	2,500	
Property tax relief	10,000	(12,500)
Taxable income		89,500

USC surcharge calculation:

	€
Rental income (gross)	12,000
Less: Case V expenses	(2,500)
Net Case V income	9,500
Less: Property tax relief (€500 c/fwd to 2022)	(9,500)
USC surcharge – €9,500 @ 5%	**475**

Note: Case V losses forward or Case V capital allowances are not allowable deductions from Case V income for USC calculation.

Note: where the additional 5% USC applies to a taxpayer in 2021, their preliminary tax for 2021 must be calculated as if this additional surcharge applied in 2020.

Questions

Review Questions

(See Suggested Solutions to Review Questions at the end of this textbook.)

Question 10.1

Peter and Andrew both work for Bosco Ltd and both are paid an annual salary of €39,000. Andrew is in receipt of a medical card due to a long-term medical condition.

Requirement

Calculate Peter and Andrew's liability to USC for 2021.

Question 10.2

Anne Bouquet works part-time as a florist with BuzyBlooms Ltd. She earned €32,000 in 2021 and paid USC of €742.65 on her salary. Anne also works in equal partnership with her spouse, Hyacinth, in a flower distribution business that made tax-adjusted profits in 2021 of €231,000. Anne and Hyacinth are jointly assessed.

Requirement

Calculate Anne's liability to USC for 2021.

Question 10.3

Gerry Brickley is a married man who works as a builder in Cavan. Gerry had the following trading income in 2021:

Trading income	€72,500
Deposit interest received (net)	€825
Dividends received (net)	€1,125

Included in Gerry's trading is a deduction for a contribution of €7,000 to his pension scheme.

Gerry's wife, Mary, works part-time as a nurse in the local hospital and earned the following for 2021:

HSE salary	€23,000
Tax deducted	€1,300
PRSI deducted	€920
USC deducted	€337

Mary also received a dividend on her credit union share account of €321 in 2021.

Requirement

Calculate the Brickleys' liability to income tax, PRSI and USC for 2021, assuming that they are jointly assessed.

The PAYE System

Learning Objectives

After studying this chapter you will understand:

■ the division of responsibilities between the employer and the taxpayer in collecting tax on employment income;
■ the administration and operation of the Pay As You Earn (PAYE) system;
■ the special rules for commencement and cessation of employments; and
■ the operation of employee tax credits and standard rate cut-off point (SRCOP) under the PAYE system.

11.1   Introduction

The PAYE (Pay As You Earn) system is the method used by the Revenue Commissioners to collect income tax, PRSI and USC on most **Schedule E** income.

Broadly speaking, it obliges an employer to deduct income tax, PRSI and USC from wages, salaries and other income assessable to tax under Schedule E **when the remuneration is actually paid**. The primary objective of the system is to collect the taxes due in respect of the relevant Schedule E payments so as to avoid a deferral of liability by the employees concerned.

The PAYE system is a good example of the principle of deduction of **tax at source** in operation, whereby the **payer**, rather than the **recipient**, of the income is liable to account for the income tax to Revenue. Under this system, it is the **employer** who is **obliged** to deduct the tax on making payments of emoluments to their employees and to account for the tax so deducted to Revenue. Payments made under Schedule E are **deemed** to have been paid **net of tax**, **PRSI and USC**. Where refunds are due to the employee, the system provides, in certain circumstances, that these are made by the employer.

Under PAYE the administration cost involved in collecting income tax, PRSI and USC due by people assessable under Schedule E is effectively put on to the employer.

The PAYE system operates on a real-time reporting basis, meaning that employers are required to report their employees' pay and deductions to Revenue on or before the date payment is made to the employee, i.e. when the payroll is run. Under real-time reporting, employers should deduct and pay to Revenue the correct amounts for:

■ income tax;
■ PRSI;
■ USC; and
■ local property tax.

Revenue, employers and employees should have available to them the most accurate, up-to-date information relating to pay and all statutory deductions and payments.

11.2   Scope of Application of the PAYE System

The PAYE system applies to all income from offices or employments (including directorships and occupational pensions). The system therefore applies to:

- Salaries, wages, directors' fees, back pay, pensions, bonuses, overtime, sales commissions, holiday pay, tea money, etc.
- **Round sum expenses** must be paid under the PAYE system. Such round-sum expenses would include, for example, a fixed sum (whether paid weekly, monthly or yearly) to cover expenses to be met by the employee, or an amount put at the disposal of the employee for which he or she does not have to account to the employer with receipts, vouchers, etc.
  Reimbursements of expenses actually incurred by employees in the performance of their duties of employment are not treated as "pay" for PAYE purposes.
- Travel expenses paid or reimbursed to a director, but excluding **non-executive** directors, to attend meetings (including board meetings), are taxable as perquisites under the PAYE system (see **Section 5.3.1**).
- Commencement/inducement payments and termination payments.
- Benefits in kind (BIKs) and perquisites ('perks') must be paid under the PAYE system (see **Section 5.3.1**).
- Share-based remuneration is included as notional pay for the calculation of PAYE.

11.3   Employer's Responsibilities

11.3.1   Registration

An employer is obliged **by law** to register for PAYE any full-time employee earning more than €8 per week (or €36 per month) or any part-time employee earning more than, €2 per week (or €9 per month). A company **must register** as an employer and operate PAYE on the pay of directors, even if there are no other employees. A qualifying domestic employer, who has only one domestic employee who is paid **less than €40** a week, is not required to register and operate PAYE.

Registration for PAYE is done **online** using the **eRegistration** system on the Revenue Online Service (ROS).

Obligation to Keep a Register of Employees
Under the Income Tax (Employments) Regulations 2018, all employers are required to keep a Register of Employees (in paper or electronic format) showing the name, address, PPS number, date of commencement and, where relevant, the date of cessation of employment of all employees.

11.3.2   Employer's Obligations Throughout the Year

At all times during the year an employer must:

- ensure that each employee's PPS number is correct;
- ensure that a PAYE record is set up for each employee for the income tax year;
- use the most up-to-date Revenue Payroll Notification (RPN) to calculate income tax, PRSI, USC and local property tax; and
- make a payroll submission to Revenue on or before the date that employees are paid.

Employers must report their payroll to Revenue on or before the date that payment is made to the employee (usually at the same time the payroll is run) by making a **payroll submission**. Revenue will issue a statement to the employer on the 5th of the following month, showing the total amount of income tax, PRSI, USC and local property tax due based on the employer's payroll submission for the previous month. The employer has until the 14th of the month to either:

1. accept the statement, at which time it becomes the statutory return; **or**
2. make corrections or amendments to the payroll submission if errors are identified.

If no action is taken, the statement will become the statutory return on the 14th of the following month.

11.3.3   Commencement of the Tax Year

Before the beginning of a new tax year, an employer should ensure that it has a RPN for **every** employee for the new tax year. Revenue should make available a RPN advising employers of the tax credits and tax and USC cut-off points (and local property tax, where applicable) for the new year for each employee. Employers with an exemption from paying and filing online will receive RPNs in paper format.

   An employer is legally obliged to request the latest RPN for its employees and must apply the tax credits and cut-off points as notified on the RPN even if they are zero. If no RPN is available (for example, where a worker does not have a PPSN or is working in Ireland for the first time), the employer must operate the **emergency basis** of tax and USC.

11.3.4   Commencement of Employment

A new employee taking up employment or resuming employment after a previous cessation will need to provide their Personal Public Service Number (PPSN). There are two possible scenarios:

1. **The new employee can provide a PPSN** – in which case the employer must take reasonable steps to ensure that the PPSN provided is valid (by using Revenue's PPSN checker, which can be accessed in ROS). If a valid PPSN is provided, the employer must assign an 'Employment Identifier' to the new employee. The Employment Identifier must be unique to the employee and it must remain unchanged where the employment is of a continuous nature. Both the PPSN and the Employment Identifier must be included on the payroll submission.
2. **The new employee cannot provide a PPSN** – in which case the employer must operate the emergency basis of tax and USC until the employee can provide a PPSN. In the absence of a PPSN, the employer must create an 'Employer Reference Number', which again should be a unique identifier, and include it on the payroll submission.

   New employees who do not have a PPSN should be referred to the DSP to obtain one. The employee should also be advised that on receipt of their PPSN they must register for myAccount and inform Revenue of their new employment using the 'Jobs and Pensions' service in myAccount. On receipt of the PPSN, an Employment Identifier can be assigned to the new employee.

For all new employees, employers must request a RPN through ROS by inputting specific details relating to the new employee. A PPSN is required to request a RPN.

   Once received, a RPN will show the tax credits, and the tax and USC cut-off points for that employee; if previously employed, pay, tax and USC details from the beginning of the year will also be shown.

11.3.5   Cessation of Employment

When an employee leaves the employment, takes a career break or dies while in employment, the employer should include the cessation date on the payroll submission for the final payment to that employee to notify

Revenue that the employee has ceased employment. It is important that the date of cessation is included on the final submission as this ensures that if an employee is commencing a new employment, all of their pay, tax and USC details from 1 January up to the date of the new employment are recorded on the cumulative RPN, which will then be issued by Revenue to the new employer.

In the case of casual employees without fixed hours or attendance arrangements, employers may not know when, or whether, the employee will attend for work again and may not know the date of leaving on the final payroll submission for that employee. Where such employees are not paid by the employer for a period of **three months**, a date of leaving equivalent to the last date the employee worked with the employer should be reported to Revenue on the payroll submission immediately after three months has elapsed.

Employees also have the option to cease the employment themselves using the 'Jobs & Pensions' service within their personal myAccount login.

11.3.6 Deduction of Local Property Tax from Salary/Pensions

Employers (including pension-providers) are required to make phased payment options available to employees who wish to pay their local property tax (LPT) (see **Chapter 13**) as a **deduction at source** from their net salary. Where this payment option is chosen by the employee, Revenue will notify the employer on the employee's RPN of the amount of LPT to be deducted **evenly** over the pay periods between **1 January and 31 December**. The employer is required to account for and remit the LPT along with the PAYE.

LPT can only be deducted where the employer has received a RPN showing the amount of LPT to be deducted, and the employer can only cease deduction of LPT from their net salary when advised to do so by Revenue, i.e. the employee cannot direct the employer to commence or cancel collection of LPT. Similarly, any queries, questions or disputes regarding LPT amounts or property valuations are a matter between the employee and Revenue.

LPT deductions are from an employee's net salary (i.e. **after** deductions under PAYE and allowable pension contributions) but take **priority** over non-statutory deductions and any deductions under a court order where the court order was made **after 30 June 2013**.

11.3.7 Payments under PAYE

Payroll submissions and the amounts collected under PAYE must be **remitted to Revenue electronically via ROS**. The payroll must be submitted to Revenue on or before the payment is made to the employee. There is no further submission date unless the employer wishes to amend its payroll submission, in which case it has up to the 14th day of the following month to do so. If there is no amended submission, the Revenue assessment generated on the 5th day of the month is deemed final.

Frequency	Payment Due Date
Monthly	14 days after the end of the month (23 days for ROS users who file and pay online)
Quarterly*	14 days after the end of each quarter (23 days for ROS)
Annual*	14 days after the end of the year (23 days for ROS)

*In certain circumstances PAYE can be paid on an annual or quarterly basis. Authorisation to do so is at the discretion of Revenue and may be terminated at any time. Employers making total annual PAYE payments of up to **€28,800 per annum** may apply to make payments on a quarterly or annual basis.

Late payments of PAYE are charged at a rate of 0.0274% for each day or part thereof (10% per annum) for which the payment is overdue.

11.3.8 Credit for Tax Paid under PAYE by Certain Employees

Employees who have a "material" interest in a company are **not** entitled to a **credit** against their income tax liability for tax deducted under PAYE from emoluments paid to them by the company, **unless** there is documentary evidence to show that the tax deducted under PAYE **has been paid** to Revenue.

An employee is deemed to have a material interest in a company if they (either on their own or with one or more connected persons) or a person with whom they are connected is the beneficial owner of, or is able to control directly or indirectly, more than **15%** of the ordinary share capital of the company.

Any tax deducted under PAYE remitted to Revenue is treated as being paid first in respect of other employees of the company.

Section 997A TCA 1997 provides that the tax deducted under PAYE remitted on behalf of proprietary directors is treated as paid in respect of each proprietary director in the **same proportion** as the emoluments paid bears to the total directors' emoluments, **provided** that the tax split does not result in a **credit exceeding** the amount of the tax actually deducted from the individual director.

11.4 Employee's Responsibilities

It is an employee's responsibility to inform Revenue about any change in circumstances that may affect their entitlement to tax credits and the amount of tax payable. In order for an employee to meet the compliance obligations they should:

- Check their tax credit certificate (TCC) on myAccount to ensure they are entitled to the tax credits allocated and that they are claiming all credits to which they are entitled. If an employee is unsure as to their entitlement to any tax credit, they should contact Revenue.
- Inform Revenue of any **change** in their basic details, including life events such as marriage, civil partnership, bereavement, change of address, etc.
- Inform Revenue of any other **non-PAYE income** from whatever source (including Government sources, e.g. DSP widow's/widower's pension).
- If requested by Revenue, complete an income tax return and return it no later than **31 October** in the year following that to which it relates.
- Keep all relevant documentation in support of claims for tax credits, reliefs, allowances, etc. for a period of **six years** from the end of the year to which the claim related (e.g. medical receipts supporting a medical expenses claim in 2021 must be kept until the end of the year 2027).

Revenue's *Compliance Code for PAYE Taxpayers* sets out Revenue's approach to PAYE compliance interventions and what PAYE taxpayers should do to ensure that they are fully tax-compliant.

11.5 Employee Tax Credits and Standard Rate Cut-off Point

11.5.1 Introduction

In myAccount, every employee can check their **tax credit certificate (TCC)**, which gives details of their tax credits and standard rate cut-off point (SRCOP) for the tax year. The TCC gives a detailed breakdown of how the total tax credits due have been calculated.

The employer is sent a RPN for each employee, which provides the same basic information but also details any local property tax (LPT) to be deducted at source from the employee's net salary. The employer is not given details of how the employee's total tax credit or SRCOP has been determined so as to preserve the confidentiality of the personal circumstances of the employee.

The employer is **obliged** to use the **latest** RPN that is held, even if the employee is disputing the amount of the tax credits or SRCOP that have been granted.

Under the tax credit-based PAYE system, tax is calculated at the 20% and/or 40% rates, as appropriate, on **gross pay**. Tax thus calculated is "gross tax", which is reduced by tax credits to arrive at net tax payable.

11.5.2 Tax Credits

As outlined in **Chapter 8**, an individual is entitled to certain tax credits depending on their personal circumstances, e.g. basic personal tax credit for a single person, married/civil partners, widowed person/ surviving civil partner, employee tax credit, single person child carer credit, etc. In addition, certain reliefs are given as a tax credit at the standard rate of tax, e.g. relief for college fees, etc.

11.5.3 Standard Rate Cut-off Point (SRCOP)

The SRCOP is the amount of the individual's **standard rate tax band** for the year. Tax is paid at the standard rate, currently 20%, up to the SRCOP. Any income in excess of the SRCOP is taxed at the higher rate, currently 40%.

Example 11.1

Liam Cotter is married with two children and his wife works full-time in the home. Liam's salary for 2021 is €48,000.

Tax credits due for 2021:	€
Basic personal tax credit (married)	3,300
Home carer tax credit	1,600
Employee tax credit	1,650
Total	6,550

Liam's tax credit certificate (TCC) will show total tax credits due to him of €6,550 for 2021. These will be expressed as a monthly tax credit amount of €545.83 (€6,550/12) and a weekly tax credit amount of €125.96 (€6,550/52).

Liam's TCC will also show a SRCOP of €44,300 (married, one income) for 2021. This will also be expressed as a monthly cut-off amount of €3,691.67 (€44,300/12) and a weekly cut-off amount of €851.93 (€44,300/52).

11.5.4 Non-PAYE Income

If an individual has small amounts of non-PAYE income and is not a "chargeable person" (see **Section 12.2**), the total tax credits due may be reduced by the non-PAYE income at the standard rate of tax and the SRCOP is reduced by the amount of the non-PAYE income. This will avoid any underpayment of tax on the non-PAYE income.

Example 11.2

If, in the previous example, Liam has UK dividend income of €1,000 for 2021 his total tax credits due to him for 2021 will be reduced by €1,000 @ 20% (i.e. €200) to €6,350. His SRCOP will also be reduced by €1,000 to €43,300. This ensures that the 40% income tax due on the dividend is collected.

Tax due by Liam Cotter for 2021

Income:	€	€
Salary	48,000	
Dividend received	1,000	
Taxable income		49,000

Tax Calculation:		
€44,300 @ 20%	8,860	
€4,700 @ 40%	1,880	10,740
€49,000		

continued overleaf

Deduct: Non-refundable tax credits:		
Basic personal tax credit	3,300	
Home carer tax credit	1,600	
Employee tax credit	1,650	(6,550)
Tax liability		**4,190**
Tax collected under the PAYE system:		
Salary		48,000
Tax Calculation:		
SRCOP (reduced)		
€43,300 @ 20%	8,660	
€4,700 @ 40%	1,880	
€48,000		10,540
Deduct: Non-refundable tax credits:		
Tax credits due (reduced)		(6,350)
Tax deducted		**4,190**

It is important to note that the onus is on the individual to inform Revenue of any non-PAYE income that is taxable.

11.5.5 Reliefs given as a Deduction from Gross Income

Certain reliefs are given as a deduction from income rather than as a tax credit, for example, pension contributions or employment expenses. Where an employee is entitled to such a relief, the total tax credits due are **increased** by the amount of the relief at the standard rate of tax and the SRCOP is **increased** by the amount of the relief.

Example 11.3

If, in the previous example, Liam is entitled to deduct Schedule E expenses relating to his employment of €1,230 for 2021, his tax credits will be increased by €246 (€1,230 @ 20%) and his SRCOP will be increased by €1,230.

Tax Payable by Liam Cotter for 2021		
Income:	€	€
Schedule E: Salary	48,000	
Less: deductible Schedule E expenses	(1,230)	
Taxable income		**46,770**
Tax Calculation:		
€44,300 @ 20%	8,860	
€2,470 @ 40%	988	
€46,770		9,848
Deduct: Non-refundable tax credits:		
Basic personal tax credit	3,300	
Home carer tax credit	1,600	
Employee tax credit	1,650	(6,550)
Tax liability		**3,298**

continued overleaf

Tax collected under PAYE for 2021			
Schedule E: Salary			48,000
Tax Calculation:			
SRCOP (increased)			
€45,530 @ 20%	(€44,300 + €1,230)	9,106	
€2,470 @ 40%		988	
€48,000			10,094
Deduct: Non-refundable tax credits:			
Basic personal tax credit		3,300	
Home carer tax credit		1,600	
Schedule E expenses	(€1,230 @ 20%)	246	
Employee tax credit		1,650	(6,696)
Tax deducted			**3,298**

11.6 Computation of Tax Liability under the PAYE System

The PAYE system obliges the employer to calculate and deduct the income tax due (if any) from the pay of every employee, including directors and any person in receipt of an occupational pension. This tax is then paid over monthly, quarterly or annually to Revenue.

PAYE tax deductions are calculated using one of the following three methods:

1. Cumulative basis
2. Non-cumulative basis (week 1/month 1 basis)
3. Emergency basis.

11.6.1 Cumulative Basis

The purpose of the real-time reporting system is to ensure that the employer calculates and deducts the correct amount of tax due each time a payment of wages/salary is made to an employee.

PAYE is normally calculated on a **cumulative basis**, meaning that when employers calculate the tax liability of an employee they actually calculate the **total tax due** from **1 January** to the date on which the payment is being made. The tax deducted in a particular period is the cumulative tax due from 1 January to that date, **reduced** by the amount of tax previously deducted. Any tax credits and/or SRCOP that are not used in a pay period can be carried forward to the next pay period within that tax year.

The cumulative basis also ensures that refunds can be made to an employee where the employee's tax credits and SRCOP have been increased.

If the employee is paid weekly, tax credits and SCROP are divided into weekly amounts; if monthly, the figures are divided into monthly amounts. These amounts are included in the Revenue Payroll Notification (RPN) sent to the employer.

Example 11.4

Joe Long's tax credits for 2021 are €3,300 (€63.46 per week) and his SRCOP is €35,300 (€678.85 per week). He is paid weekly. Joe was paid €620 for weeks 1 to 3 and was paid €950 for week 4. His payroll record (for the first 8 weeks) will show the following:

Week No.	Gross Pay	Cum. Gross Pay	Cum. Standard Rate Cut-off Point	Cum. Tax due at Standard Rate	Cum. Tax due at Higher Rate	Cum. Gross Tax	Cum. Tax Credit	Cum. Tax	Tax deducted this period	Tax refund this period
1	620.00	620.00	678.85	124.00	0.00	124.00	63.46	60.54	60.54	
2	620.00	1,240.00	1,357.69	248.00	0.00	248.00	126.92	121.08	60.54	
3	620.00	1,860.00	2,036.54	372.00	0.00	372.00	190.38	181.62	60.54	
4	950.00	2,810.00	2,715.38	*543.08	*37.85	580.92	253.84	327.08	145.46	
5			3,394.23				317.30			
6			4,073.08				380.76			
7			4,751.92				444.22			
8			5,430.77				507.68			

* *Week 4 cumulative tax: SRCOP week 4 @ 20% = €2,715.38 @ 20% = €543.08.*

Cum. Gross Pay less SRCOP week 4 @ 40% = (€2,810.00 – €2,715.38) @ 40% = €37.85.

11.6.2   Non-cumulative Basis (Week 1/Month 1 Basis)

In certain circumstances Revenue may **direct an employer** to deduct tax on a **week 1 or month 1 basis**. This instruction will be included on the RPN.

Under the week 1/month 1 basis, **neither** the pay, the tax credits **nor** the SRCOP are **accumulated**. The pay for each income tax week or month is dealt with **separately**. The tax credits and SRCOP for week 1, or month 1, are used in the calculation of tax due each week, or each month. In such cases, the employer **may not make any refunds of tax**.

11.6.3   Emergency Basis

The emergency basis of tax deduction should be used when no RPN is available for the employee. A RPN will not be provided to the employer if:

▪ the employee does not have a PPSN;
▪ the employee is not registered for PAYE.

The employer should advise the employee to contact Revenue if either of the above circumstances apply.
In such cases the employee's tax is calculated as follows:

▪ If the **employee does not provide a PPSN and no RPN is available** – tax is deducted at **40%** from gross pay (less pension contributions and permanent health contributions where relevant). No tax credit is due.
▪ If the **employee provides a PPSN but no RPN is available** – tax is applied to gross pay (less pension contributions and permanent health contributions where relevant) as follows:
  ● **Weeks 1–4, or month 1 if paid monthly** – gross tax is calculated on taxable pay, at the **standard rate** of tax (20%), up to an amount equal to **1/52nd** of the SRCOP for a single individual (2021: €35,300) if weekly paid, or **1/12th** if monthly paid. Any **balance** is taxed at the **higher rate** (40%).

* **Week 5 onwards, or month 2 onwards if paid monthly** – gross tax is calculated on the taxable pay at the **higher rate of tax** (40%) and **no tax credit** is due.

Example 11.5

Alice Casey commenced work with a new employer in January 2021. She provides her new employer with a valid PPSN, but her new employer has received a "No RPN found" message from Revenue. Alice is paid €2,650 monthly with overtime of €250 in month 2 and €400 in month 3.

Emergency Basis

Month No.	Gross Pay	Standard Rate Cut-off Point	Tax due at Standard Rate	Tax due at Higher Rate	Gross Tax	Tax Credit	Tax deducted this period	Tax refund this period
1	2,650.00	2,941.67	530.00	0.00	530.00	0.00	530.00	
2	2,900.00	0.00	0.00	1,160.00	1,160.00	0.00	1,160.00	
3	3,050.00	0.00	0.00	1,220.00	1,220.00	0.00	1,220.00	
4		0.00				0.00		
5		0.00				0.00		

Where an employee has two separate periods of employment with one employer in 2021 and the emergency basis applies in **each** period of employment, the employment is deemed to be **continuous** from the start of the first period of employment to the end of the last period of employment or to 31 December 2021, whichever is earlier.

The tax deducted should be included on the payroll submission along with an Employer Reference Number (a unique identifier allocated to the employee by the employer). The Employer Reference Number is used by Revenue to record details of the employee's pay and deductions until such time as the employee's PPSN becomes available.

It will be readily appreciated from the foregoing that the operation of the emergency basis on any employee is extremely onerous. However, the **employer is legally obliged** to operate the emergency basis and the onus is on the employee to remove themselves from the emergency basis by securing a tax credit certificate and SRCOP. Generally, registering their new employment on the Jobs and Pensions Service available on myAccount and applying for a tax credit certificate will achieve this.

If an employer is obliged to operate the emergency basis and **fails** to do so, the employer is **legally liable** for the tax that **should** have been deducted from the employee's wages and Revenue will seek to collect it from the employer.

11.7 Refunds of Tax under the PAYE System

11.7.1 Employee Taxed on Cumulative Basis

For an employee taxed on the cumulative basis, the most likely situation where they would receive a refund is where Revenue issues a **revised** Revenue Payroll Notification (RPN) showing increased tax credits and, if applicable, increased SRCOP. In such cases, the tax paid to date may **exceed** the cumulative tax due to date and a refund may need to be made. However, some tax credits are non-refundable and if tax credits to date **exceed cumulative gross tax**, the excess may not be refunded.

11.7.2 Employee Taxed under Week 1/Month 1 or Emergency Basis

Example 11.6

Alice Casey has been on the emergency tax basis for months 1–3 (as in **Example 11.5**). In month 4, a RPN issues to her employer showing cumulative tax credits of €3,300 and cumulative SRCOP of €35,300 for 2021. Alice is paid €2,650 monthly with no overtime payment for month 4.

Emergency Basis

Month No.	Gross Pay	Standard Rate Cut-off Point	Tax due at Standard Rate	Tax due at Higher Rate	Gross Tax	Tax Credit	Tax deducted this period	Tax refund this period
1	2,650.00	2,941.67	530.00	0.00	530.00	0.00	530.00	
2	2,900.00	0.00	0.00	1,160.00	1,160.00	0.00	1,160.00	
3	3,050.00	0.00	0.00	1,220.00	1,220.00	0.00	1,220.00	
Total	8,600.00	0.00				0.00	2,910.00	
5		0.00				0.00		

New Cumulative Basis

Month No.	Gross Pay	Cum. Gross Pay	Cum. Standard Rate Cut-off Point	Cum. Tax due at Standard Rate	Cum. Tax due at Higher Rate	Cum. Gross Tax	Cum. Tax Credit	Cum. Tax	Tax deducted this period	Tax refund this period
1	0.00	0.00	2,941.67	0.00	0.00	0.00	275.00	0.00	0.00	
2	0.00	0.00	5,883.33	0.00	0.00	0.00	550.00	0.00	0.00	
3	0.00	*8,600.00	8,825.00	0.00	0.00	0.00	825.00	*2,910.00	0.00	
4	2,650.00	11,250.00	11,766.67	2,250.00	0.00	2,250.00	1,100.00	1,150.00	0.00	1,760.00
5			14,708.33				1,375.00			
6			17,650.00				1,650.00			
7			20,591.67				1,925.00			

* Transferred from emergency payroll record.

11.8 Computation of Liability to PRSI and USC under the PAYE System

11.8.1 PRSI

As discussed in **Chapter 10**, employers are obliged to calculate and deduct employee PRSI from the pay of every employee. They are also obliged to calculate and pay over employer's PRSI. PRSI calculations are made on a non-cumulative basis, i.e. the gross wages for the particular week/month are categorised into the particular class that the wages fall into for that week/month and no account is taken of previous PRSI classes for prior weeks/months.

Example 11.7

Mary Deegan commenced part-time work with Pizza Slice in February 2021. Mary earns the minimum wage (2021: €10.20 per hour) and is paid weekly. She worked the following hours for the first four weeks:

Week 1   3 hours

Week 2   39 hours

Week 3   20 hours

Week 4   50 hours

Calculate the PRSI payable (employee and employer) for Mary for her first four weeks of employment.

Week 1	€	€	
Gross wages: €10.20 × 3 hours		30.60	Class J0
EE PRSI – 0%		0.00	
ER PRSI – 0%		0.00	
Total PRSI		0.00	

Week 2	€	€	
Gross wages: €10.20 × 39 hours		397.80	Class AX
EE PRSI – 4%		15.91	
Less: PRSI credit:			
Maximum credit	12.00		
Less: 1/6th × (€393.90 – €352.01)	(6.98)		
Net PRSI credit		(5.02)	
EE PRSI		10.89	
ER PRSI – 8.8%		35.00	
Total PRSI		45.89	

Week 3	€	€	
Gross wages: €10.20 × 20 hours		204.00	Class A0
EE PRSI – 0%		0.00	
ER PRSI – 8.8%		17.95	
Total PRSI		17.95	

Week 4	€	€	
Gross wages: €10.20 × 50 hours		510.00	Class A1
EE PRSI – 4%		20.40	
ER PRSI – 11.05%		56.35	
Total PRSI		76.75	

PRSI is paid on the same basis every week/month, irrespective of whether the employee is on a week 1/ month 1 or an emergency basis for income tax and USC.

11.8.2 USC

USC is collected on a cumulative basis and the RPN includes the USC rates and threshold cut-off points. The following is an extract from a RPN showing USC rates and thresholds:

Allocation of your USC Rate Bands (Subject to Rounding) for 2021				
Employer	**USC Rate Bands**			
	Rate Band	**Yearly**	**Monthly**	**Weekly**
XYZ COMPANY	Income chargeable at 0.5%	12,012.00	1,001.00	231.00
	Income chargeable at 2.0%	8,675.00	722.92	166.83
	Income chargeable at 4.5%	49,357.00	4,113.08	949.17
	Income over €70,044 in this employment is chargeable at 8%			

Cumulative and Emergency Basis for USC
- Where an employee is on the cumulative basis for tax, they will be on the cumulative basis for USC.
- Where an employee is on a week 1 basis for tax, they will also be on a week 1 basis for USC.
- Where an employee is on the emergency basis for tax, they will also be on the emergency basis for USC.

USC under the emergency basis is calculated at 8%, with no cut-off point.

Questions

Review Questions

(See Suggested Solutions to Review Questions at the end of this textbook.)

Question 11.1

Mary commenced new employment on 1 August 2021 under a contract with normal terms and conditions. The agreed monthly salary was €2,200. Mary's RPN showed the following amounts from her previous employment for the period 1 January 2021 to 31 July 2021:

Gross Salary	€16,310
Tax deducted	€1,337
Monthly tax credit	€275
Monthly SRCOP	€2,941.67
Month Number	7
Gross salary for USC purposes	€16,310
Total USC deducted	€327.16
Monthly USC cut-off point 1	€1,001.00
Monthly USC cut-off point 2	€722.92
Monthly USC cut-off point 3	€4,113.08

Requirement
Calculate the net pay receivable by Mary for August 2021, after deduction of tax, PRSI and USC, assuming that Revenue has issued a RPN for Mary.

Question 11.2

An employee, Andrew, who is paid €4,167 gross monthly, is provided with a company car by his employer for the first time from 1 June 2021. The original market value of the car is €28,000 (after allowing a 10% cash discount). Andrew's total annual travel is estimated at 51,200 km, of which 8,000 km are personal.

Andrew is required to pay €1,500 per annum to his employer for the private use of the car. This will be deducted monthly from Andrew's salary.

Requirement
Calculate Andrew's total gross taxable pay for June 2021.

Question 11.3

Sean, a married man, is employed by NEW Ltd from 1 July 2021. He is allowed unrestricted private use of a company van in respect of which he will incur business travel of 26,000 km per annum. NEW pays all the costs of running the van except diesel, which Sean pays for himself. Sean contributes €10 per month to NEW Ltd towards the running costs of the van. NEW bought the van second-hand for €10,000 on 30 June 2021. The van had a market value of €17,500 when first registered on 30 April 2016.

Requirement
(a) Calculate Sean's taxable benefit for 2021 in respect of his use of the company van.
(b) Sean's gross weekly wages are €500, inclusive of the benefit in kind on the van. Assuming the emergency basis of tax applies, calculate the tax, PRSI and USC to be deducted from Sean's first week's wages if:

   (i) NEW Ltd is provided with Sean's PPSN;
   (ii) NEW Ltd is not provided with Sean's PPSN.

Question 11.4

Paul commenced work on 12 October 2021 under a contract with normal terms and conditions, at a rate of €21 per hour for a 39-hour working week. Hours worked in excess of 39 hours are paid as overtime at time-and-a-half.

Paul's income from his previous employment for the period 1 January 2021 to 10 October 2021 is as follows:

Gross salary to date	€43,540.00	Gross salary for USC	€43,540.00
Tax deducted to date	€5,465.04	Total USC deducted	€1,355.82
Weekly Tax Credit	€95.19	USC cut-off point 1	€231.00
Week Number	45	USC cut-off point 2	€166.83
Weekly SRCOP	€851.92	USC cut-off point 3	€949.17

In his first week, ending 17 October, Paul worked 39 hours plus 11 hours overtime.

Requirement
Calculate the net pay receivable by Paul for his first week after deducting tax, PRSI and USC in each of the following scenarios:

(a) Revenue has issued an RPN on a week 1/month 1 basis.
(b) Revenue has issued an RPN on a cumulative basis.

Question 11.5

Charlotte is employed by Jolly Giants Ltd and receives a gross weekly wage of €1,050. Charlotte has a liability to LPT of €520 for 2021 and she has opted to pay for this through payroll.

Charlotte's salary details to 30 June 2021 are as follows:

Gross wages	€27,300.00
Tax deducted	€5,740.00
Weekly tax credit	€63.46
Weekly SRCOP	€678.85
Week Number 26	
Gross wages for USC purposes	€27,300.00
Total USC deducted	€879.82
Weekly USC Cut-off point 1	€231.00
Weekly USC Cut-off point 2	€166.83
Weekly USC Cut-off point 3	€949.17
Total LPT deducted	€260.00

Requirement

Calculate the net pay receivable by Charlotte for week 27 (6 July 2021) and week 28 (13 July 2021).

Question 11.6

John has been employed by Care-for-Cars Ltd for a number of years and receives a gross weekly wage of €16 per hour for a 40-hour week, i.e. €640. John has asked his employer if he can work part-time for a six-week period to help out at home as his wife, Carol, has just given birth to twin boys. Care-for-Cars agrees to continue paying John €16 per hour for the hours he works. John works the following hours for weeks 32 to 34:

Week 32 – 20 hours
Week 33 – 25 hours
Week 34 – 23 hours

John's details are as follows:

	€
Gross wages to week 31	**19,840.00**
PAYE deducted	1,017.04
USC deducted	477.07
Weekly tax credit	95.19
Weekly SRCOP	851.92
Weekly USC cut-off-point 1	231.00
Weekly USC cut-off-point 2	166.83
Weekly USC cut-off-point 3	949.17

Requirement

Calculate John's net wages for week 32 to week 34.

Self-assessment

Learning Objectives

After studying this chapter you will understand:

- the concept of self-assessment and who is a "chargeable person" for income tax purposes;
- preliminary tax requirements;
- obligations under self-assessment; and
- penalties and interest for late filings under self-assessment.

12.1 Introduction

Self-assessment is a system whereby "chargeable persons" **calculate** and **return** taxes due within the timeframes and deadlines specified by tax law.

Self-assessment applies to people, chargeable to income tax, who are in receipt of income from sources that are **not chargeable** to tax **under the PAYE** system, or where some, but **not all**, of the tax on these sources of income is paid under PAYE.

12.2 "Chargeable Persons"

For income tax purposes, self-assessment applies to the following chargeable persons:

- Self-employed persons (i.e. people carrying on their own business, including farming, professions or vocations).
- Proprietary company directors (i.e. holds or controls more than 15% of the ordinary share capital of the company) **regardless** of whether or not they have non-PAYE income.
- Individuals with gross non-PAYE income of €30,000 **or more** from all sources, even if there is **no net taxable income** from that source, for example:
  - income from rental property and investment income;
  - foreign income and foreign pensions; and
  - trading or professional income.

An individual becoming a chargeable person under this rule continues to be a chargeable person for future years, as long as the source(s) of the non-PAYE income continues to exist, **irrespective** of the amount of the annual gross income.

- Individuals with **assessable** non-PAYE income of **€5,000 or more, irrespective** of the amount of gross non-PAYE income.
- Individuals with profits arising on exercising various share options/share incentives.
- Where an Irish resident opens a **foreign bank account** of which they are the beneficial owner, they are to be regarded as a chargeable person for the years during which the account is open.
- Where a person acquires certain foreign life policies, they will be deemed to be a chargeable person.
- Where a person acquires a material interest in an offshore fund, they are deemed to be a chargeable person.
- Individuals in receipt of legally enforceable maintenance payments.

The following are not chargeable persons for the purposes of self-assessment:

- Individuals whose **only source** of income consists of income chargeable to tax under the PAYE system.
- An individual who is in receipt of income chargeable to tax under the PAYE system but who is **also** in receipt of income from other non-PAYE sources will not be regarded as a chargeable person if the total gross income from all non-PAYE sources is **less than €30,000 and** the net assessable income is **less than €5,000 and** the income is coded against PAYE tax credits (i.e collected through the PAYE system). Note that a married couple or civil partners, who are jointly assessed, are entitled to earn up to €5,000 and have that income coded before the spouse/civil partner on whom the income is assessed becomes a chargeable person. However, where a married couple/civil partners opt for separate or single assessment, each person will have a limit of €5,000.
- Non-proprietary directors **provided** they are not otherwise a chargeable person and **all** of their income is subject to PAYE.
- Directors of dormant and 'shelf' companies.
- An individual who has received a notice from an Inspector of Taxes excluding them from the requirement to make a return (i.e. an exempt person).
- An individual who is only liable to income tax in respect of tax withheld from annual payments.

12.3 Obligations under Self-assessment

An individual who is a "chargeable person" for the purposes of self-assessment income tax must:

- complete a "pay and file" income tax return, which must be filed online using the Revenue Online Service (ROS) where the individual is subject to mandatory e-filing (see **Section 14.4**), or by paper and, at the same time, pay the balance of tax outstanding for the previous year;
- pay preliminary tax for the current tax year on or before 31 October each year (i.e. preliminary tax for the year of assessment 2021 is payable by 31 October 2021).

Note that, while the due date for both returns and payments is 31 October, returns and payments that are made online qualify for an extension to the due date, which is decided on an annual basis by Revenue. The extended date for 2020 income tax returns and payments is 17 November 2021.

12.4 Preliminary Tax

Preliminary tax is the taxpayer's **estimate** of their income tax payable for the year and must be paid by **31 October** in the tax year. Preliminary tax **includes** PRSI and USC as well as income tax. Note that a time extension is given when the taxpayer pays and files online using ROS. For 2021 preliminary tax, the extension is to 17 November 2021. However, the **due date** remains **31 October** and in any event of a default or underpayment, interest and penalties are calculated from the **due date**. To avoid interest charges the amount of preliminary tax paid is not less than the **lower** of:

- **90%** of the final tax liability for the current tax year, i.e. 2021; **or**
- **100%** of the final tax liability for the immediately previous year (see Note), i.e. 2020; **or**
- **105%** of the final tax liability for the year preceding the immediately previous year, i.e. 2019. This option is **only available** where Revenue is authorised to collect tax by **direct debit**. The 105% rule does not apply where the tax payable for the pre-preceding year is nil.

Example 12.1

Paul Gasbag is a self-employed confectioner and his estimated draft accounts for the year ended 31 December 2021 show an estimated tax-adjusted profit of €44,000. The estimated capital allowances due for 2021 total €7,000. He received €450 gross interest on his AIB ordinary deposit account in October 2021, which he has held for a number of years.

His wife Sharon is employed by an insurance company and her gross salary for 2021 is €52,000 (tax deducted: €8,640). She will receive €400 gross interest on her savings account in 2021.

Paul's final tax liability for 2020 was as follows:

Case I income	€40,000	Income tax due	€6,940
Capital allowances	€2,000	USC	€1,049
Case IV interest (gross)	€350	PRSI	€1,530
		Total liability 2020	€9,519

Paul's tax liability for 2019 was €7,450 (including PRSI and USC).

Estimated Income Tax Computation 2021

	€	€
Income:		
Case I	44,000	
Less: capital allowances	(7,000)	37,000
Case IV – Paul (gross)		450
Taxable income – Paul		37,450
Schedule E – Sharon	52,000	
Case IV – Sharon	400	
Taxable income – Sharon		52,400
Total taxable income		**89,850**
Tax Calculation:		
€70,600 @ 20%	14,120	
€850 @ 33%	281	
€18,400 @ 40%	7,360	
€89,850		21,761
Deduct: Non-refundable tax credits:		
Basic personal tax credit (married)	3,300	
Earned income credit	1,650	
Employee tax credit (Sharon)	1,650	
DIRT (Paul and Sharon) (€850 @ 33%)	281	(6,881)
Tax liability		**14,880**

continued overleaf

Deduct: Refundable tax credits		
Tax deducted under PAYE deducted (Sharon)		(8,640)
Net tax liability		**6,240**

Universal Social Charge:
Paul:

€12,012 @ 0.5%	60	
€8,675 @ 2.0%	174	
€16,313 @ 4.5%	734	
€37,000		968

Sharon: USC liability will be paid under PAYE system
Case IV income not liable to USC

PRSI:

Paul: €37,450 @ 4%		1,498
Sharon: €400 @ 4% (Case IV only)		16
ESTIMATED TOTAL LIABILITY 2021		**8,722**

Note: the deposit interest (Case IV) has no further income tax liability, but is subject to PRSI, though not to USC.

Preliminary tax payment for 2021 will be:

Lower of: Year 2020 @ 100%	=	€9,519	*or*
Year 2021 @ 90%	=	€7,850	

Preliminary tax for 2021 will be €7,850 and is payable by 17 November 2021 through ROS (due date 31 October 2021). The balance of the tax due for 2021 (€8,722 – €7,850 = €872) is payable by 31 October 2022.

If Paul pays his preliminary tax by way of direct debit, his preliminary tax for 2021 will be as follows:

Lower of: Year 2019 @ 105%	=	€7,822	*or*
Year 2020 @ 100%	=	€9,519	*or*
Year 2021 @ 90%	=	€7,850	

Therefore Paul's preliminary tax for 2021 will be €7,822 and is payable by 17 November 2021 through ROS (due date 31 October 2021). The balance of the tax due (€8,722 – €7,822 = €900) is payable by 31 October 2022.

Underpayment of Preliminary Tax

Where preliminary tax paid is based on 90% of the **estimated** liability for the current year and the final tax liability is greater than the estimate, interest will be chargeable on the difference between the preliminary tax amount paid and the final tax liability at a rate of 0.0219% per day.

In addition, the ROS filing date extension is not available where the preliminary tax is underpaid. Interest will apply on any underpayment, calculated from the due date for payment of the preliminary tax, i.e. 31 October.

12.5 Self-correction and Expressions of Doubt

12.5.1 Self-correction

Where a taxpayer discovers some errors after the submission of a tax return and wishes to rectify the return, Revenue will allow a return to be self-corrected **without** penalty where, **within 12 months of the due date for filing the return**:

▪ Revenue is notified in writing or electronically through ROS of the adjustments to be made, and the circumstances under which the errors arose; **and**

> a computation of the correct tax and statutory interest payable is provided, along with a payment in settlement.

Note that a self-correction **cannot be made** if Revenue has begun to make enquiries into the return or self-assessment for that chargeable period or if an audit or investigation has commenced in relation to the tax affairs of the taxpayer for the chargeable period involved.

12.5.2 Expression of Doubt

Where a taxpayer has a **genuine doubt** over the particular interpretation of an item in a return, for example the application of a particular relief, etc., the taxpayer may:

> prepare the return for the chargeable period to the best of the taxpayer's belief as to the correct application of the law to the matter and submit it to Revenue; and
>
> complete the relevant sections on their tax return to express doubt and submit any documentation in support of the expression of doubt on or before the return filing date.

The information required to make an expression of doubt should:

> include a list of the supporting documentation being supplied;
>
> sets out in full detail the facts and circumstances of the matter in doubt;
>
> specifies the doubt and the law giving rise to the doubt;
>
> identifies the amount of tax in doubt in respect of the chargeable period to which the expression of doubt relates;
>
> provide details of any published Revenue guidelines that have been consulted regarding the application of the law in similar cases.

An expression of doubt considered "genuine" will protect the taxpayer from interest charges on any tax underpaid as a result of the expression of doubt.

An expression of doubt can only be submitted if the accompanying return is delivered to Revenue **on or before** the specified return date. Therefore an expression of doubt cannot be made if the return is filed after the due date. Revenue may refuse to accept an expression of doubt in certain circumstances. However, the taxpayer has a right to appeal against such a decision.

12.6 Self-computation of Taxes Due and Notice of Assessment

12.6.1 Self-computation of Taxes Due

Section 959R TCA 1997 requires self-assessed taxpayers to **compute the tax due** at the date of filing of the tax return. Taxpayers, however, are entitled to **rely** on the **calculation of the tax payable** by the Revenue Online Service (ROS) when submitting their return. A fixed **penalty of €250** will apply where a chargeable person fails to file the necessary self-assessment with their return.

The taxpayer's self-assessment constitutes the tax payable, but this does not in any way preclude Revenue from raising an assessment to tax where:

> a return has not been filed; **or**
>
> Revenue disagrees with the self-computation.

While most self-assessed taxpayers are obliged to file tax returns through ROS, some returns are still filed by paper. Where such a taxpayer files a return by **31 August**, Revenue will calculate the tax liability for the taxpayer and send it to them for settlement.

12.7   Interest Payable and Late Filing Surcharges

12.7.1   *Interest on Overdue Income Tax*

The rate of interest on overdue income tax is 0.0219% per day or part thereof (approximately 8% per annum).

12.7.2   *Late Filing Surcharges*

If a return of income is **not submitted** by the "specified date", i.e. 31 October, in the year following the year of assessment, the tax liability for that year is **increased** by a **surcharge** on the amount of tax assessed. The surcharge is calculated on the **full tax payable for the year** and does not take account of any tax payments already made (e.g. under PAYE). The surcharge is calculated as follows:

1.   if the return is submitted within two months of the specified return date, i.e. by 31 December, then the surcharge is 5% of the full tax payable for the year, subject to a maximum surcharge of €12,695.
2.   if the return is submitted more than two months after the specified return date, i.e. after 31 December, then the surcharge is 10% of the full tax payable for the year, subject to a maximum surcharge of €63,485.

Where an individual files a return and fails to include on the return details relating to any exemption, allowance, deduction, credit or other relief the person is claiming (referred to as "specified details") and the return states that the details required are specified details, the individual may be liable to a 5% surcharge (subject to the usual maximum of €12,695) **even if** they have filed the return **on time**. However, this surcharge may only be applied where, after the return has been filed, it has come to the person's notice (or has been brought to their attention) that the specified details were not included in the return and the person **failed to remedy** the matter.

12.7.3   *Fixed Penalty*

The penalty for a 'specified' taxpayer not making an electronic payment or not filing a return electronically, where the taxpayer is subject to mandatory e-filing (see **Section 14.4**), is €1,520 (section 917EA(7) TCA 1997). The penalty is charged in each instance where payment or filing has not been made electronically.

The fixed penalty for a self-assessed taxpayer not making a return is €3,000 (section 1052 TCA 1997) rising to €4,000 in certain circumstances.

12.8   Interest on Overpayments of Tax

Interest is paid by Revenue at **0.011% per day** or part thereof (4.015% per annum) on overpaid tax.

Under section 865A TCA 1997, the date from which interest runs will depend on whether the overpayment is as a result of Revenue's mistake or the taxpayer's. Where the overpayment arises because of a mistaken assumption by Revenue in the application of tax law, and a claim for repayment is made within the requisite time limit, interest is paid from the day after the end of the tax year to which the repayment relates or, if later, the date of payment, until the date the repayment is made.

Where the overpayment **does not arise** because of a mistaken application of the law by Revenue, the overpayment will only carry interest for the period beginning on the day which is **93 days** after the day on which a "valid claim" for repayment has been filed with Revenue. A "valid claim" is one where all the information Revenue might reasonably require to enable it to determine if and to what extent a repayment is due has been provided to Revenue.

Interest on the overpayment of tax is **not subject** to withholding tax and is **exempt** from income tax. Interest will not be paid where the overall amount due is less than €10.

Questions

Review Questions
(See Suggested Solutions to Review Questions at the end of this textbook.)

Question 12.1

The senior partner of your firm has come to you with a letter from one of the firm's clients, John Murphy, who was previously an employee and has set up his own business on 1 July 2021. Mr Murphy will prepare accounts annually to 31 December. Mr Murphy is very worried about the self-assessment system.

Requirement
You are required to write a brief letter to Mr Murphy describing the self-assessment system, paying attention to the procedure for each of the following:
    (a) income tax returns and surcharges;
    (b) preliminary tax; and
    (c) mandatory e-filing.

Question 12.2

Paul Joist is a self-employed architect and his accounts for the year ended 31 December 2021 show a tax-adjusted profit of €112,000. Capital allowances due for 2021 total €8,000. He received €1,275 gross interest on his AIB ordinary deposit account, which was subject to DIRT. Paul is a non-executive director of his brother's company in which he has a 5% stake. Paul was paid €6,000 gross in 2021, from which PRSI of €240 was deducted.

His wife, Sandra, is employed by a marketing and promotions company, and her gross salary for 2021 was €62,000 (tax deducted: €12,640). Paul's final tax liability for 2020 was €38,100 and for 2019 was €35,800. Paul and Sandra are jointly assessed.

Requirement
Calculate Paul and Sandra's preliminary tax payment for 2021 and their final tax liability for 2020.

Question 12.3

Jane Underwood is a graphic designer and works for Life Designs Ltd. Jane is married to Una Clarke and they have two children of school-going age, one of whom is incapacitated. Una is the principal carer of the children, but does some small contract jobs during school time. Jane and Una are jointly assessed. Jane and Una had the following income for 2021:

Jane	€	€
Deposit interest received (net)		592
Dividends received (net)		2,125
Medical expenses		780
Salary from Life Designs Ltd (per Employment Detail Summary)		131,500
– Tax deducted	35,490	
– USC paid	7,371	
– PRSI paid	5,260	

Una		
Consultancy fees received		8,300
Travel expenses, stationery and phone		800
Credit union dividend received (net)		635

Una estimates that she will earn approximately €8,500 in 2022, together with similar amounts for deposit interest and dividends.

Requirement

Advise Jane and Una of their responsibilities (if any) under self-assessment and calculate any amounts that may be due for tax, PRSI and USC.

Local Property Tax

13.1 Introduction

The Finance (Local Property Tax) Act 2012 provides for an annual local property tax (LPT) payable by a "liable person" in respect of certain "residential" properties. It also provides for the establishment and maintenance, by the Revenue Commissioners, of a register of residential properties in the State. Subsequent amendment acts in 2013 and 2021 provided for the exemption from LPT of certain residential properties (2013) and the revision of these exemptions and the valuation bands and tax rates (2021).

In short, the "**liable person**" in respect of a "**residential property**" at the "**liability date**" is required to pay property tax, based on the value of the residential property as of the "**valuation date**" at a rate of:

■ 0.1029% per annum on the portion of the property value up to €1,050,000;
■ 0.25% per annum on the portion of the property value between €1,050,000 and €1,750,000; and
■ 0.3% on the portion of the property value exceeding €1,750,000.

The value of the residential property at the valuation date is determined by the liable person under **self-assessment**.

13.2 Definitions

13.2.1 Liable Person

The "liable person" is responsible for the submission of the LPT return and the payment of the tax due. The liable person in most cases will be the owner of the property, but the definition is quite broad and includes the following:

- Owners of Irish residential property (irrespective of whether or not they live in Ireland).
- Holders of a life-interest in a residential property.
- Persons with a long-term right of residence (for life or for 20 years or more) that entitles them to exclude any other person from the property.
- Lessees who hold long-term leases of residential property (for 20 years or more) but excluding long leases of residential property to a local authority or social housing provider.
- Landlords or lessors, where the property is rented under a short-term lease (for less than 20 years) or where the property is let under a long-term lease to a local authority or social housing provider.
- Personal representatives for a deceased owner (e.g. executor/administrator of an estate).
- Trustees, where a property is held in a trust.
- Local authorities or social housing organisations that own and provide social housing.
- Where none of the above categories of liable person applies, the person who occupies the property on a rent-free basis and without challenge to that occupation.

Where co-ownership of a property arises, all owners will be held **jointly and severally liable** to the LPT, but only **one return** will be required which will be submitted by the designated liable person. Revenue has the discretion to designate a liable person to submit the return if this should prove necessary.

There are no exemptions from LPT available to a liable person.** However, **LPT may be deferred if the liable person satisfies certain conditions**, as outlined in **Section 13.4.3**.

13.2.2   Residential Property

For LPT purposes, residential property means any building or structure (or part of a building) which is **used as**, or is **suitable for use as**, a dwelling. This includes any co-living development, shed, outhouse, garage or other building or structure, and **grounds** of up to 0.404686 hectares (one acre) that are most suitable for occupation and enjoyment with the residence, i.e. adjoining or closest to the residence. Vacant properties are not exempt from LPT as they are "suitable for use" as a dwelling. It **excludes** a structure that is not permanently attached to the ground (e.g. caravan or mobile home).

Properties Exempt from LPT
The following are some of the properties exempt from LPT from **1 January 2022**:

- Residential properties owned by a charity or a public body and used to provide accommodation and support for people with special needs.
- Registered Nursing Homes.
- A property that has been vacated by the person for 12 months or more due to long-term mental or physical infirmity.
- Mobile homes, vehicles or vessels.
- Properties fully subject to commercial rates.
- Residential properties that have been certified as having significant pyritic damage and those damaged by the use of defective concrete blocks (mica) are exempted from LPT for a two-year period from 1 January 2022.

13.2.3   Liability Date

The liability date is **1 November** in the preceding year (i.e. for 2022, the liability date is 1 November 2021).
    A liable person of a residential property on 1 November 2021 is liable for LPT for 2022. If the liable person sells the residential property **after** 1 November 2021 but **before** 1 November 2022, they are still liable to LPT for 2022 but not for 2023. If the liable person sells the residential property after 1 November

2021 but before 31 December 2021, they are liable to LPT for 2022 even though they do not own the property in 2022.

13.2.4 Valuation Date

The valuation date is the date at which the chargeable value of the residential property is established. In the legislation this is stated as;

* 1 May 2013 for the tax years 2013 to 2021; and
* 1 November 2021 for the tax years 2022 to 2025; and
* for each consecutive four-year period after 2025, 1 November in the preceding year (i.e. for 2026, the valuation date is 1 November 2025).

From 1 November 2021, properties that are newly completed or refurbished to a habitable condition between valuation dates, are chargeable to LPT as they are completed/refurbished with a retrospective valuation to the preceding valuation date.

13.3 Calculation of LPT

13.3.1 Standard LPT Rate

* 1 May 2013 to 31 December 2021:

    * **0.18% per annum** for properties with a value up to **€1 million**; and
    * **0.25% per annum** for properties valued at **over €1 million**.

* From 1 January 2022:

    * Properties with a value up to **€1 million: 0.1029% per annum**
    * Properties with a value between **€1 million** and **€1.75 million**:

        ○ **0.1029% per annum** on the first €1.05 million; and
        ○ **0.25% per annum** on the balance between **€1.05 million** and **€1.75 million**.

    * Properties with a value **in excess** of **€1.75 million**:

        ○ **0.1029% per annum** on the first €1.05 million;
        ○ **0.25% per annum** on the balance between **€1.05 million** and **€1.75 million**; and
        ○ **0.3% per annum** on the balance in excess of **€1.75 million**.

The amount of LPT payable is based on the **market value** of the residential property at the valuation date, i.e. 1 November 2021 for years 2022 to 2025. The market value is decided by the liable person, taking into account the specific characteristics of the property. Property values are organised into 20 valuation bands and the calculation of LPT for each band is as follows:

* Bands 1 and 2 (€0 to €262,500): fixed annual LPT charge of €90 and €225, respectively.
* Bands 3–19 (€262,501 to €1.75 million): mid-point of the valuation band is taken as the property value on which the appropriate rate is applied.
* Band 20 (greater than €1.75 million): properties are assessed at the actual value (no banding will apply).

Valuation Band Number	Valuation Band €	Mid-Point of Valuation Band €	LPT 2022 at Standard Rate €
01	0 to 200,000	N/A	90
02	200,001 to 262,500	N/A	225
03	262,501 to 350,000	306,250	315
04	350,001 to 437,500	393,750	405
05	437,501 to 525,000	481,251	495
06	525,001 to 612,500	568,751	585
07	612,501 to 700,000	656,251	675
08	700,001 to 787,500	743,751	765
09	787,501 to 875,000	831,251	855
10	875,001 to 962,500	918,751	945
11	962,501 to 1,050,000	1,006,251	1,035
12	1,050,001 to 1,137,500	1,093,750	1,190
13	1,137,501 to 1,225,000	1,181,251	1,409
14	1,225,001 to 1,312,500	1,268,751	1,627
15	1,312,501 to 1,400,000	1,356,251	1,846
16	1,400,001 to 1,487,500	1,443,751	2,065
17	1,487,501 to 1,575,000	1,531,251	2,284
18	1,575,001 to 1,662,500	1,618,751	2,502
19	1,662,501 to 1,750,000	1,706,251	2,721
20	1,750,001 +	N/A	2,830 +

Example 13.1

John Corr's residential property has a market value of €530,000 as of 1 November 2021. His liability to LPT for 2022 is as follows:

Market value	€530,000
Valuation band number	06
Valuation band	€525,001 to €612,500
Mid-point of valuation band	**€568,751**

LPT 2022:

€568,751 @ 0.1029%	€585

Example 13.2

Moya Clark's residential property has a market value of €1,240,000 as of 1 November 2021. Her liability to LPT for 2022 is as follows:

Market value	€1,240,000
Valuation band number	14
Valuation band	€1,225,001 to €1,312,500
Mid-point of valuation band	**€1,268,751**

LPT:

€1,050,000 @ 0.1029%	€1,080
€218,751* @ 0.25%	€547
€1,268,751	€1,627
LPT 2022	**€1,627**

* *Mid-point of band 14 €1,268,751 less €1,050,000 = €218,751*

Example 13.3
Adeola Igoe's residential property has a market value of €2,250,000 as of 1 November 2021. Her liability to LPT for 2022 is as follows:

Market value	€2,250,000
Valuation band number	20
LPT 2022:	
€1,050,000 @ 0.1029%	€1,080
€700,000 @ 0.25%	€1,750
€500,000 @ 0.3%	€1,499
€2,250,000	€4,329
LPT 2022:	**€4,329**

13.3.2 Amendment of LPT Payable by Local Adjustment Factor

Since 2015, local authorities can vary the basic LPT percentage rate (0.1029%) on properties situated within their area. This adjustment, known as the **local adjustment factor (LAF)**, can increase or decrease the basic LPT rate by up to 15%.

For example, Clare County Council increased its rate of LPT by 15% and Dublin City Council reduced its rate by 15% in 2021. Note that the adjustments only apply to that year and are not cumulative.

Notification of any change is made by the relevant councils directly to Revenue, which will revise the amount of LPT payable.

Example 13.4
If John Corr's residential property in **Example 13.1** is situated in the area covered by Limerick County Council and they increase the rate by 15% in 2022, his liability to LPT for 2022 will be as follows:

€568,751 @ 0.1029%	€585
Limerick LAF @ 15%	€88
LPT for 2022	**€673**

13.4 LPT Returns and Payment of LPT

13.4.1 LPT Returns

The liable person in respect of the residential property, or properties, is responsible for completing the return and paying LPT. The liable person could authorise another can (e.g. a relative) to complete and submit the return on their behalf.

An LPT1 in respect of the first valuation date of **1 May 2013 was valid for the years 2013–2021**. From **1 November 2021**, the valuation date of **1 November 2021** is valid for the tax years **2022 to 2025**. For each consecutive **four-year** period after 2025, **1 November** in the preceding year is the valuation date (i.e. for 2026, the valuation date is 1 November 2025).

The **onus remains** with the liable person to **self-assess** their liability to LPT, i.e. the liable person must determine the market value of the residential property and calculate and pay the LPT accordingly.

Some points to note regarding returns:

- Where a property is newly completed or refurbished to a habitable condition **between** valuation dates, the liable person is required to deliver a return to Revenue on or before the next return date (**7 November**) following the completion/refurbishment. The corresponding liability date will become the 1 November in the **same year**.
- If a person receives a LPT1 and they are **not the liable person**, they must contact Revenue and state who the liable person is (if known).
- Where a liable person **does not receive** a LPT1 from Revenue, under self-assessment, they are **obliged** to contact Revenue to make a LPT return.
- Where an exemption is being claimed the LPT1 must be completed and filed by the return date and the owner must state which exemption condition the property satisfies (e.g. "ghost estate").
- Where a **deferral** (full or partial) is being claimed, the LPT1 must be completed and filed by the relevant deadlines and the owner must state which deferral exemption is being claimed (see **Section 13.4.3**).

If the liable person did not previously qualify for an LPT exemption but now does, the exemption can be claimed by filing a return and providing details of the exemption being claimed.

13.4.2 Payment of LPT

LPT liabilities can be paid in one single payment or phased out into equal instalments. Monthly direct debit payments for 2021 commenced on 15 January 2021 and continue on the same date each month thereafter. The payment method selected for 2020 will automatically apply for 2021 and subsequent years unless Revenue is otherwise advised.

LPT can be paid **in full** by:

- single debit authority – for 2021, payment will be deducted the bank account no earlier than 21 March 2021;
- cheque or by debit/credit card (payable on date of instruction); or
- cash payments (including debit/credit card) in equal instalments through approved Payment Service Providers.

Where the deduction at source option is chosen by the liable person, Revenue will advise the employer, pension provider or the relevant government department of the amount to be deducted. Interest does not apply to phased payments.

13.4.3 *Deferral of LPT*

There are **no exemptions** from the payment of LPT. However, **deferral arrangements** are provided whereby a person may opt to defer, or partially defer, payment of the tax if certain conditions are met. Interest will be charged on LPT amounts deferred at a rate of **3%** per annum from 1 January 2022 (2021: 4%). The deferred amount, including interest, will attach to the property and will have to be paid before the property is sold or transferred.

There are four separate categories of deferral of LPT available:

1. Income Threshold
2. Personal Representative of a Deceased Person
3. Personal Insolvency
4. Hardship.

1. Income Threshold

The income threshold that determines whether a deferral may be claimed for a particular year is based on a person's **gross income** for the year. At the liability date for a year, i.e. 1 November 2021 for 2022, a claimant must estimate what their likely gross income will be for that year, i.e. the year in which the liability date falls and not the year the LPT payment is due. For example, an owner/occupier who wishes to claim a deferral for 2022 should estimate, on 1 November 2021, what their likely income will be for **2021**, not for 2022. Gross income is all income before any deductions, allowances or reliefs that are allowed to be deducted when calculating a person's taxable income for income tax purposes. It **includes** income that is exempt from income tax and income received from the Department of Social Protection, but **excludes** child benefit.

The standard income thresholds may be **increased** where a claimant pays **mortgage interest** but from **1 January 2022**, this is restricted to those liable persons who were previously eligible for the mortgage interest increased threshold, and is not available to owner-occupiers taking out a new mortgage loan.

The increase is limited to **80% of the gross interest** that is actually paid, or that is likely to be paid, in the year the liability date falls (not the year the LPT is payable). As with gross income, a claimant must estimate at the liability date the amount of mortgage interest that is likely to be paid by the end of the year.

A property for which deferral is claimed must be the **sole or main residence** of the claimant and deferral based on income thresholds is not available for landlords or second homes.

INCOME THRESHOLD CRITERIA (FROM 1 JANUARY 2022)

	Deferral Condition Number	Condition
Full Deferral	1	Gross income for the year unlikely to exceed **€18,000** (single or widow) and **€30,000** (couple).*
Full Deferral	2	Gross income for the year unlikely to exceed the **adjusted income** limit. This adjusted income limit is calculated by **increasing** the €18,000 (single or widow) and €30,000 (couple) thresholds by **80%** of the expected gross mortgage interest payments. This increase is limited to those already eligible for the deferral and not for new claimants.
Partial Deferral (50%)	3	Gross income for the year unlikely to exceed **€30,000** (single or widow) and **€42,000** (couple).

continued overleaf

	Deferral Condition Number	Condition
Partial Deferral (50%)	4	Gross income for the year unlikely to exceed the **adjusted income** limit. This adjusted income limit is calculated by increasing the €30,000 (single or widow) and €42,000 (couple)* thresholds by **80%** of the expected gross mortgage interest payments. This increase is limited to those already eligible for the deferral and not for new claimants.

A couple includes a married couple, civil partners and certain cohabitants. For LPT deferral purposes, the required period of cohabitation is at least two years where the couple have children or at least five years where they do not have children.

Example 13.5

Brinda Lisbon is a single owner-occupier of a residential property worth €380,000. As of 1 November 2021, Brinda earns €25,000 per annum and has projected gross mortgage interest payments of €6,500 for 2021. Brinda's local authority has not adjusted the LPT rate for 2022.

Her liability to LPT for 2022 is as follows:

Market value	€380,000
Valuation band number	04
Mid-point of valuation band	**€393,750**

LPT 2022:

€393,750 @ 0.1029%	€405

Brinda wishes to opt for a deferral of some or all her LPT as she is struggling to live within her income.

Full Deferral:

Gross income threshold (single person)	€18,000
Plus: Mortgage interest @ 80% (€6,500 × 80%)	€5,200
Adjusted income threshold	€23,200

Full deferral is not available as Brinda's gross income, €25,000 is greater than her adjusted income threshold, €23,200.

Partial Deferral:

Gross income threshold (single person)	€30,000
Plus: Mortgage interest @ 80% (€6,500 × 80%)	€5,200
Adjusted income threshold	€35,200

Brinda is entitled to a partial deferral as her gross income (€25,000) is less than her adjusted income threshold, €35,200.

For 2022 Brinda must pay LPT of €202.50 and can defer €202.50.

---

2. Personal Representative of a Deceased Liable Person (Deferral Condition Number 5)

Where a liable person who was the sole owner of a property dies, that person's personal representative may apply for a full deferral of LPT for a maximum period of three years commencing from the date of death.

3. Personal Insolvency (Deferral Condition Number 6)
A person who enters into any debt arrangement under the Personal Insolvency Act 2012 may apply for a deferral of LPT for the periods for which the insolvency arrangement is in place. The deferred LPT plus interest will become due when the particular insolvency arrangement ceases to have effect.

4. Hardship (Deferral Condition Number 7)
Where a liable person suffers an **unexpected** and **unavoidable** significant financial loss or expense within the current year and is unable to pay the LPT without causing excessive financial hardship, that person can apply for a full or partial deferral. Revenue will determine whether or not to grant a deferral (full or partial) but **will not** refund any payments made by the liable person up to that point.

To be considered for a deferral, the loss suffered by the liable person must reduce the remainder of their income to the **income threshold levels** at 1. above, **or**, the total loss suffered must be at least **20%** of their **gross income**. However, it does not follow that, if either or both conditions are met, deferral will be granted automatically. The onus is on the liable person to demonstrate that payment of the tax would cause **excessive financial hardship**.

13.5 Compliance

13.5.1 Penalties and Interest for Non-filing/Late payment

Penalty for non-filing of LPT1 Return
Where a liable person does not file a LPT return the penalty is the LPT due, subject to a maximum of €3,000.

Penalty for undervaluing property
Where a liable person **knowingly** undervalues their property for the purpose of calculating LPT due, the penalty is the correct amount of LPT, subject to a maximum of €3,000.

Interest Due on Late Payments
The rate of interest due on late payments (excluding amounts deferred and amounts payable under phased payments options) is **0.0219%** per day or part thereof (approximately 8% per year).

13.5.2 Additional Sanctions for Self-Assessed Taxpayers

- A self-assessed liable person who fails to submit a LPT return or to pay their LPT liability on time may incur a **surcharge** for the late submission of their **income tax return**, **regardless** of whether or not the income tax return is submitted on time. The surcharge amounts to 10% of the income tax liability.
- Where a self-assessed liable person fails to pay LPT, Revenue will not issue a **tax clearance certificate**.
- Where a self-assessed liable person fails to send back the LPT return form and the assessment of LPT liability, the tax set out in the Revenue estimate will be collected using normal collection/enforcement options – sheriff, court action, attachment orders, etc.
- Where LPT remains outstanding a charge will attach to that property. This charge will have to be discharged on the sale/transfer of the property.

13.6   Appeals

Where there is a disagreement between an individual and Revenue on matters relating to LPT, such as whether the property is residential, who the liable person is, disputed valuations, denial of deferrals etc. that cannot be resolved, Revenue will issue a formal **Notice of Assessment** or a formal decision or determination. The individual may appeal to:

- the Land Values Reference Committee in respect of valuation disputes; or.
- the Tax Appeals Commission against non-valuation disputes; and
- request a determination.

As with other self-assessed taxes, to appeal Revenue's assessment or decision the individual must have made an LPT return and paid the assessment of the tax due (even if this is disputed).

Questions

Review Questions
(See Suggested Solutions to Review Questions at the end of this textbook.)

Question 13.1

Bill and Frida are married and own and occupy their home in Wicklow. Their estimated gross income for 2021 is €42,000 and they expect that their gross mortgage interest payments for 2021 will be €6,000. They have no other properties. Bill and Frida's house was estimated to be valued at €560,000 at 1 November 2021.

Requirement
(a) Calculate the amount of LPT payable by Bill and Frida for 2022, assuming no local authority adjustment in 2022.
(b) Establish if Bill and Frida qualify for a deferral of LPT.

Question 13.2

Theo and Emer Rohan are a cohabiting couple who own their own home. They have two children for whom they receive child benefit. Their estimated income and expenses for 2021 are:

Income:

Gross Case I income	€35,000
Schedule E income	€13,500
Illness Benefit (DSP)	€10,491
Child Benefit	€3,360

Expenses:

Mortgage interest	€16,000

Theo had a serious accident and incurred unexpected medical expenses of €19,000 in 2021, for which he was not reimbursed.

Requirement
Calculate whether Theo and Emer can make a claim for deferral of LPT for 2022.

Question 13.3

Kevin Ryan's residential property, situated in Co. Mayo, was valued by an auctioneer as having a market value of €1,400,000 as of 1 November 2021.

Requirement
Calculate the amount of LPT payable in 2022.

Administration and Procedures

Learning Objectives

After studying this chapter you will understand:

- the special tax collection arrangements for certain activities – relevant contracts tax (RCT) and payments in respect of professional services; and
- how the Revenue Online Service (ROS) works, what returns are required to be filed electronically (mandatory e-filing), and the incentives for using ROS.

This chapter looks at the system for the administration of tax in the State through the use of the Revenue Online Service (ROS) for electronic filing, as well as the operation of specialist tax collection schemes for the construction sector (relevant contracts tax (RCT)) and in respect of certain professional services supplied (professional services withholding tax (PSWT)).

14.1 Relevant Contracts Tax

Relevant contracts tax (RCT) was introduced with the primary objective of reducing the perceived level of tax evasion by subcontractors in the construction, forestry and meat-processing industries. The RCT system is an electronic system, all communication between the principal contractor and Revenue being conducted online using ROS. Subcontractors are not obliged to register for ROS, but if they do they can view all transactions on their RCT account using eRCT.

14.1.1 General Scheme

The general rule is that a **"principal contractor"** is required to deduct RCT from payments made to subcontractors under a **"relevant contract"** at one of three rates **to be advised by Revenue**, as follows:

- **rate of 0%** will likely apply where a subcontractor is registered with Revenue and is fully tax compliant;
- **rate of 20%** will apply where a subcontractor is registered for tax and has a record of tax compliance; and
- **rate of 35%** will apply to subcontractors who are not registered with Revenue or where there are serious compliance issues to be addressed.

14.1.2 Operation of the RCT Scheme

Contract Notification

When a principal contractor enters into a relevant contract with a subcontractor, the principal contractor is obliged to provide Revenue, online, with details of the subcontractor and the contract, including a declaration that the contract is **not a contract of employment**.

Where the **tax reference number of the subcontractor is known, the contract notification** will include the following:

- subcontractor's name and tax reference number;
- details of the contract (i.e. sector, nature and location of work, start/end date, value of contract);
- details of the subcontractor's fixed place of business;
- details of whether the subcontractor will supply materials, plant and machinery;
- details of whether the subcontractor will provide their own insurance; and
- details of whether the subcontractor will engage other people to work on the contract at the subcontractor's own expense.

Where the tax reference number of the subcontractor is **not provided or is unknown**, the following details must be provided in addition to the information above:

- the subcontractor's address, date of birth, country, e-mail address, mobile and telephone numbers;
- if registered for tax outside Ireland, state the country and their tax registration number in that country; and
- details regarding the type of contractor, e.g. individual, company or partnership.

Payment Notification

Prior to making any payment under the contract, the principal contractor must notify Revenue, **online**, of their intention to make the payment and provide details of the gross amount to be paid.

Deduction Authorisation

On receipt of a payment notification Revenue will issue a deduction authorisation, which will detail the **rate of tax** and the **total amount of tax** to be deducted from the payment. The principal contractor can only pay the subcontractor in accordance with this notification and must provide a copy of the deduction authorisation to the subcontractor.

Deduction Summary

The deduction summary is created by Revenue from the payment notifications received from the principal contractor during the return period. Depending on the principal contractor's filing frequency, the summary will be available online to the principal contractor shortly after the end of the return period.

Payment of RCT Deducted

The principal contractor should check the deduction summary and make any amendments necessary and arrange for the RCT to be paid on or before the due date which, as electronic filers, will be the **23rd of the month** following the end of the return period. If the deduction summary is amended after the due date, the return will be late and a surcharge will apply.

For subcontractors any tax deducted will be credited against other tax liabilities which the subcontractor may have. Any excess will only be refunded after the tax return for the chargeable period has been filed and paid.

Penalties for Failing to Operate RCT Correctly

A principal contractor is obliged to deduct tax from payments to subcontractors in accordance with the **deduction authorisation** issued by Revenue.

Where a principal contractor fails to operate RCT on relevant payments to subcontractors, in each instance the principal contractor will be liable to the following penalties:

- Where the subcontractor is liable to an RCT deduction **rate of 0%**, the principal contractor will be liable to a **penalty of 3%** of the relevant payment.
- Where the subcontractor is liable to an RCT deduction **rate of 20%**, the principal contractor will be liable to a **penalty of 10%** of the relevant payment.
- Where the subcontractor is liable to an RCT deduction **rate of 35%**, the principal contractor will be liable to a **penalty of 20%** of the relevant payment.
- Where the subcontractor to whom the payment was made is not known to Revenue, the principal contractor will be liable to a **penalty of 35%** of the relevant payment.

In all the above instances, the principal contractor is required to submit an unreported payment notification to Revenue.

14.1.3   Definitions

Principal Contractor

A "principal contractor" is a person who takes on a subcontractor and who carries on a business in the construction, forestry or meat-processing industries. A local authority, government minister or any Board funded primarily by public money is also a principal contractor. **Note:** a principal contractor in the provision of construction services is subject to the VAT reverse charge rules (see **Section 21.9.5**).

Relevant Contract

A "relevant contract" is defined as a contract (not being a contract of employment) whereby a person is liable to another person:

1. to carry out relevant operations;
2. to be responsible for the carrying out of such operations by others; or
3. to furnish their own labour or the labour of others in the carrying out of such operations, or to arrange for the labour of others to be furnished for the carrying out of such operations.

Where a principal contractor engages the same subcontractor on various or multiple contracts, they will be required to notify each contract separately, unless the contracts can be considered to be part of one ongoing relevant contract with the subcontractor.

Relevant Operations

The main "relevant operations" are:

1. the construction, alteration, repair, extension, demolition or dismantling of buildings, including site preparation and haulage;
2. meat processing; and
3. forestry.

RCT applies to payments for relevant operations carried out within the Republic of Ireland and in designated areas of its continental shelf.

RCT does not apply where relevant operations are performed wholly abroad. If the contract is partly performed in the State and partly abroad, and if the foreign aspect of the contract is merely incidental, then the RCT is regarded as applying to the full contract.

14.2 Professional Services Withholding Tax

14.2.1 Introduction

Professional services withholding tax (PSWT) is a **tax of 20%** that is **deducted at source** from payments made by certain bodies in respect of professional services. PSWT is deducted by "**accountable persons**" from "**relevant payments**" made by them to "**specified persons**" in respect of "**professional services**".

Accountable Persons
For the purposes of PSWT, the following public bodies are "accountable persons":

- Government departments and offices;
- local authorities;
- the Health Service Executive;
- authorised health insurers; and
- commercial and non-commercial semi-State bodies and their subsidiaries.

A list of accountable persons is set out in Schedule 13 TCA 1997.

Relevant Payments
"Relevant payments" are payments made by accountable persons in respect of **professional services**. The payments need not be in respect of services provided to the accountable person. PSWT applies to the **entire payment**, including any element which is in respect of the reimbursement of expenses incurred by the specified person, **except** for stamp duties, Land Registry and Deed of Registration fees, Companies Office and Court fees. **VAT charged by the specified person should be excluded when calculating PSWT.**

Excluded Payments
PSWT should **not be** deducted from the following payments:

- payments which are subject to PAYE;
- payments which come within the RCT scheme;
- payments to other accountable persons:
  - in reimbursement of payments for professional services, **or**
  - where the income of the accountable person receiving the payment is exempt from income tax or corporation tax;
- payments to charities which have been granted an exemption from tax by the Revenue Commissioners; and
- where the payment is made by a foreign-based branch or agency of an accountable person to a person resident abroad.

Specified Persons
"Specified persons" are persons who provide professional services in respect of which relevant payments are made to them by accountable persons. Specified persons can be individuals, companies or partnerships and includes non-residents. PSWT deducted is available for **offset** against the specified person's final **income tax/corporation tax liability** for the period in which the relevant payment is charged to tax.

Tax Clearance

Suppliers of goods or services who enter into a public sector contract with a value of €10,000 (inclusive of VAT) or more, must produce a tax clearance certificate (see **Section 14.3**) to the public body with whom the contract is being entered into.

PSWT **must be deducted** from relevant payments made by an accountable person to a specified person, **irrespective** of the fact that the specified person produces a tax clearance certificate.

Professional Services

Section 520 TCA 1997 provides that professional services that are subject to PSWT include:

- services of a medical, dental, pharmaceutical, optical, aural or veterinary nature;
- services of an architectural, engineering, quantity surveying or surveying nature, and related services;
- services of accountancy, auditing or finance and services of financial, economic, marketing, advertising or other consultancies;
- services of a solicitor or barrister or other legal services;
- geological services; and
- training consultancy services, including advice on training requirements and syllabus design and development, but **excluding** teaching or lecturing services.

The above is not an exhaustive list. In some cases a service may not of itself attract PSWT, but where a service forms **part of a wider consultancy service**, it would then come within the scope of PSWT, e.g. where printing a brochure forms part of an overall professional service provided to an accountable person, it is an expense incurred in the **provision** of that service. The **full amount** of the payment (including the printing costs) in respect of the overall service is subject to PSWT.

Services that are not regarded as professional services for the purposes of PSWT include:

- teaching, training or lecturing services;
- translation services, including the services of an interpreter;
- proof-reading services;
- services of stenographers;
- setting and assessing oral, aural or written examinations;
- contract cleaning services; and
- maintenance and repair work.

14.2.2 Administration

Where a person provides professional services to an accountable person, they must supply the following to the accountable person:

1. their PPSN or corporation tax number; and
2. if the payment includes VAT, their VAT reference number.

If the specified person does not reside in the State or have a permanent establishment in the State, they must supply details of their country of residence and their tax reference number in that country.

When the specified person has supplied the above information, the accountable person must, when making a payment, complete **Form F45**, which contains the following information:

1. the name and address of the specified person;
2. the person's tax reference number;
3. the amount of the relevant payment;

4. the amount of PSWT deducted from the payment;
5. the date on which payment is made; and
6. the amount of VAT charged.

The specified person also gets a copy of the completed Form F45.

Form F45 must be issued in respect of **each relevant payment** made, including a relevant payment to a specified person who has not supplied their tax reference number. Only one Form F45 should ever be issued for a relevant payment. If a Form F45 issued to a specified person is lost or destroyed or where the details entered require amendment, **Form F43** can be issued by the accountable person.

The accountable person must make a monthly return (**Form F30**) to Revenue, declaring the total amount of PSWT deducted in that month. The return and payment of PSWT due must be made online within 23 days from the end of each income tax month. Where no PSWT is deducted by an accountable person in a month, a "NIL" return should be made. An **annual return (Form F35)** declaring the PSWT liability for a tax year must be returned online by 23 February following the end of the tax year.

14.2.3 Credit for PSWT

Credit will be given to the specified person for PSWT deducted (as confirmed in Form F45) against their income tax or corporation tax liabilities.

Income Tax

PSWT deducted in the basis period may be set against the income tax liability for that year of assessment. Any excess PSWT over and above the income tax liability will be refunded.

Where the basis period for two tax years overlap, the overlapping period is deemed to form part of the second tax year only.

Example 14.1

An individual commences to trade on 1 July 2021 and makes up accounts for the year ended 30 June 2022. The period 1 July to 31 December 2021 will form part of the basis period for the tax year 2021 and 2022. For PSWT purposes this period will be deemed to form part of the 2022 basis period only. Accordingly, credit for PSWT deducted from payments included in the period 1 July to 31 December 2021 will be given against the individual's tax liability for 2022.

Where a period falls into a gap between two basis periods, it is deemed to fall into the **later basis period**.

Example 14.2

An individual makes up accounts annually to 30 September. The individual ceases to trade on 30 June 2021. Actual profits for 2020 were less than those originally assessed; therefore, there is no revision of 2020 profits to actual. The period 1 October 2020 to 31 December 2020 does not form part of the basis period for 2020 or 2021. Credit will be given for PSWT deducted from payments relating to the period 1 October 2020 to 31 December 2020 against the individual's tax liability for 2021.

Where the PSWT deducted refers to two or more persons, for example in the case of a partnership, the PSWT suffered is apportioned in the partner profit-sharing ratios.

The taxpayer must submit Form F45, given to the taxpayer by the accountable person, when making a claim for an interim refund of PSWT (see below). Form F45 no longer needs to be submitted with the taxpayer's annual tax return, but they should be retained as they may be requested by Revenue for verification purposes at a later date.

Preliminary Tax

PSWT can be taken into account as a credit in computing the amount of tax **payable** for the year. However, PSWT deducted may not be treated as a payment (or part-payment) of the preliminary tax that is required to be paid directly to Revenue.

Example 14.3

Mary Burns estimates that her income tax liability for 2021 amounts to €54,000. She paid PSWT of €10,000 in 2021. Her figures for 2020 were as follows:

Income tax liability	€28,000
PSWT	€15,000

Calculation of Preliminary Tax for 2021:

Lower of:

Year 2021 @ 90% = (€54,000 – €10,000) @ 90%	€39,600 **or**
Year 2020 @ 100% = (€28,000 – €15,000) @ 100%	€13,000

Preliminary tax is calculated by reference to the net amount of tax payable after deducting PSWT.

14.2.4 Refunds of PSWT

Where a taxpayer considers that the amount of PSWT deducted from payments is in excess of their likely final liability to tax, an application may be made to the taxpayer's Revenue office for an interim refund of any excess, instead of waiting to have it credited against final liability. The application is made on **Form F50**.

Ongoing Business

An interim refund of PSWT may be given to a person who satisfies the following requirements:

1. the profits of the basis period for the tax year immediately preceding the tax year in question must have been finally determined;
2. the amount of tax due in respect of the tax year immediately preceding the tax year in question must have been paid; and
3. the individual must provide Form F45 in respect of the withholding tax reclaimed.

The amount of the interim refund that can be made is calculated as:

> Tax withheld, according to Form F45
> *Less*: tax liability for previous tax year
> *Less*: any outstanding VAT, PAYE or PRSI due by the individual.

Example 14.4

Jason makes up accounts to 30 September each year. In order for Jason to be able to claim a refund of tax withheld from receipts included in his accounts for the year ended 30 September 2021, he must have filed a return for 2020 and paid his tax liability for 2020. Jason files his return for 2020 on 31 October 2021 and pays the balance of tax due for 2020 on the same day.

During the year ended 30 September 2021, Jason received €128,000 after deduction of PSWT of €32,000 in respect of services provided during the year ended 30 September 2021. Provided that Jason has no arrears of VAT or PAYE, and has Form F45 in respect of the PSWT paid of €32,000, he may submit a claim for an interim refund of PSWT of €5,500, i.e. €32,000 – €26,500.

Commencing Businesses

Where an individual wishes to make a claim for an interim refund of PSWT in the year in which they commenced business, they do not have to satisfy requirements 1. and 2. above. Instead, the Inspector of Taxes may make an interim refund to the individual of 20% of an amount calculated using the following formula:

$$E \times \left(\frac{A}{B} \times \frac{C}{D} \right)$$

where:

A = the estimated amount of payments from which PSWT will be deducted to be included as income in the basis period for the tax year;

B = the estimated total receipts to be included in income in the basis period for the tax year;

C = the estimated number of months or fractions of months in the period in respect of which the claim is being made;

D = the estimated number of months or fractions of months in the basis period for the tax year; and

E = the estimated expenses to be incurred by the individual in the basis period for the tax year.

Example 14.5

John commences to trade on 1 June 2021. He intends to make up accounts annually to 31 December. His first set of accounts will be made up for the seven months to 31 December 2021. Up to 30 September 2021, he has received payments of €16,000, from which PSWT of €4,000 was deducted. It is estimated that his accounts for the seven months to 31 December 2021 will include income of €100,000 and expenses of €45,000. €40,000 of his total income will be paid under deduction of PSWT. In October 2021, he makes a claim for an interim refund of €2,057, calculated as follows:

$$20\% \times \left(€45,000 \times \frac{€40,000}{€100,000} \times \frac{4}{7} \right)$$

If the actual PSWT suffered was less than €2,057, his refund would be restricted to the amount of tax withheld.

Cases of Particular Hardship

Where an individual claims and proves particular hardship, Revenue can waive all or some of the conditions outlined above governing the payment of interim refunds. In such circumstances, the amount of the refund to be made to the individual is at the discretion of the Inspector of Taxes.

14.3 Tax Clearance

Tax clearance is a confirmation from Revenue that a person's tax and customs affairs are in order at the date of issue of the tax clearance certificate. Tax clearance is required in certain circumstances including, but not limited to, the following:

1. **Public Sector Contracts** The Department of Finance requires a contractor to produce a general tax clearance certificate in order to qualify for a public sector contract of a value of €10,000 or more (inclusive of VAT) within any 12-month period. Such contracts include the purchase, hiring and leasing of goods, services or property by public authorities. The tax clearance requirement applies even where the provision of goods or services is not the subject of a formal written contract.

2. **Grant Payments** An applicant must hold a general tax clearance certificate in order to qualify for State/public authority grants, subsidies and similar type payments of a value of €10,000 or more within any 12-month period.

3. **Licences and Certain Schemes** A current tax clearance certificate is required by law for the operation of certain types of business situations, for example, liquor, gaming or auctioneer's licences.
4. **Members of the Houses of the Oireachtas** The Standards in Public Office Act 2001 (SIPO) provides for a tax clearance requirement for members of the Dáil and Seanad.

If upon review a taxpayer is found to be non-compliant with their obligations, tax clearance can be **rescinded** or withdrawn.

14.3.1 eTax Clearance

An electronic tax clearance system **(eTC)** is in operation for the online processing of tax clearance applications, the issuing of certificates and for verification by third parties.

eTC is available to businesses, PAYE and non-resident taxpayers with a PPSN/tax reference number. The system provides new online application screens for business taxpayers using ROS and for PAYE taxpayers using myAccount. Taxpayers who are tax compliant will receive a Tax Clearance Access Number (TCAN) which, along with their PPSN/tax reference number, they give to a third party to enable that third party to verify their tax clearance through ROS.

eTC **does not** apply to Standards in Public Office applicants or those not registered for Irish tax (e.g. non-residents or community/voluntary groups). These applications require a paper tax clearance form to be submitted to the Collector-General's office.

14.4 Revenue Online Service (ROS)

14.4.1 Introduction

The Revenue Online Service (ROS) allows taxpayers or their agents to file tax returns, pay tax liabilities and access their tax details online. Some of the main features of ROS include the facility to:

- file returns and declarations online;
- make payments;
- calculate tax liabilities; and
- claim repayments.

ROS also provides taxpayers with access to their tax account information, including the facility to view details of returns filed and due, payments made, view and amend tax credits, etc.

14.4.2 Mandatory e-Filing

Companies, trusts, partnerships, the self-employed and taxpayers registered for VAT and PAYE are **required** to pay and file returns electronically. Some PAYE taxpayers availing of certain reliefs, such as pensions relief, are also required to pay and file **online**.

14.4.3 Online Returns

The following is a list of returns and tax liabilities (income tax, VAT and PAYE) that must be paid and filed using ROS (mandatory e-filing):

Tax Head	Specified Return	Specified Tax Liability
Partnership	Form 1 (Firms)	–
Income Tax	Form 11	Preliminary tax and balance due
High Earner Restriction	Form RR1	–
Employer PAYE	Payroll submissions under PAYE Modernisation	All amounts due under PAYE
Value-added Tax	Form VAT 3 Annual Return of Trading Details (RTD)	VAT due
	VAT on e-services Quarterly Return	Quarterly VAT due on e-services

The above list is not exhaustive as some other taxes, e.g. registered contractors tax (RCT), can **only** be filed and paid electronically.

An electronic version of **Form 12 (eForm 12)** is available through Revenue's myAccount facility. This allows a person whose main source of income is from a PAYE employment or pension to complete a return and claim tax credits, allowances and reliefs electronically.

The following services are also available through ROS:

▨ A facility for ROS business customers and agents to apply for and check if a tax clearance certificate is valid (eTax clearance).

▨ eRegistration allows the taxpayer to register for a new tax. A tax agent can also register a client for a certain tax or set up a link with a new client. A facility is also available to de-register for a tax head or as a tax agent for a client.

14.4.4   Off-line Returns

All returns are also available to upload to ROS. These have to be created off-line via the **ROS Off-line Application**, which has to be downloaded from ROS. Some of the returns can be created off-line using compatible third-party software. Once created and saved, these files can be **uploaded** to ROS.

14.4.5   Registration

In order to use ROS, the taxpayer must first **register** with the service.

Self-employed Individuals, Businesses and Practitioners
This is a three-step process, which is completed online on the ROS home page.

Step 1: Apply for a ROS Access Number (RAN)
The taxpayer enters one of their tax registration numbers. If an agent is applying for a RAN, they should enter their Tax Advisor Identification Number (TAIN). Revenue will post the ROS Access Number to the taxpayer at their registered address.

Step 2: Apply for a "Digital Certificate"
The taxpayer enters their RAN and registration number together with an e-mail address. Once processed by Revenue, a password will be generated and sent to the taxpayer by email or text. The taxpayer will use this password to retrieve their "digital certificate".

Step 3: Retrieve Digital Certificate

The taxpayer will enter their ROS system password (from Step 2 above), which is valid for one hour from the time it is sent, and install the digital certificate on their computer in a password-protected file. The taxpayer becomes a ROS customer once the digital certificate is installed.

Correspondence from ROS

A ROS customer will be provided with a secure ROS Inbox. Correspondence posted to this inbox includes reminders to file returns, copies of returns, statements of account and payment receipts. Customers are notified upon accessing ROS if there are any new items of correspondence that have not been viewed. Approaching the due date for filing relevant returns, ROS issues notification to file to customers and/or tax agents acting on behalf of customers. This notification is issued in the form of an e-mail to the designated e-mail address provided by the customer and/or tax agent.

Registering for myAccount

'myAccount' is Revenue's online service that allows non-ROS taxpayers access to a full range of services, including:

- PAYE services, including managing and reviewing their tax or adding a job or pension;
- eForm 12;
- local property tax (LPT); and
- the Help to Buy incentive.

In order to avail of the full range of myAccount services, the taxpayer will need to register and have their personal details verified. If the taxpayer is already registered for other business taxes with Revenue (e.g. VAT or self-employed income tax), they will not be able to access these with the myAccount registration. Instead they will require a ROS digital certificate.

14.4.6 Payments to Revenue

The RevPay service from Revenue is a method by which taxpayers can make certain tax payments online. ROS and myAccount users may pay their taxes by:

- **Debit/credit card** – payment is taken as soon as the transaction is authorised.
- A once-off debit known as a '**single debit instruction**' (SDI) drawn on a bank account (normally a current account) capable of accepting a direct debit. This can take up to seven days to be processed by the bank. If a taxpayer files their tax return early, Revenue **will not** debit the payment amount from the bank account **before** the due date for payment, provided the taxpayer specifies that date as the payment date.
- A **ROS debit instruction** (RDI) drawn on a bank account (normally a current account) capable of accepting a direct debit. The taxpayer determines the amount of the payment and when the payment is to be made. RDI does not confer on Revenue **any right** to take money from a taxpayer's bank account.
- A **direct debit instruction** (DDI) to make monthly payments to Revenue for current taxes.

14.4.7 Incentives for using ROS and myAccount

ROS taxpayers who are obliged to meet "pay and file" obligations for self-assessed income tax on 31 October 2021, will be entitled to have the due date extended to 17 November 2021 when they **file their**

2020 income tax return (Form 11) **and submit their payment online** using ROS for both the income tax balance due for 2020 and preliminary tax for 2021.

If the payment is specified online at any date before 17 November 2021, the taxpayer's bank account will not be debited until 17 November 2021, **provided** the taxpayer **specifies that date** as the payment date.

Note: the extended deadline for return and payment will only apply where the taxpayer files the Form 11 *and* makes the payment online, i.e. it is necessary to do both transactions online. Where only one of these actions is completed through ROS, the extension will not apply.

Taxpayers who pay or file by means **other** than ROS are required to submit both payments and returns on or before 31 October 2021.

Where a return and associated payment are not made electronically by the extended deadlines, the extended time limits will be disregarded so that, for example, any interest imposed for late payment will run from the former due dates and not the extended dates.

Questions

Review Questions
(See Suggested Solutions to Review Questions at the end of this textbook.)

Question 14.1

John Bricks is a self-employed carpenter who employs two full-time employees. John has recently been employed as a subcontractor on the building of a new office block by OMG Ltd. John is registered for VAT and for PAYE and is registered with ROS. For his accounting year ended 30 September 2021, John received the following Deduction Authorisations from OMG Ltd.

Date of Payment	Gross Payment	Net Payment	Deduction Amount	RCT Rate
	€	€	€	€
28/02/2021	20,000	16,000	4,000	20%
05/05/2021	19,500	15,600	3,900	20%
31/07/2021	12,500	10,000	2,500	20%
12/10/2021	28,950	23,160	5,790	20%

John estimates that his tax liability for accounts year ended 30 September 2021 is €5,500 and he owes €3,500 for VAT and €2,950 for PAYE as of that date. John wishes to make a claim for a repayment of RCT and has requested your assistance in processing his claim.

Requirement
Advise John of the position regarding income tax and relevant contracts tax paid.

Part Two

Corporation Tax

Corporation Tax: Introduction and General Principles

Learning Objectives

After studying this chapter you will understand:

- how to determine and apply the appropriate rate of corporation tax for each profit source;
- how to advise on and calculate corporation tax payments and reporting requirements of a company, depending on its size and accounting period; and
- the principles and conditions of the three-year tax exemption for start-up companies.

> Chartered Accountants Ireland's *Code of Ethics* applies to all aspects of a Chartered Accountant's professional life, including dealing with corporation tax issues. As outlined at the beginning of this book, further information regarding the principles in the *Code of Ethics* is set out in **Appendix 3**.
>
> Students should also be aware of the issues around tax planning, tax avoidance and tax evasion, which are discussed in **Appendix 4**.

15.1 Overview

Irish corporation tax is levied on the worldwide income of companies resident in Ireland for tax purposes and on the trading income of non-resident companies to the extent that it arises in Ireland. A non-resident company is liable to income tax on Irish-source income if it is not trading in the State through a branch or an agency.

Under the Taxes Consolidation Act 1997 (TCA 1997), corporation tax is charged on the income and chargeable gains that together constitute the **profits** of companies. The period for which corporation tax is charged is the **accounting period**. This is the period for which the company makes up its accounts but, for corporation tax purposes, an accounting period **cannot exceed 12 months,** but can be less than 12 months.

As with income tax, income and gains are classified according to **source**, which are defined by the Schedules in the TCA 1997. This stage is crucial because, depending on the income classification, different rules apply to the taxation of the income and the applicability of reliefs and deductions against it. For companies all transactions, irrespective of classification, are included in the financial statements.

15.2 Classification of Income and Gains

Under the Schedule system, the various sources of income and gains are classified as follows:

▦ **Schedule D**

- **Cases I and II:** Trading income and income from professions.
- **Case III:** Investment income and foreign income that has not suffered Irish tax at source.
- **Case IV:** Taxed Irish income and miscellaneous income.
- **Case V:** Rents and income from property in the Republic of Ireland.

▦ **Franked Investment Income (FII)**

- Distributions from most Irish resident companies.

▦ **Chargeable Gains**

- Capital disposals (excluding development land).

15.3 Rates of Corporation Tax

There are two different rates of corporation tax, depending on the classification of the income and gains:

1. **Trading rate of corporation tax @ 12.5%**
   This applies to the following income and gains:

   - Schedule D Case I and Case II profits;
   - capital gains (as adjusted); and
   - certain foreign dividends.

2. **Passive rate of corporation tax @ 25%**
   This applies to the following sources of income:

   - Case III income, i.e. foreign income and untaxed Irish interest (excluding certain foreign dividends taxable at 12.5%);
   - Case IV income, i.e. taxed Irish income and miscellaneous income not taxed under any other Case of Schedule D;
   - Case V income, i.e. Irish rental income; and
   - income from an "excepted trade".

Example 15.1
High-Rise DAC, a company involved in the construction of office buildings, has the following income for the year ended 31 December 2021:

	€
Case I – construction operations	800,000
Case III interest	20,000
Case V rental income	150,000
Total	970,000

continued overleaf

The corporation tax payable by High-Rise DAC is as follows:

	€
Case I: €800,000 @ 12.5%	100,000
Case III and Case V: €170,000 @ 25%	42,500
Total corporation tax payable	142,500

15.4 The Charge to Corporation Tax

The question of whether, and how, a company is to be charged to corporation tax depends on whether or not it is **resident** in the State.

15.4.1 Resident Company

In the case of a company resident in the State, the charge to corporation tax is imposed on all its income and chargeable gains (excluding gains on development land which are subject to CGT) **wherever** arising. A company is deemed to be tax resident in the State if it was **incorporated in Ireland** on or after 1 January 2015, unless it is treated as a tax resident company in another country under a double taxation agreement. A company incorporated in another country but **managed and controlled** in Ireland is resident in Ireland for tax purposes.

Example 15.2
Pants Ltd is a UK incorporated company that manufactures clothes in England, France and Germany. It has a warehouse and offices in Ireland and all directors' and shareholders' meetings take place in Ireland. It has the following sources of income:

- UK profits;
- French profits;
- German profits;
- New Zealand deposit interest; and
- rental income in the USA.

As the company's controlling body and management are located in Ireland, its place of residence is Ireland. **All** sources of profits are liable to Irish corporation tax.

15.4.2 Non-resident Company

A non-resident company is chargeable to corporation tax on any income attributable to the trade of a branch or agency in the State. For example, if a German resident company sets up a factory in Ireland, the German company would be liable to Irish corporation tax on any income or gains attributable to the Irish factory.

15.5 Payment of Corporation Tax

Corporation tax is assessed on the profits of companies for accounting periods. Accordingly, the concept of the basis period for income tax does not apply in the corporation tax system. The due dates for paying and filing corporation tax are determined by the date of the **accounting period**. Corporation tax includes not only the tax due on profits and chargeable gains but also any income tax payable.

A company, regardless of its size, is required to file its corporation tax return (Form CT1) electronically using ROS, and pay the balance of corporation tax by the 23rd day of the **ninth month after** the end of the accounting period. For example, a company with an accounting period ended 31 December 2021 must pay the balance of corporation tax and file its corporation tax return by 23 September 2022 (see **Section 15.7**).

15.6 Preliminary Tax

A company is required to pay preliminary tax **before** the end of the accounting period. The number of preliminary tax instalments, and the amount to be paid at each instalment, is based on whether the company is deemed to be a **large** or a **small** company for preliminary tax purposes for that particular accounting period.

15.6.1 Preliminary Tax: Small Companies

A company is deemed to be a small company for preliminary tax purposes if its "corresponding corporation tax liability for the preceding accounting period of a year" does **not exceed €200,000** (pro-rata where the accounting period is less than 12 months). Preliminary tax is payable in one instalment, **31 days** before the end of the accounting period, but not later than the **23rd day** of the preceding month.

The amount of preliminary tax payable is the lower of either:

- **90%** of the corporation tax liability of the company for the current accounting period; **or**
- **100%** of the corresponding corporation tax liability of the company for the preceding accounting period of same length.

Example 15.3

Acme DAC's corporation tax for the year ended 31 December 2021 is expected to be €120,000. Its liability for 2020 was €90,000.

As a small company, Acme's preliminary tax should be paid by 23 November 2021 and is calculated as the lower of:

90% current year: 2021	€108,000 **or**
100% preceding year: 2020	€90,000

Acme must pay the balance of the corporation tax due and file its CT1 return by 23 September 2022.

15.6.2 Preliminary Tax: Large Companies

A company is deemed to be a large company for preliminary tax purposes if its "corresponding corporation tax liability for the preceding accounting period of a year" **exceeds €200,000** (pro-rata where the accounting period is less than 12 months). Preliminary tax is payable in **two** instalments.

1. The **first instalment** is payable in the **sixth month** of the accounting period (e.g. 23 June for a company with calendar year accounts) and the amount payable is the **lower** of either:
   - **45%** of the corporation tax liability for the current accounting period; **or**
   - **50%** of the corresponding corporation tax liability of the preceding accounting period of same length.

2. The **second instalment** is payable in the **11th month** of the accounting period (e.g. 23 November for a company with calendar year accounts) and the amount payable should bring the total preliminary tax paid to **90%** of the **current** corporation tax liability.

Example 15.4

Geeno DAC's corporation tax for the year ended 31 December 2021 is expected to be €220,000. Its liability for 2020 was €230,000. As a large company, Geeno's preliminary tax should be paid in the following instalments:

1st instalment due 23 June 2021

	€
45% current liability (2021: €220,000 × 45%)	99,000 **or**
50% of preceding period (2020: €230,000 × 50%)	115,000

The lower amount should be paid, i.e. €99,000.

2nd instalment due 23 November 2021

90% of final liability for 2021 (€220,000 @ 90%)	198,000
Deduct: amount paid in the 1st instalment	(99,000)
Amount to be paid	99,000

Form CT1 must be filed and the balance of the corporation tax due, i.e. €32,000 (€230,000 – €99,000 – €99,000), must be paid by 23 September 2022.

Where the accounting period is less than **seven months**, preliminary tax of 90% of the current-year tax liability is payable in one instalment, as for small companies.

15.7 Corporation Tax Filing Requirements

15.7.1 Corporation Tax Return

A company must file its corporation tax return (Form CT1) using ROS by the 23rd day of the **ninth month after** the end of the accounting period. For example, a company with an accounting period ended 30 June 2021 must file its Form CT1 by 23 March 2022.

Companies that are dealt with by Revenue's Large Corporates Division are required to file their returns using iXBRL, a computer language that allows the presentation of financial information in a computer-readable format. iXBRL filing is also required for companies that do not satisfy **all** of the following criteria:

- the balance sheet total (i.e. aggregate assets before deduction of liabilities) of the company does not exceed **€4.4 million**;
- the turnover of the company does not exceed **€8.8 million**; and
- the average number of persons employed by the company does not exceed **50**.

Form CT1 must include a 'self-assessment', i.e. a statement that sets out the income, profits and gains of the company for the accounting period, the company's tax liability and the balance of tax payable. When Form CT1 is submitted, Revenue will issue an acknowledgement of the self-assessment submitted.

Where a company is in doubt as regards any matter to be included in a return, the company should specify the doubt in the return and retain supporting documentation to submit to Revenue if requested. If the company does this and the doubt is accepted as genuine, the company is regarded as having made a full and true return and accordingly is protected from the penalties that apply where a company fails to make a full and true return.

15.7.2 Country-by-Country (CbC) Reporting

There is an additional filing requirement for an Irish-resident parent company of a large multinational enterprise (MNE), i.e. one where consolidated turnover **exceeds €750** million in the preceding accounting period. The parent company is required to provide a country-by-country (CbC) report to Revenue within 12 months of the fiscal year end for **each tax jurisdiction** in which it does business.

The CbC report is based on guidance published in the OECD/G20 Action Plan on Base Erosion and Profit Shifting (BEPS). The report must contain details of the MNE's revenue, profit before income tax and income tax paid, income tax accrued, stated capital, accumulated earnings, number of employees and tangible assets in each tax jurisdiction. It also requires the tax identification numbers of all entities within the MNE, each company's tax residence and an indication of the business activities engaged in by each entity. Revenue will share the report with other tax administrations under mandatory automatic exchange of information provisions.

15.8 Interest Payable and Late Filing Surcharges

15.8.1 Interest on Overdue Corporation Tax

If there is a default in payment of corporation tax, interest is charged at **0.0219%** per day or part of a day (approximately 8% per annum). Interest on late payment of tax is not tax deductible. Where a **small company** defaults in the payment of preliminary tax, does not pay sufficient preliminary tax or does not pay its preliminary tax by the due date, interest is calculated on the **total** of the corporation tax for that accounting period. This total is deemed to be due on the date the preliminary tax was due, but on the **21st** day rather than the 23rd day of the month.

Example 15.5
Dimm DAC has a corporation tax liability of €20,000 for the year ended 31 December 2021. It paid no preliminary tax but paid its entire corporation tax liability on 23 September 2022.

The company will have an interest liability on the total of €20,000 deemed due on 21 November 2021, calculated as follows:

€20,000 × 0.0219% × 306 days = €1,340

Where a **large company** defaults in the payment of preliminary tax, does not pay sufficient preliminary tax or does not pay its preliminary tax by the due date, interest on late payment arises at 0.0219% per day or part of a day. A proportion, **45%**, of the corporation tax liability for that accounting period is deemed to be due on the 21st day of the month the first preliminary tax instalment was due. The remaining **55%** of its corporation tax liability is deemed due on the 21st day of the month its second instalment of preliminary tax was due.

Example 15.6
Dimmer DAC, a large company, has a corporation tax liability of €250,000 for the year ended 31 December 2021. The company paid its entire liability on 31 December 2021 rather than paying €112,500 (45%) on 23 June 2021, paying €112,500 (45%) on 23 November 2021 and €25,000 at 23 September 2022.

Although the whole tax liability was discharged by 31 December 2021, even though €25,000 was not payable until September 2022, because Dimmer DAC did not make any preliminary tax payment, the following situation arises:

continued overleaf

- 45% of the full corporation tax liability of €250,000 is deemed due and unpaid at 21 June 2021 (€112,500); and
- 55% (€137,500) is deemed due and unpaid from 21 November 2021.

The company will therefore have an interest liability on the late payment of corporation tax as follows:

Deemed due 21 June 2021:
€112,500 @ 0.0219% × 193 days (to 31 December 2021)   €4,755

Deemed due on 21 November 2021:
€137,500 @ 0.0219% × 40 days (to 31 December 2021)   <u>€1,205</u>

   Total interest liability   **€5,960**

15.8.2 Late Filing Penalties and Surcharges

Surcharge for Late Filing of Corporation Tax Return

If Form CT1 is filed within two months after the due filing date, the surcharge is 5% of the tax due for the period, subject to a maximum of €12,695. If the delay is two months or more, the surcharge is 10%, subject to a maximum of €63,485.

Example 15.7

A company had a tax-adjusted Case I profit of €500,000 for the year ended 31 December 2021. If Form CT1 is filed within nine months, i.e. by 23 September 2022, the tax liability is €62,500, i.e. €500,000 @ 12.5%.

If Form CT1 is not filed until 10 October 2022, the liability is €65,625 (€62,500 + €3,125) (5% surcharge).

If Form CT1 were not filed until 1 December 2022, the liability would be €68,750 (€62,500 + €6,250) (10% surcharge).

The surcharge payable is treated as part of the company's corporation tax liability for the accounting period, which could mean that as a result of having to pay a surcharge the company has underpaid its preliminary tax and so could be liable for interest charges (see **Section 15.8.1**).

Penalty for Non-filing of Corporation Tax Return

The fixed penalty for a company not making a corporation tax return is €2,000, rising to €4,000 in certain circumstances.

Penalty for Late Filing of Country-by-Country Return

Under the legislation, Revenue may impose a penalty for failure to make a country-by-country (CbC) return, or where an incorrect or incomplete CbC return is filed. The penalty is €19,045, plus €2,535 for each day the failure continues.

15.9 Interest on Overpayment of Corporation Tax

Interest is paid by Revenue at **0.011% per day** or part thereof (4.015% per annum) on overpaid tax. Under the legislation, the date from which interest runs will depend on whether the overpayment is as a result of a mistake made by Revenue or by the taxpayer. Where the overpayment arises because of a mistaken assumption by Revenue in the application of tax law, interest is payable from the day after the end of the accounting period to which the repayment relates or, if later, when the tax was overpaid, until the date the repayment is made. A claim for repayment must be made to Revenue within four years of the end of the period to which it relates.

Where the overpayment **does not arise** because of a mistaken application of the law by Revenue, the overpayment will only carry interest for the period beginning on the day which is **93 days** after the day on which a "valid claim" for repayment has been filed with Revenue. A valid claim is one where all the information Revenue might reasonably require to enable it to determine if and to what extent a repayment is due has been provided to Revenue.

Interest on the overpayment of tax is **not subject** to withholding tax and is **exempt** from tax. Interest will not be paid where the overall amount due is less than €10.

15.10 Three-year Tax Exemption for Start-up Companies

15.10.1 Overview

Section 486C TCA 1997 provides relief from corporation tax for new companies (including companies incorporated in the United Kingdom) commencing to trade in the period **1 January 2009 to 31 December 2021**. The exemption is granted in respect of the profits of a new trade and chargeable gains on the disposal of any assets used for the purposes of a new trade, subject to the following limits:

- **full relief** is granted where the total amount of corporation tax payable by a company for a 12-month accounting period **does not exceed €40,000**; **or**
- **partial relief** is granted where the total amount of corporation tax payable by a new company for a 12-month accounting period exceeds **€40,000** but **does not exceed €60,000**.

However, both full and partial reliefs are limited to the total amount of Employers PRSI paid for accounting period commencing on or after 1 January 2011 (see below). In addition

- **No relief** applies where corporation tax payable **exceeds €60,000**.
- The exemption is available for a period of **three years** from the commencement of the new trade and separate exemptions are available for each new trade.

15.10.2 Qualifying and Non-qualifying Trades

A qualifying trade, for the purposes of this exemption, means a trade that is set up and commenced by a new company in the period 1 January 2009 to 31 December 2021.

A non-qualifying trade is a trade:

- that was previously carried on by another person. This means that where a sole trader transfers a business to a new company, the company cannot avail of this exemption on income from this trade;
- that is an "excepted trade", i.e. land development or exploration and extraction of petroleum or minerals;
- that is a professional service company;
- the activities of which are excluded due to an EU Regulation on state aid (e.g. certain fishery, agricultural, transport, coal and export activities).

15.10.3 Calculation of Relief

The relief applies to corporation tax:

1. payable by the company for an accounting period in respect of income from the **qualifying trade** for that accounting period (broadly, income taxed at 12.5%); **and**

2. payable in respect of chargeable gains on the disposal of qualifying assets in relation to the trade. Qualifying assets are assets (including goodwill but not investments) used for the new trade.

Limit on Relief – Employers' PRSI

Where the amount of qualifying Employers' PRSI paid by a company in an accounting period is **less** than the corporation tax on the income and gains of the new trade, the relief is restricted to the total Employer's PRSI, subject to a **limit of €5,000** for each employee, or a **total** PRSI limit of **€40,000**.

Effective from **1 January 2013**, where a company has an excess of Employers' PRSI contributions over corporation tax payable in the first three years, the excess may be **carried forward** to the fourth year and claimed then or in later years, subject to having sufficient Employers' PRSI paid in that year.

Example 15.8

Start-UP DAC was incorporated on 1 November 2020 and commenced to trade on 1 January 2021. Trading income for the year ended 31 December 2021 is €100,000.

The company paid the following Employers' PRSI:

Employee 1	€2,000
Employee 2	€4,000
Employee 3	€6,000

Calculation:

	€	€
Corporation tax payable (€100,000 @ 12.5%)		12,500
Specified contributions		
Employee 1	2,000	
Employee 2	4,000	
Employee 3 (maximum)	5,000	
Total specified contributions	11,000	
Relief limited to		(11,000)
Corporation tax payable		**1,500**

As Start-UP DAC commenced to trade on 1 January 2021, the exemption applies for 2021, 2022 and 2023. The company will not be entitled to the exemption in 2024.

15.10.4 Carry Forward of Relief to Years After the Qualifying Relevant Period

Many companies may not have sufficient corporation tax payable in the first three years of trading to utilise the total Employer's PRSI paid during those years due to losses or very low trading profits.

Effective from 1 January 2013, where a company qualifies for **full exemption** from corporation tax on the new trade but total Employers' PRSI exceeds the relevant corporation tax, this excess can be used to reduce the company's corporation tax liability in the fourth (and subsequent) year of trading, provided sufficient Employers' PRSI has been paid in those years also.

Example 15.9

Get-Up DAC was incorporated on 11 November 2020 and commenced its retail trade on 1 January 2021. It has the following profits and qualifying Employers' PRSI:

	2021	2022	2023	2024	2025
	€	€	€	€	€
Trading profits	14,000	12,000	70,000	100,000	115,000
Qualifying Employers' PRSI	10,000	10,000	10,500	11,000	12,000

The start-up relief available to Get-Up DAC is calculated as follows:

	2021	2022	2023	2024	2025
	€	€	€	€	€
Trading profits	14,000	12,000	70,000	100,000	115,000
Corporation tax @ 12.5%	1,750	1,500	8,750	12,500	14,375
Qualifying Employers' PRSI	10,000	10,000	10,500	11,000	7,500
Tax due after relief applied	0	0	0	1,500	6,875
Unused relief	8,250	8,500	1,750	-	-
Unused relief cumulative	8,250	16,750	18,500	7,500	0

Notes:

1. As all the conditions for the start-up exemption are satisfied and qualifying Employers' PRSI is greater than the corporation tax for each of the first three years, the company has no corporation tax to pay and it has the excess Employers' PRSI to carry forward to the fourth year or later (2024 or later).
2. While €18,500 is available for carry forward to 2024 and the corporation tax on trading income is €12,500, the claim in 2024 cannot exceed the qualifying Employers' PRSI for that year of €11,000. The unclaimed amount of €7,500 is carried forward to 2025.

Where a company claims partial relief (i.e. corporation tax between €40,000 and €60,000) excess Employers' PRSI can also be carried forward.

Questions

Review Questions
(See Suggested Solutions to Review Questions at the end of this textbook.)

Question 15.1

The Willis brothers own and manage Lemmon DAC, a distribution company, which prepares accounts annually to 31 December. In January 2021 it decided to change its accounting date to 28 February and accordingly a 14-month set of accounts was made up to 28 February 2022.

The brothers also own a property rental company, Rentco Ltd, whose year-end is 31 December. On 1 August 2021 the Willis brothers acquired all the share capital of another distribution company, Yann DAC.

Results for the three companies, as adjusted for tax purposes, are as follows:

	Lemmon 14 months ended 28/02/2022	Rentco Year ended 31/12/2021	Yann 8 months ended 31/03/2022
	€	€	€
Schedule D Case I	308,000	–	20,000
Schedule D Case III (Note 1)	5,000	–	–
Schedule D Case V	–	50,000	–
Chargeable gain (as adjusted for corporation tax)	5,156	–	–

Note

1. Case III income received: €3,000 on 31 December 2021; and €2,000 on 28 February 2022.

Requirement
(a) Calculate the corporation tax liabilities for all three companies for the above accounting periods.
(b) State the latest date by which all corporation tax liabilities are to be paid (assuming that all the companies are "small") and the dates by which returns must be filed for the above periods.

Corporation Tax Computation

16.1 Overview

Corporation tax is charged on the total profits of a company for an accounting period, i.e. on the income and gains contained in its financial statements for the accounting period. The basic rule for the calculation of income is that, apart from certain special provisions relevant only to companies, it is to be computed in accordance with **income tax principles**. The computation will therefore be made for each class of income under the same Schedules and Cases as apply for income tax purposes (see **Part One**). CGT principles, as covered in **Part Three** of this book, supplemented by some company-specific provisions, apply to the calculation of chargeable gains.

16.2 Schedule D, Cases I and II Income – Trading Income

A company carrying on a trade or profession will prepare financial statements, based on accounting principles, to arrive at profit before tax for a particular accounting period. However, as previously noted, the accounting profit before tax is not necessarily the taxable Case I or Case II income as this may require adjustment to arrive at the tax-adjusted Case I or Case II profits for corporation tax purposes.

In calculating Case I and Case II profits, income earned is included on an **accruals basis**. Two fundamental principles in deciding whether an item is included when calculating Case I and Case II adjusted profits apply:

1. If an item is of a capital nature it must be disallowed.
2. Even if an item is of a revenue nature, it may be specifically disallowed by statute.

16.2.1 Income and Gains Not Taxable under Cases I and II

In accordance with the aforementioned fundamental principles, the following items are not taxable under Cases I and II for corporation tax purposes:

▧ Grants – most employment grants and capital grants paid by State bodies are exempt from corporation tax.
▧ Interest on tax overpaid is specifically exempt from corporation tax.
▧ Investment income – interest, royalties and dividends are assessed under Case III or Case IV. Irish dividends (franked investment income) are exempt.
▧ Rental income is assessed under Case V; foreign rental income is assessed under Case III.
▧ Profits/gains on disposal of non-current assets (e.g. property or shares) are ignored when calculating the adjusted Case I and Case II profits. Chargeable gains are assessed to corporation tax (as outlined in **Section 16.6**) unless they relate to the disposal of development land, in which case CGT applies.

16.2.2 Capital Expenditure and Losses

Capital expenditure and losses are not deductible when calculating the adjusted Case I and Case II profit. Therefore, depreciation, purchase of non-current assets and related expenses (e.g. legal fees), improvements to premises, losses on disposal of non-current assets and related expenses and finance lease interest charges must be added back.

The income tax scheme of capital allowances and balancing charges is brought into the corporation tax system (see **Chapter 4**). However, **capital allowances** due to trading companies are **treated as trading expenses** for corporation tax purposes and not as a deduction from the assessable income as in the case of income tax. Similarly, balancing charges are treated for corporation tax purposes as trading receipts. Furthermore, the capital allowances are calculated by reference to assets in use/expenditure incurred in each accounting period. Capital allowances in respect of intangible assets (e.g. patents, trademarks) are discussed in **Section 16.2.4**.

16.2.3 Allowable and Disallowable Items under Cases I and II

As with income tax, the main statutory provision disallowing expenditure is section 81 TCA 1997. Expenditure not **wholly and exclusively** laid out for the purpose of the trade is disallowed, including:

▧ political donations;
▧ fines, penalties and interest for late payment of tax;
▧ payments from which tax is deducted (e.g. patent royalties). These may be allowed as a charge (see **Chapter 17**).

Treatment of Certain Specific Items
The rules around allowable and disallowable items are identical to those for income tax purposes (see **Sections 3.3.5** and **3.3.6**). Other items, specific to corporation tax, are detailed below.

Donations
Companies are entitled to a deduction, as a trading expense, for qualifying donations to eligible charities, educational institutions, schools, churches, research foundations and other approved organisations that satisfy certain conditions. The eligible organisation can be established anywhere in the European Economic Area (EEA) or the European Free Trade Association. Similarly, donations to an approved sports body (in the State) to enable it to purchase, construct or improve facilities and/or equipment are eligible. To qualify for a tax deduction, the donation to an organisation or sports body in a 12-month accounting

period must amount to at least €250. If the accounting period is less than 12 months, the €250 minimum is proportionately reduced. There is no upper limit.

Directors: Salaries and Company Cars

Bona fide directors' salaries, fees and benefits payable for directors are deductible, unlike the drawings/ salary of a self-employed person. Such income is, of course, assessable in the hands of the individual director under Schedule E. Remuneration paid to directors is tax deductible, provided that it is not excessive.

Where a director has a company car available for private use, the full amount of motor expenses (other than restricted leased motor charges) is deductible. There is no deduction for the "personal element" for corporation tax purposes, unlike the personal element of a self-employed person. Again, a director with the use of a company car for private purposes will suffer tax on the benefit in kind.

Transfer Pricing

The legislation sets out the transfer pricing rules that apply the arm's length principle to trading transactions between associated persons. In the absence of these rules, associated companies all over the world could buy and sell goods/services from each other at prices that maximise their taxable profits in low-tax jurisdictions and minimise their profits in high-tax jurisdictions.

Companies are **associated** if one controls the other, or both are controlled by the same person. Transfer pricing **does not apply** to groups that:

- employ less than 250 employees; and
- have a turnover not exceeding €50 million; or
- total assets not exceeding €43 million.

In Ireland, the transfer pricing rules apply to trading and, effective from 1 January 2020, non-trading transactions between associated companies that result in the understatement of Case I and Case II income for Irish corporation tax purposes. If the amount payable exceeds the arm's length amount, or the amount receivable is less than the arm's length amount, then the Case I and Case II profits must be adjusted to reflect the arm's length amount.

Example 16.1

Clifden DAC sells goods to its subsidiary, Evergreen Ltd, at a price of €250 per unit. The arm's length price would have been €380 per unit. During the accounting period ended 31 December 2021, Clifden sold 1,000 of these items to Evergreen Ltd.

A transfer pricing adjustment is made on the basis that the arm's length price was not received. As a result, Clifden's taxable income for corporation tax is increased by €130,000 (1,000 units × (€380 – €250)) as its profit was originally understated for tax purposes.

Evergreen Ltd can adjust its allowable expenditure, reducing its taxable profit by €130,000 to reflect the arm's length price.

It is necessary to retain records that may reasonably be required to determine whether or not an arrangement exists for transfer pricing purposes.

16.2.4 Capital Allowances

Items of a capital nature are not deductible for corporation tax purposes. This means that, when arriving at the tax-adjusted trading profits of a business, depreciation for accounting purposes is specifically disallowed and is added back to the net profit or loss. This, therefore, may deny a business a tax deduction for the depreciation or amortisation of capital expenditure used in the generation of taxable income. To offset this, companies can claim a capital allowances deduction for the net cost of certain capital assets employed for the purposes of the business or trade. The calculation of capital allowances is considered in detail in **Chapter 4**.

Tangible Assets

In summary, a company can claim capital allowances at the following rates:

- Plant and machinery (including motor vehicles) at **12.5% straight line**.
- Qualifying industrial buildings at **4% straight line**.
- Accelerated Capital Allowances (ACA) of **100%** can be claimed for the following:
  - energy-efficient equipment including electric and alternative fuel vehicles;
  - gas vehicles and refuelling equipment;
  - equipment in a crèche or gym provided by the company for its employees.
- A company can also claim capital allowances at a rate of **15%** over seven years on the cost of a building used as a crèche or gym by its employees.

Intangible Assets

Intangible assets or intellectual property includes patents, registered designs, trademarks, brands, copyrights, domain names, customer lists, know-how and related goodwill.

Section 291A TCA 1997 allows for capital allowances against taxable income on capital expenditure incurred by companies on the provision of intangible assets for the purposes of a trade. If the expenditure is incurred before trading commences, it will be allowed when the relevant trade commences.

An asset may only be recognised as an intangible asset in the financial statements if:

- the cost of the asset can be reliably **measured**; **and**
- it is probable that future economic benefits attributable to the asset **will flow to the company**.

The writing-down allowance available can be either:

- the standard accounting treatment of the amortisation of the intangible asset; **or**
- a fixed write-down period of 15 years at a rate of **7% per annum and 2% in the final year**.

The aggregate amount of capital allowances and related interest that may be claimed in any accounting period is limited to **80% of the trading income** of the relevant trade where the asset is acquired **after 11 October 2017**, or limited to the trading income of the relevant trade if acquired before that date. Related interest in this context is interest incurred as a trading expense on borrowings to fund expenditure on intangible assets for which capital allowances are claimed.

Example 16.2		
	Example 1	Example 2
	€m	€m
Income from relevant trade before allowances	10	15
Capital allowances available under scheme	11	10
Allowances carried forward from previous accounting period	NIL	4
Computation of income		
Income from relevant trade before allowances	10	15
Deduct: Capital allowances (max. 80%)	(8)	(12)
Income chargeable	2	3
Allowances carried forward to next accounting period	3	2

16.2.5   *Cases I and II Loss Relief*

Relief for Trading Losses (other than Terminal Losses)
Where a company incurs a trading loss, it may obtain relief from corporation tax as follows:

1.   By set-off against relevant trading income, on a euro-for-euro basis (section 396A TCA 1997):

  (a) in the **same** accounting period; and
  (b) in the immediately **preceding** period of the same length.

Example 16.3
DEF Ltd, a distribution company, had the following results for the years ended 31 December 2020 and 2021.

	2020	2021
	€	€
Case I profit/(loss)	30,000	(55,000)
Corporation tax computation		
Taxable income (Case I)	30,000	Nil
Less: section 396A relief	(30,000)	=
Taxable income	Nil	Nil
Loss forward		(25,000)

---

2.   By claiming relief for the loss against **non-trading income** on a value basis (section 396B TCA 1997):

  (a) in the same accounting period; and
  (b) in the immediaetely preceding period of the same length.

Example 16.4
As **Example 16.3**, but with non-trading income of €10,000.

	2020	2021
	€	€
Case I profit/(loss)	30,000	(55,000)
Case V income	10,000	8,000
Corporation tax computation		
Taxable income (Case I)	30,000	Nil
Less: section 396A relief	(30,000)	=
Taxable income	Nil	Nil
Case V income	10,000	8,000
Corporation tax @ 25%	2,500	2,000
Less: section 396B relief (Note 1)	(1,125)	(2,000)
Corporation tax payable	1,375	Nil

continued overleaf

Note 1. Loss available for relief on a value basis:

	€
Total loss 2021	55,000
2020 relief under section 396A	(30,000)
Loss available for relief under section 396B	25,000
Tax value of losses: €25,000 @ 12.5%	3,125
Section 396B claim – 2021: €8,000 @ 25%	(2,000)
	1,125
Section 396B claim – 2020: balance	(1,125)
Remaining tax value	**Nil**

---

3. Any unused trading losses can be carried forward again **trading profits** in future periods and utilised at the first opportunity (section 396(1) TCA 1997).

Example 16.5
ABC Ltd, a distribution company, had the following results for the years ended 31 December 2020 and 2021.

	2020	2021
	€	€
Case I profit/(loss)	(50,000)	60,000
Corporation tax computation		
Taxable income (Case I)	Nil	60,000
Less: section 396(1) relief	–	(50,000)
Taxable income	Nil	10,000
Corporation tax payable @12.5%	Nil	1,250

A section 396A claim must be made before a claim under section 396B and the claim for loss relief under these sections must be made within **two years** of the end of the accounting period in which the loss occurs. There is no time limit for claiming section 396(1) loss relief as the loss can be carried forward indefinitely.

A loss forward must be set-off against the first available income of the same trade for an earlier future accounting period in priority to a later future accounting period (i.e. a future accounting period cannot be skipped). When carried forward, a section 396(1) loss is deducted from the income from the same trade in priority to any section 396A loss.

If the accounting period in which the loss is incurred is shorter than the accounting period to which the loss is to be offset, then only a proportion of the relevant trading income will be available for offset.

Example 16.6: Accounting periods of different lengths

MNO Ltd, a distribution company, had the following results for the year ended 31 March 2020, the nine months ended 31 December 2020 and for the year ended 31 December 2021.

	Year ended 31/03/20 (12 months)	Period ended 31/12/20 (9 months)	Year ended 31/12/21 (12 months)
	€	€	€
Case I profit/(loss)	30,000	20,000	(60,000)
Corporation tax computation:			
Taxable income (Case I)	30,000	20,000	Nil
Less: section 396A relief (Note)	(7,500)	(20,000)	–
Taxable income	22,500	Nil	Nil
Loss forward			32,500

Note: as the loss-making period was 12 months long, the loss can only be offset against a 12-month period. As the immediately preceding accounting period was nine months long, relevant trading income for three months only of the previous accounting period can be relieved, i.e. 3/12ths of Case I income for the year ended 31 March 2020.

The remaining loss of €32,500 may be carried forward against future profits from the same trade, or used on the value basis if the company has non-trading income in the current or preceding period of equal length.

Relief for Terminal Losses

When a company ceases to trade a carry forward of unutilised trading losses is not possible and a company may therefore claim **terminal loss relief** under section 397 TCA 1997. Any trading losses incurred in the final 12 months of trading, which have not otherwise been used (against trading income or on a value basis), can be set against trading income of the same trade for the **36 months** preceding the final 12-month period.

In calculating terminal loss relief, charges paid wholly and exclusively for the purposes of the trade (i.e. relevant trade charges) in the final 12 months of trading are included in the terminal loss claim, to the extent that they have not already been claimed. The terminal loss is to be set against income of a later period in priority to an earlier period and is not to displace relief already given for losses carried forward from earlier periods.

Example 16.7

Bust-up DAC ceases to trade on 31 December 2021. The accounts show the following results:

	Trading profit/(loss)	Other income
	€	€
Year to 31 December 2017	14,000	1,600
Year to 31 December 2018	12,000	3,000
Year to 31 December 2019	10,000	2,000
Year to 31 December 2020	19,000	2,560
Year to 31 December 2021	(75,000)	3,840

continued overleaf

A loss can only be utilised as a terminal loss if it has not or cannot be otherwise relieved. The loss for the year to 31 December 2020 can be relieved as follows:

	€
By set-off 2020 (section 396A):	
Against trading profits of the preceding accounting period to 31/12/2020	19,000
On a value basis 2021 (section 396B):	
Against corporation tax – €3,840 @ 25% = €960	
Loss used €7,680 @ 12.5% = €960	7,680
On a value basis 2020 (section 396B):	
Against corporation tax – €2,560 @ 25% = €640	
Loss used €5,120 @ 12.5% = €640	5,120
Loss used	31,800

The unrelieved loss of the accounting period is thus €43,200 (i.e. €75,000 – €31,800).

Terminal loss relief (section 397):
Available for three-year period commencing on 01/01/2018 and ending on 31/12/2020:

	€
1. Trading income of the accounting period to 31/12/2020 (already relieved)	Nil
2. Trading income of the accounting period to 31/12/2019	10,000
3. Trading income of the accounting period to 31/12/2018	12,000
	22,000

The balance of the loss, i.e. €21,200 (€43,200 – €22,000), cannot be relieved in any way.

Restriction of Loss Relief on Late Submission of Returns

The due date for filing company accounts to Revenue is within nine months after the end of the accounting period, provided no later than day 23 of that month.

If a company fails to submit its income return on or before the specified return date, then claims to offset trading losses against trading income, or on a value basis, are reduced by the following:

- If the delay is **greater** than two months – **reduction of 50%** subject to a maximum of €158,715 in each case.
- If the delay in filing a return is **less than** two months – **reduction of 25%** subject to a maximum amount restricted of €31,740.

Example 16.8
HIJ Ltd had the following results for the years ended 31 December 2020 and 2021:

	2020	2021
	€	€
Case I profit/(loss)	60,000	(100,000)
Case V income	45,000	50,000

continued overleaf

	2020	2021
	€	€
Corporation tax computation:		
Case I	60,000	Nil
Less: section 396A relief	(60,000)	–
Taxable Case I income	Nil	Nil
Case V income	45,000	50,000
Taxable profits	45,000	50,000
Corporation tax @ 12.5% – Case I	Nil	Nil
Corporation tax @ 25% – Case V	11,250	12,500
Less: section 396B relief on a value basis (Note)	–	(5,000)
Corporation tax payable	11,250	7,500

Note: €100,000 – €60,000 = €40,000 @ 12.5% = €5,000.

If HIJ Ltd files its return **more than two months** after the due date for filing its return, relief under sections 396A and 396B will be restricted as follows:

	2020	2021
	€	€
Case I profit/(loss)	60,000	(100,000)
Case V income	45,000	50,000
Corporation tax computation		
Case I	60,000	Nil
Less: section 396A relief @ 50% (Note 1)	(30,000)	–
Taxable Case I income	30,000	Nil
Case V income	45,000	50,000
Taxable profits	75,000	50,000
Corporation tax @ 12.5% - Case I	3,750	Nil
Corporation tax @ 25% - Case V	11,250	12,500
Less: section 396B relief on a value basis (Note 2)	–	–
Corporation tax payable	15,000	12,500

Notes:

1. Relief under section 396A: reduction in profits because of relief is restricted to 50%.
2. Relief under section 396B: the trading loss is reduced by 50% (€100,000 × 50% = €50,000). Then from this must be deducted the claim which could have been made under section 396A if the return had been filed on time, i.e. €60,000. Therefore, as this amount of €60,000 exceeds €50,000, no relief may be claimed under section 396B. The loss available for carry forward to 2022 against future income of this trade is €100,000 − €30,000 = €70,000.

16.3 Schedule D – Cases III and IV

The following income is charged under Case III and Case IV Schedule D:

- Case III untaxed Irish income and income from foreign sources.
- Case IV income that has been subject to Irish tax at source and miscellaneous income. Corporation tax is charged on the gross amount of the Case IV income. The income tax suffered by deduction may be set against the corporation tax chargeable. Companies have the option to receive interest income **without the deduction of DIRT** by simply completing a written declaration and providing their Irish tax reference number to the relevant deposit-taker, stating that the company is within the charge to corporation tax and interest will be included in the profits chargeable to corporation tax.

16.3.1 Basis of Assessment

Strictly, tax is charged under Case III and Case IV on the income **received** during the accounting period. In practice, however, interest that is received gross is taxed on an accruals basis.

16.3.2 Case III and Case IV Losses

Case III losses are only available against profits in a similar category and can only be carried forward against future profits in that category. For example, foreign rental losses are only allowable against foreign rental income.

Case IV losses may be set-off against the amount of any other income assessable to corporation tax under Case IV for the same accounting period. Case IV losses, so far as unrelieved, may be carried forward and set against corresponding income of subsequent accounting periods.

16.4 Schedule D – Case V

The following income is charged under Case V Schedule D:

- rents in respect of any premises or lands in the State, i.e. offices, shops, factories, land, etc.; and
- certain premiums received for the granting of a lease.

16.4.1 Basis of Assessment

Tax is charged under Case V on the income **arising** during the accounting period. The rental income taken into account is the amount receivable in the accounting period, whether or not it is actually received.

16.4.2 Premiums on Short Leases

Previously it had been possible for a landlord to avoid being taxed on income from let property by letting the property at a large 'once-off' premium in the first year and charging a nominal rent thereafter. This once-off premium was treated as a capital receipt and was not within the charge to income tax. Legislation was introduced so that a certain proportion of a premium on a short lease, i.e. one that does not exceed 50 years, is taxable under Case V.

Calculation of Taxable Portion of Premium
Where a landlord receives a premium on the creation of a short lease, a portion of the premium will be treated as rental income in the first year (see **Chapter 7**, **Example 7.1**).

16.4.3   *Allowable and Disallowable Items – Case V*

The following amounts may be deducted from the gross rental income:

- Rent payable.
- Rates (if any).
- Cost of goods or services that the landlord company is obliged to provide and for which it receives no separate consideration, e.g. gas, electricity, waste disposal, etc.
- Cost of repairs, excluding improvements and items treated as capital expenditure.
- Interest on money borrowed for the purchase, improvement or repairs to a commercial property – but interest charges incurred prior to the first letting are not deductible.
- Interest on money borrowed for the purchase, improvement or repairs to a residential property where the taxpayer has satisfied the registration requirements of the RTB (Residential Tenancies Board). Generally, interest charges incurred prior to the first letting are not deductible but, if the residential letting qualifies for relief for pre-letting expenses in respect of vacant premises, some interest incurred may be allowed as a deduction.
- Accountancy fees incurred in drawing up rental accounts and keeping rental records. Strictly, such expenses are not allowable as they relate more to the management of the landlord's affairs than to the receipt of rent or the management of the premises. In practice, however, Revenue allows a deduction for such expenses as it recognises that the efficient running of a business of letting premises requires that financial accounts should be prepared.
- Mortgage protection policy premiums. Generally, financial institutions insist on a mortgage protection policy being taken out by a borrower before they will approve a loan in respect of a property. Like accountancy fees, premiums on such policies would not be strictly allowable, being more to do with the landlord's financial affairs than to the management of the property or the receipt of rent. Revenue allows a deduction for such premiums.
- Pre-letting expenses in respect of vacant premises of **up to €5,000** incurred in the 12 months before the date of the first residential letting are allowable as a deduction against rental income. This applies only to expenditure on a premises that has been **vacant for at least 12 months** and which is then let as a residential premises between 25 December 2017 and 31 December 2021.

    If the person who incurs the expenditure ceases to let the property as a residential premises within **four years** of the first letting, the deduction will be clawed back in the year in which the property ceases to be let as a residential premises. The cessation can be either on sale of the property or change of use from rented residential property.
- Wear and tear allowances. A wear and tear allowance of **12.5% per annum** on a straight-line basis for eight years is available on the cost of furniture and fittings in the case of furnished lettings.
- Expenses incurred after the termination of one lease and before the commencement of another lease in respect of the property are deductible provided the following three conditions are satisfied:
    1. the expenses would otherwise be deductible;
    2. the person who was the lessor of the property does not occupy the premises during the period when the property is not let; and
    3. the property is let by the same lessor at the end of the period.

Allowable expenses are normally deducted on an accruals basis rather than on a paid basis. In order to be deductible, the expense must be incurred wholly and exclusively for the purpose of earning the rent and must be revenue, rather than capital, in nature.

Expenses **not deductible** against property income include:
- Local property tax payable by the owners of residential property.
- Expenses incurred before a lease commences on the property, other than legal or advertising expenses, and qualifying pre-letting expenditure on vacant residential property outlined above.

- Interest or rent payable before the property is first occupied by a lessee other than qualifying pre-letting expenditure on vacant residential property outlined previously.
- Expenses incurred after the termination of a lease unless followed by another lease to a new tenant, as outlined above.

Example 16.9

A company purchased a vacant rental residential property on 1 February 2021. The previous occupants had vacated the property in June 2020. Between the date of purchase and 30 June 2021 the company spent €25,000 refurbishing the property. On 1 July 2021 the property was leased for €1,900 per month, payable in advance.

The following expenses were incurred up to 30 June 2021:

	€	€
Auctioneers' and advertising fees for first tenants	1,180	
Repairs and maintenance	300	
Light and heat	450	
Security and insurance	800	
Interest on loan	2,750	5,480

The following expenses were incurred in the period 1 July to 31 December 2021:

	€	€
Insurance	100	
New furniture and fittings	6,420	
Management and letting fees	1,540	
Interest (property was registered with RTB on 25 July 2021)	2,300	
RTB registration costs	90	
Local property tax (LPT)	495	10,945

Case V rental computation

	€	€
Gross rents (€1,900 × 6)		11,400
Less: qualifying expenses:		
Pre-letting expenses (maximum)	5,000	
Insurance	100	
Management and letting fees	1,540	
Interest	2,300	
RTB registration costs	90	(9,030)
Wear and tear allowance: €6,420 @ 12.5% × 6/12ths		(401)
Net Case V income		1,969

16.4.4 Case V Losses

Case V losses (which are defined as losses after offset against any Case V income of the accounting period) may be set against Case V income of a **preceding period** of the same length. A claim for this relief in respect of a Case V loss must be made **within two years** after the end of the accounting period of loss.

Case V losses, so far as unrelieved, may be carried forward and set against Case V income of subsequent accounting periods.

Example 16.10
Upland Ltd makes up accounts to 31 December. Recent results are as follows:

	2018	2019	2020	2021
	€	€	€	€
Trading income	100,000	110,000	120,000	130,000
Interest on government securities	10,000	11,000	12,000	13,000
Rental income (loss)	20,000	(30,000)	5,000	20,000

Starting with earliest loss:

		€		€
2019:				
Case I				110,000
Case III				11,000
Case V				Nil
				121,000
Loss Memo – Case V				
2019 loss		30,000		
2018:				
Case I				100,000
Case III				10,000
Case V		20,000		
Less: loss 2019		(20,000)		Nil
				110,000
Loss Memo – Case V				
2019 loss		30,000		
Less: used 2018		(20,000)		
Losses forward		10,000		
2020:				
Case I				120,000
Case III				12,000
Case V		5,000		
Less: loss forward from 2019		(5,000)		Nil
				132,000
Loss Memo – Case V				
2019 loss forward		10,000		
Less: used 2020		(5,000)		
Losses forward		5,000		

continued overleaf

2021:		
Case I		130,000
Case III		13,000
Case V	20,000	
Less: 2020 loss forward	(5,000)	15,000
		158,000
Loss Memo – Case V		
2020 loss forward	5,000	
Less: used 2021	(5,000)	
Losses forward	Nil	

16.4.5   Case V Capital Allowances

Capital allowances available to lessors of industrial buildings (Case V allowances) are to be treated primarily as deductions from the relevant income, i.e. the lease rentals. Any excess of such allowances over the relevant income may be:

- Set-off against total profits (including chargeable gains) for the same accounting period or for an immediately preceding period of the same length. A claim must be made within two years of the end of the accounting period in which the excess occurs.
- Carried forward and treated as an allowance for a later accounting period.

Example 16.11
Takeaway Ltd has the following income and allowances:

Year Ended	Case I	Case III	Case V	Case V Capital Allowances
	€	€	€	€
31 December 2020	20,000	40,000	80,000	30,000
31 December 2021	100,000	20,000	25,000	160,000

Corporation Tax Year Ended 31 December 2021

	€	€
Case I		100,000
Case III		20,000
Case V	25,000	
Less: Case V allowances	(25,000)	Nil
		120,000
Less: Excess Case V allowances		(120,000)
		Nil

Balance of Case V capital allowances available for set-off against 2020 profits:

€160,000 − €25,000 − €120,000 = €15,000

continued overleaf

Corporation Tax Year Ended 31 December 2020

	€	€
Case I		20,000
Case III		40,000
Case V	80,000	
Less: Case V 2020 allowances	(30,000)	50,000
		110,000
Less: Excess Case V allowances in 2021		(15,000)
Taxable income		95,000

Corporation tax:	€
€20,000 @ 12.5%	2,500
€75,000 @ 25%	18,750
Total	21,250

Note: the excess Case V capital allowances are offset against total profits. Takeaway Ltd will choose to offset them against the profits taxed at the highest rate, i.e. 25%.

16.5 Franked Investment Income

Irish dividends received are exempt from corporation tax when received by an Irish-resident company from an Irish-resident company. They are referred to as franked investment income (FII). Consequently, no deduction is allowed for dividends paid by a company (or any item treated as a distribution of profits under corporation tax rules) when computing taxable profits.

16.6 Computation of Chargeable Gains

Chargeable gains of a company, other than those arising from disposals of development land, are subject to corporation tax rather than capital gains tax (CGT). The exception is any gain on the disposal of development land, which is subject to CGT. The gain is calculated after deducting capital losses from the current accounting period and any losses brought forward from earlier periods.

CGT computation principles apply to the calculation of the gain (as set out in **Part Three**). If an individual made the disposal, the chargeable gain would be taxed at **33%**, but the corporation tax rate applicable to chargeable gains is only **12.5%**. Therefore, to avoid inequity, the chargeable gain subject to corporation tax needs to be **adjusted** so that when the adjusted chargeable gain is taxed at 12.5%, the amount of the tax arising equals the amount of tax that would arise if the disposal had been subject to CGT at 33%. The adjusting formula is:

$$\text{Adjusted chargeable gain} = \text{chargeable gain} \times 33\%/12.5\%$$

The adjusted chargeable gains are added to total income in the corporation tax computation.

Example 16.12

XIT DAC prepares accounts to 31 December each year. In the year ended 31 December 2021 the tax-adjusted Case III profit was €20,000. During that year the company bought an asset for €10,000 and sold it for €15,000 in June 2021.

Corporation tax computation	€	€
Case III	20,000	
Adjusted chargeable gain: €5,000 × 33%/12.5%	13,200	
		33,200
Corporation tax due @ 12.5% – chargeable gain	1,650	
Corporation tax due @ 25% – Case III	5,000	
Total corporation tax		6,650
Proof:		
Case III €20,000 @ 25%	5,000	
Capital gain €5,000 @ 33%	1,650	
Total tax payable		6,650

16.6.1 Capital Losses

While trading losses may be set-off against trading profits and utilised on a value basis, capital losses can only be set-off against current chargeable gains on other assets, or carried forward against chargeable gains in subsequent accounting periods.

Questions

Review Questions

(See Suggested Solutions to Review Questions at the end of this textbook.)

Question 16.1

Telstar DAC commenced trading in 2001 and makes up its accounts each year to 31 December. The income statement to 31 December 2021 is as follows:

	Notes	€	€
Gross profit			239,800
IDA grant for extension of premises			10,000
IDA employment grant			1,000
Patent royalty (net)	1.		1,600
Discount received			3,300
Dividends from Irish quoted shares			1,300
Profit on sale of van	2.		1,000
Profit on sale of shares	3.		2,000

continued overleaf

Bank deposit interest (paid gross)			<u>600</u>
			260,600
Less: Discount given		3,000	
Goods stolen		3,000	
Business overdraft interest		5,800	
Depreciation		15,149	
Van expense		3,400	
Motor expenses	4.	6,800	
Bad debts		2,300	
Obsolete inventories – written off		2,600	
Salaries and wages		93,840	
Telephone		2,311	
Entertainment	5.	2,700	
Finance lease charges	6.	1,300	
Legal fees	7.	2,400	(<u>144,600</u>)
Profit before tax			116,000

Notes:

1. The patent royalty was received in December 2021.
2. Profit on sale of van – the van was acquired second-hand on 03/02/2014 for €12,000. It was sold on 05/05/2021 for €4,000. The net book value of the van at 31/12/2020 was €3,000.
3. Profit on sale of shares – these shares were acquired on 31/03/2003 for €4,000 and sold on 30/04/2021 for €6,000.

4.	There are two cars:	€
	Mercedes purchased second-hand on 30/06/2021	
	Cost	28,000
	Expenses	800
	Category B car leased on 01/02/2019	
	Cost	25,000
	Operating lease payments	6,000
5.	The charge for entertainment is made up as follows:	€
	Prizes for top salesperson of the year	900
	Christmas party for staff	750
	Christmas gifts for suppliers	150
	Reimbursement of managing director for costs incurred entertaining customers at home	350
	General customer entertainment	<u>550</u>
		<u>2,700</u>

6. Finance lease charges – these relate to a machine leased in 2019, the cost of which is capitalised in the company's accounts. The lease agreement states that the burden of wear and tear remains with the lessor. Total repayments made during the year ended 31 December 2021 were €9,400, which included both capital repayments and finance charges.
7. The legal fees relate to the extension of the premises.
8. Capital allowances for the year are €7,272.
9. The company paid €80,000 of corporation tax on its 2020 profits.

Requirement

Calculate the corporation tax liability for the year ended 31 December 2021 and show the dates on which it is payable.

Question 16.2

The income statement of Zaco Ltd for the year ended 30 September 2021 is as follows:

	Notes	€	€
Sales			2,450,000
Cost of sales			(1,959,750)
Gross profit			490,250
Less: Salaries and wages		62,500	
Rent and rates		5,400	
Repairs	1.	16,100	
Insurance		1,720	
Professional fees	2.	1,600	
Depreciation		13,000	
Audit Fees		1,000	
Subscriptions	3.	2,400	
Entertainment	4.	600	
Staff award	5.	1,000	
Discount allowed		320	
Bank interest		7,060	
Light and heat		12,250	(124,950)
Add: Dividends	6.	3,000	
Bad debts recovered		300	
Profit on sale of investments	7.	5,200	
Interest on tax overpaid		1,200	
Profit on sale of fixtures and fittings	8.	3,100	12,800
Profit before tax			378,100

Notes:

1. Repairs: includes improvements to offices of €5,200.
2. Professional fees: includes debt collection fees of €200 and architect's fees re. office improvements of €300.
3. Subscriptions: includes political donations of €750 and staff race sponsorship of €1,000.
4. Entertainment: made up as follows:

	€
Customer entertainment	450
Supplier entertainment	150
	600

5. Staff award: a special award of €1,000 was made to an employee who achieved first place in Ireland in his engineering examinations during the year.
6. Dividends: Irish dividends – cash amount = €3,000.
7. Sale of investments:

Irish Treasury Bonds – Irish Government Security	€	€
Cost May 2016	2,148	
Proceeds June 2020	2,800	652
Shares in quoted investment company		
Cost June 1998	1,000	
Proceeds July 2020	5,548	4,548
		5,200

8. Profit on sale of fixtures and fittings: cost €8,000 in August 2019 and sold for €11,100 in September 2021. Net book value was €6,800 on 30 September 2020.
9. The capital allowances (including balancing allowances and charges) are €9,846.
10. There are capital losses forward of €10,000.

Requirement
Calculate the company's corporation tax liability for the year.

Question 16.3

Overseas Ltd, a distribution company resident in Taxland and under the control of individuals resident in Taxland, has been trading in Ireland for many years through a branch.

The company has the following income during the year ended 31 December 2021:

	€
Trading profits (including Irish branch trading profits of €600,000)	900,000
Interest income from surplus funds invested by branch (received gross)	20,000
Dividends received from Australian subsidiary	10,000

The Irish branch had chargeable gains, before adjustment, on the sales of premises out of which the branch traded of €32,000 in December 2021.

Requirement

Calculate the relevant Irish tax liabilities of Overseas Ltd.

Question 16.4

Enya Ltd had the following profits/losses for the years in question.

	Rents	Trading profits/(losses)	Case III
	€	€	€
Year ended 31/03/2018	5,000	60,000	10,000
Year ended 31/03/2019	(4,000)	70,000	5,000
Year ended 31/03/2020	6,000	(130,000)	10,000
Year ended 31/03/2021	8,000	10,000	3,500

Requirement

Using the above figures for Enya Ltd, show how the Case V and Case I losses may be used. Assume a tax rate of 12.5% on trading income and 25% for Cases III and V for all years.

Question 16.5

Hells Bells Ltd shows the following results:

	Year ended 31 March 2021	Nine months ended 31 December 2021
	€	€
Trading profit/(loss)	167,000	(190,000)
Rents	4,000	(4,000)
Capital gains/(losses) (non-development land)	(19,000)	10,000
Case III	10,000	20,000

Requirement

Calculate the tax payable for each accounting period, claiming the earliest possible loss relief.

Question 16.6

Monk Ltd prepares annual accounts to 31 December each year. Recent results were as follows:

	Year ended	
	31/12/2020	31/12/2021
	€	€
Adjusted Case I profit/(loss) (Note)	340,000	(400,000)
Interest on Government stocks	5,000	30,000
Rental income	15,000	20,000
Capital gains as adjusted for CT (non-development land)	12,000	26,000
Capital gain on development land (1 June)	–	100,000

Note: Monk Ltd has an unutilised Case I loss forward from the year ended 31 December 2019 of €20,000. The company wishes to claim the loss reliefs available so as to maximise the benefit of the losses.

Requirement

Compute the corporation tax payable for each of the above years and indicate the amount (if any) of unutilised losses available for carry forward to the year ending 31 December 2022.

Question 16.7

Monaghan Ltd prepares annual accounts to 30 June each year. Recent results were as follows:

	Year ended 30 June		
	2019	**2020**	**2021**
	€	€	€
Adjusted Case I profit/(loss)	180,000	(530,000)	140,000
Trade charges paid (Note)	10,000	10,000	6,000
Interest on Government stocks	5,000	30,000	10,000
Rental income	10,500	20,000	20,000
Capital gains as adjusted for CT	10,200	40,000	50,000
Cash dividend from subsidiary	10,000	30,000	Nil
Non-trade charges paid	–	–	50,000

Monaghan Ltd has an unutilised Case I loss forward from the year ended 30 June 2018 of €20,000.

Note: trade charges of €4,000 relating to the year ended 30 June 2021 were paid in July 2021 and are not included in the figures above.

Requirement

Compute the corporation tax for each of the above years and indicate the amount (if any) of unutilised losses available for carry forward to the year ending 30 June 2022.

Annual Payments and Charges on Income

17.1 Annual Payments and Patent Royalty Payments

A company must deduct income tax at 20% when making certain annual payments and patent royalty payments. This income tax must be paid over to Revenue by the company on behalf of the payee and is treated as part of the paying company's corporation tax liability.

Conversely, where a company receives income from which Irish income tax has been deducted, such income is assessed under Case IV on the **gross amount**. A tax credit against its corporation tax liability will be allowed for the income tax withheld at source.

Annual payments include:

■ annual interest, including interest paid to close company directors and their associates;
■ patent royalties;
■ rents paid to non-residents in respect of property in the State; and
■ loans to participators in close companies.

17.2 Charges on Income

17.2.1 General

Certain payments, such as interest, annual payments and patent royalties, rank as charges on income and are allowed as deductions in the accounting period in which they are **paid**. Charges on income incurred before a trade commences are treated as paid when the trade commences, and are deductible in the first year of trading. Where income tax is withheld from the payment, the **gross** amount is deductible when calculating taxable profits for corporation tax. The income tax withheld by the company is then added to the corporation tax liability of the accounting period in which the payment is made.

Charges can be:

1. **Relevant trade charges**, i.e. those wholly and exclusively for trade purposes, such as patent royalties, are allowed **against trading income** in the accounting period in which they are paid.
2. **Non-trade charges**, i.e. charges other than relevant trade charges, such as protected interest, may be offset against total profits (including chargeable gains) in the period in which they were paid. Non-trade charges are generally offset against income taxed at 25%, in priority to profits taxed at 12.5%.

17.2.2   Amounts Treated as Charges

For the purposes of this discussion, the following amounts, subject to the above, are treated as "charges on income":

1. Yearly interest (other than interest allowable in computing profits chargeable under Case I and Case V).
2. Patent royalties.
3. Any other interest payable in the State on an advance from a bona fide bank or a bona fide discount house or a bona fide stock exchange member in the EU.

17.2.3   Interest Qualifying as a Charge – Section 247 Interest Relief

Section 247 TCA 1997 provides relief for interest as a non-trade charge against total profits where the borrowings are used to acquire shares in, or lend money to, certain companies. This type of interest, sometimes referred to as 'protected interest', qualifies as a non-trade charge if it cannot be deducted in computing trading profits or rental income and the following conditions are satisfied:

1. The investing company uses the borrowings to:
    (a) acquire part of the ordinary share capital of a company
        (i)   which exists wholly or mainly for the purpose of carrying on a trade or whose income consists wholly or mainly of rental income; or
        (ii) whose business consists wholly or mainly of holding shares in a company as described above, and the company into which the investment is made uses the funds received for the purpose of its trade or rental business; or
    (b) lend to such a company at (a) where the money is used by the borrower, or a connected company, wholly and exclusively for the purpose of their trade or rental business; or
    (c) pay off another loan applied for the purposes of (a) or (b) above.
2. At the time the interest is paid, the investing company must have a "material interest" in the company that uses the money, i.e. owns or controls **more than 5% of the ordinary share capital of the other company**.
3. At least one **director** of the investing company must be a director of the company that uses the money throughout the period from the application of the proceeds of the loan until the interest is paid, i.e. they share a "common director".
4. During the period of the loan, there must be no recovery of capital by the investing company. An investing company is regarded as recovering capital from the company if:
    (a) the investing company sells any of its shares or the company repays any share capital;
    (b) the company or a connected company repays a loan to the investing company;
    (c) the investing company receives consideration for the assignment of any debt due to it by the company.

Example 17.1
ONX Ltd had the following results for the year ended 31 December 2021:

	€
Case I income	100,000
Case V income	50,000
Trade charges (patent royalties paid under deduction of tax)	10,000 (gross)
Non-trade charges (interest paid under deduction of tax)	30,000 (gross)

Corporation tax computation	
Case I income	100,000
Deduct: Trade charges	(10,000)
	90,000
Case V income	50,000
Total profits	140,000
Non-trade charges	(30,000)
Taxable	110,000
€90,000 @ 12.5%	11,250
(€50,000 – €30,000) = €20,000 @ 25%	5,000
	16,250
Add: Income tax withheld from charges:	
€40,000 @ 20%	8,000
Corporation tax payable	**24,250**

17.3   Relief for Excess Charges

17.3.1   Relevant Trading Charges

Where the amount of the relevant trading charges exceeds Case I income, relief for the excess trade charges is given in one of two ways:

1. by claiming relief for the excess in the same accounting period on a value basis (section 243B TCA 1997); or
2. by carrying the excess forward as a trading loss (section 396(7) TCA 1997).

Claim for Relief on a Value Basis
Section 243B allows relief for excess trade charges against the relevant corporation tax liability of the company in the current accounting period on a value basis, i.e. the relevant corporation tax liability can be reduced by the tax value of the excess trade charges. The tax value of the excess trade charges is 12.5% of the excess. The relevant corporation tax of the company is the corporation tax liability not including any withholding.

The **sequence of claims** (see also **Section 16.2.5**) is:

- section 396(1), i.e. trading losses forward from earlier periods against income of the same trade;
- section 396A, i.e. trading losses against trading income;
- section 243A, i.e. trading charges against trading income;
- section 243B, i.e. trading charges against corporation tax on a value basis; and
- section 396B, i.e. trading losses against corporation tax on a value basis.

Example 17.2

YZA Ltd, a distribution company, had the following results for the years ended 31 December 2020 and 2021:

	2020	2021
	€	€
Case I profit/(loss)	30,000	(70,000)
Relevant trading charges	20,000	15,000
Case V income	15,000	20,000

Corporation tax computation:

	2020	2021
Case I	30,000	Nil
Less: section 396A relief	(30,000)	–
Taxable Case I income	Nil	Nil
Case V income	15,000	20,000
Corporation tax @ 25%	3,750	5,000
Less: Relief on a value basis:		
Excess trading charges (section 243B) (Note 1)	(2,500)	(1,875)
Less: section 396B relief (Note 2)	(1,250)	(3,125)
Corporation tax payable	Nil	Nil

Notes:

1. Excess 2020 charges are:

	€
Case I	30,000
Less: section 396A relief	(30,000)
Less: relevant charges	(20,000)
Excess charges	(20,000)

    Tax value of excess charges: €20,000 × 12.5% = €2,500

    Excess 2021 charges are:

	€
Case I	Nil
Less: relevant charges	(15,000)
Excess charges	(15,000)

    Tax value of excess charges: €15,000 × 12.5% = €1,875

continued overleaf

2. Section 396B relief is claimed after relief for excess charges.

   Tax value of 2021 losses: €70,000 – €30,000 = €40,000 × 12.5% = €5,000

   Losses available to carry forward and offset against profits arising in subsequent years from the same trade are as follows:

	€
Total loss	70,000
Utilised by way of section 396A relief 2020	(30,000)
Utilised by way of section 396B relief:	
2021: €25,000 @ 12.5% = €3,125	(25,000)
2020: €10,000 @ 12.5% = €1,250	(10,000)
Losses available to carry forward	5,000

   That is: €5,000 – €3,125 – €1,250 = €625/12.5% = €5,000

17.3.2 Non-trade Charges

As outlined above, non-trade charges may be offset against a company's total profits. Where non-trade charges exceed a company's total profits, no relief may be obtained for the excess. In addition, where relief is claimed for losses under section 396B (i.e. relief for losses on a value basis), in calculating trading losses available for carry forward to subsequent years, the company is deemed to have used up any additional loss relief under section 396B instead of claiming any relief for non-trade charges, expenses of management and other amounts deductible against total profits (except excess Case V capital allowances).

Questions

Review Questions

(See Suggested Solutions to Review Questions at the end of this textbook.)

Question 17.1

Nifty Investments Ltd had the following results for the year ended 31 March 2021:

	€
Trading profits	90,000
After charging the following amounts:	
Depreciation	10,000
Patent royalties (paid August 2020) (Net)	8,000
Interest paid to an Irish bank on monies borrowed to invest in a company – conditions satisfied to qualify as protected interest	9,000
After crediting:	
Loan interest received October (Net €4,800 actually received)	6,000
Bank interest received October (Gross)	1,000
Chargeable gain before adjustment (January 2021)	10,000

Requirement

Compute the corporation tax payable by Nifty Investments Ltd for the year ended 31 March 2021.

Question 17.2

The following information relates to Alpha Ltd for the year ended 31 December 2021.

Income Statement of Alpha Ltd for the year ended 31 December 2021

	Notes	€	€
Sales			3,450,000
Cost of sales			(2,850,000)
Gross profit			600,000
Less: Salaries and wages	1	71,300	
Rent and rates	2	7,600	
Repairs	3	18,500	
Insurance	4	1,350	
Loss on sale of investments	5	600	
Legal expenses	6	2,700	
Commissions		9,209	
Depreciation		13,260	
Audit fees		1,550	
Subscriptions	7	3,400	
Discounts allowed		900	
Bank interest	8	3,300	
Other interest	9	7,000	
Light and heat		11,234	
Motor expenses	10	33,126	
Sundry	11	3,740	
Entertainment expenses	12	1,191	
Finance lease charges	13	1,700	(191,660)
Add: Irish dividends received	14	4,500	
Gain on sale of Irish shares	15	1,000	
Enterprise Ireland employment grant		240	
Interest on tax overpaid		475	
Interest on Irish treasury bonds		2,500	
Rent received		6,000	
Deposit interest (received gross)		1,500	
Bad debts		50	16,265
Net profit before tax			**424,605**

Notes:

1. Salaries and wages include €25,000 in respect of staff bonuses relating to the year ended 31 December 2021, which were not paid until 5 January 2022.
2. Rent and rates include an amount of €1,000 relating to part of the company's premises which has been let to a sub-tenant.
3. Repairs include an amount of €15,000 for an extension to the factory premises.
4. Insurance includes an amount of €350 relating to the let premises.
5. Loss on sale of investments:

UK shares purchased 2014	€
Cost	10,000
Proceeds	(9,400)
Net loss	600

6. Legal expenses:

	€
Debt collection	700
Extension to factory	2,000
	2,700

7. Subscriptions:

	€
Chamber of commerce	430
Local football club	20
Trade association	1,135
Political	1,815
	3,400

8. Bank interest – includes an amount of €1,500 relating to borrowings taken out to finance the extension to the factory premises.
9. Other interest – interest on monies borrowed from bank to acquire shares in a trading subsidiary, where Alpha Ltd is represented on the board and there has been no recovery of capital. €7,000 gross was paid during the year.
10. Motor expenses – the company leased six new motor cars on 1 April 2020, CO_2 emissions category B. The retail price of each, at the time the lease contracts were entered into, was €25,000. The motor expenses can be analysed as follows:

	€
Leasing charges on leased cars	21,126
Running costs of leased cars	12,000
	33,126

11. Sundry:

	€
Interest on late payments of VAT	1,630
Parking fines	30
Staff Christmas party	500

Gifts to customers	541
General office expenses	<u>1,039</u>
	<u>3,740</u>

12. Ententertainment: €

Hotel and accommodation for overseas customers	<u>1,191</u>

13. Finance lease charges – relate to new machinery leased in 2019, the cost of which is capitalised in the company's accounts. The lease agreement states that the burden of wear and tear remains with the lessor. Total repayments made during the year ended 31 December 2021 were €12,200, which included both capital repayments and finance charges.

14. Irish dividends: €

Dividend on quoted shares	1,500
Dividend from subsidiary	<u>3,000</u>
	<u>4,500</u>

15. Sale of Irish quoted shares: €

Cost (July 2013)	19,000
Proceeds (January 2021)	<u>20,000</u>
Gain	<u>1,000</u>

16. Capital allowances for the accounting period are €26,006.

Requirement

Calculate the corporation tax liability for Alpha Ltd for the year ended 31 December 2021.

Distributions and Dividend Withholding Tax

Learning Objectives

After studying this chapter you will understand:

- how to identify and advise on company distributions; and
- the dividend withholding tax implications for persons making or receiving distributions.

18.1 Distributions

A distribution for tax purposes refers to any payment out of the assets of a company in respect of shares, **except a repayment of capital**, including:

- dividends paid by a company, including a capital dividend;
- scrip dividends – where a shareholder in a quoted resident company opts to take shares instead of a cash dividend;
- redemption of bonus securities;
- certain share buy-back schemes;
- sale of assets by a company at undervalue, or purchase of assets by a company at overvalue, from a shareholder;
- certain interest paid to non-resident parent companies;
- interest paid to certain directors of close companies that exceeds a prescribed limit; and
- certain expenses, incurred by a close company in the provision of benefits for a participator.

Distributions **paid** by an Irish resident company are **not an allowable deduction** when calculating corporation tax and may be subject to dividend withholding tax.

Distributions **received** by an Irish resident company from an Irish resident company are **exempt from corporation tax**. Distributions received by an Irish resident individual from an Irish resident company are assessed under Schedule F for income tax purposes. Distributions received by an Irish resident person from a non-resident company are assessed to tax under Schedule D Case III.

18.2 Dividend Withholding Tax

Dividend withholding tax (DWT) is payable in respect of all relevant distributions made by an Irish resident company, with certain exceptions. The rate of DWT is currently **25%** of the distribution made.

DWT is deducted **at source** by the company and paid over to Revenue on behalf of the shareholder. The shareholder can claim a **tax credit** for the DWT against their tax liability.

Example 18.1

ABD Ltd, an Irish resident company, is owned by three Irish resident individuals, Joe, Frank and Bob. ABD Ltd is to make an interim dividend payment of €10,000 on 1 October 2021 to each of its shareholders for the year ended 31 December 2021.

	Joe	Frank	Bob	Total
	€	€	€	€
Dividend paid 1 October 2021	10,000	10,000	10,000	30,000
DWT 25%	(2,500)	(2,500)	(2,500)	(7,500)
Net dividend paid	7,500	7,500	7,500	22,500

18.2.1 Relevant Distributions

DWT applies to all relevant distributions made by an Irish resident company. Relevant distributions are all dividends and distributions made by a company, including:

1. cash dividends;
2. any non-cash distributions;
3. expenses incurred by close companies in providing certain benefits for a participator in the company;
4. interest in excess of a specified amount paid by close companies to directors; and
5. scrip dividends of quoted and unquoted companies (where shares are taken instead of a cash dividend).

The amount of the relevant distribution to which the DWT applies is the cash amount, where a cash payment is made, or the market value of the distribution where a non-cash distribution is made.

Example 18.2

As in **Example 18.1**, ABD Ltd owns shares in another company, ZEE Ltd. ABD Ltd distributes all its shares in ZEE Ltd to Joe, Frank and Bob. At the time the shares in ZEE Ltd are distributed, they have a market value of €90,000.

ABD Ltd is required to pay DWT as follows:

	Joe	Frank	Bob	Total
	€	€	€	€
Deemed distribution	30,000	30,000	30,000	90,000
DWT 25%	(7,500)	(7,500)	(7,500)	(22,500)
Net distribution	22,500	22,500	22,500	67,500

ABD Ltd is entitled to **recover** the DWT of €22,500 from Joe, Frank and Bob. If it does not recover the DWT from its shareholders, the distribution will have to be grossed up as the non-recovered amount is also deemed a distribution to the shareholders.

18.2.2 Exemptions from DWT

DWT should not be deducted from distributions made to the following:

1. most Irish resident companies;
2. a pension scheme, approved minimum retirement fund and approved retirement fund;

3. a charity;
4. certain non-resident persons; and
5. dividends paid out of exempt profits (beyond the scope of this textbook).

In order to qualify for exemption from DWT, those listed at 1. to 3. above must make a declaration of entitlement to relief to the company making the distribution, confirming that the declarer is beneficially entitled to the distribution and entitled to an exemption. The declaration remains valid until the person ceases to qualify as an excluded person.

However, in the case where an Irish resident company makes a distribution to its **Irish resident parent** (i.e. it is a 51% subsidiary), a declaration is not required.

18.2.3 Payment of DWT and Filing a Return

Companies must use ROS to pay DWT and file the return for **any month** they make, or are deemed to have made, a relevant distribution.

The date for paying and filing is the **14th day of the month** following the month in which the distribution is paid. For example, if a distribution is paid on 28 May, the pay and file due date is 14 June. A return must be filed even if no DWT was deducted from the distribution. The date of distribution is the date that the **dividend was paid** to the shareholder.

The company, including any Authorised Withholding Agent (AWA), making a relevant distribution must give each recipient a statement that includes:

- the name and address of the company making the distribution;
- the name and address of the AWA, if it was involved;
- the name and address of the person to whom the distribution is made;
- the date the distribution is paid;
- the amount of the distribution; and
- the DWT amount, if any, that was deducted from the distribution.

Questions

Review Questions
(See Suggested Solutions to Review Questions at the end of this textbook.)

Question 18.1

Lance Investments Ltd, an Irish resident company, is to pay a dividend of €500,000 on 1 November 2021. Its shareholders are as follows:

	Number of Ordinary Shares
Mr C (resident in the State)	3,000
National Investments Ltd (resident in the State)	18,000
Irish registered charity	1,000
Local Investments Ltd (resident in the State)	3,000
Total share capital	25,000

Requirement
(a) Compute the DWT payable by Lance Investments Ltd assuming all declarations necessary to obtain exemption are given.
(b) Indicate when the DWT is payable assuming the dividend is paid on 1 November 2021.
(c) Indicate the declarations to be made and the certificates to be provided by shareholders of Lance Investments Ltd in order to obtain exemption from DWT.

Part Three

Capital Gains Tax

Capital Gains Tax: Introduction, General Principles and Administration

Chartered Accountants Ireland's *Code of Ethics* applies to all aspects of a professional accountant's professional life, including dealing with capital gains tax issues. Further information regarding the principles in the *Code of Ethics* is set out in **Appendix 3**.

Students should also be aware of the issues around tax planning, tax avoidance and tax evasion, and these are discussed in **Appendix 4**.

19.1 The Charge to Capital Gains Tax

Capital gains tax (CGT) arises from the disposal of chargeable **assets**. The charge to CGT is contained in section 28 of the Taxes Consolidation Act 1997 (TCA 1997).

There are four basic elements that must apply before the provisions relating to the taxation of capital gains come into operation:

1. there must be a **disposal**;
2. of an **asset**;
3. by a **chargeable person**;
4. after **5 April 1974**.

The extent to which gains are chargeable, and losses are allowable, depends on the location and nature of the asset and the person's tax residence, ordinary residence and domicile (see **Chapter 1**).

19.2   Disposal of an Asset

In order for a liability to CGT to arise, a disposal of an asset must take place or must be deemed to take place. A disposal for these purposes will occur in each of the following situations:

1. On the sale of an asset.
2. On the sale of part of an asset (part disposal – see **Section 19.6.5**).
3. On the gift of the whole or part of an asset.
4. On the receipt of a capital sum resulting from the ownership of an asset, e.g. compensation received for damage or forfeiture or surrender of rights, etc.
5. On the receipt of a capital sum received as consideration for the use or exploitation of assets.
6. On the transfer of an asset to a trust or a corporate body.
7. On an exchange of assets in a barter transaction.
8. On the occasion of the entire loss or destruction of an asset, e.g. if a painting is destroyed in a fire, there is a disposal of the painting whether or not any insurance proceeds are received.
9. Where an asset becomes negligible in value and Revenue allows a claim for loss relief, there is a deemed disposal of the asset.

19.3   Assets

For the purpose of CGT all forms of property are assets, including options and property created by the person disposing of it (e.g. copyrights, patents and goodwill), debts and foreign currency. Specifically included is an interest in property, e.g. a lease. The basic rule is that any capital asset of an individual or company is a chargeable asset unless it is specifically exempt from CGT or corporation tax on chargeable gains.

A **non-wasting chattel** is also an asset for CGT purposes. This is defined as "tangible movable property" that has a predictable useful life of **more than 50 years** and includes works of art, e.g. paintings, antiques, postage stamps, books, manuscripts, sculpture jewellery, furniture or similar objects, etc.

19.4   Chargeable Persons

CGT is charged on gains realised by individuals, partnerships and trusts. Companies are assessed to CGT on disposals of development land only. Other capital gains realised by companies are also chargeable gains but are assessed to corporation tax and not CGT.

19.4.1   Spouses and Civil Partners

Each spouse or civil partner is a separate person for CGT purposes and their gains or losses should be computed separately. The residence and domicile status of each spouse or civil partner must be considered individually to decide whether or not that person is chargeable to CGT. (All further references to spouses and married couples include civil partners.)

Disposal by One Spouse to the Other
A disposal of an asset from one spouse to the other **does not give rise to a CGT liability**, provided that the couple are **living together** for tax purposes, i.e. they are not separated. The asset is deemed to have passed from one to the other at a value that gives rise to no gain or no loss. The **whole period** of ownership by both spouses is taken into account when determining the indexation date on a subsequent disposal.

Losses

Where a married couple are living together in the year of assessment, the net chargeable gains accruing to one spouse for that year of assessment should be reduced by any unutilised allowable losses accruing to the other spouse (including losses brought forward) for the same year.

Example 19.1: Year of Marriage

John and James married on 1 October 2021. They had the following capital gains and losses for 2021:

	John	James	
	€	€	
1 January 2021 to 30 September 2021:			
Net chargeable gains	4,800	1,000	
Net allowable losses		(2,000)	Disposal prior to marriage
1 October 2021 to 31 December 2021:			
Net chargeable gains	0	250	
Taxable gains	4,800	(750)	Net losses
Set off of net loss	(750)	750	
Net chargeable gain	4,050	NIL	
Less: Annual exemption	(1,270)	N/A	
Net taxable gain	**2,780**		

19.4.2   Separated and Divorced Couples

Although technically a couple must be living together for the exemption on disposal of a capital asset between spouses to apply, Revenue practice is that any assets transferred in the **year of separation** are transferred at no gain/no loss. If there is a loss in the year of separation, the loss of one spouse may be used by the other.

Years Following Separation

CGT does not arise where a person disposes of an asset to a spouse as a consequence of a legal obligation under a **deed of separation** or a **Court order**, including on a divorce or dissolution. This means that each asset is treated as being disposed of for an amount that gives rise to neither a gain nor a loss in the hands of the disposing spouse. The acquiring spouse is deemed to acquire the asset on the same day and at the same cost as the spouse who originally acquired it.

All disposals between spouses following a separation that takes place after the year of separation, or outside of a legal deed of separation/Court order, will be deemed to be at **market value** regardless of the actual consideration and CGT will be calculated in the normal way. Following a divorce or dissolution, a couple cease to be connected persons as they are no longer married or in a civil partnership.

Example 19.2

Joe and Anne separate. As part of a deed of separation, Joe transfers the following assets to Anne:

- shares worth €100,000 (which he had purchased 10 years previously for €20,000);
- his interest in the family home (cost €30,000 20 years previously).

Joe will not be liable for any CGT on either of these disposals to Anne, regardless of whether the transfers take place in the year of separation or subsequently.

If Anne subsequently sells any of the shares, she will be liable for any CGT which arises. The gain will be calculated as if she had purchased the shares herself, 10 years previously, at the original cost of €20,000.

19.4.3   Cohabiting Couples

Cohabiting couples are treated as single individuals, but where assets are received or disposed of under a **Court order**, the following applies:

▨   If an asset is transferred under a Court order, the transferring cohabitant will not have to pay CGT on the transfer and the receiving cohabitant will not be liable for CAT.

▨   Where a cohabitant receives an asset under a Court order and sells it at a later date, CGT is calculated from the time the asset was received under the order.

A qualifying cohabitant is one who has been cohabiting for at least:

▨   two years if the parents of dependent children; or

▨   five years for all other cases.

If an asset was received from a previous cohabitant and sold at a later date, the seller will have to pay CGT. CGT is calculated on the basis that the seller owned the asset from the time they received it.

19.5   Rate of Tax, Date of Payment and Returns

19.5.1   Rate of CGT

CGT is charged by reference to the **year of assessment for individuals**. A CGT year is the same as an income tax year, i.e. the **calendar year**.

    The rate of **CGT for 2021 is 33%**. The rates of CGT for previous years are listed in **Appendix 1**.

19.5.2   Annual Exemption

Individuals (not companies) are entitled to an annual exemption of **€1,270**. If the **chargeable gains** do not exceed €1,270 for 2021, no tax is due. If the gains exceed €1,270, only the excess is chargeable.

    If an individual is married, **each** spouse is entitled to the €1,270 allowance. If one spouse does not avail of the allowance, it **cannot** be transferred to the other spouse. Furthermore, this allowance cannot be carried forward to subsequent years if it is not used in the current year.

Example 19.3
Holly and Robin are married. During 2021 they had the following disposals:

▨   on 5 July, Holly sold shares for €12,000 – original cost was €11,500 on 5 March 2012;

▨   on 8 August, Robin sold a building for €350,000 – original cost was €290,000 on 7 January 2008.

	Holly	Robin
	€	€
Original cost of asset	11,500	290,000
Proceeds on disposal	12,000	350,000
Profit on disposal	500	60,000
Deduct: Annual exemption	(1,270)	(1,270)
Net gain/(loss)	Nil	58,730
CGT @ 33%	Nil	19,380

Both Holly and Robin can claim an annual exemption of €1,270. However, Robin cannot claim for the part of Holly's exemption that she could not use (€770).

19.5.3 Date of Payment

CGT is operated by means of self-assessment. Any liability due is payable in two amounts:

1. The first amount, known as "tax payable for the initial period", is payable on or before **15 December in the tax year**. Tax payable for the initial period means the tax which would be payable for the tax year if it ended on **30 November** in that year instead of 31 December. By deeming the tax year to end on 30 November, all reliefs, e.g. losses carried forward from previous years or the annual exemption amount, are taken into account when calculating the person's chargeable gains and, thus, their CGT liability for the period.
2. The second amount, known as "tax payable for the later period", is payable on or before **31 January after the end of the tax year**. Tax payable for the later period means the tax payable for the **tax year** less tax payable for the initial period.

Example 19.4

Denis disposes of an asset in June 2021, giving rise to a chargeable gain of €10,000. He disposes of a second asset in December 2021, giving rise to a chargeable gain of €8,000.

Denis had a loss forward of €3,000 from the disposal of shares in 2020. CGT is payable by Denis as follows:

	€
Tax payable for initial period	
Chargeable gains 01/01/2021–30/11/2021	10,000
Less: losses from 2020	(3,000)
Less: annual exemption	(1,270)
Taxable gain	5,730
CGT @ 33%	1,891
Tax payable for later period	
Total chargeable gains in 2021	18,000
Less: losses from 2020	(3,000)
Less: annual exemption	(1,270)
Total Taxable gains	13,730
CGT @ 33%	4,531
Less: tax payable for initial period	(1,891)
Tax payable for later period	2,640

CGT for 2021 is payable as follows:

On or before 15 December 2021	1,891
On or before 31 January 2022	2,640

It should be noted that tax due for the initial period is calculated **ignoring any losses that might arise in the tax year after 30 November**. Accordingly, where capital losses arising in the period 1 December to 31 December exceed chargeable gains arising in the same period, a refund of CGT will be due. Assuming the asset disposed of by Denis in December 2020 gave rise to an allowable loss of €4,000, he would still be required to pay CGT of €1,891 on 15 December 2021. However, after the end of the tax year he would be entitled to claim a refund as follows:

continued overleaf

	€
Total chargeable gains in 2021	10,000
Less: allowable losses in 2021	(4,000)
Less: losses from 2020	(3,000)
Less: annual exemption	(1,270)
Taxable gains	1,730
CGT @ 33%	571
Less: tax payable for initial period	(1,891)
Refund due	(1,320)

19.5.4 Returns

A return of chargeable gains must be made on or before 31 October in the year following the year of assessment, i.e. for 2021 the return must be made by 31 October 2022. If filing using the Revenue Online System (ROS), the 31 October deadline is usually extended to mid-November. This return will normally be made on a **Form 11** (the self-assessment annual income tax return) where the individual pays income tax under the self-assessment system; or on **Form CG1** where the individual is not within the self-assessment system for income tax purposes.

Failure to submit this return on time will result in the application of a **surcharge** of 5% of the CGT liability or €12,695, whichever is the lower, if filed within two months of the due date. The surcharge is 10% or €63,485, whichever is the lower, if the return is filed more than two months after the due date.

With effect from 1 July 2009, interest on overdue tax is charged at the rate of 0.0219% per day or part of a day (approximately 8% per annum).

19.6 Computation of Gain or Loss

19.6.1 General

The capital gain is the difference between:

1. the **consideration** on disposal of the asset or the **deemed** consideration (e.g. market value in the case of a gift or disposal between connected persons); and
2. the **cost of acquisition** of the asset or its **market value** if not acquired at arm's length (e.g. property acquired by way of gift).

If any part of the sales consideration is taken into account in computing income tax profits or losses, it is excluded from the amount under 1. above.

Any expenditure that is allowable as a deduction from income tax profits is excluded from 2. above. Allowable expenditure for CGT purposes is confined to capital expenditure and excludes expenditure deductible in calculating income. It includes the following:

1. Incidental **costs of acquisition or disposal**, e.g. agent's commission, stamp duty, valuation costs, cost of transfer or conveyance, auctioneers', accountants' or solicitors' fees and advertising costs.
2. Any cost associated with the **creation of an asset** that was not acquired, e.g. copyright, goodwill of a business.

3. Expenditure incurred for the purposes of **enhancing the value** of the asset and which is reflected in the state of the asset at the time of disposal, e.g. improvements to property. Expenditure incurred in establishing, preserving or defending an owner's title or interest in an asset is allowable within this definition.

Any contingent liability is ignored and the gain or loss is calculated as if this liability did not exist. If the contingency happens after the CGT liability has been paid, then at that stage the gain or loss is recalculated to include a deduction for the liability. This will typically lead to a repayment of CGT overpaid.

19.6.2 Indexation Relief

Indexation relief applies to allow the effects of inflation to be taken into account when computing chargeable gains on disposals of assets. It is only available for assets acquired **before 2003** and is only available for the period of ownership up to 1 January 2003.

The relief operates by permitting the cost of any asset (including enhancement expenditure) to be adjusted for inflation by reference to the increases in the Consumer Price Index over the period of ownership of the asset. The table of indexation factors for CGT is included in the tax reference material included at **Appendix 1** at the end of this textbook.

For valuation purposes, any asset owned at **6 April 1974** is deemed to have been disposed of and immediately re-acquired at market value at that date and, therefore, its base cost is its 6 April 1974 market value.

The following important points should be noted about indexation relief:

1. Indexation relief applies to all assets without exception, but is restricted to a significant degree in the case of development land.
2. Indexation relief cannot increase an allowable loss to an amount greater than the actual monetary loss. The allowable loss is restricted to the actual loss.

Example 19.5
Mary bought shares for €1,000 in June 2000. She sold them for €800 in August 2021. What is the allowable loss?

	€
Proceeds	800
Deduct: Cost × indexation factor for year 2000:	
Cost: €1,000 @ 1.144	(1,144)
"Loss"	(344)

As Mary made an actual loss of €200, the allowable loss is €200.

---

3. Indexation relief cannot convert a monetary gain into an allowable loss. In these circumstances, the disposal is at "no gain/no loss", i.e. effectively the disposal is ignored for tax purposes.

Example 19.6
Joe bought shares for €1,000 in June 2001. He sold them for €1,050 in May 2021. What is the taxable gain?

	€
Proceeds	1,050
Cost: €1,000 @ 1.087	(1,087)
"Loss"	(37)

As Joe made an actual monetary gain, the disposal is at "no gain/no loss".

---

4. The interaction of indexation relief and the use of a 6 April 1974 valuation instead of cost can result in an actual monetary gain or loss being increased. In such circumstances, as at 2. above, the taxable gain or allowable loss is restricted to the actual gain or loss. Similarly, the interaction of indexation relief and the use of a 6 April 1974 valuation instead of cost can result in the conversion of an actual monetary gain into a loss, or an actual monetary loss into a gain. In such a scenario, as at 3. above, the disposal is deemed to be at no gain/no loss.

19.6.3 Enhancement Expenditure

Where enhancement expenditure has been incurred on an asset and is **reflected in the asset at the date of disposal**, the original cost and the cost of each subsequent item of enhancement expenditure is deductible. The chargeable gain is calculated as the difference between the various items of expenditure (i.e. both original cost and enhancement expenditure as adjusted for indexation) and the sale proceeds. Enhancement expenditure is **indexed** from the date **when it was incurred**.

Example 19.7
A public house was acquired in November 1998 at a cost of €450,000. Enhancement expenditure was incurred as follows:

		€
1.	November 1999	100,000
2.	November 2001	15,000
3.	November 2003	10,000

The public house was sold in September 2021 for €1,850,000.

Computation of taxable gain

		€	€
Sale proceeds			1,850,000
Deduct: Allowable costs × indexation factors:			
1998/99 expenditure:	€450,000 @ 1.212	545,400	
1999/00 expenditure:	€100,000 @ 1.193	119,300	
2001 expenditure:	€ 15,000 @ 1.087	16,305	
2003 expenditure:	€ 10,000 @ 1.000	10,000	(691,005)
			1,158,995
Deduct: Annual exemption			(1,270)
Taxable gain			1,157,725

19.6.4 Special Rules Relating to Allowable Deductions

1. Treatment of Interest

Interest payments in general are not allowable deductions in the computation of capital gains, **except** where a company incurs interest on money borrowed to finance the construction of any building, structure or works. Such interest will be allowed as a deduction where the interest was not availed of by the company as a deduction in computing its profits for the purposes of corporation tax.

2. Value-added Tax (VAT)

Where a person acquires a chargeable asset and the acquisition is liable to VAT, the cost of the asset for CGT depends on whether or not the acquirer is entitled to claim "input credit" in respect of the VAT. If the acquirer cannot claim input credit, the cost of the asset is the VAT-inclusive price. Where the acquirer can claim input credit, the cost of the asset is the VAT-exclusive price. In other words, if VAT can be reclaimed it is no longer a cost.

3. Insurance Premiums
Insurance premiums paid to protect against damage to an asset are specifically not an allowable deduction.

4. Foreign Tax
Where the person making a disposal of a foreign asset incurs a charge to foreign tax and the foreign tax is incurred in a country with which Ireland has a **double taxation treaty**, relief is given by deducting the foreign tax paid from the Irish CGT, i.e. **credit relief**.

Example 19.8

Jones realised a gain of €500,000, after annual exemption, on the disposal of a property in Paris in March 2021. The French CGT payable was €80,000. The CGT computation is as follows:

	€
Chargeable gain	500,000
Irish CGT payable @ 33%	165,000
Less: credit for French CGT paid	(80,000)
Balance of Irish CGT payable	85,000

Where the person making a disposal of a foreign asset incurs a charge to foreign CGT on the gain arising and **no double taxation relief** is available for the foreign CGT suffered, then the **foreign CGT may be deducted** in computing the amount of the gain that is chargeable to Irish CGT.

Example 19.9

Smith sold a capital asset located in Libya, a country with which Ireland does not have a double taxation treaty, for €900,000. The indexed cost of the asset was €398,730. The Libyan tax paid on the capital gain was €80,000. The CGT computation is as follows:

	€
Total sale proceeds	900,000
Less: foreign CGT	(80,000)
Net proceeds	820,000
Less: indexed cost	(398,730)
Less: annual exemption	(1,270)
Taxable	420,000
Irish CGT @ 33%	**138,600**

---

5. Grants
When computing chargeable gains, no deduction is allowed for any expenditure that has been met by the provision of government, public or local authority grants (whether Irish or foreign).

19.6.5 Part Disposal of an Asset

A partial disposal of an asset is a chargeable event for CGT purposes. Where a portion of an asset is sold, the sale proceeds are known but the issue arises as to how much of the original cost of the asset is allowable as a deduction when computing the chargeable gain or allowable loss arising on the part disposal.

Section 557 TCA 1997 provides that the portion of the original cost allowed against the consideration received on the part disposal is based on the following formula:

$$\text{Original cost} \times \frac{A}{(A + B)}$$

where:

A = amount of the proceeds (or market value) of the part disposal, and
B = the market value of the portion of the asset that is **retained**.

Example 19.10

Assume an asset cost €1,000 on 1 September 2021 and that nine months later part of the asset was sold for €600. The market value of the remainder of the asset is €700. The chargeable gain in respect of the disposal would be computed as follows:

	€
Sale proceeds	600
Less: allowable cost: $€1,000 \times \dfrac{€600}{(€600 + €700)}$	(462)
Chargeable gain	138

Note: the balance of the cost of €538 (€1,000 – €462) will be carried forward against any future disposal of the remainder of the asset and will be the allowable cost deductible in calculating any gain arising on the disposal of the remainder of the asset.

Example 19.11

Asset cost €10,000 on 10 April 1982. Part of the asset was sold on 10 November 2006 for €27,000. At that time, the market value of the remainder of the asset was €50,000. The remainder of the asset was sold on 1 November 2021 for €30,000.

The individual is married. Calculate the CGT liability for 2021.

Value of asset at time of 2006 sale:		€
Sale proceeds		27,000
Less: allowable cost: $€10,000 \times \dfrac{€27,000}{(€27,000 + €50,000)} = 3,506$		
Cost × 1982/83 indexation factor – 2.253		(7,899)
Chargeable gain		19,101
Value of remaining asset (€10,000 – €3,506)		6,494
2021 disposal:		
Proceeds		30,000
Less: allowable cost: value of remaining asset	6,494	
Cost × 1982/83 indexation factor – 2.253		(14,630)
		15,370
Less: Annual exemption		(1,270)
Taxable gain		14,100
CGT due @ 33%		**4,653**

The marital status of the individual has no bearing on the final tax due.

19.6.6 *Application of Market Value*

Normally where a disposal is at arm's length, the **consideration**, in money terms, is accepted for CGT purposes. However, the **market value** is deemed to be the consideration for the purpose of determining the chargeable gain/loss where the transaction is:

1. between connected persons, as defined in law, the *main* people being:
    - (a) **spouse**, **civil partner** and **relatives** (brother, sister, uncle, aunt, niece, nephew, ancestor or lineal descendant (including stepchild or adopted child) but excluding cousins);
    - (b) **in-laws**;
    - (c) **business partners**;
    - (d) a **company** where a person has **control** of the company.
2. not at arm's length (e.g. gift);
3. for a consideration that is not valued in money terms or that is a barter transaction;
4. for a consideration that cannot be valued;
5. the acquisition of an asset in a winding up situation; or
6. the acquisition of an asset in connection with an office or employment, or in recognition of past services from an office or employment,

19.7 Date of Disposal

The date of disposal determines the rate of CGT that applies and when the CGT must be paid, e.g. CGT arising on gains accruing in October 2021 must be paid by 15 December 2021. The date of disposal and the date a gain accrues is the **same** date. Briefly, the rules for the date of disposal are as follows:

1. In the case of an **unconditional contract**, the date of the contract is the relevant date irrespective of the date of the conveyance or transfer of the asset.
2. In the case of a **conditional contract**, the general rule is that the date of the disposal for the purposes of CGT is the date on which the condition is satisfied. A conditional contract is a contract that is subject to a condition that must be satisfied before there is a binding contract between the parties, e.g. a contract for the sale of land that is subject to planning permission being granted in respect of the land.
3. In the case of **gifts**, the date of disposal is the date on which the property effectively passes.
4. In the case of **compulsory purchase orders**, the date of disposal is the date the compensation is received.
5. In **compensation cases**, the effective date is usually the date of receipt of the compensation.

19.8 Development Land

19.8.1 *Introduction*

Disposals of development land made on or after 28 January 1982 are subject to special CGT treatment involving restrictions of indexation relief and loss relief. Irish resident companies are only assessed to CGT on disposals of development land; all other disposals by Irish resident companies are assessed to corporation tax.

Development land is land which, at the time a disposal is made, the consideration or market value exceeds the **current use value (CUV)** of that land. The CUV is the market value of the land if it was illegal to carry out any development. For example, a farm worth approximately €10,000 an acre as farmland but sold for €50,000 an acre, as it has outline planning permission for housing, is development land.

A similar definition is also provided in relation to shares in an **unquoted** company that derive their value, or the greater part of their value, directly or indirectly from land.

The rate of CGT applicable to development land is the normal rate, i.e. **33%**.

19.8.2 Restriction of Indexation Relief

In the case of development land acquired **prior** to 6 April 1974, indexation relief may only be applied to the **CUV** portion of the market value of the asset at 6 April 1974. The difference between the market value and the current use value can be deducted as an allowable cost but without indexation relief.

Enhancement expenditure incurred after acquisition can be treated as an allowable cost when calculating the CGT liability but is not available for indexation relief.

Example 19.12

	€	€
Sale proceeds: development land 1 August 2021		<u>150,000</u>
Original cost of acquisition 1 January 1968	10,000	
Total market value 6 April 1974	30,000	
CUV at 6 April 1974	14,000	
Enhancement expenditure May 1986	5,000	

CGT computation 2021

	€	€
Sale proceeds		150,000
Deduct: CUV at 6 April 1974:		
€14,000 indexed @ 7.528 (1974/75)	(105,392)	
Balance of market value at 6 April 1974	(16,000)	
Enhancement expenditure May 1986	<u>(5,000)</u>	<u>(126,392)</u>
Chargeable gain		23,608
Deduct: annual exemption		<u>(1,270)</u>
Taxable gain		<u>22,338</u>
CGT due @ 33%		<u>7,372</u>

In the case of development land acquired **after** 6 April 1974, indexation relief may only be applied to the CUV portion of the consideration paid together with the appropriate portion of total incidental costs of acquisition at that date. As before, enhancement expenditure incurred after acquisition can be treated as an allowable cost when calculating the CGT liability but is not available for indexation relief.

Example 19.13

	€	€
Sale proceeds: development land 1 August 2021		<u>200,000</u>
Original cost of acquisition 1 July 1982	40,000	
Current use value 1 July 1982	21,000	
Incidental costs of acquisition	1,000	
Enhancement expenditure June 1986	3,000	

continued overleaf

CGT Computation 2021		
	€	€
Sale proceeds		200,000
Deduct: CUV on purchase		
€21,000 indexed @ 2.253 (1982/83)	(47,313)	
Incidental costs referable to CUV:		
$€1,000 \times \dfrac{€21,000}{€40,000} = €525$ indexed @ 2.253	(1,183)	
Balance of original cost (€40,000 – €21,000)	(19,000)	
Balance of incidental costs (€1,000 – €525)	(475)	
Enhancement expenditure	(3,000)	(70,971)
Chargeable gain		129,029
Deduct: annual exemption		(1,270)
Taxable gain		127,759
CGT due @ 33%		42,160

19.8.3 Restriction of Loss Relief

Normally, allowable losses for CGT may be set-off against other chargeable gains realised in the same year of assessment or, alternatively, carried forward against chargeable gains in future years. The legislation relating to development land provides that allowable losses on assets other than development land **may not be set-off** against gains arising on the sale of development land. However, allowable losses arising on the disposal of development land may be offset against the gains arising on any type of **chargeable asset**.

19.8.4 Disposals of Development Land for €19,050 or Less

The special CGT rules relating to restriction of indexation and loss reliefs that normally apply to sales of development land do not apply where **the total sales consideration** (not the amount of the gain) for disposals of development land by an individual **does not exceed €19,050 in any year of assessment**. It should be noted that this special relief is restricted to individuals and is not available to companies.

Questions

Review Questions

(See Suggested Solutions to Review Questions at the end of this textbook.)

Question 19.1

1. Maurice purchased a holiday home for €20,000 on 2 February 1985 and subsequently sold it on 30 November 2021 for €80,000. Incidental legal costs on purchase amounted to €600, and €750 on sale.

2. Vincent bought shares in a Plc in December 1991 for €1,200. He sold the shares for €9,300 on 1 April 2021.
3. The following capital assets were sold on 31 December 2021:

Sold by	Cost	Date of Purchase	Market Value @ 06/04/74	Sale Proceeds
	€		€	€
(a) John	7,600	June 2001	N/A	7,800
(b) Philip	3,000	July 1980	N/A	2,700
(c) Paul	5,700	June 1973	5,800	5,500
(d) Oliver	15,000	July 1980	N/A	18,000

Requirement

Compute the CGT due or allowable losses in each case. Assume that the individuals had no other realised gains or losses during the year.

Question 19.2

1. James constructed a hotel in July 1992 for €260,000. He received a capital grant from the State of €10,000. Additional expenditure was incurred as follows:

		€
August 2001	Repair to roof	3,000
May 2004	Three new bedrooms added	90,000

James sold the hotel on 31 May 2021 for €650,000. James had no other capital gains during 2021.

2. Declan purchased a public house on 6 April 1998 for €85,000. Additional expenditure was incurred as follows:

	€
Additional games room (6 August 2001)	20,000
Additional lounge bar (1 February 2003)	39,250

Declan sold the public house for €400,000 on 1 July 2021. Declan had no other capital gains during 2021.

Requirement

Compute the CGT payable by James and Declan in each case (assume that the 33% rate of CGT applies).

Question 19.3

Michael Gain made the following disposals of Plc shares on 6 October 2021.

	Cost	Date Purchased	Proceeds
	€		€
1,000 Courtaulds Plc	888	06/11/1974	1,162
1,550 Box Plc	1,732	07/05/1981	1,662
500 Cox Plc	1,693	07/12/1993	16,000
400 Nox Plc	623	01/03/2005	1,305

Michael is not married and had no other chargeable gains during 2021.

Requirement

Compute chargeable gains (if any) made by Michael and the CGT payable (if any) for 2021.

Question 19.4

Derek Cotter is 49 years old and has completed the following capital transactions for the year ended 31 December 2021. He has lived in Ireland all his life.

1. On 12 January 2021 he sold a 5% holding, with a market value of €50,000, in the family tanning business to his sister for €40,000. Derek had inherited the shares from his father in January 2000 when they had a market value of €8,000.
2. On 5 February 2021 he sold his holiday home in Florida for €320,000. Derek had acquired the property for €110,000 on 30 October 1999.
3. On 5 May 2021 he sold shares in a Plc for €30,000. Derek had purchased the shares for €50,000 in April 2002.
4. On 10 December 2021 he sold a house (not his principal private residence) in Foxrock, Dublin, for €2,000,000. Derek had acquired the house and garden in December 1992 for €300,000. Derek sold the garden of one acre for €500,000 on 30 April 2001. The remainder of the house and garden was valued at €1,000,000 on 30 April 2001. The house did not have any development value at 10 December 2020.
5. On 21 December 2021 he gifted an antique chair to his nephew, Tom. The chair had been purchased for €2,600 on 3 December 2001. On 21 December 2021 the chair was valued at €3,500.

Requirement

Compute Derek's CGT liability for the tax year 2021 and state the due dates for the payment of this liability (assume that the 33% rate of CGT applies to all gains).

Exemptions, Reliefs and Capital Losses

Learning Objectives

After studying this chapter you will understand:

- how to identify, advise on and apply the appropriate CGT treatment to disposals of particular assets that qualify for exemptions or relief, including:
  - government securities;
  - chattels;
  - site to a child;
  - certain land and buildings acquired from 7 December 2011 to 31 December 2014;
  - miscellaneous property;
  - principal private residence relief; and
- how to determine and apply the appropriate treatment for capital losses.

20.1 Gains Exempt from CGT

The following gains are **exempt** from CGT.

- Winnings from betting, lotteries, sweepstakes or games with prizes.
- Bonuses under the National Instalments Savings Scheme.
- Securities of government, local authorities and semi-State bodies.
- Sums obtained as compensation or damages for any wrong or injury suffered by an individual including libel and slander.
- Certain life assurance policies.
- A gain arising on the disposal of tangible movable property (i.e. a **wasting** chattel with a life of **less** than 50 years) does not give rise to a charge to tax, but chattels that are business assets qualifying for capital allowances are excluded (see **Section 20.2** below).
- A gain arising to an **individual** on the disposal of **non-wasting** chattels (i.e. a chattel with a life of **greater** than 50 years is exempt if the consideration (after sale expenses) does not exceed €2,540.
- Gains on disposals of fine art objects with a market value of at least €31,740 and which were on loan and displayed in an approved gallery or museum for not less than 10 years.

20.2 Wasting and Non-wasting Chattels

A chattel is defined as "tangible movable property" that has a predictable useful life.

20.2.1 Wasting Chattels

A wasting chattel is a chattel with a **predictable life not exceeding 50 years**, for example, livestock, bloodstock, private motor car, yachts, aeroplanes and caravans. These assets include durable consumer goods that waste away over their lifetime and whose residual value is negligible so that gains will not normally arise on their ultimate disposal. Plant (other than plant that is a work of art) and machinery is always to be regarded as having a predictable life of less than 50 years and is always a wasting asset. Accordingly, antique plant or machinery, e.g. an antique clock or a vintage car, is deemed for tax purposes to have a predictable life of less than 50 years, even though in reality such an asset may be older.

A work of art, such as a picture, print, book, manuscript, sculpture, piece of jewellery, furniture or similar object, is **not** a wasting asset and therefore is subject to the treatment outlined at **Section 20.2.2.**

A gain arising on the disposal of tangible movable property that is a wasting asset **does not** give rise to a charge to tax.

The exemption is **not** given where the chattels are **business assets** used in a trade or profession **and** which qualify for capital allowances. This is because capital allowances, up to the full cost of those assets, are given for income tax purposes and even if capital allowances were not claimed, the exemption will still not operate if the allowances **could** have been claimed.

20.2.2 Treatment of Wasting Chattels that have Qualified for Capital Allowances

As outlined above, the exemption from CGT on gains realised from the disposal of wasting chattels does not apply to the extent that the chattels have qualified for capital allowances.

If the entire asset has qualified for capital allowances and the allowances have not been restricted due to private usage, then any loss arising on disposal of the asset will not be allowable for CGT purposes as it will have been effectively relieved for income tax or corporation tax purposes.

Example 20.1

	€
Business equipment cost	10,000
Tax WDV at date of sale	2,000
Sale proceeds	4,500
Computation	
Sale proceeds	4,500
Cost	(10,000)
Loss	(5,500)
Loss allowed for CGT purposes	Nil

The loss of €5,500 has already been fully relieved for income tax purposes as follows:

	€
Original cost	10,000
Less: tax WDV at date of sale	(2,000)
Capital allowances granted during period of ownership	8,000 **(A)**

continued overleaf

Sale proceeds	4,500
Less: tax WDV at date of sale	(2,000)
Balancing charge on disposal	2,500 **(B)**
Capital allowances granted A – B	5,500

If a wasting asset is sold and the asset has qualified without restriction for capital allowances purposes, then any gain arising after indexation relief has been taken into account is fully chargeable to CGT.

Example 20.2

	€
Business equipment cost	1,000
Tax WDV at date of sale	Nil
Sale proceeds	4,500

Asset owned by single individual for four years.
Indexation factor to be applied is 1.8.

Computation of gain

	€
Sale proceeds	4,500
Cost €1,000 @ 1.8	(1,800)
Chargeable gain	2,700

Note: the total capital allowances granted during the period of ownership will be recaptured on sale by means of a balancing charge.

20.2.3   Non-wasting chattels

A non-wasting chattel is a chattel that has a predictable life of **more than 50 years**. Though the term "tangible movable property" is not defined, it covers, for example, paintings, antiques, postage stamps, etc.

A gain arising on the disposal of tangible movable property, which is a non-wasting asset, **does** give rise to a charge to tax.

20.2.4   Relief for Non-wasting Chattels Sold for €2,540 or Less

A gain arising to an **individual**, after the deduction of expenses of sale, on the disposal of non-wasting chattels is exempt if the consideration does not exceed €2,540.

Where the consideration exceeds €2,540, there is **a marginal relief** that restricts the tax payable to 50% of the excess of the proceeds over €2,540. The CGT is first calculated as if no marginal relief applies, deducting the annual exemption of €1,270, if applicable. This figure is then compared to the maximum CGT payable as calculated using the marginal relief formula and the lesser amount is the CGT liability. The annual exemption is only taken into account to the extent that it cannot be used against other chargeable gains.

Example 20.3
Assume that assets were acquired in 2005 and that the annual exemption had already been used against other chargeable gains.

	Asset 1	Asset 2
	€	€
Sale proceeds	2,550	2,590
Cost of asset	(1,400)	(2,550)
Chargeable gain	1,150	40
Less: exemption	(Nil)	(Nil)
Gain	1,150	40
CGT @ 33%	379	13
Compare with:		
Half the excess of sale proceeds over €2,540	5	25
CGT payable	5	13

Where a loss is incurred on the disposal of a chattel for less than €2,540, the allowable loss is restricted by deeming the **consideration** to be exactly €2,540.

Example 20.4
Two works of art with the following details:

	€	€
Sale proceeds	1,400	1,900
Cost	(2,600)	(2,720)
Actual loss	(1,200)	(820)
Allowable loss – in each case cost less €2,540	(60)	(180)

Note: in such circumstances, expenses of sale are added to the allowable loss and not deducted from the consideration for the purpose of the €2,540 limit. If the expenses on each sale were €30, the allowable loss would be increased to €90 and €210.

Note: the €2,540 exemption rule does not apply to currency and commodity futures in addition to **not** applying to wasting assets.

20.3 Disposal of a Site to a Child

A CGT exemption exists, under section 603A TCA 1997, where a parent disposes of a site to their child (or certain foster children), on or after **6 December 2000**, for the purpose of enabling the child to **construct a dwelling** house on the land and which is to be occupied by the child as their **only or main residence**. Such a disposal by the parent is **exempt** from CGT **provided** the market value of the site at the date of the disposal does not exceed €500,000. The site area is limited to one acre (0.4047 hectare) (excluding the area of the house to be built).

Where the child subsequently disposes of a site that qualified for exemption to any person, other than a spouse or civil partner, and the land does not contain a dwelling house that:

1. was constructed by the child since the time of the acquisition of the land; **and**
2. had been occupied by the child as their only or main residence for a period of three years,

then the chargeable gain, that would have accrued to the parent, is treated as accruing to the child.

Where the transfer of a site to a child has qualified for exemption, a further transfer of another site to that child will **not qualify** for exemption unless the chargeable gain that would have accrued on the transfer of the first site to the child is treated as accruing to the child.

20.4 Certain Land and Buildings Acquired between 7 December 2011 and 31 December 2014

Section 604A TCA 1997 provides an exemption from CGT on gains arising on the disposal of land and buildings in the State and the EEA (EU plus Norway, Iceland and Liechtenstein) if the property was acquired **between 7 December 2011** and **31 December 2014** and held for **seven years**, with tapered relief if the asset was sold after that date. For disposals on or after **1 January 2018** the holding period is **four years**. The legislation maintains full exemption for properties sold up to seven years after acquisition, with tapered relief after that date.

To qualify for relief the property must be:

- acquired in the period 7 December 2011 to 31 December 2014;
- at a consideration equal to its market value or, if acquired from a relative, at a consideration not less than 75% of the market value at the date of acquisition; and
- continue in the ownership of the person who acquired that land or buildings for at least four years from the date of acquisition; and
- the income, profits or gains from the land or buildings must be within the charge to Irish taxation.

Example 20.5

In October 2014, Patrick, who is Irish resident, acquired an investment property in Dublin for €250,000. Patrick pays Irish income tax on the rental income. In September 2017 he received an offer of €425,000 for the property.

What are the CGT implications if Patrick were to accept the offer?

If Patrick were to accept the offer in September 2017, the disposal would not have been exempt from CGT as he had not held the property for at least seven years. Ignoring the annual exemption, he would have paid CGT of €57,750, (i.e. €425,000 – €250,000 @ 33%).

If Patrick decides to accept the offer in February 2019, how would this affect his CGT liability?

In February 2019 the gain on disposal would be exempt from CGT as he would have held a qualifying property for at least **four** years.

Example 20.6

Sheila acquired an investment property in Dublin on 1 March 2014 for €180,000. She pays Irish income tax on the rental income. On 1 March 2022, Sheila sells the property for €315,000. What are the CGT implications (ignoring the annual exemption)?

A portion of the gain will be exempt (i.e. reflecting seven years' "exempt" ownership):

Ownership: 1 March 2014 to 1 March 2022 = 8 years

Exempt: 1 March 2014 to 1 March 2021 = 7 years

	€
Sale proceeds	315,000
Cost	(180,000)
Gain	135,000
Deduct: Exempt gain: €135,000 × 7/8	(118,125)
Chargeable gain	16,875
CGT @ 33%	**5,569**

20.5 Principal Private Residence Exemption

20.5.1 Introduction

The general rule is that a gain accruing on the disposal of an individual's principal private residence (PPR) is exempt from CGT. Grounds up to one acre (exclusive of the site of the house) around the house are also exempt. If there is more than one acre of land, then the acre to be taken is that which would be most suitable for occupation and enjoyment with the residence.

Only one house per person qualifies for exemption, and spouses or civil partners **count as one person** for this purpose. A person with two or more residences will nominate which one will qualify for relief by giving notice to the Inspector of Taxes within two years of the beginning of the period of ownership of the two or more residences. Unless such notice is given, the Inspector may decide the matter, subject to the taxpayer's rights of appeal within 21 days to the Tax Appeals Commission.

If the owner rents out a room in the PPR and qualifies for rent-a-room relief, this will not reduce any relief due under these provisions.

20.5.2 Occupation and Deemed Occupation of PPR

Full exemption from CGT is granted only where the owner has occupied the house throughout the period of ownership. Where occupation has been only for **part** of the period of ownership, the exempt part of the gain is the proportion given by the formula:

$$\frac{\text{Period of occupation} \times \text{Chargeable gain}}{\text{Total period of ownership}}$$

Any period of ownership before 6 April 1974 is ignored.

The period of occupation is deemed to include **certain periods of absence,** provided:

1. the individual had **no other exempt residence** at the time; and

2. the period of absence was both preceded by, and followed by, a period of occupation.

It is not necessary for the periods of occupation to immediately precede and follow the periods of absence. It is enough that there was occupation at some time before and after absence. The periods of absence deemed to be periods of occupation subject to the above condition are:

- **any periods** in which the owner was required by their employment to **work wholly outside Ireland**; and
- any period **not exceeding four years**, or periods that together do not exceed four years, as condition of employment or place of work, the individual had to reside away from home. Where such periods exceed four years, only four years are deemed to be periods of occupation.

There is also a general rule whereby the **last 12 months of ownership** are included in the period of occupation as long as the owner was in occupation at some time during the period of ownership.

Revenue also provides for two further periods of deemed occupation as follows:

- where an individual was receiving care in a hospital, nursing home or convalescent home, or was resident in a retirement home on a fee-paying basis, and the private residence remained unoccupied (or only occupied by a relative, rent-free, for the purpose of security or maintaining the house in a habitable condition); **or**
- where an individual has a house constructed on land they already own, provided the house is completed within a year of the acquisition of the land and occupied as the individual's PPR by the individual. The period from the date the land was acquired and the house was first occupied shall be treated as a period of occupation of the house as a main residence.

It should be noted that in the case where full exemption is not available, partial relief will apply to reduce the liability of any chargeable gain arising.

Example 20.7

Owen Gough bought a freehold house for €6,000 on 1 April 1987. He lived in it until 30 September 1997 when he moved into a rented flat. He let the house until he sold it on 1 October 2021 for €220,000.

In the period 30 September 1997 to 1 October 2021, there is one year's deemed occupation, i.e. the last 12 months of ownership. Therefore, the CGT liability is:

	€
Proceeds	220,000
Deduct: Cost: €6,000 @ 1.637	(9,822)
Chargeable gain	210,178
Less: exempt portion:	
$\dfrac{10.5 \text{ years} + 1 \text{ year}}{34.5 \text{ years}} \times €210{,}178$	(70,059)
Chargeable gain	140,119
CGT @ 33%	**46,239**

It is assumed that the annual exemption has been utilised against other gains.

Alternatively, a loss on the PPR is not allowable. However, where the house had only been a PPR for part of the period of ownership, then a similar part of the loss is allowable.

Example 20.8
Una bought a house for €250,000 on 1 May 2010. She lived in it until 1 May 2012 when she let it. On 1 May 2021 she sold the house.

If she sold it for €210,000, her capital loss would be:

	€
Proceeds	210,000
Deduct: Cost	(250,000)
Loss	(40,000)
Reduce by: PPR exempt portion:	
$\dfrac{2 \text{ years } + 1 \text{ years}}{11 \text{ years}} \times €40,000$	10,090
Allowable loss	**(29,910)**

This would be allowed against any other gains and her CGT for 2021 would be calculated, net of the annual exemption.

If a portion of the house is used for the purpose of a trade or profession, the gain must be apportioned as the part used for the trade is not exempt. The PPR relief is calculated as:

$$\frac{\text{Period of occupation}}{\text{Period of ownership}} \times \text{Gain} \times \% \text{ used as residence}$$

20.5.3 House Occupied by Dependent Relative

The legislation extends the PPR exemption to a gain arising on the disposal of a private residence **owned** by an individual and occupied by a dependent relative as their PPR where:

- the house must be occupied by a dependent relative of the individual claiming the relief;
- the house must have been provided to the dependent relative free of any charge and without any other consideration; or
- the house must have been occupied by the dependent relative as their sole private residence throughout the full period of ownership.

For any particular individual, only one house can qualify for the relief at a particular time. However, in the case of spouses or civil partners, relief can be claimed by each spouse or civil partner in respect of a disposal of a PPR owned by them and occupied by a dependent relative **of that spouse or civil partner**. For example, a married couple could have three PPRs: their own, and one for a dependent relative of each spouse.

20.5.4 Restriction of PPR Exemption – Development Land

A PPR and land up to **one acre** around it may be sold for development value. In this case, the exemption will only apply to the current use value of the house or land, i.e. without its development value. The balance of the gain arising is effectively treated as a gain on disposal of development land.

20.6   Capital Losses

20.6.1   General

Capital losses are computed in the same manner as gains. Where an asset (that is not an exempt asset) is sold for less than the allowable cost of acquiring and enhancing the asset, an allowable loss arises. An allowable loss may also arise where the asset is not sold but where the asset value becoming negligible (see **Section 20.6.5** below).

Allowable losses can be set-off against chargeable gains arising in the **same year** of assessment. Any unutilised balance of losses can be carried forward and set-off against chargeable gains arising in the earliest **subsequent** year.

Loss relief must be utilised before the €1,270 annual exemption may be taken.

Example 20.9
Janet has the following gains/losses for 2021:

	€
15 January Asset 1 Gain	4,000
23 May Asset 2 Gain	2,000
17 August Asset 3 Loss	(4,000)
29 November Asset 4 Gain	3,000

Janet has allowable losses forward of €2,000 from 2020. Loss relief will be claimed as follows:

	€
Chargeable gains 2021	9,000
Less: 2021 allowable losses	(4,000)
Deduct: allowable losses forward 2020	(2,000)
	3,000
Deduct: annual exemption	(1,270)
Taxable gains	1,730
CGT due @ 33%	**571**

20.6.2   Carry-back of Losses – Terminal Relief

While the general rule is that capital losses cannot be carried back to earlier years, an exception to this rule is made in the case of losses that accrue to an individual **in the year in which they die** but not on death (see **Section 20.7** below). These losses may be carried back and set against gains of the **three years** of assessment proceeding the year of assessment in which the individual died.

Example 20.10
Mr Marat dies on 31 August 2021. In the period 1 January 2021 to 31 August 2021 he made disposals of assets and made allowable losses of €5,000.

The losses of €5,000 will first be available for set-off against any chargeable gains assessed on Mr Marat in 2020, then against any chargeable gains in 2019 and, finally, against any chargeable gains in the tax year 2018. Any overpaid tax will be repaid by Revenue.

20.6.3 Losses between Connected Persons

Where a disposal to a connected person results in an allowable loss, that loss may only be **set-off against chargeable gains on disposals to the same connected person**.

20.6.4 Losses on Assets Qualifying for Capital Allowances

Expenditure which qualifies for capital allowances represents an allowable cost for CGT purposes. However, to the extent that a loss on an asset has been covered by capital allowances no further relief is allowed for CGT purposes.

Example 20.11

	€
Cost of factory (qualifying for industrial buildings allowance)	150,000
Sale proceeds	120,000
Capital losses	30,000

Assuming the tax written down value of the building is €100,000, a balancing charge of €20,000 will arise. The capital loss allowable is restricted as follows:

	€	€
Capital loss		30,000
Allowances claimed	50,000	
Less: Balancing charge	(20,000)	
Net allowances granted		(30,000)
Allowable capital loss		Nil

If the written down value of the building was nil, then the allowable capital loss would still be nil, i.e.:

	€	€
Capital loss		30,000
Allowances claimed	150,000	
Balancing charge	(120,000)	
Net allowances granted		(30,000)
Allowable capital loss		Nil

In general, capital losses arising on the sale of assets qualifying for capital allowances will only be allowable for CGT purposes to the extent, if any, by which **they exceed the capital allowances granted for income tax purposes** (including any balancing allowance). Such an unlikely situation might arise, e.g. in the case of a sole trader who used an asset partly for business and partly for private use. In such a case, a capital loss arising on disposal would not be fully relieved by way of a balancing allowance (due to restriction for private element) and some measure of CGT loss relief might then be available.

20.6.5 Negligible Value Claims

Where a person owns a capital asset, the value of which is now negligible, the person may make a claim to Revenue for relief for the unrealised loss. Even though there is no disposal of an asset, if Revenue is satisfied that the value of an asset has become negligible, they may allow relief for the loss. The loss relief is allowed when the claim is made. On a strict interpretation of the law, a loss under this provision is allowable only in the year of claim. In practice, however, a claim made within 12 months of the end of the year of assessment (or accounting period for a company) for which relief is sought will be allowed by Revenue, provided that the asset was of negligible value in the year of assessment or accounting period concerned. Negligible is not defined and has its normal meaning, i.e. not worth considering; insignificant.

Example 20.12

Joe owns 1,000 shares in BigBank DAC, which he bought for €15 per share and which are now only worth 50c per share. He also owns 1,500 shares in Defunct Ltd, which he bought for €10 per share. A liquidator has been appointed to Defunct Ltd and it is insolvent. Joe had other CGT gains of €23,000 in 2021.

CGT computation 2021

	€
Chargeable gains 2021	23,000
Less: 2021 allowable losses:	
BigBank DAC	Nil
Defunct Ltd – 1,500 @ €10	(15,000)
	8,000
Deduct: annual exemption	(1,270)
Taxable gains	6,730
CGT due @ 33%	**2,221**

Note: Joe is entitled to make a claim for the loss of €15,000 in Defunct Ltd as the shares have negligible value. While he has suffered a very significant unrealised loss on the shares in BigBank DAC, the shares have more than negligible value and, therefore, he cannot get relief for the unrealised loss. He can only get relief when he sells the bank shares.

20.7 Death

Any assets of a deceased person are deemed to be acquired on their death, by the personal representatives or by the beneficiary, at the **market value at the date of death**. The deemed transfer at market value at date of death **does not** give rise to a chargeable disposal for CGT purposes and, accordingly, no liability will attach to the estate of the deceased in respect of any gains realised on the asset over their lifetime. The converse is also true in that no allowable losses are crystallised on a death. The **base cost** for the purposes of a subsequent disposal, by the personal representatives or by the beneficiaries, of an asset acquired on death is the market value at the **date of death**.

Questions

Review Questions

(See Suggested Solutions to Review Questions at the end of this textbook.)

Question 20.1

Philip Even is married, and during the tax year 2021, he completed the following transactions:

1. On 1 July 2021 he gave a gift of a painting to his wife. He bought the painting in June 1988 for €8,000 and its current market value is €17,000.
2. On 1 September 2021 he sold two acres of development land to his son, John, for €10,000. The land has planning permission for residential development. The market value of the land on 1 September 2021 was €200,000. He originally bought it on 1 June 1982 for €5,000. At that date the current use value of the land was €3,000.
3. He sold a small farm for €260,000 on 1 June 2021. He originally acquired the farm by gift from his wife on 25 December 1992. The market value of the farm at that date was €50,000. The farm has been let by Philip for the last 10 years. The farm is not development land. His wife originally acquired it for €32,000 on 1 July 1990.
4. He sold his entire holding of Irish Government National Loan Stock on 1 July 2021 for €8,000. He had originally acquired it for €6,100 on 1 February 2011.
5. He sold an antique necklace for €1,500 on 7 August 2021. He had bought the necklace nine months earlier for €1,100.
6. He sold a painting on 8 August 2021 for €900. He had bought the painting in January 2005 for €1,200.
7. He gifted one of his commercial properties to his mother on 1 August 2021. The market value of the property at that date was €875,000. He originally bought the property on 1 January 1983 for €50,000. In June 1989 he extended the property at a cost of €60,000. In March 2007 he further extended the property at a cost of €50,000.
8. He sold a second piece of development land on 1 October 2021 for €18,000. He had acquired this land four months earlier for €10,000.
9. On 1 June 2021 he sold an antique vase for €1,800. He had bought the vase for €700 in June 1992.

Philip had agreed unutilised losses forward at 1 January 2021 of:

(a) losses unrelated to development land of €6,000;
(b) losses in respect of disposals of development land of €1,500.

Requirement
Compute Philip Even's CGT liability for 2021.

Question 20.2

(a) Mrs O'Sullivan sold a large freehold commercial property on 6 October 2021. She had owned it for many years and it had been continuously let to tenants at a commercial rent. The details given to you are:

	€
Disposal proceeds	1,585,000
Legal costs of disposal	12,500
Agent's commission	7,000

The property had been extended on 6 June 1994 at a cost of €162,000. The agreed value at 6 April 1974 was €60,000.

Requirement (a)
Calculate the chargeable gain in respect of the above disposal.

(b) Mrs O'Sullivan had 10 acres of development land adjoining a housing estate. She acquired the land in June 1970 for €5,000. She has received an offer for the land of €1.8 million. The market value of the land at April 1974 was €25,000 and its current use value at that date was €12,500.

Requirement (b)
Calculate the CGT payable on the assumption the land is sold for €1.8 million on 31 May 2021. (Ignore the annual exemption.)

Question 20.3

Bill O'Rourke bought a substantial residence on one acre of land in Rathgar, Dublin, on 6 April 1986 for €75,000. His incidental costs on purchase were €4,251.

Bill accepted an offer from a developer and signed a contract for sale on 10 June 2021 for the residence and one acre at a selling price of €1.68 million. Incidental costs of disposal were €18,000. The value of the property as a residence at the date of disposal was €800,000.

Throughout the period of ownership, Mr O'Rourke had used the property as his PPR.

Requirement
Compute the chargeable gain in respect of Bill's disposal.

Question 20.4

On 5 January 2021, Mr Smart, a single man, sold a shop premises that he had owned as an investment. The sale price was €695,000 and costs of disposal amounted to €7,000. He had never occupied the premises himself and had never carried on a trade in the property.

The premises had been purchased in 1973 and was professionally valued at €10,000 as at 6 April 1974. Enhancement expenditure of €12,000 was incurred on 6 December 1991.

On 1 October 2021, Mr Smart reinvested €580,000 in an investment property let in four units.

On 1 June 2021, Mr Smart also sold a holiday cottage to his nephew for €16,000. Mr Smart had purchased the cottage on 6 July 1987 for €25,000. The market value of the cottage on 1 June 2021 was €20,000.

Requirement
Advise Mr Smart of his CGT liability, if any, for the tax year 2021, giving reasons for your conclusions.

Question 20.5

Christine Martin, a single woman, entered into the following transactions during 2021.

1. On 1 August 2021, she disposed of a derelict shop for €224,000. The property was adjacent to a shopping centre that wished to expand. The current use value of the property at the date of disposal was €80,000. Auctioneer's fees amounted to €3,100. Christine had purchased the property in March 1992 for €63,000, its then current use value, and it has been vacant since then. Christine used €40,000 of the sale proceeds to repay the outstanding mortgage on the property.
2. On 5 May 2021, she disposed of a painting for €2,600. She had inherited the painting on the death of her mother on 20 December 2003, at which date it had a value of €1,900. The painting was a family heirloom that was considered to have a value of €100 on 6 April 1974.

Requirement
Compute the CGT payable by Christine Martin for 2021.

Part Four
Value-added Tax

Value-added Tax (VAT): Introduction

Learning Objectives

After studying this chapter you will understand:

- the general principles of value-added tax (VAT);
- the importance and distinction between the supply of goods and the supply of services;
- how to compute the value of the goods or services on which VAT is chargeable; and
- the administration of VAT – books and records to be kept and tax payment dates.

Chartered Accountants Ireland's *Code of Ethics* applies to all aspects of a professional accountant's professional life, including dealing with VAT issues. Further information regarding the principles in the *Code of Ethics* is set out in **Appendix 3**.

Students should also be aware of the issues around tax planning, tax avoidance and tax evasion, and these are discussed in **Appendix 4**.

21.1 General Principles of VAT

21.1.1 Introduction

VAT is a tax on consumer spending. It is chargeable on:

- the supply of goods and services within the State by a taxable person in the course of any business carried on by the taxpayer;
- goods imported into the State from outside the EU (VAT at the point of entry);
- intra-Community acquisition of goods by VAT-registered persons; and
- intra-Community acquisition of new means of transport, e.g. motor vehicles, boats, etc. by either a registered or unregistered person.

VAT-registered persons collect VAT on the **supply of goods and services** to their customers. Each such person in the chain of supply, from manufacturer through to retailer, **charges VAT on their sales** and is entitled to **deduct** from this amount the **VAT paid on their purchases** (input credit). The effect of offsetting purchases against sales is to impose the tax on the **value added** at each stage of production – hence value-added tax. The final consumer, who is often not registered for VAT, absorbs VAT as part of the purchase price.

21.1.2   Legislation and Directives

The main legislation governing the Irish VAT system comprises the:

- Value-Added Tax Consolidation Act 2010 (VATCA 2010);
- Value-Added Tax Regulations (Statutory Instruments);
- EU Regulations and Directives; and
- annual Finance Acts.

European Union Directives and Case Law

VAT is the only tax where the operational rules are decided by the EU. The State is permitted to set the rates of VAT (within certain parameters), but the rules in relation to the operation of the system and the categorisation of goods and services for VAT charging purposes are set by the EU.

The EU issues VAT Directives to Member States and the Member State must give effect to the intention of EU Directives in its national legislation. As a result, a person may rely on the Directive if their national legislation differs in some way.

Member States may have derogations in certain areas, which would allow them to impose national VAT legislation that is not in line with the Directive. In the event of any inconsistency, **EU law takes precedence**. Any decision from the Court of Justice of the European Union is binding on the Member State.

21.1.3   "Taxable Persons" and "Accountable Persons"

A **"taxable person"** is one who independently (i.e. other than as an employee) carries on a business in the EU or elsewhere.

An **"accountable person"** is a taxable person who engages in the supply, within the State, of taxable goods or services. An accountable person may also be someone who is in receipt of certain services or goods **in the State** from a supplier established **outside of the State** and the recipient has to **self-account** for VAT as if they were the supplier, i.e. **reverse charge**.

The State and public bodies are regarded as accountable persons for certain activities.

Note: 'accountability' is a key concept in VAT, as persons who are accountable must register for the tax, submit tax returns and payments, keep records and comply with the provisions of VATCA 2010.

21.1.4   The Charge to VAT

VAT is chargeable on the following:

- the supply of goods or services for consideration within the State by a taxable person;
- the importation of goods into the State from **outside** the EU (VAT is usually charged at the point of entry by Customs);
- the intra-Community acquisition by an accountable person of goods (other than new means of transport) when the acquisition is made within the State;
- the intra-Community acquisition of new means of transport by either an accountable or non-accountable person.

21.2   Registration

"Taxable persons" are obliged to register for VAT if any of the VAT thresholds outlined below are exceeded, or are likely to be exceeded, in a **12-month** period:

- **€37,500** for persons supplying **services**.
- **€75,000** for persons supplying **goods**, including persons supplying both goods and services, where **90% or more** of sales is derived from supplies of goods.

- **€37,500** for persons supplying goods liable at the 13.5% or 23% rates which they have manufactured or produced from **zero-rated** materials.
- **€35,000** for persons making mail order or distance sales into the State.
- **€41,000** for persons making intra-Community acquisitions.
- A **non-established** person supplying taxable goods or services in the State is **obliged** to register and account for VAT, **irrespective** of the level of turnover (i.e. **nil threshold**).
- Persons receiving services from abroad for business purposes in the State must register irrespective of the level of turnover.

For the purposes only of deciding if a person is obliged to register for VAT, the **actual turnover** may be **reduced** by an amount equivalent to the **VAT borne** on purchases of stock for resale. Therefore a person whose annual purchases of stock for resale are €61,000 (€49,593 plus €11,407 VAT at 23%) and whose actual turnover is €75,000 inclusive of VAT is not obliged to register. This is because the turnover, after deduction of the €11,407 VAT charged on the purchases of stock, is below the registration limit of €75,000.

No threshold applies in the case of taxable services received from abroad and in the case of cultural, artistic, sporting, scientific and educational, entertainment or similar services received from a person **not established** in the State. All such services are liable to VAT on a reverse-charge basis.

Suppliers of goods and services that are exempt from VAT and non-taxable entities, such as State bodies, charities, etc. are **obliged to register** for VAT where it is **likely** that they will acquire **more than** €41,000 of intra-Community acquisitions in any 12-month period.

A taxable person established in the State is not required to register for VAT if their turnover does not reach the appropriate threshold, although they may **opt to register** for VAT.

21.3 VAT Rates

There are a number of different VAT rates in the State. Generally the standard rate of VAT applies to the supply of goods and services and the reduced rates apply to a number of labour-intensive services, while the zero rate applies to many foods, oral medicines, children's shoes and children's clothes. Special schemes apply to livestock and agricultural supplies by non-VAT-registered traders.

In addition to these rates there are a number of activities that are exempt from VAT. These include many services supplied in the public interest, such as education, public transport and areas of childcare.

Standard Rate – 23%
This applies to all goods and services that are not exempt or liable at the zero or reduced rates.

Reduced Rate – 13.5%
Goods and services which attract VAT at 13.5% include bakery products (excluding bread), food supplements, certain fuels, building services, insemination services for all animals, repair, cleaning and maintenance services generally and certain photographic supplies.

Second Reduced Rate – 9%
This rate applies to the following services:

- Facilities for taking part in sporting activities, including subscriptions charged by non-member-owned golf clubs (excluding green fees).
- Printed newspapers, e-newspapers, magazines and periodicals, and e-books.

From **1 November 2020 to 31 December 2021**:

- Catering and restaurant supplies, including vending machines and hot take-away food (excluding alcohol and soft drinks sold as part of the meal).
- Hotel lettings, including guest-houses, caravan parks, camping sites, etc.
- Cinemas, theatres, certain musical performances, museums, art gallery exhibitions, fairgrounds or amusement park services.

- Facilities for taking part in sporting activities, including subscriptions charged by non-member-owned golf clubs (excluding green fees).
- Printed matter, e.g. brochures, leaflets, programmes, maps, catalogues, printed music (excluding books).
- Hairdressing services.

Livestock Rate – 4.8%
This applies to livestock in general, and to horses intended for use in foodstuffs or agricultural production.

Farmer's Flat-rate Addition – 5.6%
This applies to the sale of agricultural produce and services by non-registered farmers to VAT-registered persons (from 1 January 2021).

Zero-rated Goods and Services
These include exports, certain food and drink, oral medicine but excluding food supplements, certain books, nursing home services, etc.

Exempted Goods and Services
These include financial, medical and educational activities; and green fees and membership fees charged by member-owned golf clubs.

A full list of applicable VAT rates is available at www.revenue.ie

Difference between Exempt and Zero-rated
These terms appear to have the same meaning, but only to the extent that both exempt and zero-rated supplies do not attract what is referred to as a positive rate of VAT. They are different, however, in that a VAT-registered trader making zero-rated supplies (e.g. a book shop or food store) is entitled to a refund of VAT on the taxable business purchases (e.g. shop fittings, wrapping materials, cash registers, etc.), while normally a VAT-exempt trader is **not entitled** to any refund of VAT on purchases in respect of the business. It is a crucial difference.

21.4 Amount on which VAT is Chargeable

21.4.1 General Rules

In the case of the supply of goods or services and the intra-Community acquisition of goods, the amount on which VAT is chargeable is normally the **total sum** paid or payable to the person supplying the goods or services, including all taxes, commissions, costs and charges whatsoever, but **not including** the VAT chargeable in respect of the transaction. However, section 38 VATCA 2010 provides an anti-avoidance measure, which states that **Revenue** may determine that the **value** on which tax is charged in relation to certain transactions **between connected persons** is the **open market value**.

21.4.2 Specific Rules

1. Imports
VAT on imports is charged on the cost, **plus** transport cost, **plus** duty payable on the goods (customs value).

2. Goods/Services Supplied otherwise than for Money
Where a customer agrees to pay the supplier in kind, the amount on which VAT is chargeable is the **open market** or arm's length value of the goods or services supplied.

In the UK case of *Boots Company plc v. ECJ*, it was held that money-off vouchers that were given to customers by Boots to enable them to buy other products at a discount did not form part of the consideration for the purchase.

3. Credit Card Transactions

The taxable amount is the total amount actually charged to the customer by the trader. Any amount withheld by the credit card companies from their settlement with the trader forms part of the taxable amount.

4. New Motor Vehicles

The amount on which VAT is chargeable on a new motor vehicle is normally the price of the vehicle **before** vehicle registration tax (VRT) is applied.

5. Intra-EU Services

The amount on which VAT is chargeable in relation to intra-EU services received from abroad will normally be the **amount payable** in respect of those services.

6. Packaging and Containers

When goods are supplied packed for sale and **no separate charge** is made for the packaging in which the goods are contained, the rate of VAT chargeable is that **applying to the goods**. If containers are charged for **separately** from the goods, the transaction is regarded as consisting of separate sales of goods and of packages and **each** such **separate sale** is chargeable at the appropriate rate.

Where containers are returnable and a separate charge in the nature of a deposit is included on an invoice, the containers are regarded as being the property of the supplier and the **deposit** is **not** subject to VAT. VAT **is** payable on the value of containers which are **not returned** to the supplier. This VAT may be accounted for at the time when the containers' account is being balanced and a charge is being raised by the supplier against the customer for the value of containers not returned.

7. Postage and Insurance

Where a separate charge is made for postage and insurance and paid over in its **entirety** to the carrier or to the insurer on behalf of customers, suppliers may treat such charges as not being subject to VAT. If, for example, a trader charges an extra €1 for posting an order and such amount of postage is actually paid over, the €1 may be treated as exempt. Similarly, if a car hire company charges €50 for motor insurance, and that amount is actually paid over in full to insurers in the name of the lessee, the €50 may be treated as exempt. However, if a charge is made for posting and/or insurance, and a **lesser amount** is paid over by the supplier to the carrier or the insurer, the charge made to the customer is regarded as part of the total price of the goods/service supplied, and is subject to the VAT rate applicable to the goods/service in question.

8. Mixed Transactions (Package Rule)

A "package" comprises two or more elements that attract different VAT rates.

Composite Supply   Where there is a **principal element** and an **ancillary supply** the VAT rate is that attaching to the principal element. The main feature of an ancillary supply is that it has no standalone value or use other than in the context of the principal component. For example, the provision of an instruction booklet (VAT 0%) with an MP3 player (VAT 23%) is an ancillary supply to the principal supply of the MP3 player.

Multiple Supply   Where a number of individual supplies are **grouped together** for a single **overall** consideration, the consideration should be apportioned between the various individual supplies and taxed at the appropriate VAT rate. The main feature of an individual supply is that it is physically and economically distinct from the other elements of the multiple supply. For example, a meal sold at an all-inclusive price that includes food and wine – the food is liable to VAT at 9% and the wine at 23%.

9. Bad Debts

Relief for VAT on bad debts is allowed, subject to Revenue's agreement, where:

- all reasonable steps to recover the bad debt have been taken;
- the bad debt is allowable as a deduction in arriving at the tax-adjusted profits of the business;

- the bad debt has been written off in the financial accounts of the accountable person and the obligation to keep relevant records in relation to the debt have been fulfilled; and
- the person from whom the debt is due is not connected to the accountable person.

21.5   Supply of Goods or Services

VAT becomes due, or a liability for VAT arises, at the time when a supply of goods or services takes place, or on receipt of payment, if an earlier date.

21.5.1   *Supply of Goods*

A taxable supply of goods means the **normal transfer of ownership** of goods (including developed property) by one person to another and includes the supply of goods liable to VAT at the zero rate. This includes:

- The transfer of ownership of goods by agreement.
- The sale of movable goods on a commission basis by an auctioneer or agent acting in their own name but on the instructions of another person.
- The handing over of goods under a hire-purchase contract.
- The handing over by a person to another person of immovable goods (property) which have been developed.
- The seizure of goods by a sheriff or other person acting under statutory authority.
- The application or appropriation (**self-supply**) by the taxable person of materials or goods to some private or exempt use, e.g. if a builder uses building materials to build or repair their private house, this is a self-supply.
- The provision of electricity, gas and any form of power, heat, refrigeration or ventilation.
- With some exceptions, the transfer of goods from a business in the State by a taxable person to the territory of another Member State for the purposes of the business.
- The transfer of ownership of immovable goods by way of very long leases is a supply of goods.
- Gifts of taxable goods made in the course or furtherance of business are liable to VAT where the cost to the donor, excluding VAT, is €20 or **more**.
- Where vouchers and tokens having a face value are supplied at a discount to an intermediary with a view to their ultimate re-sale to private consumers, such tokens or vouchers become liable to VAT at the standard rate of 23% at the time the consideration is received. VAT is also chargeable on the re-sale of the vouchers by the intermediary to the private customer. However, this rule only applies where the intermediary who purchases the voucher for resale is VAT-registered in Ireland, i.e. they must be an accountable person.
- Gift vouchers are subject to VAT at the rate applicable to goods or services supplied in exchange for the voucher at the time the voucher is redeemed by the customer. The retailer must generally only account for VAT on the consideration received for the sale of vouchers at the time the voucher is redeemed by the customer.

A taxable supply is **not affected** where:

- Gifts of taxable goods are made in the course or furtherance of business where the cost to the donor, excluding VAT, is €20 or **less**.
- Special offers, such as two for the price of one and promotional items given away free with the sale of another item, are not treated as gifts. Rather, they are considered to be simply a reduction in price for the relevant items and regular VAT rules therefore apply to such supplies.

- Advertising goods and industrial samples are given free to customers in reasonable quantities, in a form **not ordinarily available for sale** to the public, even where the €20 limit is exceeded.
- Replacement goods are supplied free of charge in accordance with **warranties** or **guarantees** on the original goods.
- Goods change ownership as **security** for a loan or debt.
- A business is transferred from one taxable person to another.

21.5.2 Supply of Services

For VAT purposes a "service" is any commercial activity **other than** a supply of goods. Typical services include:

- The services of caterers, mechanics, plumbers, accountants, solicitors, consultants, etc.
- The hiring or leasing of goods.
- The supply of digitised goods delivered online as well as the physical supply of customised software.
- Refraining from doing something and the granting or surrendering of a right.
- Contract work, i.e. the handing over by a contractor, to a customer, of movable goods made or assembled by the contractor from goods entrusted to them by the customer.
- A self-supply of a catering or canteen service (e.g. a vending machine).

Insurance agents, banking agents and certain related agents are **exempt** from VAT.

Services Taxable as Supplies of Goods (the "Two-thirds" Rule)
A transaction which may **appear** to be a **supply of a service** is nevertheless taxable as a **supply of goods** if the value of the goods (i.e. cost excluding VAT) used in carrying out the work **exceeds two-thirds** of the total charge, exclusive of VAT. For example, where the VAT-exclusive cost of materials used by a plumber in the repair of a washing machine is €120, and the total charge for the repair work is €150, the 23% rate applicable to the materials applies, rather than the 13.5% rate which normally applies to repair services. The repair and maintenance of motor vehicles and agricultural machinery is **not subject** to the "two-thirds" rule.

The two-thirds rule does not apply where principal contractors operate the **reverse charge** rule with sub-contractors (see **Section 21.9.5**) or to supplies of construction services between **connected persons** to whom the reverse charge rule for VAT applies.

21.6 Place of Supply of Goods or Services

Goods and services are liable to VAT **in the place where they are supplied** or deemed to be supplied. If the place of supply is outside or is deemed to be outside the State, then Irish VAT **does not** arise. The complexity of the supply of goods or services outside the State is beyond the scope of this textbook. The general rules that you should be aware of at this point are outlined below.

21.6.1 Place of Supply of Goods

The place of supply of goods is deemed to be as follows:

- Where goods are not dispatched or transported, the place of supply is deemed to be the place where the goods are **at the time** of their supply.
- Where goods are installed or assembled by or on behalf of the supplier, the place of supply is the place where the goods **are installed or assembled**. For example, a French-based company supplies and installs a machine in an Irish company's factory in the State. The place of supply is Ireland and the

recipient Irish company self-accounts for the VAT on the supply and can claim a simultaneous input credit if the goods are used for the taxable business.

- Where goods are supplied on board **sea vessels, aircraft and trains** (during intra-Community transport), the place of supply is the place where the **transport begins**. For example, if a person buys goods on board the Dublin–Holyhead ferry leaving from Dublin, the place of supply is Ireland and Irish VAT arises.
- In all other cases, the **location** of the goods at the time of supply determines the place of supply.

21.6.2   Place of Supply of Services

There are two general "place of supply" rules, depending on whether the recipient is a **business** or a **consumer**:

- For supplies of "**business to business** (B2B)" services, the place of supply is the place where the **recipient is established**.
- For supplies of "**business to consumer** (B2C)" services, the place of supply is where the **supplier is established**.

Where an Irish supplier makes a supply to an Irish customer in Ireland, irrespective of whether or not the customer is a business or a consumer, the place of supply is Ireland and the supplier must account for VAT.

The supply of services rule is more complex when the supplier and the recipient are in different EU Member States.

21.7   Recovery of VAT

21.7.1   Deductible VAT

In computing the amount of VAT payable in respect of a taxable period, a person may **deduct** the VAT charged on most goods and services that are used for the purposes of their **taxable business**. To be entitled to the deduction, the trader must have a proper VAT invoice or relevant customs receipt as appropriate.

While a deduction of VAT is allowable only on purchases which are for the purposes of a taxable business, a situation may arise where a **portion** of a person's purchases may be for the purposes of the taxable business and the remaining portion for the person's **private use** (e.g. electricity, telephone charges, heating expenses, etc. where the business is carried on from the trader's private residence). It may also arise that inputs may be used for **both taxable and non-taxable** activities. In such cases, only the amount of VAT **that is appropriate to the taxable business** is deductible. Similarly, where a person engages in both taxable and exempt activities (dual-use inputs), it will be necessary to **apportion the credit** in respect of these dual-use inputs.

In general, VAT is deductible against a taxable person's liability in any of the following situations:

- VAT charged to a taxable person by other taxable persons on supplies of goods (including fixed assets) and services.
- VAT paid by the taxable person on goods imported.
- VAT payable on self-supplies of goods and services provided that the self-supplies are for business purposes.
- VAT payable on purchases from flat-rate farmers.
- VAT on intra-Community acquisitions.
- VAT payable under **reverse charge rules**, provided the goods or services are used for the purposes of their taxable business (e.g. goods that are installed or assembled in the State by a foreign supplier, etc.).

▨ Reduction in VAT input credit for unpaid amounts – where an accountable person has claimed a VAT input credit in relation to a supply to them but the consideration for such a supply remains partially or fully outstanding six months after the period the initial input credit was claimed, the accountable person must reduce the amount of VAT deductible by the amount of VAT relating to the unpaid consideration.

Where the accountable person makes a subsequent payment or part payment, they may claim a VAT input credit for the consideration paid (section 62A VATCA 2010).

▨ **Qualifying Vehicles** – section 62 VATCA 2010 allows any VAT-registered person (other than motor dealers, car-hire companies, driving schools, etc.) to recover **20%** of the VAT charged on the purchase or hire of vehicles **coming within VRT Category A**, subject to the following conditions:

- The vehicle must have been registered on or after **1 January 2009**.
- A maximum of **20% of the VAT** incurred on the cost or on the monthly hire/lease charge can be reclaimed.
- VAT can only be reclaimed for vehicles that have a level of CO_2 emissions of less than **156g/km** (i.e. CO_2 emission bands A, B and C) on vehicles registered between **1 January 2009 and 31 December 2020**.
- For vehicles registered on or after **1 January 2021**, VAT can only be reclaimed where vehicles have CO_2 emissions of less than **140g/km** (i.e. CO_2 emission bands A and B).
- At least **60%** of the vehicle's use must be for business purposes.
- If the business is exempt from VAT (e.g. taxi, limousine and other passenger transport), then no VAT can be reclaimed. Partly exempt businesses can reclaim some, but not all, of the 20%.
- If VAT is reclaimed on a vehicle purchased under this provision, some or all of the VAT must be repaid to Revenue if the vehicle is disposed of within two years.
- There is no need to charge VAT on the disposal of the vehicle, even though VAT was reclaimed under this provision.
- If the vehicle is sold or traded-in to a motor dealer, the margin scheme for second-hand vehicles will apply.

21.7.2 Non-deductible VAT

No deduction is allowed in respect of VAT paid on expenditure on any of the following:

▨ The provision of food, drink, accommodation or other personal services supplied to the taxable person, their agent or employees, **except** to the extent that the provision of such services represent a taxable supply by the taxable person. For example, where a hotel incurs expense in providing accommodation for its own employees, this would be a taxable supply and the VAT arising would be a deductible input. A taxable person can claim VAT on "qualifying accommodation" in connection with the attendance at a "qualifying conference" by the taxable person or their representative, **except** where it was supplied under the Travel Agent Margin Scheme (TAMS). Where the accommodation is supplied and invoiced **directly** to the taxable person, a deduction for the VAT applies.

▨ Entertainment expenses incurred by the taxable person, their agent or their employees.

▨ The acquisition, hiring or leasing of motor vehicles that are not "qualifying vehicles" (as above), **other** than as stock-in-trade or for the purpose of a business that consists, in whole or in part, of the hiring of motor vehicles, or for use in a driving school business for giving driving instruction.

▨ The purchase of petrol other than as stock-in-trade.

▨ Expenditure incurred on food, drink, accommodation or other entertainment service, as part of an advertising service, is not deductible in the hands of the person providing the advertising service.

▨ VAT in respect of goods or services used by the taxable person for the purposes of an exempt activity or for the purposes of an activity not related to their business.

21.8 Basis of Accounting of VAT

21.8.1 Invoice Basis of Accounting for VAT

Generally an accountable person becomes liable for VAT at the time of the **issue** of **sales invoices** to their customers **regardless** of whether they have received payment for the supplies made. Accordingly, an accountable person must, for example in their January/February 2021 VAT return, include VAT on **all sales invoices issued** during January and February 2021. This is known as the **invoice basis of accounting** for VAT.

21.8.2 Cash Receipts Basis

Under the cash receipts basis of accounting, persons **do not** become liable for VAT until they have actually **received payment** for the goods or services supplied.

The cash receipts basis **does not apply** to transactions between **connected** persons. VAT on such transactions must be accounted for on the normal invoice basis. VAT on **property transactions** must always be accounted for on an invoice basis.

An accountable person who opts for the cash receipts basis of accounting is liable for VAT at the **rate ruling at the time the supply is made** rather than the rate ruling at the time payment is received.

For example, Joe, operating under the cash receipts basis, made a supply of goods in December 2020 when the rate of VAT was 21%. He received payment of €1,000 for those goods in March 2021 when the rate had changed to 23%. Joe accounts for the VAT on the supply at 21% (i.e. €1,000 × 21/121 = €173.55) in his March–April 2021 VAT return.

In addition, where such a person receives a payment from which PSWT or RCT has been deducted, the person is deemed to have received the **gross amount due** and is liable to pay the **full amount** of the VAT due. For example, if an architect receives a payment of €800, being €1,000 less PSWT at 20%, he is deemed to have received €1,000 and must account for VAT on this amount.

Accountable persons accounting for VAT on the basis of moneys received must issue to a VAT-registered customer, or other person entitled to a VAT invoice, a credit note showing VAT if there is a discount or price reduction allowed subsequent to the issue of an invoice. The effect of the credit note is to reduce any VAT deduction available to the customer on the basis of the original invoice. The accountable person accounts for VAT on the money received.

It should be noted that the cash receipts basis of accounting **only applies to sales and supplies** and VAT on purchases is still claimed on an invoice basis.

Entitlement to Cash Receipts Basis

The cash receipts basis of accounting for VAT may be used by persons engaged in the supply of taxable goods or services if:

- at least **90%** of the supplies are to **unregistered** persons; **or**
- the trader's turnover is not likely to **exceed €2 million** per annum.

Formal Election

Any accountable person who finds that they are eligible to use this basis of accounting and wishes to use it should apply to the local Revenue district for authority to do so. Such persons may not change from the invoice basis of accounting to the cash receipts basis, or vice versa, without such authority.

Persons who are applying for VAT registration for the first time, and find that they are eligible for the cash receipts basis, should indicate in the appropriate box on the eRegistration forms, TR1 or TR2, whether or not they wish to use it.

21.8.3 Change of Basis of Accounting

A person who has been accounting for VAT on the cash receipts basis and now wishes to revert to the invoice basis (or who ceases to be a taxable person) will have to make an adjustment. The adjustment must be made by reference to the **VAT due on outstanding debtors**.

21.9 Administration of VAT

21.9.1 Registration Procedure

In the majority of cases, VAT registration must be completed online using the Revenue's eRegistration Service using the online forms:

- **Form TR1** for individuals, sole traders, trusts and partnerships.
- **Form TR2** for limited companies.

In exceptional circumstances only, applicants who cannot access the eRegistration Services must complete a paper version of these forms. Those who are already registered for ROS or myAccount are obliged to register online.

Registration is effective from the beginning of the next taxable period of two months after the date on which the completed application is received, or from such earlier date as may be agreed between Revenue and the applicant. In the case of a person not obliged to register but who is opting to do so, the effective date **will be not earlier** than the beginning of the taxable period during which the application is made.

A person who is setting up a business, but who has **not yet commenced** supplying taxable goods or services, **may** register for VAT as soon as it is clear that they will become a taxable person. This will enable them to obtain credit for VAT on purchases made before trading actually commences.

21.9.2 VAT Returns and Payment of VAT

An accountable person normally accounts for VAT on a two-monthly basis (January–February, March–April, etc.). The return is made on Form **VAT 3,** and this form, together with a payment for any VAT due, should be submitted electronically (through ROS) to Revenue on or before the **23rd day** of the month following the **end** of the taxable period (e.g. a return for the VAT period January–February 2021 is due by 23 March 2021). The VAT return shows the **gross amount** of the tax due by the person, the amount of **input tax deductible** and the **net VAT due** to Revenue or **VAT refund** due to the accountable person.

In addition, accountable persons are required to submit an **annual** "VAT Return of Trading Details" (Form RTD EUR), which gives details of purchases and sales for the year, broken down by VAT rates.

Payment of VAT
VAT is payable through ROS on or before the **23rd day** of the month following the **end** of the taxable period along with the Form VAT 3.

An accountable person may pay VAT by **direct debit** in monthly instalments. If a business is seasonal, an accountable person can vary the amounts paid each month to reflect cash flow. Where a person pays a VAT liability by direct debit, the person is only required to make an **annual VAT 3** return, together with the annual VAT Return of Trading Details. At the end of the year, if a shortfall arises, the balance must be included when submitting the annual return of trading (RTD EUR). Where insufficient amounts are paid by direct debit and, as a result, the **balance of tax payable** with the annual return is **more than 20% of the annual liability for VAT**, then an accountable person will be liable to an **interest charge** backdated to the mid-point of the year.

Reduced Frequency for Filing VAT Returns

Eligible businesses may be allowed, with authorisation from the Collector-General, to reduce their number of VAT filings. Eligible businesses are:

- Businesses making total annual VAT payments of less than **€3,000** can file VAT returns and make payments on a **six-month** basis.
- Businesses making total annual VAT payments of **between €3,000 and €14,400** can file VAT returns and make payments on a **four-month** basis.

VAT Returns on an Annual Basis

There is a provision whereby VAT can be returned and paid on an annual basis. Authorisation to do so is at the discretion of Revenue, and this authorisation may be terminated at any time. The VAT returns and payment must be submitted electronically to Revenue between the 10th and 23rd days of the month following the end of the year.

Interest on Late Payments of VAT

If VAT is not paid within the proper period, interest is chargeable (as a fiduciary tax) for each day at the rate of 0.0274% per day. This interest also applies where a refund of VAT has been made on the basis of an incorrect return, and where all or part of the tax refunded was not properly refundable. Where a person fails to make returns, Revenue is entitled to make estimates of tax payable and to recover the amount so estimated, subject to the usual appeal procedures.

21.9.3   VAT Records

Records to be Maintained

A VAT-registered trader must keep **full records** of all transactions that affect the liability to VAT. The records must be kept up to date and be sufficiently detailed to enable a trader to accurately calculate liability or repayment and also to enable Revenue to check the calculations, if necessary.

Purchases Records

The purchases records should **distinguish** between purchases of goods for **resale** and goods or services **not for resale** in the ordinary course of business. The records should show the date of the purchase invoice and a consecutive number (in the order in which the invoices are filed), the name of the supplier, the cost **exclusive** of VAT and the amount of VAT. Purchases at **each rate** must be recorded **separately**. The same information should be recorded in respect of imports, intra-EU acquisitions and services received.

Sales Records

The sales records must include the amount charged in respect of every sale to a registered person and a daily entry of the total amount charged in respect of sales to unregistered persons, **distinguishing in all cases** between transactions liable at each **different VAT rate** (including the zero rate) and **exempt** transactions. All such entries should be cross-referenced to relevant invoices, sales dockets, cash register tally rolls, delivery notes, etc. Traders who are authorised to account for VAT on the cash receipts basis are also obliged to retain all documents they use for the purposes of their business. Persons involved in intra-EU trade also have requirements in relation to retention of records as regards certain transfers of goods to other Member States.

Retention of Records

An accountable person **must retain** all books, records and documents relevant to the business, including invoices, credit and debit notes, receipts, accounts, cash register tally rolls, vouchers, stamped copies of customs entries and other import documents and bank statements. These business records must be retained for **six years** from the date of the latest transaction to which they refer, unless written permission from Revenue has been obtained for their retention for a shorter period.

There is no requirement to retain the paper originals of any third-party record where an electronic copy of the original record is generated, recorded and stored in accordance with Revenue's information technology and procedural requirements.

21.9.4 *VAT Invoices and Credit Notes*

Information to be included on VAT Invoices/Credit Notes

Revenue imposes strict requirements on the information given on invoices and credit notes. This information establishes the VAT **liability** of the supplier of goods or services and the **entitlement** of the customer to an **input deduction** for the VAT charged.

Accountable persons who issue invoices and credit notes, and persons to whom these documents are issued, should ensure that the documents **accurately represent** the transactions to which they refer. For example, if an incorrect rate of VAT is used on an invoice, both the supplier and the customer are liable for VAT at the correct rate, unless the supplier has **overcharged** VAT and is therefore liable for the total amount of VAT invoiced.

Form of VAT Invoice/Credit Note

The VAT invoice/credit note should show the following:

- Name and address of the supplier issuing the invoice.
- Supplier's VAT registration number.
- Name and address of the customer.
- Date of issue of the invoice.
- Date of supply of the goods or services.
- Full description of the goods or services.
- Quantity or volume and unit price of the goods or services supplied.
- The amount charged **exclusive** of VAT (in €).
- The rate (including zero rate) and amount of VAT at each rate.
- The total invoice/credit note amount exclusive of VAT (in €).
- A person who makes zero-rated intra-Community supplies is obliged, in addition to the above, to show the **VAT registration number of the customer** in the other EU Member State.

If a VAT invoice is required to be issued, it must be issued **within 15 days** of the end of the month in which goods or services are supplied. Where payment in full is made **before** the completion of the supply, the person receiving payment must also issue an invoice within 15 days of the end of the month in which the **payment** was **received**.

Allowances, Discounts, etc.

When the amount of VAT payable, as shown on an invoice, is reduced because of an allowance or discount or similar adjustment, the accountable person who issued the VAT invoice must issue a credit note stating the amount of the reduction in the price and the appropriate VAT. This person may then reduce their VAT liability by the amount credited in the accounting period in which the credit note is issued. Likewise, the customer or recipient of the credit note must increase their VAT liability by the same amount. All credit notes must contain a reference to the corresponding invoices.

Where a VAT-registered supplier and a VAT-registered customer **agree** in respect of a transaction **not to make any change** in the VAT shown on the original invoice, even though the price charged may subsequently be reduced, there is **no obligation** to issue a credit note in respect of the VAT. Such a practice saves trouble for both seller and purchaser. For example, if the discount taken by the purchaser is only on the goods, and the amount of VAT originally invoiced is allowed to stand, no adjustment for VAT is necessary and a VAT credit note is not required.

21.9.5 VAT Reverse Charge

Under the VAT reverse charge rules, it is the **receiver** of the relevant supply, and **not the supplier**, who accounts for and pays the VAT to Revenue.

Under section 16 VATCA 2010, VAT reverse charge applies mainly to a principal contractor in receipt of construction operations from a subcontractor subject to relevant contracts tax (RCT).

Procedures under the VAT Reverse Charge Rule

- The supplier issues the recipient a reverse charge invoice that includes all of the information required on a VAT invoice, except the VAT rate and the VAT amount. It also includes an indication that it is the recipient who is accountable for the VAT.
- If there is prior agreement between the supplier and the recipient, the recipient may issue the reverse-charge invoice, subject to agreed procedures being in place for the acceptance by the supplier of the validity of the invoice (e.g. invoice is signed by both parties).
- The recipient does not pay the VAT to the supplier but, instead, accounts for it in the VAT return for the relevant period in "VAT on Sales" (T1).
- The recipient can claim a simultaneous input credit in "VAT on Purchases" (T2) for that VAT if the recipient has valid documentation and would have been entitled to an input credit if that VAT had been charged by the supplier.
- The recipient pays the supplier for the VAT-exclusive value of the supply, less RCT if applicable.

Example 21.1

Allen Ltd is renovating a factory building for a manufacturing company. Allen Ltd invoices the manufacturing company in October 2021 as follows:

	€
Construction services	740,740
VAT @13.5%	100,000
Total	840,740

These services do not come within the reverse charge since Allen Ltd is not a subcontractor to the manufacturing company for RCT purposes.

Burke, a building contractor, supplies services to Allen Ltd. Allen Ltd is the principal contractor and Burke is the subcontractor.

Burke incurred €13,000 VAT on purchases in September–October 2021 for the purposes of his business.

Burke charges Allen Ltd €600,000 in September 2021 for the building services but does not charge any VAT on this amount.

Allen Ltd VAT Return

Allen Ltd accounts for the VAT on the construction services from Burke. VAT chargeable on the services is €600,000 @13.5% = €81,000.

As the construction services provided by the subcontractor to the principal were invoiced during September–October 2021, the VAT on these services is accounted for by reverse charge.

In its September–October 2021 VAT return, Allen Ltd includes VAT €181,000 as VAT on sales (i.e. VAT on its own sales of €100,000 plus reverse charge VAT €81,000 on services received from Burke).

continued overleaf

---

311 Value-added Tax (VAT): An Introduction

Allen Ltd can claim input credit for €81,000 reverse charge VAT in the same return.

Allen Ltd should pay Revenue €100,000.

Allen Ltd notifies Revenue of the gross payment to Burke (Payment Notification) online. Revenue issues a Deduction. Authorisation, which states that RCT @ 35% should be deducted from the payment.

Allen Ltd should deduct RCT from the payment due to Burke (amount deducted €600,000 @ 35% = €210,000) and pay Burke net €390,000.

Burke's VAT Return
Burke does not account for VAT on the services supplied to Allen Ltd. As Burke only works for a principal contractor, his VAT on sales figure is nil.

Burke is entitled to his input credit of €13,000; and so should receive a VAT repayment for that amount.

Example 21.2
Axel Ltd supplies scrap metal to Breakers Ltd for €1,000 (excl. VAT). Both companies are registered for VAT.

Axel Ltd raises an invoice (or, if agreed, Breakers Ltd may raise the invoice), which shows that the recipient (Breakers Ltd) is accountable for the VAT. The VAT amount or rate is not shown on the invoice.

Breakers Ltd calculates the VAT (€1,000 × 23% = €230) and accounts for it in the VAT return for that period as VAT on Sales (T1). Breakers Ltd, subject to deductibility rules, can claim input credit, in the same return for that VAT (T2).

Questions

Review Questions
(See Suggested Solutions to Review Questions at the end of this textbook.)

Question 21.1

With regard to VAT, set out:

(a) the criteria for determining the obligation to register, and
(b) the records to be maintained and the information required to complete a VAT 3 return.

Question 21.2

Outline the VAT rules for determining the tax point or time when a supply of goods or services is treated as taking place.

Question 21.3

Michael, a friend of yours, has recently set up business in Ireland selling computers. He has already registered for VAT.

Requirement
Advise Michael on:

(a) what records he should keep for VAT purposes in relation to purchases and sales; and
(b) when VAT returns and related VAT payments should be returned to Revenue and the consequences if he defaults.

Question 21.4

John Hardiman's business consists partly of the supply of VAT-exempt services and partly of services liable to VAT at 23%. He is authorised by the Revenue Commissioners to account for VAT on the cash receipts (money received) basis.

John's records for the VAT period September–October 2021 provide the following information:

1. Sales and cash receipts: €

	€
Supplies of services at 23% VAT (gross)	24,000
Supplies of services exempt from VAT	2,000
Cash receipts relating to supplies of services at 23% VAT (gross)	30,250
Cash receipts relating to supplies of exempt services	3,000

2. Purchases €

	€
Purchases of goods and services at 23% VAT (gross)	6,150
Purchases of goods and services at 13.5% VAT (gross)	2,270

3. It has been agreed with the Revenue Commissioners that 10% of John's input credits relate to his exempt activities.
4. Included in the purchases figures at 2. above are the following items:
    (i)   An invoice for the servicing of his motor car amounting to €160 plus VAT at 13.5%. It has been agreed with the Revenue Commissioners that the private use of his car is 25%.
    (ii) An invoice for the lease of the motor car referred to in (i) above. The invoice is for €300 plus VAT at 23%. The car is a "qualifying vehicle".
    (iii) An invoice for the purchase of stationery amounting to €123 was included with purchases at 23% VAT. A closer examination of the invoice revealed that it had no supplier VAT number listed and no details of VAT rates or amounts.
    (iv) An invoice for the building of a new office. The invoice was in respect of an instalment payment and amounted to €1,000 plus VAT at 13.5%.
    (v)   A petty cash voucher for postage, amounting to €64, was included with purchases at 23% VAT.

Requirement

On the basis of the above information, calculate the VAT liability/refund of John Hardiman for the VAT period September–October 2021.

Question 21.5

Mr Byte supplies computers to business and retail outlets. You are given the following information in connection with his VAT return for the period July–August 2021.

	€
Invoiced sales July–August (excluding VAT)	100,000
Cash received July–August (including VAT)	75,000
Purchases invoices received July–August (excluding VAT)	40,000
Purchase invoices paid July–August (excluding VAT)	50,000
Other expenses:	
Stationery (excluding VAT @ 23%)	6,000
Wages (VAT-exempt)	20,000
Electricity (excluding VAT @ 13.5%)	2,000
Hotel bills (excluding VAT @ 9%)	1,000
Rent (VAT-exempt)	2,400

Requirement

Compute the liability to VAT of Mr Byte for the period July–August 2021 assuming he is authorised to account for VAT on the cash receipts basis.

Question 21.6

Joe, who is a baker, supplies you with the following information from his books for the months of May and June 2021 (all figures are **exclusive** of VAT).

		May €	June €
Sales of bread	zero-rated	10,000	8,000
Purchase of ingredients	zero-rated	5,000	2,000
Expenditure on petrol	23%	1,000	1,000
Purchase of mixing machine	23%	–	6,000
Lease rentals – vans	23%	2,000	2,000
Bank interest	exempt	400	400

Requirement

Compute the VAT liability for the period in question, and show the date on which the VAT returns should be submitted.

Question 21.7

State the categories of persons who may apply for voluntary registration for VAT and discuss the reasons why such persons might choose to apply for voluntary registration.

Question 21.8

(a) Discuss the place where goods and services are deemed to be supplied for VAT purposes.
(b) Explain what you understand the term "self-supply" to mean for VAT purposes.

Question 21.9

Andrew opened a coffee shop on 17 March 2021 and the transactions undertaken during the first VAT period March–April 2021 were as follows:

Sales and Receipts

1. Receipts in respect of supplies of goods and services, inclusive of VAT @ 23%, amounted to €1,815 for the period.
2. Receipts in respect of supplies of goods and services, inclusive of VAT @ 9%, amounted to €2,837.50 for the period.

Purchases and Payments

1. Purchase of stock for resale: €605 inclusive of VAT @ 23%.
2. Purchase of stock for resale: €334 @ zero-rate VAT.
3. Purchase of tables and chairs: €440 excluding VAT @ 23%.
4. Payment of rent to landlord: €373. No invoices have been received.
5. Purchase of second-hand cash register on three months' credit. The invoice, dated 3 March 2021, was for €665.50 in total and included VAT @ 23%.
6. Payment of €200 plus VAT @ 13.5% to the tiler on 16 March 2021.
7. On 5 March 2021, Andrew signed a lease for shop fittings requiring a monthly payment of €700 plus VAT @ 23%. The monthly payments are debited to Andrew's bank account on the 30th of each month.
8. Payment of €750 on account to a solicitor for legal fees on foot of a bill received for €1,452 inclusive of VAT @ 23%.
9. Purchase for the business of a commercial van for €9,840 inclusive of VAT @ 23%.
10. Purchases of petrol for the van totalling €98 inclusive of VAT @ 23%.

All invoices relating to the above transactions have been received unless otherwise stated. Assume that Andrew was registered for VAT prior to incurring any expenditure.

Requirement
Calculate the VAT liability/refund for the VAT period March–April 2021.

Appendix 1

Taxation Reference Material for Tax Year 2021

Table of Contents

INCOME TAX, USC & PRSI

Income Tax Rates 2021

Single/Widowed/ Surviving Civil Partner with Qualifying Children	Rate	Single/Widowed/ Surviving Civil Partner without Qualifying Children	Rate	Married Couple/ Civil Partners	Rate
First €39,300	20%	First €35,300	20%	First €44,300/€70,600[1]	20%
Balance	40%	Balance	40%	Balance	40%

[1] Depending on personal circumstances of married couple/civil partners.

Non-refundable Tax Credits 2021

	Tax Credit €
Single person	1,650
Married couple/civil partners	3,300
Widowed person/surviving civil partner (year of bereavement)	3,300
Widowed person/surviving civil partner tax credit – no dependent children	2,190
Widowed person/surviving civil partner tax credit – with dependent children	1,650
Single Person Child Carer Credit (additional)	1,650
Widowed parent/surviving civil partner tax credit – with dependent children	
Year 1 after the year of bereavement	3,600
Year 2 after the year of bereavement	3,150
Year 3 after the year of bereavement	2,700
Year 4 after the year of bereavement	2,250
Year 5 after the year of bereavement	1,800
Employee tax credit	1,650
Earned Income Tax Credit	1,650
Fisher Tax Credit (maximum)	1,270
Age tax credit – single/widowed/surviving civil partner	245
Age tax credit – married/civil partners	490
Incapacitated child tax credit	3,300
Dependent relative – income limit €15,740	245
Home carer's credit – income limit €7,200 (lower)/ €10,400 (upper)	1,600
Blind person	1,650
Both spouses/civil partners blind	3,300

continued overleaf

	Tax Credit
	€
Third-level education fees[1]:	
Full-time course	800
Part-time course	1,100

[1] There is a maximum level of qualifying fees, per academic year, of €7,000 per student, per course, subject to the first €3,000 (full-time) or €1,500 (part-time) being disallowed (per claim, not per course). Relief is at the standard rate of tax on the amount of the qualifying fees.

Income Tax Allowances and Reliefs 2021

Deduction for employed person taking care of incapacitated person (maximum)	– €75,000
Provision of childcare services	– income limit €15,000
Rent-a-Room relief (maximum)	– €14,000

Income Tax Exemption Limits for Persons Aged 65 and Over 2021

	€
Single/widowed/surviving civil partner	18,000[1]
Married/civil partners	36,000[1]

[1] Dependent children: increase exemption by €575 for each of first two, and by €830 for each additional child.

Pension Contributions

The maximum amount on which tax relief may be claimed in 2021 in respect of qualifying premiums is as follows:

Age	% of Net Relevant Earnings[1]
Under 30 years of age	15%
30 to 39 years of age	20%
40 to 49 years of age	25%
50 to 54 years of age	30%
55 to 59 years of age	35%
60 years and over	40%

[1] The earnings cap for 2021 on net relevant earnings is €115,000.

Preferential Loans

The specified rates for 2021 are:

- 4% in respect of qualifying home loans;
- 13.5% in respect of all other loans.

Motor Car Benefit in Kind

Annual Business Kilometres	Cash Equivalent (% of OMV)
24,000 or less	30%
24,001–32,000	24%
32,001–40,000	18%
40,001–48,000	12%
48,001 and over	6%

Motor Vehicle Category Based on CO_2 Emissions

Vehicle Category	CO_2 Emissions (CO_2 g/km)
A, B and C	0g/km up to and including 155g/km
D and E	156g/km up to and including 190g/km
F and G	191g/km and upwards

Restricted Cost for Motor Lease Expenses

Restricted Cost of Passenger Motor Vehicle for Capital Allowances and Motor Leases Expenses Restriction Purposes

Specified Limit	€
From 1 January 2007	24,000

Restricted Cost for Motor Vehicles bought on/after 1 July 2008

Category	CO_2 Emissions	Restriction
A	0–120g/km	Use the specified amount regardless of cost.
B and C	121–155g/km	
D and E	156–190g/km	Two steps to calculate limit: 1. take the lower of the specified limit or cost; 2. limit is 50% of this amount.
F and G	191+g/km	No allowance available.

Capital Allowances

Plant and Machinery

Expenditure incurred on or after 4 December 2002:

Plant and machinery	12.5% straight-line
Cars other than those used as a taxi or in car-hire business	12.5% straight-line

Industrial Buildings

Expenditure incurred on or after 1 April 1992	4% straight-line

Civil Service Mileage and Subsistence Rates

Motor Car Travel Rates (effective from 1 April 2017)

Official Motor Travel in a calendar year	Engine Capacity		
	Up to 1,200cc	**1,201cc–1,500cc**	**1,501cc and over**
0–1,500km	37.95 cent per km	39.86 cent per km	44.79 cent per km
1,501–5,500km	70.00 cent per km	73.21 cent per km	83.53 cent per km
5,501–25,000km	27.55 cent per km	29.03 cent per km	32.21 cent per km
Over 25,001km	21.36 cent per km	22.23 cent per km	25.85 cent per km

Motor Cycle Travel Rates

Official Motor Travel in a calendar year	Engine Capacity			
	Up to 150cc	**151cc to 250cc**	**251cc to 600cc**	**601cc and over**
Up to 6,437km	14.48 cent per km	20.10 cent per km	23.72 cent per km	28.59 cent per km
Over 6,437km	9.37 cent per km	13.31 cent per km	15.29 cent per km	17.60 cent per km

Subsistence Rates

Overnight Allowances[1] (from 1 October 2018)			Day Allowances[2] (from 1 July 2019)	
Normal rate (up to 14 nights)	Reduced rate (next 14 nights)	Detention rate (next 28 nights)	10 hours or more	5 hours (but less than 10 hours)
€147.00	€132.30	€73.50	€36.97	€15.41

[1] Night allowance: the employee is at least 100km away from their home or place of work and covers a period of up to 24 hours from the time of departure, and any further period not exceeding five hours.
[2] Day allowance: the employee is at least 8km away from their home or normal place of work.

Universal Social Charge 2021

Employment Income
The rates of USC (where gross income is greater than €13,000 per annum) are:

Rate of USC	Annual Income	Monthly Income	Weekly Income
0.5%	First €12,012	First €1,001	First €231
2.0%	€12,013–€20,687	€1,002–€1,724	€232–€398
4.5%[1,2]	€20,688–€70,044	€1,725–€5,837	€399–€1,347
8.0%[1,2]	Balance	Balance	Balance

[1] Persons aged 70 years and over with income of €60,000 or less are not liable at the 4.5%/8% rates but instead pay at 2.0%.
[2] Persons who hold a full medical card and with income of €60,000 or less are not liable at the 4.5% or 8% rates but instead pay at 2.0%.

Exempt Categories

▪ Where an individual's total income for a year does not exceed €13,000.
▪ All Department of Social Protection payments.
▪ Income already subjected to DIRT.

Self-assessed Individuals

The rates of USC (where gross income is greater than €13,000 per annum) are:

	Aged under 70/Aged 70 and over with income >€60,000/Full medical card holder with income >€60,000	Aged 70 and over with income of €60,000 or less/Full medical card holder with income of €60,000 or less
First €12,012	0.5%	0.5%
Next €8,675	2.0%	2.0%
Next €49,357	4.5%	2.0% (max. €39,313)
Balance[1]	8.0%	N/A

[1] An additional USC charge of 3% is payable by individuals on self-assessed income (excluding employment income) in excess of €100,000 in a year, regardless of age.

Surcharge on Use of Property Incentives

There is also an additional USC surcharge of 5% on investors with gross income greater than €100,000 where certain property tax reliefs have been used to shelter taxable income.

PRSI 2021

Employees' and Employers' Rates

Employee's income	Employee rate	Employers' rate
Income of €38–€352 per week	Nil	8.8%
Income of €352–€398 per week	4%	8.8%
Income greater than €399 per week	4%	11.05%

Employee PRSI Credit

An employee PRSI credit of a maximum of €12 per week is available to Class A employees with gross earnings between €352.01 and €424 per week. The credit is reduced by one-sixth of gross earnings in excess of €352 per week. The reduced credit is then deducted from the employee PRSI liability calculated at 4% of gross weekly earnings.

Self-employed

Individuals in receipt of income of €5,000 or less in 2021 will not be subject to PRSI. Where income is greater than €5,000, PRSI at 4% is payable subject to a minimum contribution of €500. For those with an annual self-employed income of in excess of €5,000 but who have no net liability to tax, the minimum contribution is €300 for 2021.

LOCAL PROPERTY TAX

Valuation Table 2022

Valuation Band Number	Valuation Band €	Mid-Point of Valuation Band €	LPT 2022 at Standard Rate €
01	0 to 200,000	N/A	90
02	200,001 to 262,500	N/A	225
03	262,501 to 350,000	306,250	315
04	350,001 to 437,500	393,750	405
05	437,501 to 525,000	481,251	495
06	525,001 to 612,500	568,751	585
07	612,501 to 700,000	656,251	675
08	700,001 to 787,500	743,751	765
09	787,501 to 875,000	831,251	855
10	875,001 to 962,500	918,751	945
11	962,501 to 1,050,000	1,006,251	1,035
12	1,050,001 to 1,137,500	1,093,750	1,190
13	1,137,501 to 1,225,000	1,181,251	1,409
14	1,225,001 to 1,312,500	1,268,751	1,627
15	1,312,501 to 1,400,000	1,356,251	1,846
16	1,400,001 to 1,487,500	1,443,751	2,065
17	1,487,501 to 1,575,000	1,531,251	2,284
18	1,575,001 to 1,662,500	1,618,751	2,502
19	1,662,501 to 1,750,000	1,706,251	2,721
20	1,750,001 +	N/A	2,830 +

CORPORATION TAX

Rates of Corporation Tax

Trading Rate of Corporation Tax

The trading rate of corporation tax is **12.5**% and applies to the following income and gains:

- Schedule D, Case I and Case II profits;
- capital gains (as adjusted); and
- certain foreign dividends.

Passive Rate of Corporation Tax

The passive rate of corporation tax is 25% applies to the following sources of income:

- Case III income, i.e. foreign income and untaxed Irish interest (excluding certain foreign dividends taxable at 12.5%);
- Case IV income, i.e. taxed Irish income and miscellaneous income not taxed under any other Case of Schedule D;
- Case V income, i.e. Irish rental income; and
- income from an "excepted trade".

CAPITAL GAINS TAX

Rates and Annual Exemption

	Rate
Disposals on or after 6 December 2012	33%
Disposals on or after 7 December 2011 and before 6 December 2012	30%
Disposals on or after 8 April 2009 and before 7 December 2011	25%
Annual exempt amount for 2021 is €1,270	

Where revised entrepreneur relief applies:

Disposals on or after 1 January 2017	10%
Disposals on or after 1 January 2016 and before 1 January 2017 20%	20%

Indexation Factors

Year of Assessment in which Expenditure Incurred	Multiplier for Disposal in Period Ended							
	5 April 1997	5 April 1998	5 April 1999	5 April 2000	5 April 2001	31 Dec 2001	31 Dec 2002	31 Dec 2003 et seq.
1974/75	6.017	6.112	6.215	6.313	6.582	6.930	7.180	7.528
1975/76	4.860	4.936	5.020	5.099	5.316	5.597	5.799	6.080
1976/77	4.187	4.253	4.325	4.393	4.580	4.822	4.996	5.238
1977/78	3.589	3.646	3.707	3.766	3.926	4.133	4.283	4.490
1978/79	3.316	3.368	3.425	3.479	3.627	3.819	3.956	4.148
1979/80	2.992	3.039	3.090	3.139	3.272	3.445	3.570	3.742
1980/81	2.590	2.631	2.675	2.718	2.833	2.983	3.091	3.240
1981/82	2.141	2.174	2.211	2.246	2.342	2.465	2.554	2.678
1982/83	1.801	1.829	1.860	1.890	1.970	2.074	2.149	2.253
1983/84	1.601	1.627	1.654	1.680	1.752	1.844	1.911	2.003
1984/85	1.454	1.477	1.502	1.525	1.590	1.674	1.735	1.819
1985/86	1.369	1.390	1.414	1.436	1.497	1.577	1.633	1.713
1986/87	1.309	1.330	1.352	1.373	1.432	1.507	1.562	1.637
1987/88	1.266	1.285	1.307	1.328	1.384	1.457	1.510	1.583
1988/89	1.242	1.261	1.282	1.303	1.358	1.430	1.481	1.553
1989/90	1.202	1.221	1.241	1.261	1.314	1.384	1.434	1.503
1990/91	1.153	1.171	1.191	1.210	1.261	1.328	1.376	1.442

continued overleaf

Year of Assessment in which Expenditure Incurred	5 April 1997	5 April 1998	5 April 1999	5 April 2000	5 April 2001	31 Dec 2001	31 Dec 2002	31 Dec 2003 et seq.
1991/92	1.124	1.142	1.161	1.179	1.229	1.294	1.341	1.406
1992/93	1.084	1.101	1.120	1.138	1.186	1.249	1.294	1.356
1993/94	1.064	1.081	1.099	1.117	1.164	1.226	1.270	1.331
1994/95	1.046	1.063	1.081	1.098	1.144	1.205	1.248	1.309
1995/96	1.021	1.037	1.054	1.071	1.116	1.175	1.218	1.277
1996/97	-	1.016	1.033	1.050	1.094	1.152	1.194	1.251
1997/98	-	-	1.017	1.033	1.077	1.134	1.175	1.232
1998/99	-	-	-	1.016	1.059	1.115	1.156	1.212
1999/00	-	-	-	-	1.043	1.098	1.138	1.193
2000/01	-	-	-	-	-	1.053	1.091	1.144
2001	-	-	-	-	-	-	1.037	1.087
2002	-	-	-	-	-	-	-	1.049
2003 et seq.	-	-	-	-	-	-	-	1.000

Multiplier for Disposal in Period Ended

VAT

VAT Rate	Examples
Exempt	▪ Medical, dental and optical services ▪ Insurance services ▪ Certain banking services ▪ Educational services ▪ Funeral services ▪ Gambling and lotteries ▪ Transport of passengers (and their baggage) ▪ Certain lettings of immovable goods
Zero rate	▪ Supply of most foodstuffs (excluding those specifically liable at the standard rate) ▪ Printed books and booklets (excluding stationery, brochures, etc.) ▪ Most clothing and footwear for children under 11 years of age ▪ Oral medicine (excluding food supplements) ▪ Exported goods (i.e. despatched outside the EU) ▪ Sea-going ships (more than 15 tonnes) ▪ Fertilizer ▪ Animal feed, other than pet food

continued overleaf

VAT Rate	Examples
Standard rate (23%)	All goods and services that are not exempt or zero-rated, or are not liable at the other specific rates. Includes: ■ Alcohol, soft drinks, bottled drinking water, juices ■ Chocolate and confectionery, biscuits, crisps, ice cream and similar ■ Adult clothing and footwear ■ Office equipment and stationery
Reduced rate (13.5%)	■ Fuel for power and heating (coal, peat, etc.) ■ Supply of electricity and gas ■ Waste disposal services ■ Non-residential immovable goods, including supply and development ■ Supply of concrete and concrete goods ■ Repair and maintenance of movable goods ■ General agricultural and veterinary services ■ Short-term hire of cars, boats, caravans, etc. ■ Food supplements ■ Driving instruction ■ Supply and hire of live horses and greyhounds
Second reduced rate (9%)	■ Subscriptions for certain sporting activities ■ Hairdressing services ■ Printed newspapers, e-newspapers, magazines and periodicals and e-books ■ Supply of hot food, including take-away food ■ Hotel/holiday accommodation, including caravan parks and camping sites ■ Admission to cinemas, theatres, certain musical performances, museums and fairground amusements
Farmer flat-rate addition (5.6%)	Supply of agricultural products and services by non-VAT-registered farmers to VAT-registered customers
Livestock rate (4.8%)	■ Supply of livestock ■ Supply of horses intended for foodstuffs

Code of Practice for Determining Employment or Self-Employment Status of Individuals[1]

This leaflet was prepared by the Employment Status Group set up under the Programme for Prosperity and Fairness. The group was set up because of a growing concern that there may be increasing numbers of individuals categorised as 'self-employed' when the 'indicators' may be that 'employee' status would be more appropriate. The leaflet has been updated in 2007 by the Hidden Economy Monitoring Group under Towards 2016 Social Partnership Agreement. The purpose of the document is to eliminate misconceptions and provide clarity. It is not meant to bring individuals who are genuinely self-employed into employment status.

In most cases it will be clear whether an individual is employed or self-employed. However, it may not always be so obvious, which in turn can lead to misconceptions in relation to the employment status of individuals.

The criteria below should help in reaching a conclusion. It is important that the job as a whole is looked at, including working conditions and the reality of the relationship, when considering the guidelines. An important consideration in this context, will be whether the person performing the work does so "as a person in business on their own account". Is the person a free agent with an economic independence of the person engaging the service? This consideration can be a useful indicator of the person's status and should be considered in conjunction with the other criteria listed in this code of practice.

The Safety, Health and Welfare at Work Act, 2005 is the cornerstone of health and safety regulation in Ireland. Employers and Employees all have duties under the act. The legislation treats self-employed persons in a similar manner to employers. It places on them an onus to manage, plan and conduct all work activities to ensure the health and safety of all persons at a workplace. Generally speaking self-employed persons and contractors have a greater responsibility to manage health and safety issues than employees. However, regardless of a person's status, health and safety management and practice is essential in all work operations. More information is available from www.hsa.ie

Criteria on Whether an Individual is an Employee

While all of the following factors may not apply, an individual would normally be an employee if he or she:

- Is under the control of another person who directs as to how, when and where the work is to be carried out.
- Supplies labour only.

---

[1] *Report of the Employment Status Group* – PPF, available from the Revenue Commissioners, see www.revenue.ie/en/self-assessment -and-self-employment/documents/code-of-practice-on-employment-status.pdf

- Receives a fixed hourly/weekly/monthly wage.
- Cannot subcontract the work. If the work can be subcontracted and paid on by the person sub-contracting the work, the employer/employee relationship may simply be transferred on.
- Does not supply materials for the job.
- Does not provide equipment other than the small tools of the trade. The provision of tools or equipment might not have a significant bearing on coming to a conclusion that employment status may be appropriate having regard to all the circumstances of a particular case.
- Is not exposed to personal financial risk in carrying out the work.
- Does not assume any responsibility for investment and management in the business.
- Does not have the opportunity to profit from sound management in the scheduling of engagements or in the performance of tasks arising from the engagements.
- Works set hours or a given number of hours per week or month.
- Works for one person or for one business.
- Receives expense payments to cover subsistence and/or travel expenses.
- Is entitled to extra pay or time off for overtime.

Additional Factors to be Considered

- An individual could have considerable freedom and independence in carrying out work and still remain an employee.
- An employee with specialist knowledge may not be directed as to how the work is carried out.
- An individual who is paid by commission, by share, or by piecework, or in some other atypical fashion might still be regarded as an employee.
- Some employees work for more than one employer at the same time.
- Some employees do not work on the employer's premises.
- There are special PRSI rules for the employment of family members.
- Statements in contracts considered in the *Denny* case, such as *"You are deemed to be an independent contractor"*, *"It shall be your duty to pay and discharge such taxes and charges as may be payable out of such fees to the Revenue Commissioners or otherwise"*, *"It is agreed that the provisions of the Unfair Dismissals Act 1977 shall not apply, etc."*, *"You will not be an employee of this company"*, and *"You will be responsible for your own tax affairs"*
  are not contractual terms and have little or no contractual validity. While they may express an opinion of the contracting parties, they are of minimal value in coming to a conclusion as to the work status of the person engaged.

Criteria on Whether an Individual is Self-employed

While all of the following factors may not apply to the job, an individual would normally be self-employed if he or she:

- Owns his or her own business.
- Is exposed to financial risk, by having to bear the cost of making good faulty or sub-standard work carried out under the contract.
- Assumes responsibility for investment and management in the enterprise.
- Has the opportunity to profit from sound management in the scheduling and performance of engagements and tasks.
- Has control over what is done, how it is done, when and where it is done and whether he or she does it personally.
- Is free to hire other people, on his or her terms, to do the work which has been agreed to be undertaken.

- Can provide the same services to more than one person or business at the same time.
- Provides the materials for the job.
- Provides equipment and machinery necessary for the job, other than the small tools of the trade or equipment which in an overall context would not be an indicator of a person in business on their own account.
- Has a fixed place of business where materials, equipment, etc. can be stored.
- Costs and agrees a price for the job.
- Provides his or her own insurance cover, e.g. public liability, etc.; or
- Controls the hours of work in fulfilling the job obligations.

Additional Factors to be Considered

- Generally an individual should satisfy the self-employed guidelines above, otherwise he or she will normally be an employee.
- The fact that an individual has registered as self-employed or for VAT under the principles of self-assessment does not automatically mean that he or she is self-employed.
- An office holder, such as a company director, will be taxed under the PAYE system. However, the terms and conditions may have to be examined by the Scope Section of the Department of Social Protection to decide the appropriate PRSI class.
- It should be noted that a person who is a self-employed contractor in one job is not necessarily self-employed in the next job. It is also possible to be employed and self-employed at the same time in different jobs.
- In the construction sector, for health and safety reasons, all individuals are under the direction of the site foreman/overseer. The self-employed individual controls the method to be employed in carrying out the work.

Consequences Arising from the Determination of an Individual's Status

The status as an employee or self-employed person will affect:

- The way in which tax, PRSI and USC is payable to the Collector-General.
- An employee will have tax and PRSI deducted from his or her income.
- A self-employed person is obliged to pay preliminary tax and file income tax returns whether or not he or she is asked for them.
- Entitlement to a number of social welfare benefits, such as unemployment and disability benefits.
- An employee will be entitled to unemployment, disability and invalidity benefits, whereas a self-employed person will not have these entitlements.

Other rights and entitlements, for example, under Employment Legislation:

- An employee will have rights in respect of working time, holidays, maternity/parental leave, protection from unfair dismissal, etc. A self-employed person will not have these rights and protection.
- Public liability in respect of the work done.

Deciding Status: Getting Assistance

Where there are difficulties in deciding the appropriate status of an individual or groups of individuals, the following organisations can provide assistance.

Tax and PRSI

- The Local Revenue Office or The Local Social Welfare Office.
- Scope Section in the Department of Employment Affairs and Social Protection.

If there is still doubt as to whether a person is employed or self-employed the Local Revenue Office or Scope Section of Department of Employment Affairs and Social Protection should be contacted for assistance. Having established all of the relevant facts, a written decision as to status will be issued. A decision by one Department will generally be accepted by the other, provided:

- all relevant facts were given at the time
- the circumstances remain the same
- it is accepted that the correct legal principles have been applied to the facts established.

However, because of the varied nature of circumstances that arise and the different statutory provisions, such a consensus may not be possible in every case.

The National Employment Rights Authority

The National Employment Rights Authority was established in February 2007 in accordance with a commitment under Towards 2016. NERA's mission is to drive the achievement of a national culture of employment law compliance in order to protect sustainable enterprises and statutory employment rights. NERA's core activities include: dissemination of information on employment rights to both employers and employees; compliance inspections and where necessary, prosecution and enforcement activity.

Relevant Contracts Tax - Form RCT 1

Relevant Contracts Tax (RCT) applies where a Subcontractor enters into a contract with a Principal Contractor (Principal) to carry out relevant operations (construction,forestry or meat processing operations). The Principal and Subcontractor must jointly complete Form RCT 1, declaring that the contract is a Relevant Contract(and not a contract of employment). Form RCT 1 has been revised to require further information from both Principal and Subcontractor as to why a proposed contract is considered to be a Relevant Contract. An incorrect designation of the contract as a Relevant Contract will have consequences for both the Principal and the Subcontractor. Further information is available from www.revenue.ie.

Employment which is not Insurable

The 2003 and 2006 Employment Permits Acts provide for a large number of employer obligations and offences which include specifically the employment of nonEEA(non-European Economic Area) nationals except in accordance with an employment permit, where required. In this regard, a contract of employment between such a migrant worker and an employer which is not covered by a valid employment permit is an illegal contract and that employment is not consequently insurable under the Social Welfare Consolidation Act, 2005. Further information regarding Employment Permits legislation is available at www.dbei.gov.ie or by calling LoCall 1890 220 222.

Useful contacts for information and leaflets

The Report of the Employment Status Group is available for viewing on the websites of:

- Revenue Commissioners
- Department of Employment Affairs and Social Protection
- Department of Business, Enterprise, & Innovation
- Irish Congress of Trade Unions
- Irish Business and Employers Confederation

Taxation and the *Code of Ethics*

Under the Chartered Accountants Ireland *Code of Ethics* (applicable from 1 December 2020), a Chartered Accountant shall comply with the following fundamental principles.

1. **Integrity** – to be straightforward and honest in all professional and business relationships.
2. **Objectivity** – to not compromise professional or business judgements because of bias, conflict of interest or undue influence of others.
3. **Professional Competence and Due Care** – to attain and maintain professional knowledge and skill at the level required to ensure that a client or employing organisation receives competent professional service based on current technical and professional standards and relevant legislation; and to act diligently and in accordance with applicable technical and professional standards.
4. **Confidentiality** – to respect the confidentiality of information acquired as a result of professional and business relationships and, therefore, not disclose any such information to third parties without proper and specific authority, unless there is a legal or professional right or duty to disclose, nor use the information for the personal advantage of the Chartered Accountant or third parties.
5. **Professional Behaviour** – to comply with relevant laws and regulations and avoid any conduct that the professional accountant knows, or should know, might discredit the profession.

The Institute's "Five Fundamental Principles, Five Practical Steps" is a useful resource for members and students and is available at www.charteredaccountants.ie. As a Chartered Accountant, you will have to ensure that your dealings with the tax aspects of your professional life are also in compliance with these fundamental principles. You may be asked to define or list the principles and also must be able to identify where these ethical issues arise and how you would deal with them.

In the context of tax, examples of situations that could arise where these principles are challenged are outlined below.

Example 1
You are working in the tax department of ABC & Co. and your manager is Jack Wilson. He comes over to your desk after his meeting with Peter Foley. He gives you all the papers that Peter has left with him. He asks you to draft Peter's tax return. You know who Peter is as you are now living in a house that your friend Ann leased from Peter. As you complete the return, you note that there is no information regarding rental income. What should you do?

Action
As a person with integrity, you should explain to your manager that your friend, Ann, has leased property from Peter and that he has forgotten to send details of his rental income and expenses. As Peter sent the information to Jack, it is appropriate for Jack to contact Peter for details regarding rental income and related expenses.

Example 2

You are working in the tax department of the Irish subsidiary of a US-owned multinational. You are preparing the corporation tax computation, including the R&D tax credit due. You have not received some information from your colleagues dealing with R&D and cannot finalise the claim for R&D tax credit until you receive this information. Your manager is under pressure and tells you to just file the claim on the basis of what will maximise the claim. He says, "It is self-assessment, and the chance of this ever being audited or enquired into is zero." What should you do?

Action

You should act in a professional and objective manner. This means that you cannot do as your manager wants. You should explain to him that you will contact the person in R&D again and finalise the claim as quickly as possible.

Example 3

Anna O'Shea, financial controller of Great Client Ltd, rings you regarding a VAT issue. You have great respect for Anna and are delighted that she is ringing you directly instead of your manager. She says that it is a very straightforward query. However, as you listen to her, you realise that you are pretty sure of the answer but would need to check a point before answering. What should you do?

Action

Where you do not know the answer, it is professionally competent to explain that you need to check a point before you give an answer. If you like, you can explain which aspect you need to check. Your client will appreciate you acting professionally rather than giving incorrect information or advice.

Example 4

The phone rings, and it is Darren O'Brien, your best friend, who works for Just-do-it Ltd. After discussing the match you both watched on the television last night, Darren explains why he is ringing you. He has heard that Success Ltd, a client of your Tax Department, has made R&D tax credit claims. Therefore, you must have details regarding its R&D. Darren's relationship with his boss is not great at present, and he knows that if he could get certain data about Success Ltd, his relationship with his boss would improve. He explains that he does not want any financial information, just some small details regarding R&D. What should you do?

Action

You should not give him the information. No matter how good a friend he is, it is unethical to give confidential information about your client to him.

Example 5

It is the Friday morning before a bank holiday weekend, and you are due to travel from Dublin to West Cork after work. Your manager has been on annual leave for the last week. He left you work to do for the week, including researching a tax issue for a client. He has advised you that you are to have an answer to the issue by the time he returns, no matter how long it takes. It actually took you a very short time and you have it all documented for him.

Your friend who is travelling with you asks if you could leave at 11am to beat the traffic and have a longer weekend. You have no annual leave left, so you cannot take leave. You know that if you leave, nobody will notice, but you have to complete a timesheet. Your friend reminds you that the research for the client could have taken a lot longer and that you could code the five hours to the client. What should you do?

Action

It would be unprofessional and would display a lack of integrity if you were to charge your client for those five hours.

Tax Planning, Tax Avoidance and Tax Evasion

The global financial and economic crash of 2008 and the ensuing worldwide recession led to a fall in tax collected by many governments and pushed tax and tax transparency higher up the agenda. Subsequent events further increased the focus and attention of the wider public – as well as governments – on both tax avoidance and the evasion of taxes: the revelations in the 'Paradise Papers' and the 'Panama Papers', the EU's state aid decision against Ireland and Apple Inc. and the 'tax shaming' of many multinational brand names and famous people led to tax, and tax ethics, appearing in media headlines almost on a daily basis. As a result, a number of international and domestic initiatives to try and address the fundamental issues have dramatically changed the tax planning and tax compliance landscape and brought tax transparency to the fore in many businesses and boardrooms.

The tax liability of an individual, partnership, company or trust can be reduced by tax planning, tax avoidance or tax evasion. Although the overriding objective of each is to reduce the taxpayer's tax bill, the method each adopts to do so is different. Each is also vastly different from an ethical and technical perspective.

Tax receipts are used to fund public services such as education, hospitals and roads. Individuals and businesses in a country benefit from these services directly and indirectly and it is therefore seen as a social and ethical responsibility for them to pay their fair share of taxes. Evading or avoiding paying your taxes is viewed as unacceptable as a result.

Tax Planning

Tax planning is used by taxpayers to reduce their tax bill by making use of provisions within domestic tax legislation. For example, any company with good tax governance will seek to minimise its tax liability by using the tools and mechanisms – allowances, deductions, reliefs and exemptions for example – made available to them by the government.

Planning can also take the form of simple decisions, such as delaying disposal of an asset when a fall in the rate of capital gains tax is expected so that the person pays a lower rate of tax on its taxable profits. Or a taxpayer may consider what type of assets to buy to maximise capital allowances. Any tax planning decision should work not just from a tax planning and legislative perspective, it should also make commercial sense.

The Irish government accepts that all taxpayers are entitled to organise their affairs in such a way as to mitigate their tax liability – as long as they do so within the law and within the spirit in which government intended when setting the law. Tax planning is both legally and ethically acceptable.

Tax Avoidance

Tax avoidance is often viewed as a grey area because it is regularly confused with tax planning. Tax avoidance is the use of loopholes within tax legislation to reduce the taxpayer's tax liability. Although tax avoidance may seem similar to tax planning because the taxpayer is using tax law to reduce their overall tax burden, the key difference is that the taxpayer is using tax legislation in a way not intended, or anticipated, by government.

TCA 1997 section 811C provides general anti-avoidance legislation. A transaction shall be a tax avoidance transaction if it would be reasonable to consider that the transaction gives rise to a tax advantage and it was not undertaken primarily for purposes other than to give rise to a tax advantage. These provisions are designed to counteract certain transactions which have little or no commercial reality but are carried out primarily to create an artificial tax deduction or to avoid or reduce a tax charge.

In addition, TCA 1997 sections 817D–817T provide mandatory disclosure of certain transactions that could result in a tax advantage. The regime seeks to force advisors, promoters and taxpayers who implement schemes designed to procure a tax advantage, to inform Revenue of the details of such schemes. The mandatory disclosure regime also has penalties for advisors who do not comply. The users of such schemes are also required to notify Revenue that they have used a particular scheme by including the scheme notification number on the relevant tax return or submission.

While tax avoidance is arguably legal, it is generally viewed as ethically unacceptable behaviour. Tax avoidance behaviour that is successfully challenged by Revenue will lead to the original tax saving being paid, in addition to interest and penalties.

Tax Evasion

At the extreme end of the spectrum is tax evasion. Tax evasion involves breaking the law deliberately and either not paying any of the taxes that fall due or underpaying the taxes that fall due when the law clearly states that they must be paid. Tax evaders intend to deliberately break rules surrounding their tax position in order to avoid paying the correct amount of tax they owe.

A tax evader illegally reduces their tax burden, either by a misrepresentation to Revenue or by not filing tax returns at all thereby concealing the true state of their tax affairs. Tax evasion can include onshore (within the State) and offshore deliberate behaviour.

Examples of tax evasion include, *inter alia*:

- failure to file a tax return and pay the relevant tax arising;
- failure to declare the correct income;
- deliberately inflating expenses, which reduces taxable profits or increases a loss;
- hiding taxable assets;
- wrongly claiming a tax refund or repayment by being dishonest;
- not telling Revenue about a source of income;
- not operating a PAYE scheme for employees/pensioners; and
- not registering for VAT when required to do so.

In all cases the Exchequer suffers a loss of tax. This is known as tax fraud. Tax evasion, and the tax fraud that flows from this behaviour, is a criminal offence prosecutable by Revenue. It is viewed as ethically unacceptable behaviour. The error will generally fall into the deliberate behaviour resulting in the original tax saving being paid, in addition to interest and penalties.

As Chartered Accountants, we must be cognisant of the activities of clients and potential clients, particularly in cases of tax avoidance and tax evasion.

Suggested Solutions to Review Questions

Chapter 2

Question 2.1

Income Tax Computation – Pat and Una 2021	Pat €	Una €	Total €
Taxable income	15,000	47,000	62,000
Tax payable: (married persons)			
Una – First €44,300 @ 20%		8,860	8,860
Pat – €15,000 @ 20%	3,000		3,000
Una – Balance €2,700 @ 40%		1,080	1,080
Gross income tax liability	3,000	9,940	12,940
Deduct: Non-refundable tax credits			(6,600)
Net tax due			**6,340**

Question 2.2

Income Tax Computation – Paul and Jason 2021	Paul €	Jason €	Total €
Taxable income	47,000	41,000	88,000
Tax payable: (civil partners)			
First €70,600 @ 20%			14,120
Balance €17,400 @ 40%			6,960
Gross income tax liability			21,080
Deduct: Non-refundable tax credits			(6,600)
Net tax due			**14,480**

Question 2.3

Income Tax Computation of Seán and Norah 2021	€
Taxable income	82,000
Tax payable: (married, one income)	
First €44,300 @ 20%	8,860
Balance €37,700 @ 40%	15,080
Gross income tax liability	23,940
Deduct: Non-refundable tax credits	(6,550)
Net tax due	**17,390**

Chapter 3

Question 3.1

Year of Assessment		Basis	Original Figure €	Final Figure €
2020	1st year:	Actual 01/06/2020–31/12/2020 7/12 × €48,000	28,000	N/A
2021	2nd year:	12-month accounting period ending in tax year 01/06/2020–31/05/2021	48,000	N/A
2022	3rd year:	12-month accounting period ending in the year of assessment – year ended 31/05/2022	39,000	33,750*
2023	4th year:	12-month accounting period ending in the year of assessment – year ended 31/05/2023	37,200	N/A

* Amount assessed in the second year (2021)		48,000
Less: Actual profits for the second year (2021)		
(€48,000 × 5/12) + (€39,000 × 7/12)		42,750
	Excess	5,250
Final 2021 assessment: €39,000 – €5,250		33,750

Question 3.2

Year of Assessment		Basis	Initial Figure €	Final Figure €
2020	1st year:	Actual 01/05/2020–31/12/2020 €44,800 + (2/12 × €54,400)	53,867	N/A
2021	2nd year:	12-month accounting period ending in tax year y/e 31/10/2021 (Note 1)	54,400	N/A
2022	3rd year:	12-month accounting period ending in tax year y/e 31/10/2022 (Note 2)	53,600	53,467

Notes:

1. Amount initially assessed in the 2nd year (2021)   €54,400

   Less: Actual profits for the 2nd year

      (€54,400 × 10/12) + (€53,600 × 2/12)   €54,267

   Excess   €133

2. As the amount assessed for the 2nd year exceeds the actual profits for the 2nd year, a claim may be made for a deduction of €133 against the profits of the 3rd year of assessment (2022):

           y/e 31/10/2022   53,600

           Excess for 2021   (133)

           Final assessment   53,467

Question 3.3

Year of Assessment	Basis	€
1st tax year 2020	01/05/2020–31/12/2020	
	8/12 × €48,000	32,000
2nd tax year 2021	12-month accounting period ending in tax year y/e 30/04/2021	48,000
3rd tax year 2022	Y/e 30/04/2022	60,000
4th tax year 2023	Y/e 30/04/2023	9,600

Note: profits assessable for 2nd year: €48,000

      Actual profits for 2nd year, 2021: (€48,000 × 4/12) + (€60,000 × 8/12) = €56,000

      Therefore no reduction for 3rd year, 2022.

Question 3.4

Year of assessment	Basis	€
1st tax year 2021	01/05/2021–31/12/2021	
	8/12 × €179,400	119,600
2nd tax year 2022	12-month accounting period ending in tax year y/e 30/04/2022	179,400

Donna Ross Income Tax Computation	2021	2022
	€	€
Schedule D, Case I	119,600	179,400
Schedule E salary	20,300	–
Total income	139,900	179,400

continued overleaf

Tax payable – single parent:

€39,300 @ 20%		7,860		7,860
Balance @ 40%	(€100,600)	40,240	(€140,100)	56,040
Deduct: Non-refundable tax credits		(4,950)		(4,950)
Tax deducted under PAYE		(3,850)		–
Income tax due		39,300		58,950

MEMO

To: Donna Ross	**Date: 3 January 2023**
From: Your Accountant	**Re: Taxable Trading**

I refer to our meeting last week. I have calculated your income tax liability for 2021 and 2022 at €39,300 and €58,950, respectively. The computations are attached.

I have considered the facts around your eBay activity for 2019 and 2020. To be liable to income tax, your eBay activity must constitute trading. There is no definition of trading in the Irish income tax legislation (TCA 1997), but guidance is available in case law and from the UK Royal Commission Rules. The rules or "Badges of Trade" help determine if your activity constitutes trading for Irish tax purposes. These are:

"Badges of Trade"	**Your circumstances**
Subject matter – if ownership does not give income or personal enjoyment, then sales indicate trading.	As your sales were of items bought originally for your enjoyment, this is not indicative of trading.
Length of ownership – short period indicates trading.	The 2020 job lot purchase and sale had a very quick turnaround, indicating trading.
Frequency – more over a long period indicates trading.	Transactions appear infrequent and opportunistic, not indicative of trading.
Supplementary work indicates trading.	As you didn't have an eBay "shop" until 2021, there is no indication of an effort to obtain customers.
Circumstances, if opportunistic or unsolicited, refute trading.	Sales until 2021 were opportunistic and the items sold personal in nature. This would counteract the trading suggestion.
Motive.	The evidence suggests the activity was merely a hobby until the business was established in 2021.

In deciding if trading is carried on, all rules are evaluated and the whole picture is taken into account. The overriding evidence in your case suggests that no trading took place during 2019 and 2020, and the activity involved was an attempt to declutter your home. However, for 2021 and 2022 you would be considered to be trading and therefore subject to Irish income tax on the income derived from your eBay sales.

Question 3.5

Year of Assessment	Original Basis Period	Original Figures €	Revised Figures €	
2019	Year ended 31/05/2019	64,000	N/A	
2020	Year ended 31/05/2020	72,000	N/A	(Note 1)
2021	Actual 01/01/2021–31/12/2021	16,000	N/A	(Note 2)

Notes:

1. Actual profits 2020: (€72,000 × 5/12) + (€9,600 × 7/12) = €35,600, therefore no revision.
2. Actual profits 2021: €12,000 + (5/12 × €9,600) = €16,000.

Question 3.6

Year of Assessment	Original Basis Period	Original Figures €	Revised Figures €	
2019	Year ended 31/07/2019	32,000	N/A	
2020	Year ended 31/07/2020	60,000	N/A	(Note 1)
2021	Actual 01/01/2021–31/05/2021	20,000	N/A	(Note 2)

Notes:

1. Actual profits 2020: (€60,000 × 7/12) + (€40,000 × 5/10) = €55,000. Therefore, original assessment will not be revised.
2. Actual profits 2021: €40,000 × 5/10 = €20,0000.

Question 3.7

			€
Final year 2021	01/01/2021–30/09/2021	9/12 × €240,000	180,000
Penultimate year 2020	01/01/2020–31/12/2020	(Note)	78,000

Note: actual profit 2020: (€24,000 × 9/12) + (€240,000 × 3/12) = €78,000

This figure will be assessed for 2020, as it is higher than the profits of €24,000 that were originally assessed for the year ended 30 September 2020.

Alex – Income Tax Computation for 2021	€
Income:	
Schedule D, Case I	180,000
Schedule E salary	15,000
Total income	195,000
Tax payable – single person:	
€35,300 @ 20%	7,060

continued overleaf

€159,700 @ 40%	63,880
€195,000	70,940
Deduct: Non-refundable tax credits	(3,300)
Deduct: Refundable tax credits: tax paid under PAYE	(3,410)
Income tax due	64,230

Question 3.8

As J. Cog retired on 30 September 2021, his last year of assessment is 2021. The requirement is therefore to calculate his assessable income for 2020 and 2021. The tax years 2018 and 2019 don't change.

Year of Assessment	Basis	€
2021	9/11 × 24,000 (9 months to 30/09/2021)	19,636
2020	y/e 31/10/2020	64,000 (Note)
2019	y/e 31/10/2019	65,000 – no change
2018	y/e 31/10/2018	40,000 – no change

Note: actual profit 2020: (€64,000 × 10/12) + (€24,000 × 2/11) = €57,697. The 2020 assessment will therefore not be revised to an actual basis.

Question 3.9

Distribution of Profits

	Total	Alex	Bill	Colin
	€	€	€	€
Year ended 30/09/2017	20,000	10,000	10,000	Nil
Year ended 30/09/2018	25,000	10,000	10,000	5,000
Year ended 30/09/2019	30,000	12,000	12,000	6,000
Year ended 30/09/2020	30,000	Nil	15,000	15,000
Year ended 30/09/2021	35,000	Nil	17,500	17,500

Assessments will be raised as follows:

Alex		Profits Assessable
Year of Assessment	Final Basis Period	€
2017	y/e 30/09/2017	10,000
2018	Actual (Note)	10,500
2019 Cessation	01/01/2019–30/09/2019 (€12,000 × 9/12)	9,000

Note: 2018 actual profits: (€10,000 × 9/12) + (€12,000 × 3/12) = €10,500. As this is higher than profits of the original basis period, year ended 30 September 2018, the assessment will be revised and actual profits will be assessed.

Bill			Profits Assessable
	Year of Assessment	**Final Basis Period**	**€**
	2017	y/e 30/09/2017	10,000
	2018	y/e 30/09/2018	10,000
	2019	y/e 30/09/2019	12,000
	2020	y/e 30/09/2020	15,000
	2021	y/e 30/09/2021	17,500

Colin			Profits Assessable
	Year of Assessment	**Basis Period**	**€**
	2017 Commencement	01/10/2017–31/12/2017 (3/12 × €5,000)	1,250
	2018	y/e 30/09/2018	5,000
	2019	y/e 30/09/2019 (Note)	6,000
	2020	y/e 30/09/2020	15,000
	2021	y/e 30/09/2021	17,500

Note: 2018 actual profits: (€5,000 × 9/12) + (€6,000 × 3/12) = €5,250. As this is greater than the profits assessable for the second year, the third year does not require amendment.

Question 3.10
Allocation of profits

	June	Mary	Karen	Jill	Louise	Total
	€	**€**	**€**	**€**	**€**	**€**
Y/e 30/06/2017	16,000	12,000	12,000			40,000
Y/e 30/06/2018	24,000	18,000	18,000			60,000
Y/e 30/06/2019	21,600	16,200		16,200		54,000
Y/e 30/06/2020	20,000	15,000		15,000		50,000
Y/e 30/06/2021	9,000	9,000		9,000	9,000	36,000
Six months to 31/12/2021	5,000	5,000		5,000	5,000	20,000

2017		€
June:	Year ended 30/06/2017	16,000
Mary:	Year ended 30/06/2017	12,000
Karen:	Actual (Note 1)	15,000

2018

June:	Year ended 30/06/2018	24,000
Mary:	Year ended 30/06/2018	18,000
Karen:	Actual (Note 2) (cessation)	9,000
Jill:	Actual (Note 3) (commencement)	8,100

2019

June:	Year ended 30/06/2019	21,600
Mary:	Year ended 30/06/2019	16,200
Jill:	Year ended 30/06/2019	16,200

2020

June:	Year ended 30/06/2020 (Note 6)	20,000
Mary:	Year ended 30/06/2020 (Note 6)	15,000
Jill:	(Note 4)	14,400
Louise:	Actual (Note 5) (commencement)	4,500

2021	Year of cessation – all partners on actual basis	
June:	01/01/2021–30/06/2021 (€9,000 × 6/12)	4,500
	01/07/2021–31/12/2021	<u>5,000</u>
		9,500
Mary:	As above	9,500
Jill:	As above	9,500
Louise:	As above	9,500

Notes:

1. Karen:	2017: original assessment: y/e 30/06/2017	<u>12,000</u>
	Actual profits 2017: (€12,000 × 6/12) + (€18,000 × 6/12)	<u>15,000</u>
	Penultimate year revised to actual	
2. Karen:	2018: final year actual: 01/01/2018–30/06/2018 (€18,000 × 6/12)	<u>9,000</u>
3. Jill:	2018 first year actual €16,200 × 6/12	<u>8,100</u>
4. Jill:	Second year 2019: assessment y/e 30/06/2019	16,200
	Actual profit for second year: (€16,200 × 6/12) + (€15,000 × 6/12)	(15,600)
	Excess	600
	Final third year assessment: €15,000 – €600	<u>14,400</u>
5. Louise:	2020: First year actual: €9,000 × 6/12 = €4,500	

6. There will be no revision of 2020 (penultimate year) profits to actual as actual profits were less than those assessed, i.e.:

> June actual 2020 (€20,000 × 6/12) + (€9,000 × 6/12) = €14,500
> Mary actual 2020 (€15,000 × 6/12) + (€9,000 × 6/12) = €12,000
> Jill actual 2020 – as for Mary €12,000

Question 3.11

Computation of Tax-adjusted Case I Profit for Joseph Murphy y/e 31 December 2021	€	€
Profit per accounts		9,874
Add back: Drawings (Note)	8,500	
Interest on VAT	1,121	
Interest on PAYE	1,238	
Depreciation	13,793	
Subscription (political, football, old folks, sports)	525	
Repairs (€6,480 – €2,335)	4,145	
Bad debts – increase in general provision (€7,975 – €5,100)	2,875	
Legal fees (capital)	1,009	33,206
		43,080
Deduct: Dividend from Irish Co.	2,813	
National loan stock interest	2,250	
Deposit interest	170	
Profit on fixed assets	5,063	(10,296)
Case I profit		**32,784**

Note: Disallow Mr Murphy's salary of €7,500 and the €1,000 holiday trip as these are drawings.

Question 3.12

Computation of Tax-adjusted Case I Profit for Andy Reilly y/e 31 December 2021	€
Net profit before taxation	36,050
Add back: Disallowed expenses:	
Motor vehicles (Note)	2,400
Depreciation – Equipment	2,500
– Vehicles	3,000
– Office equipment	900
Construction of garages (capital)	3,150
General bad debt provision	275
Drawings	20,000
Entertainment – Holiday	1,200
– Tickets (non-business)	300
– Customer business meals	1,200
Case I Tax-adjusted profit	**70,975**

Note: Disallowed motor expenses:	€	
Expenses for Andy Reilly's car	4,000	
Disallow personal element 60% × €4,000	2,400	

Question 3.13

(a) Computation of adjusted profit for Tony for the 15 months ended 31 December 2021 and the 12 months ended 31 December 2022:

	15 months ended 31/12/2021		12 months ended 31/12/2022	
	€	€	€	€
Net loss per accounts		(4,350)		(7,400)
Add back:				
Depreciation	3,000		2,400	
General provision for bad debts	2,500		(2,500)	
Entertaining	1,500		700	
Political donations	100			
Charitable donations	50			
Interest on late payment of VAT	250		–	
Drawings	15,000		12,000	
		22,400		12,600
Adjusted profit		**18,050**		**5,200**

(b) Tony's Case I taxable profit for 2021:

His first year of trading is 2020; 2021 is his second tax year of trading. An accounting period for a period in excess of 12 months ends in that year, namely the 15-month period ending 31 December 2021. Accordingly, Tony is taxable on the profits for the year ending on 31 December 2021. Therefore taxable Case I profits for 2021 are €18,050 × 12/15 = €14,440.

Question 3.14

Computation of Adjusted Profit for John Smith for the year ended 30 April 2022	€	€
Profit per accounts		2,820
Add back:		
Drawings (wages to self)	5,200	
Own PRSI	200	
Depreciation	1,250	
Motor expenses (Note 1)	924	
Leasing charges (Note 2)	1,994	
Extension	1,500	
Provision for repairs	1,000	
Interest on late payment of tax	120	

continued overleaf

Donation to church (Note 3)		260	
Expenses for son		710	
Retirement annuity premiums		1,100	
Life assurance		<u>460</u>	<u>14,718</u>
			17,538
Deduct: Interest received			<u>(390)</u>
Adjusted trading profits			**<u>17,148</u>**

Notes:

1.
		Add back
Motor expenses	1,860	
Less: parking fine	<u>(100)</u>	100
	1,760	
Plus car insurance	<u>300</u>	
	2,060	
Less: private element 40%	<u>(824)</u>	824
	1,236	___
Total disallowed		924

2.
		Add back
Lease charges on car	2,800	
Less: private element 40%	<u>(1,120)</u>	1,120
Lease charges restriction (category D):	1,680	
1,680 × (25,000 – (24,000 × 50%))		<u>874</u>
25,000		<u>1,994</u>

3. A donation made to an eligible charity is not a deduction from Case I or Case II income.

4. The accrued bonus for the sales assistant should be added back if it remains unpaid six months after the year-end.

Question 3.15

Computation of Adjusted Profit for Polly Styrene for the year ended 31 December 2021	€	€
Profit per accounts		22,000
Add back:		
Wages to self	8,000	
Light, heat and telephone (5/6 × 1,500)	1,250	
Repairs and renewals (extension to shop and general provision)	3,400	
Legal and professional fees (purchase of property)	300	
Bad debts (decrease in general reserve)	(600)	
Travel and entertainment (Note 1)	1,100	

continued overleaf

Lease interest (Note 3)	2,000	
Sundries (Note 2)	<u>1,549</u>	
		16,999
Deduct: Lease repayments (Note 3)		<u>(18,600)</u>
Case I adjusted profits year ended 31/12/2021		<u>**20,399**</u>

Notes:

1. Travel and entertainment	**€**	
Motor expenses (private 1/3 × €1,500)	500	
Entertaining customers	<u>600</u>	
	<u>1,100</u>	
2. Sundries		
Political party	1,000	
Parking fines	49	
Charitable donation	<u>500</u>	
	<u>1,549</u>	
3. Lease interest		
Deduct: total repayments for the year (allowable)	18,600	
Add back: lease interest deducted from profit	2,000	

Question 3.16

Case II Computation of Adjusted Profit for Jack and John	€	€	€
Net profit y/e 30/01/2021		46,000	
Add back:			
Disallowed expenses	26,000		
Partner salaries	41,000		
Partner interest	<u>13,000</u>	80,000	
Assessable profit		126,000	

Partnership Allocation	**Total**	**Jack**	**John**
Salaries (actual)	41,000	20,000	21,000
Interest (actual)	13,000	6,000	7,000
Balance (50:50)	<u>72,000</u>	<u>36,000</u>	<u>36,000</u>
Total	<u>126,000</u>	<u>62,000</u>	<u>64,000</u>
Case II taxable profits for 2021		<u>**62,000**</u>	<u>**64,000**</u>

Chapter 4

Question 4.1

Computation	Motor Vehicles 12.5% €	Plant and Equipment 12.5% €	Total €
Asset cost	*12,000	2,500	14,500
Additions 2021	0	4,500	4,500
Cost of assets qualifying for capital allowances	12,000	7,000	19,000
TWDV 01/01/2021	10,500	1,875	12,375
Additions y/e 30/04/2021			
(Basis period for 2021)	0	4,500	4,500
	10,500	6,375	16,875
Wear and tear 2021	(1,500)	(875)	(2,375)
TWDV 31/12/2021	9,000	5,500	14,500

*Cost €35,000 – restricted to €24,000. Wear and tear allowance for the car is further restricted by 50%, i.e. €1,500 as the car is a Category D car for CO_2 emissions.

Question 4.2

Year of Acquisition	Cost €	TWDV 01/01/2021 €	Wear and Tear 12.5% €	TWDV 31/12/2021 €
2018	15,000	9,375	(1,875)	7,500
2019	9,000	6,750	(1,125)	5,625
2021	5,100	0	(637)	4,463
		16,125	(3,637)	17,588

Question 4.3

Tax Year of Acquisition	Cost	TWDV 01/01/2021 €	Wear and Tear 12.5% €	TWDV 31/12/2021 €
2017	10,000	5,000	1,250	3,750
2021 - assets not in use	2,300			2,300
2021	9,920		1,240	8,680
		5,000	2,490	14,730

Note: the printer ink cartridges are not a capital item.

Question 4.4

First tax year for which business assessed: 2021
Basis period for 2021: 01/10/2021–31/12/2021 (3 months)

Second tax year for which business assessed: 2022
Basis period for 2022: 01/10/2021–30/09/2022 (12 months)

Asset bought and put into use during basis period for 2021.

Wear and tear allowances for 2021 and 2022 computed as follows:

	€	
Qualifying cost	1,000	
Wear and tear 2021 @ 12.5% (basis period 3 months)	(31)	$\left(12.5\% \times 1,000 \times \dfrac{3 \text{ months}}{12 \text{ months}}\right)$
TWDV as at 31 December 2021	969	
Wear and tear 2022 @ 12.5% (basis period 12 months)	(125)	
TWDV at 31 December 2022	844	

Question 4.5

	€	
Qualifying cost	10,000	
Wear and tear 2021 @ 12.5% (basis period 7 months)	(729)	$\left(12.5\% \times 10,000 \times \dfrac{7 \text{ months}}{12 \text{ months}}\right)$
TWDV 31/12/2021	9,271	
Wear and tear 2022 @ 12.5% (basis period 12 months)	(1,250)	
TWDV 31/12/2022	8,021	

Question 4.6

Basis period for 2021: 01/05/2021–31/12/2021 (8 months)
Basis period for 2022: y/e 30/04/2022

		Plant and Machinery (12.5%)
		€
TWDV	01/01/2021	–
Additions (basis period for 2021)	01/05/2021–31/12/2021	9,000
Wear and tear 2021 (8 months)	€9,000 @ 12.5% × 8/12	(750)
TWDV 31/12/2021		8,250
Additions 01/01/2022–30/04/2022		1,700
		9,950
Wear and tear 2022 (Note)		(1,337)
TWDV 31/12/2022		8,613

Note: €9,000 + €1,700 = €10,700 @ 12.5% = €1,337

Question 4.7

	Motor Vehicle (12.5%) €	Allow (3/4) €	
Cost/specified limit (restricted by 50% Category D)	10,500		
Wear and tear 2021 €10,500 @ 12.5%	(1,312)	984	(75%)
TWDV 31/12/2021	9,188		

Question 4.8

	Motor Vehicles (12.5%) €	Allow (2/3) €
Cost (restricted) 2021	24,000	
Wear and tear €24,000 @ 12.5%	(3,000)	2,000
TWDV 31/12/2021	21,000	

Car cost restricted to €24,000.

As the vehicle is emissions Category C, no emissions restriction applies.

Question 4.9

Allowances Computation for 2021

	Motor Vehicles (12.5%) €	Allow (70%) €	Office Equipment (12.5%) €
TWDV @ 01/01/2021			7,500
Acquired in y/e 31/12/2021 (restricted)	24,000		1,000
Disposals 2021 @ TWDV			(7,500)
Wear and tear 2021	(3,000)	(2,100)	(125)
TWDV 31/12/2021	21,000		875

Car cost restricted to €24,000.

As the car is emissions Category A, no emissions restriction arises.

Balancing Allowance (Charge) assessable:

Office equipment	€
TWDV 01/01/2021	7,500
Proceeds	(3,500)
Balancing allowance	4,000

Capital Allowance Claim	€
Wear and tear	2,225
Balancing allowance	4,000
Total 2021	6,225

Question 4.10

Capital Allowance Computation 2021

	€
Proceeds: $20,000 \times \dfrac{24,000}{27,000}$	17,778
TWDV @ 01/01/2021 (Note)	(18,000)
Balancing allowance	222
Business use 70%	155

Note:	€
Motor vehicle (Oct 2018) allowable cost	24,000
Wear and tear 2019 (basis period 30/09/2019)	(3,000)
Wear and tear 2020 (basis period 30/09/2020)	(3,000)
	18,000

Question 4.11

Capital Allowances Computation for 2021

	Plant (12.5%)	Lorries (12.5%)	Motor vehicle* (12.5%)	Total
	€	€	€	€
Cost at 01/01/2021	52,000	26,000	24,000	102,000
Additions at cost 2021	50,000	20,000	0	70,000
Disposals at cost 2021	(42,000)	0	0	(42,000)
Cost at 31/12/2021	60,000	46,000	24,000	130,000

	Plant (12.5%)	Lorries (12.5%)	Motor vehicle* (12.5%)	Total
	€	€	€	€
TWDV 01/01/2021	8,750	0	15,000	23,750
Additions	50,000	20,000	0	70,000
	58,750	20,000	15,000	93,750
Disposals at TWDV	0	0	0	0
	58,750	20,000	15,000	93,750

continued overleaf

Wear and tear:

Allowance 2021	(7,500)	(2,500)	(3,000)	(13,000)
TWDV at 31/12/2021	51,250	17,500	12,000	80,750
Allowance 2022	(7,500)	(2,500)	(3,000)	(13,000)
TWDV at 31/12/2022	43,750	15,000	9,000	67,750

*Motor Vehicle (12.5%)

Cost 16/07/2017 i.e. y/e 30/04/2018	24,000	(restricted)
Wear and tear 2018	(3,000)	(restricted to 1/3 for business use)
TWDV 31/12/2018	21,000	
Wear and tear 2019	(3,000)	(restricted to 1/3 for business use)
TWDV 31/12/2019	18,000	
Wear and tear 2020	(3,000)	(restricted to 1/3 for business use)
TWDV 31/12/2020	15,000	

Balancing Charge/Allowance 2021

TWDV of plant sold	0
Proceeds	2,200
Balancing charge	2,200

Cannot be offset as no replacement plant purchased.

Asset sold for €1,500 with a nil TWDV ignored as proceeds < €2,000.

Summary

2021 €

Wear and tear: €7,500 + €2,500 + (€3,000 × 1/3)	11,000
Balancing charge	(2,200)
Total allowances	8,800

2022

Wear and tear: €7,500 + €2,500 + (€3,000 × 1/3)	11,000

Question 4.12

Assessable Profits

Tax Year	Basis Period	Profits
		€
2018	01/06/2018–31/12/2018	34,417 (7/12 × €59,000)
2019	Year ended 31/05/2019	59,000
2020	Year ended 31/05/2020	38,417 (Note)
2021	Year ended 31/05/2021	120,000

continued overleaf

Note: profits assessable for the second year 2019:

	59,000
Less: Actual profits (€59,000 × 5/12) + (€46,000 × 7/12)	51,417
Excess	7,583

Final third year 2020 assessment: €46,000 – €7,583 = €38,417

Capital Allowances Computation for 2021

	Equipment (12.5%) €	Car (12.5%) €	Allow (60%) €	Total €
Additions at Cost 2018:				
General equipment	26,000			26,000
Hairdryers	800			800
Additions at Cost 2019:				
Chairs	1,400			1,400
Motor car (specified amount)	0	24,000	____	24,000
Cost at 31/12/2021	28,200	24,000	____	52,200
Wear and Tear Calculation				
01/06/2018–31/12/2018:				
Additions	26,800	–	–	
Wear and tear (7 months)	(1,954)	–	–	(1,954)
TWDV 31/12/2018	24,846	–	–	
Additions 2019	1,400	24,000		
Wear and tear 2019	(3,525)	(3,000)	(1,800)	(5,325)
TWDV 31/12/2019	22,721	21,000		
Wear and tear 2020	(3,525)	(3,000)	(1,800)	(5,325)
TWDV 31/12/2020	19,196	18,000		
Wear and tear 2021	(3,525)	(3,000)	(1,800)	(5,325)
TWDV 31/12/2021	15,671	15,000		

Question 4.13

(a)   Computation of taxable case/income for the year ended 31 December 2021

	€	€
Loss per accounts to 31 December 2021		(310)
Adjustments – add back:		
Wages to self (drawings)	5,200	
Motor expenses 25% × €1,750 (private element)	437	
Light and heat 25% × €1,200 (private element)	300	
Christmas gifts (entertainment – n/a)	300	
Depreciation	900	

continued overleaf

Covenant	105	
Cash register (fixed asset)	380	
Deposit on shelving (fixed asset)	1,000	
Display freezer (fixed asset)	600	
Flat contents insurance (private element)	100	
Hire-purchase instalments	1,920	
Notional rent (drawings)	<u>2,000</u>	<u>13,242</u>
		12,932
		<u>(376)</u>
Deduct: Hire-purchase charges		
		12,556
Deduct: Building society interest received	210	
Sale proceeds of equipment	<u>1,500</u>	<u>(1,710)</u>
Adjusted profits	<u>10,846</u>	
Case I taxable income for 2021	<u>10,846</u>	

(b) Capital allowances claim 2021

	Plant (12.5%) €	Motor car (12.5%) €	Allow (75%) €	Total €
Cost at 01/01/2021	2,500	24,000*		26,500
Additions at cost 2021:				
Cash register 01/02/2021	380			380
Shelving 10/02/2021	5,633			5,633
Freezer 01/03/2021	600			600
Disposals at cost 2021	(2,500)	0		(2,500)
Cost at 31/12/2021	6,613	24,000		30,613
TWDV 01/01/2021	**1,250**	**9,000**		**10,250**
Additions at cost	6,613			6,613
Disposals at TWDV	(1,250)			(1,250)
Wear and tear 2021	(827)	(3,000)	(2,250)	(3,827)
TWDV 31/12/2021	**5,786**	**6,000**		**11,786**

*Specified amount.

Balancing Charge/Allowance calculation

Proceeds of sale	1,500
Less: TWDV	(1,250)
Balancing charge – ignored as proceeds < €2,000	250
Capital allowances due 2021	
Wear and tear €2,250 + €827	3,077

Question 4.14

Mr Goa

2017   Basis period y/e 30/06/2017:

Annual allowance of €140,000 × 4% = €5,600 claimed

2018   Basis period 30/06/2018 balancing charge as set out below:

	€
Sale proceeds (€190,000 – €25,000)	165,000
TWDV (€140,000 – €5,600)	134,400
Balancing charge	30,600
Restricted to allowances actually claimed:	
(€140,000 – €134,400)	5,600

Mrs Statham

Qualifying expenditure	140,000

2018   Basis period: 01/05/2018–31/12/2018

$$\frac{8}{12} \times \frac{1}{25-1} \times 140,000 = €3,889$$

Basis period is less than 12 months

2019   Basis period y/e 30/04/2019

$$\frac{12}{12} \times \frac{1}{25-1} \times 140,000 = €5,883$$

2020   Basis period y/e 30/04/2020

$$\frac{12}{12} \times \frac{1}{25-1} \times 140,000 = €5,883$$

2021   Basis period y/e 30/04/2021

$$\frac{12}{12} \times \frac{1}{25-1} \times 140,000 = €5,883$$

Question 4.15

Calculate eligible items

	€	
Site purchase cost	0	
Site development costs	5,000	
Construction of factory	95,000	
Construction of adjoining office	0	(Note 1)
Construction of adjoining showroom	0	(Note 1)
Total cost	100,000	

continued overleaf

Note:

1. The 10% rule for eligible items applies to the showroom and office as follows:

$$\frac{10,000+15,000}{(135,000-10,000)} = 20\%$$

IBAA @ 4% of €100,000 = €4,000

Question 4.16

Capital Allowances Computation 2021

	Plant (12.5%)	Motor Vehicles (12.5%)	Trucks (12.5%)	Total
	€	€	€	€
Cost at 01/01/2021	25,500	24,000	18,750	68,250
Additions at cost 2021:				
(1) Office furniture	10,000			10,000
(2) Truck			25,000	25,000
(4) Car (restricted to 50% Category D)		12,000		12,000
(5) New machinery (net of grant)	20,000			20,000
Disposals at cost 2021	0	(24,000)	0	(24,000)
Cost at 31/12/2021	55,500	12,000	43,750	111,250
TWDV 01/01/2021	**15,937**	**9,000**	**14,062**	**38,999**
Additions	30,000	12,000	25,000	67,000
Disposals at TWDV	0	(9,000)	0	(9,000)
	45,937	12,000	39,062	96,999
Wear and tear 2021	(6,938)	(1,500)	(5,469)	(13,907)
TWDV 31/12/2021	**38,999**	**10,500**	**33,593**	**83,092**

(3) Deposits on Machinery No allowance is available in 2021 as assets not in use at 31 December 2021.

(6) Industrial Building Allowance

Original cost €75,000

IBAA €75,000 × 1/15 = €5,000

(7) Extension to Factory Premises   IBAA not due as extension was not in use at the end of the basis period.

(4) Balancing Allowance Charge Computation – car   €

TWDV at 01/01/2021		9,000
Sale proceeds:	$7,500 \times \dfrac{24,000}{26,000}$	(6,923)
		2,077
Balancing allowance	$2,077 \times 75\%$	1,558

continued overleaf

Summary of Capital Allowances 2021

Plant	6,938
Car (€1,500 × 75%)	1,125
Trucks	5,469
IBAA	5,000
Balancing allowance	1,558
	20,090

Question 4.17

	Plant and Machinery (12.5%) €	Trucks (12.5%) €	Vehicles/ Cars (12.5%) €	TOTAL €
Original cost 01/01/2021	45,000	17,000	24,000	86,000
Additions at cost	25,000		48,000	73,000
Disposals at cost	(35,000)		(24,000)	(59,000)
Remaining cost	35,000	17,000	48,000	100,000
				–
TWDV 01/01/2021	5,000	2,125	12,000	19,125
Additions y/e 31/05/2021	25,000		48,000	73,000
Disposals y/e 31/05/2021			(12,000)	(12,000)
	30,000	2,125	48,000	80,125
Wear and tear 2021	(4,375)	(2,125)	(6,000)	(12,500)
TWDV 31/12/2021	25,625	–	42,000	67,625

Balancing allowances charges:

		€	
Machinery:	Sold for	14,000	
	TWDV	Nil	
	Potential balancing charge	14,000	Offset as replacement
Replacement machinery:	Cost	49,000	
	Grant	(10,000)	
	Replacement option	(14,000)	
	Plant addition	25,000	
Sale of car:	TWDV	12,000	
	Proceeds €12,500 × €24,000/€24,000	12,500	
	Balancing charge	500	

Wear and tear is not due for the photocopier as it was not in use at the end of the 2021 basis period.

continued overleaf

IBAA:

Second-hand industrial building: $\dfrac{120,000}{25-11} = €8,571$ IBAA per annum.

Sale of office building: no balancing charge as does not qualify as an industrial building.

Extension to industrial building: €70,000 × 4% = €2,800 IBAA per annum. The offices qualify for IBAA as they did not cost more than 10% of the overall cost.

Summary

	€
Wear and tear	12,500
Balancing charge	(500)
IBAA	8,571
IBAA	2,800
Total capital allowances due 2021	23,371

Question 4.18

Assessment 2021	€
Case I	–
Schedule E	80,000
	80,000
Less: section 381 loss	(60,000)
Taxable income 2021	20,000

As Linda is involved in the business in an "active capacity", i.e. more than 10 hours a week, there is no restriction on the section 381 relief available.

Question 4.19

Mr Jones Assessment 2021	€
Case I	0
Case III (government securities)	25,000
Schedule E	55,000
Gross statutory income	80,000
Deduct: section 381 loss (restricted)	(31,750)
Taxable income 2020	**48,250**
Loss available under section 382	8,250

As Mr Jones is only involved in the business for seven hours a week, he is not involved in the business in an "active capacity", i.e. more than 10 hours a week, and therefore the section 381 relief is restricted to €31,750.

Question 4.20

This gives rise to a loss of €7,000 (27,000 – 20,000), which can be claimed under section 381.

	€	€
Profit y/e 31/12/2021		20,000
Less: capital allowances	(37,000)	
Deduct: balancing charge	10,000	(27,000)
Section 381 loss 2021		(7,000)

Question 4.21

John – Capital Allowances 2021: Section 381 Claim

	€
Tax-adjusted Case I profit y/e 30/09/2021	9,000
Deduct: capital allowances forward (limited)	(9,000)
Net Case I	Nil
Balancing charge	3,000
Deduct: balance of unused capital allowances forward (€9,600 – €9,000)	(600)
Net balancing charge	2,400
Deduct: 2021 capital allowances claim	(7,500)
Section 381 loss (available to reduce total income for 2021 or carried forward to 2022 as a section 382 loss)	(5,100)

Note: capital allowances carried forward from previous year cannot be used to create or augment a section 381 loss claim directly. However, they may be used to wipe out any current year balancing charges and to reduce current year profits and in this way may result in increasing a section 381 claim.

Question 4.22

	2019	2020	2021	Total
	€	€	€	
Case I	Nil	17,000	50,000	
Deduct: Case I losses forward (section 382)	——	(17,000)	(1,000)	(18,000)
Assessable Case I	Nil	Nil	49,000	

Jim is obliged to take relief for the loss forward in the first year in which Case I profits from the same trade are available. This occurs in 2020 and results in a waste of his personal tax credits for that year. Jim would have preferred to defer relief for some of the loss until 2021 to avoid wasting his 2020 tax credits and to avail of relief from the tax that will be suffered in 2021. Unfortunately, this is not permitted.

Question 4.23

Assessments		€
2019	Case I	80,000
	Case IV	1,000
	Case V	20,000
	Taxable 2019	**101,000**
2020	Case I	Nil
	Case IV	1,200
	Case V	30,000
		31,200
	Less: section 381	(31,200)
	Taxable 2020	**Nil**
2021	Case I	45,000
	Section 382 relief (€37,000 – €31,200)	(5,800)
		39,200
	Case IV	1,200
	Case V	25,000
	Taxable 2021	**65,400**

Chapter 5

Question 5.1

(a) Calculation of Taxable Benefit in Kind – Sid Harvey

Car:	€
OMV = €35,000	
Rate for 26,400 business km 24%	8,400
Deduct: fuel and insurance reimbursed	(1,300)
Sid's personal contribution €100 × 12	(1,200)
Net benefit in kind	5,900
Free use of apartment:	
Annual value 8% × €110,000	8,800
Add: expenses paid by company	890
	9,690

Meals: exempt as provided free of charge to all staff.

Loan: waiver of loan is treated as additional benefit in February 2021 of €1,000.

Loan interest: $€1,000 \times 13.5\% \times \dfrac{1 \text{ month}}{12 \text{ months}} = €11$

(b)

Sid Harvey – Income Tax Computation for 2021		€	€
Schedule E income:			
Salary 2021			40,000
Round sum expense allowance: €100 × 12			1,200
Benefit in kind:	Car	5,900	
	Apartment above	9,690	
	Meals	Exempt	15,590
Perquisites:	Loan waived	1,000	
	Deemed preferential interest paid:		
	$€1,000 \times 13.5\% \times \dfrac{1 \text{ month}}{12 \text{ months}}$	11	1,011
Gross income			57,801
Tax payable (single):	€35,300 @ 20%	7,060	
	€22,501 @ 40%	9,000	
	€57,801	16,060	
Deduct: Non-refundable tax credits		(3,300)	12,760
Deduct: Refundable tax credits: tax paid under PAYE			(12,760)
Tax payable			**NIL**

Question 5.2

(a)   Benefit in kind – Rich Bank plc

	€
Mortgage loan: €125,000 @ 4%	5,000
Less: €125,000 @ 2% (actual interest paid)	(2,500)
Benefit in kind assessable	2,500
Preferential loan: Golf club €10,000 @ 13.5%	1,350
Company car: Cash equivalent percentage: (business km 36,000)	
€30,000 @ 18%	5,400
Less: reimbursement by employee: 10,400 km @ 15c	(1,560)
Benefit in kind assessable	3,840
Taxable benefits:	
Mortgage loan	2,500
Other loan	1,350
Golf club membership	3,500
Car	3,840
Total benefits assessable in 2021	11,190
Tax payable @ 40% €4,476 = cost of benefits provided	

(b)

Terry – Income Tax Computation 2021		New Job €		Current Job €
Schedule E salary		70,000		75,000
Benefit in kind		11,190		0
Taxable income		81,190		75,000
Tax payable (married, one income):				
€44,300 @ 20%		8,860		8,860
Balance @ 40%	(36,890)	14,756	(30,700)	12,280
		23,616		21,140
Deduct: Non-refundable personal tax credits		(6,550)		(6,550)
Net tax liability		17,066		14,590
Net Pay Calculation:				
Salary		70,000		75,000
Deduct: tax		(17,066)		(14,590)
		52,934		60,410
Add: value of benefits:				
– Mortgage interest saved (Note 1)		3,750		0
– Car running costs (Note 2)		9,564		0
Value received by Terry		**66,248**		**60,410**

Notes:

1. Interest paid @ 5%	€125,000 @ 5%	6,250
Interest paid @ 2%	€125,000 @ 2%	(2,500)
Saving		3,750
2. Car running cost: current estimate		10,500
Less: reimbursed to bank (€1,560 – 40%)		(936)
Saving		9,564

Question 5.3

Mr Stodge – Income Tax Computation 2021	€	€
Schedule E:		
Salary (actual)	41,600	
Salary (spouse)	15,500	
Sales commission (receipts basis)	9,000	
Lump sum expense allowance 12 × €100	1,200	
		67,300
Schedule E expense claim (Note 1)		(10,675)
Total/taxable income		56,625

continued overleaf

Tax payable (married, two incomes):

(€41,125 + €15,500 = €56,625) @ 20%	11,325	
Deduct: Non-refundable tax credits	(6,600)	
Net tax liability		4,725
Deduct: Refundable tax credits: tax paid under PAYE (€5,410 + €1,450)		(6,860)
Tax Refund due		**(2,135)**

Notes:

1. Schedule E expense claim 2021

Motor car operating costs 2021	6,450	
Less: related to private use (10%)	(645)	
Allowable running costs		5,805
Lease charges:		
Total lease charges	5,700	
Less: personal element (10%)	(570)	
	5,130	
Less: restricted amount: €5,130 × (27,000 – 24,000)/27,000	(570)	4,560

Other expenses tax year 2021:		
Total per schedule	910	
Disallow: Suit	(450)	
Correspondence course	(150)	310
Total allowable Schedule E expenses		10,675

Note: as Philip's car is a Category B car, there is no further restriction to the lease allowances based on CO_2 emissions.

Question 5.4

(a) **Frank – Income Tax 2021: Current Arrangement**	€	€
Schedule E:		
Salary		50,000
Sales commission		8,000
		58,000
Schedule E expense claim:		
Motor expenses (Note 1)	6,944	
Lease charges (Note 2)	0	(6,944)
Total/taxable income		51,056

continued overleaf

Tax payable (single):

€35,300 @ 20%	7,060	
€15,756 @ 40%	6,302	13,362
€51,056		
Deduct: Non-refundable personal tax credits		(3,300)
Tax liability		10,062

Notes:

1. Allowable motor expenses:

Petrol	4,300
Insurance	1,500
Motor tax	1,480
Repairs and services	1,400
	8,680
Disallow private use $€8,680 \times \dfrac{8,960 \text{ km}}{44,800 \text{ km}}$	(1,736)
Allowable motor expenses	6,944

2. Allowable lease charges:

Total lease charges	6,600
	(1,320)
Disallow personal element: $6,600 \times \dfrac{8,960 \text{ km}}{44,800 \text{ km}}$	
	5,280
	(5,280)
Less: restriction (emissions Category F): $5,280 \times \dfrac{(51,000 - 0)}{51,000}$	
Allowable lease charges	0

(b)

Frank – Income Tax 2021: New Arrangement		€
Schedule E:		
Salary		50,000
Sales commission (two-thirds)		5,333
BIK (Note)		5,580
Taxable total income		60,913
Tax payable:		
€35,300 @ 20%	7,060	
€25,613 @ 40%	10,245	17,305
€60,913		
Deduct: Non-refundable personal tax credits		(3,300)
Tax liability		14,005

Note:

Benefit in kind – car	€31,000
18% (business 35,840 km)	€5,580

continued overleaf

After-tax position	Option (a)	Option (b)
Gross salary	58,000	55,333
Less: tax	(10,062)	(14,005)
Less: car running costs (€8,680 + €6,600)	(15,280)	0
Net cash	32,658	41,328

Conclusion: Frank has more disposable income under option (b).

Chapter 6

Question 6.1

Income Tax Computation for Maeve 2021	€	€
Income:		
Schedule D, Case IV (Note 1)	12,418	
Schedule E: Contributory Widow's Pension	12,912	
Schedule F (Note 2)	26,827	
Taxable income		52,157
Tax payable: (widowed without dependent children)		
€12,418 @ 33%	4,098	
€35,300 @ 20%	7,060	
€4,439 @ 40%	1,776	
€52,157		12,934
Deduct: *Non-refundable tax credits:*		
Personal tax credits	4,085	
DIRT paid	4,098	(8,183)
		4,751
Deduct: *Refundable tax credits:*		
DWT paid		(6,707)
Net tax refundable		**(1,956)**

Notes:

1. Schedule D, Case IV		**Gross**	**DIRT @ 33%**
		€	€
PTSB	€6,400/0.67	9,552	3,152
Credit Union	€1,200/0.67	1,791	591
AIB interest account	€720/0.67	1,075	355
		12,418	4,098

continued overleaf

2. Schedule F dividends

		Gross	**DWT @ 25%**
		€	€
Tyson	€17,520/0.75	23,360	5,840
Holyfield	€2,600/0.75	3,467	867
		26,827	6,707

Question 6.2

Income Tax Computation 2021 for Anthony and Sandrine Kelly		**€**	**€**
Income: Schedule D:	Case IV – Anthony (Note 1)	310	
	Case IV – Sandrine	2,000	2,310
Schedule E:	Anthony	50,000	
	Sandrine	28,000	78,000
Schedule F:	Gross dividend (Note 2)		3,333
Total/taxable income			83,643
Tax payable (married, two incomes):			
	€2,310 @ 33%	762	
	€70,600 @ 20%	14,120	
	€10,733 @ 40%	4,293	19,175
Deduct: Non-refundable tax credits:			
	Personal tax credits	9,900	
	DIRT paid: €2,310 @ 33%	762	(10,662)
Net tax liability			**8,513**
Deduct: Refundable tax credits:			
	Tax paid under PAYE – Anthony	6,340	
	Tax paid under PAYE – Sandrine	2,300	
	DWT	833	(9,473)
Net tax refundable			**(960)**
Notes:		**€**	
1. Case IV income – Anthony:			
Credit Union interest, ordinary deposit account		80	
Credit union interest, share account		100	
AIB interest, ordinary deposit account		130	
		310	
Case IV income – Sandrine:			
KBC interest gross		2,000	
2. Schedule F income:			
Dividends net of DWT		2,500	
DWT @ 25%		833	
Gross		3,333	

Question 6.3

David Lee – Income Tax 2021	€	€
Schedule D, Case III: Interest on government stock	1,130	
Schedule D, Case IV: €500 + €140 + €29 = €669 @ 100/67	998	
Schedule E salary	42,000	
Taxable income		44,128
Tax payable (single parent):		
€39,300 @ 20%	7,860	
€998 @ 33%	329	
€3,830 @ 40%	1,532	9,721
€44,128		
Deduct: Non-refundable tax credits:		
Personal tax credits	4,950	
DIRT paid: €998 @ 33%	329	(5,279)
Tax liability		**4,442**
Deduct: Refundable tax credits: Tax paid under PAYE		(3,990)
Tax payable		**452**

Chapter 7

Question 7.1

			Properties		
Mr O'Reilly Case V Computation		**A**	**B**	**C**	**D**
		Res.	Comm.	Res.	Res.
		€	€	€	€
	Rent receivable during 2021	6,000	5,000	3,500	9,600
	Premium on lease (Note 1)		6,000		–
		6,000	11,000	3,500	9,600
Less:	Allowable expenses (Note 2):				
	Bank interest	(5,500)	(3,000)	–	(6,167)
	Storm damage	–	(1,400)	–	–
	Pre-letting expenses	–	–	–	(4,993)
	Advertising	–	–	(130)	–
	Roof repairs	–	–	–	(160)
	Blocked drains and painting	–	–	(790)	–
	Net rents	500	6,600	2,580	(1,720)

continued overleaf

Summary (Note 3):

Property A	500
Property B	6,600
Property C	2,580
Property D	(1,720)
Net assessable Case V 2021	7,960

Notes:

1. Rent Receivable
    Property A
    Although the rent for December was not received until after the end of the tax year, it is still taken into account in 2021 as Case V is assessed on rents receivable.

    Property B
    Let from 1 August 2021, i.e. 5 months @ €1,000 per month = €5,000
    Premium on lease:
    Assessable portion of premium: $€10,000 \times \dfrac{51 - 21}{50} = €6,000$

    Property C
    €6,000 × 4/12 = 2,000   (4 months to 30 April)

    $€9,000 \times 2/12 = \dfrac{1,500}{3,500}$ (2 months to 31 December)

2. Allowable Expenses
    Property A
    As the property is registered with the PRTB, a full deduction for interest of €5,500 is allowable.

    Property B
    Pre-letting expenses are not allowable. These include bank interest paid in June 2021 of €1,800 and the interest relating to the period 1 July 2021 to 31 July 2021. Interest allowable:

    $$\left(€3,600 \times \frac{5}{6}\right) = €3,000$$

    Expenses incurred in April and June are also disallowed as those are pre-letting expenses.

    Property C
    Although the property was vacant when the expenditure was incurred, this was only a temporary period of vacancy and the expenditure is allowed in full.

    Property D
    As the property is registered with the PRTB, a full deduction for interest paid is allowable. Post-letting interest allowable is:

    €9,250 × 8/12ths = €6,167

continued overleaf

As property D was vacant for more than 12 months and this is its first letting, the following pre-letting expenses are allowable:

	€
Replace broken window	100
Painting and decorating	1,100
Cleaning	420
Interest: €9,250 × 4/12ths	3,083
Total pre-letting expenses allowed	4,993

3. Summary
    Losses on one property may be offset against the rental profits arising on other properties.

Question 7.2

(a) Sonya – Case V Assessable Income 2021

Rent Account 2021	Property 1	Property 2	Property 3	Property 4
	€	€	€	€
Gross rents	16,000	8,000	9,600	4,500
Expenses	(4,300)	(1,200)	(800)	–
Interest	–	–	(1,400)	–
Net rents	11,700	6,800	7,400	4,500
Total Case V 2021	30,400			

Notes:
1. The rent to be brought into account is that receivable in the tax year 2021 whether or not rent is actually received in the year, i.e. for Property 4 = 6/12 × €9,000.
2. The income from Property 5 is excluded on the grounds that the rent receivable under the lease, taking one year with another, is not sufficient to meet the allowable expenses connected with the property and it is an uneconomic letting. Losses may be accumulated and set off against future rental income from that property only.
3. Because all properties are commercial, there is no restriction to the interest allowable against the rents.

(b) Tax Effects of Investments

(i) *National Instalment Savings Scheme*
Any bonus or interest payable to an individual under an instalment savings scheme is exempt from income tax.

(ii) *Government Securities*
Interest on government securities is paid without deduction of tax and, accordingly, is assessable under Schedule D, Case III on an actual basis.

Question 7.3

Under Rent-a-Room relief the costs associated with providing the accommodation are not allowable against the rents received.

2021	**€**
Income: €450 × 4 students × 4 months (September–December)	7,200
Costs: €711 × 4 months	(2,844)
Net income	4,356

As the gross rent received of €7,200 for 2021 does not exceed €14,000, this income is exempt from income tax but must be included in Liz's tax return for 2021.

2022	**€**
Income: €450 × 4 students × 9 months	16,200
Costs: €711 × 9 months	(6,399)
Net income	9,801

While Liz's net income is below the threshold of €14,000, the costs of providing the accommodation are not allowable deductions under the Rent-a-Room scheme. As the gross income of €16,200 exceeds the scheme threshold of €14,000, the full amount of the income is taxable under Case V. However, Liz is allowed a deduction for the expenses incurred and the taxable amount for 2022 under Case V is €9,801.

If Liz ceased providing meals and reduced the rent by €100 per month per student, her situation for 2022 would be as follows:

	€
Income: €350 × 4 students × 9 months	12,600
Costs: €250 × 9 months (laundry and light and heat only)	(2,250)
Net income	10,350

As the gross income is below the €14,000 Rent-a-Room threshold it is exempt from income tax for 2022.

Chapter 8

Question 8.1

(a) As only one spouse has income, the Joyces are entitled to the married couple, one income standard rate band. Their income tax liability for 2021 is as follows:

Income Tax Computation 2021 – Joyces	**€**	**€**
Taxable income		46,000
Tax payable:		
€44,300 @ 20%	8,860	
€1,700 @ 40%	680	9,540
€46,000		
Deduct: Non-refundable tax credits		
Basic personal tax credit (married)	3,300	
Employee tax credit	1,650	
Home carer tax credit	1,600	(6,550)
Tax liability		2,990

continued overleaf

(b) If the home carer had income of €10,600 in 2022, i.e. above the income limit for the home carer tax credit in 2022, the carer tax credit can still be claimed as the home carer was entitled to the tax credit in 2021. The maximum home carer tax credit claimable would be the tax credit claimed for the tax year 2021.

However, it will be more beneficial for the increased standard rate band to be claimed, i.e. the tax saving by claiming the increased standard rate band (i.e. €10,600 @ (40% − 20%) = €2,120) will be more than the reduction due to claiming the €1,600 home carer tax credit.

Question 8.2

As both spouses have income, they are entitled to the increased standard rate tax band. As one spouse has income of less than €10,400, they also qualify for the home carer tax credit. If the increased standard rate tax band is claimed, their income tax liability for 2021 will be as follows:

Income Tax Computation 2021 – Roches	€	€
Schedule E salary		46,000
Schedule F		8,000
Taxable income		54,000
Tax payable:		
€52,300* @ 20%	10,460	
€1,700 @ 40%	680	11,140
€54,000		
Deduct: Non-refundable tax credits		
Basic personal tax credit (married)	3,300	
Employee tax credit	1,650	(4,950)
Deduct: Refundable tax credits		
DWT		(2,000)
Tax liability		4,190

* The standard rate band of €44,300 is increased by the lower of €26,300 or the total income of the lower income spouse, i.e. €8,000 in this case.

If the home carer tax credit is claimed instead of the increased standard rate band, their liability will be as follows:

Income Tax Computation 2021 – Roches	€	€
Taxable income		54,000
Tax payable:		
€44,300 @ 20%	8,860	
€9,700 @ 40%	3,880	12,740
€54,000		
Deduct: Non-refundable tax credits		
Basic personal tax credit (married)	3,300	
Employee tax credit	1,650	
Home carer tax credit: €1,600 − ((€8,000 − €7,200)/2)	1,200	(6,150)

continued overleaf

Deduct: Refundable tax credits

DWT	(2,000)
Tax liability	4,590

As their tax liability is lower if the increased standard rate tax band is claimed, the Roches should claim the increased standard rate tax band instead of the home carer tax credit.

Question 8.3

Medical Expenses	**€**
Mr Murray	80
Michael Murray	200
David Murray	210
Sean Ryan	650
	1,140

Medical expenses allowable for 2021 are €1,140. Relief is at the standard rate of 20% = tax credit of €228.

Mr Murray is also entitled to a deduction from net statutory income in respect of the €13,200 he pays towards nursing home care for his mother. Therefore, if Mr Murray's marginal rate of tax is 40%, tax relief @ 40%, i.e. €5,280, will be available. If the nursing home did not provide 24-hour nursing care on-site, then no deduction would be available.

Mr Murray should submit a claim either using Form Med 1 or online on myAccount using PAYE Services after the end of the tax year to claim the tax credits available for both the medical expenses and the nursing home charges.

Question 8.4

Rachel's net relevant earnings and allowable pension contribution for 2021:

Net Relevant Earnings 2021 – Rachel	**€**
Case II	320,000
Less: capital allowances	(10,000)
Less: charges – covenant	(6,000)
Net relevant earnings	304,000
Premium paid	**75,000**
Maximum claim allowed:	
Net relevant earnings ceiling restricted to	115,000
Relief restricted to €115,000 × 25%	**28,750**

Question 8.5

Income Tax Computation 2021 – Mr Frost	**€**	**€**
Salary		46,000
VHI (gross) (Note 1)		1,160
Taxable income		47,160

continued overleaf

Tax payable:

€35,300 @ 20%	7,060	
€11,860 @ 40%	4,744	11,804
€47,160		

Deduct: Non-refundable tax credits

Basic personal tax credit	1,650	
Employee tax credit	1,650	(3,300)
		8,504
Tax deducted from VHI €1,000 (max.) @ 20%		(200)
Tax liability		8,304

Note:

1. VHI – 1st €1,000 @ 20% tax credit net   €800
   Balance €160 @ Nil tax credit net   €160
   Gross €1,160   Net   €960

Question 8.6

Income Tax Liability 2021 – June	€	€
Schedule E income:		
Salary	43,000	
Less: Retirement annuity premium paid	(2,000)	41,000
Widow's pension		10,842
Taxable income		51,842
Tax payable: (widowed)		
€39,300 @ 20%	7,860	
€12,542 @ 40%	5,017	12,877
€51,842		
Deduct: Non-refundable tax credits		
Basic personal tax credit (widowed)	1,650	
Single person child carer credit	1,650	
Widowed parent (third year after year of death)	2,700	
Incapacitated child tax credit × 2	6,600	
Employee tax credit	1,650	
College fees (€3,000 + €2,300 – €1,500) @ 20%	760	
Medical expenses €500 @ 20%	100	
Total tax credits due		(15,110)
Net tax liability		(2,223)
Restrict as tax credits are non-refundable		0

continued overleaf

Deduct: Refundable tax credits

Tax paid under PAYE		(1,690)
Tax refund due		**(1,690)**

Notes:

1. Medical expenses incurred for David of €500 are allowable. Expenditure incurred on eye test and spectacles for John is not allowable.
2. The income received by John and Mary has no effect on June's entitlement to tax credits.
3. VHI premium paid is ignored. Tax relief is given at source.
4. The first €1,500 of college fees, where all of the students are part-time, is not allowable.
5. No relief is available in 2021 for rent paid.

Question 8.7

Income Tax Computation 2021 – John Fitzpatrick	€	€
Schedule E:		
Pension (gross)		29,400
Tax payable:		
€29,400 @ 20%		5,880
Deduct: Non-refundable tax credits		
Widowed person tax credit	2,190	
Age tax credit	245	
Employee tax credit	1,650	
Medical expenses (€590 – €200) @ 20%	78	(4,163)
Tax liability		1,717
Deduct: Refundable tax credits		
Tax paid under PAYE		(2,040)
Refund due		**(323)**

Notes:

1. Donation to eligible charity is ignored. Charity will claim tax relief.
2. VHI premium paid is ignored as tax relief is given at source.

Question 8.8

Income Tax Computation 2021 – Jason and Damien	€	€
Schedule E income – pension (gross)		35,000
Tax payable (civil partners – one income):		
€35,000 @ 20%		7,000
Deduct: Non-refundable tax credits		
Basic personal tax credit – civil partners	(3,300)	
Age tax credit (Note)	(490)	
Employee tax credit	(1,650)	(5,440)
Initial tax liability		1,560

continued overleaf

Income exemption limit €36,000

Final tax liability	0
Deduct: Refundable tax credits	
Tax paid under PAYE	(2,050)
Refund due	**(2,050)**

Note: it is the older civil partner's age that is relevant.

Question 8.9

	2020	2021
	€	€
Retirement Annuity Relief – Bob		
Relevant earnings – Salary	50,980	54,480
Reduced by:		
Charges (covenant)	3,000	3,000
Less: Deposit interest	(1,160)	(1,195)
	(1,840)	(1,805)
Net relevant income	49,140	52,675
Maximum allowable premium (30% in 2020, 35% in 2021)	14,742	18,436
2020: Premium paid	15,000	
Restricted to	14,742	
Balance carried forward to 2021	258	
2021: Premium paid		16,000
Plus balance carried forward from 2020		258
Premium allowed		16,258

Question 8.10

Maria's Income Tax Computation 2021	€	€
Schedule E: Salary		35,000
Less: Charges on income:		
Covenant (€4,000/0.8)		(5,000)
Taxable income		30,000
Tax payable: €30,000 @ 20%		6,000
Deduct: Non-refundable tax credits		
Basic personal tax credit	(1,650)	
Employee tax credit	(1,650)	(3,300)
Add: tax on covenant €5,000 @ 20%		1,000
Tax liability		3,700

continued overleaf

Deduct: Refundable tax credits

Tax paid under PAYE	(3,700)
Tax refund due	**NIL**

Jim's Income Tax Computation 2021	
Schedule D, Case IV	5,000
Schedule D, Case V	8,000
	13,000
Tax payable: €13,000 @ 20%	2,600
Deduct: Non-refundable tax credits	
Widowed person tax credit	(2,190)
Initial tax liability	410
Income exemption limit €18,000, thus tax liability	Nil
Deduct: Refundable tax credits	
Tax paid on covenant €5,000 @ 20%	(1,000)
Tax refund due	**(1,000)**

Question 8.11

Income Tax Computation 2021 – Robert		€	€
Income:			
Schedule D, Case IV (€1,600/0.67)			2,388
Case V (Note 1)			2,219
Schedule E salary		84,000	
Less: pension contribution (Note 2)		(16,800)	67,200
Schedule F (Note 3)			6,933
Gross income			78,740
Deduct: Charges	Covenant: brother (€3,200/0.8)		(4,000)
	Covenant: father (Note 4)		(3,737)
Total income			71,003
Tax payable:			
€35,300 @ 20%		7,060	
€2,388 @ 33%		788	
€33,315 @ 40%		13,326	21,174
€71,003			
Deduct: Non-refundable tax credits			
	Basic personal tax credit	(1,650)	
	Employee tax credit	(1,650)	

continued overleaf

Medical expenses (€845 @ 20%)	(169)	
DIRT paid	(788)	(4,257)
Add: tax on covenant paid (Note 5)		1,700
Tax liability		18,617
Deduct: Refundable tax credits		
Tax paid under PAYE	(14,120)	
DWT (€6,933 @ 25%)	(1,733)	(15,853)
Tax payable		**2,764**

Notes:

1. Computation of Case V income	€	€
Rental income		14,400
Less expenses:		
Mortgage interest	3,200	
Management fee	3,100	
Expenses	2,600	
Capital allowances (€2,250 × 12.5%)	281	(9,181)
Case V income		5,219
Less: loss forward		(3,000)
Net Case V income		2,219

2. Pension contribution allowed – net relevant earnings calculation:		
Schedule E income		84,000
Reduced by: Charges (covenants × 2)	(8,500)	
Less: Case VI	2,388	
Case V	2,219	
Schedule F (Note 3)	6,933	Nil
Net relevant earnings		84,000
Maximum pension allowed 20%		16,800

3. Net dividend received from Independent News €5,200/0.75	6,933

4. Covenant to father is restricted to 5% of total income as follows:	
Schedule D, Case IV (€1,600/0.67)	2,388
Case V	2,219
Schedule E salary	84,000
Less: pension contribution (Note 2)	(16,800)
Covenant to brother (€3,200/0.8)	(4,000)
Schedule F (Note 3)	6,933
Total income	74,740
Covenant to parent restricted to 5%	3,737

continued overleaf

5. Covenant paid to brother		4,000
Covenant paid to father		4,500
		8,500
Tax deducted @ 20%		1,700

Question 8.12

Income Tax Computation 2021 – Jenny McFee	€	€
Income:		
Schedule D:		
Case IV €1,200/0.67		1,791
Case V – room rental (Note 1)		NIL
Schedule E:		
Salary	55,000	
Pension	12,150	
BIK – VHI (Note 2)	1,740	68,890
Total income		70,681
Less: employment of carer		(12,500)
Taxable income		**58,181**
Tax payable:		
€39,300 @ 20%	7,860	
€17,090 @ 40%	6,836	
€1,791 @ 33%	591	
€58,181		15,287
Deduct: Non-refundable tax credits:		
Basic personal tax credit (widowed)	1,650	
Single person child carer credit	1,650	
Widowed parent (first year after year of bereavement)	3,600	
Employee tax credit	1,650	
College fees (Note 3)	1,148	
Training courses – maximum	254	
DIRT paid	591	(10,543)
Tax liability		4,744
Deduct: Refundable tax credits		
Tax deducted from VHI €1,000 (max.) @ 20%	200	
Tax paid under PAYE (€5,590 + €2,550)	8,140	(8,340)
Tax refund due		**(3,596)**

continued overleaf

Notes:

1. Room rental

    Rent from student letting is not taxable under the Rent-a-Room relief, i.e. gross receipts are less than €14,000 in 2021.

2. BIK – VHI

First	€1,000 @ 20% tax credit	800
Balance	€740 @ nil tax credit	740
Gross	€1,740	Net 1,540

3. College fees

	€
Maria: fees €8,500 – limited to	7,000
John: fees	1,740
Total	8,740
Less: amount disallowed	(3,000)
Allowable	5,740
Relief @ 20%	**1,148**

    Colm's fees are for an approved training course and qualify for relief under Training Courses, maximum amount allowable at the standard rate €1,270 @ 20% = €254.

Chapter 9

Question 9.1

(a) **Joint Assessment**

Income Tax Computation 2021	**Patrick**	**Helen**	**Total**
	€	**€**	**€**
Income: Schedule E	10,500	50,000	60,500
Schedule E – BIK	–	2,100	2,100
Total income	10,500	52,100	62,600
Less: Permanent Health Insurance	–	(950)	(950)
Taxable income	**10,500**	**51,150**	**61,650**
Tax payable:			
€44,300 @ 20%		8,860	8,860
€10,500 @ 20%	2,100		2,100
€6,850 @ 40%	–	2,740	2,740
€61,650	2,100	11,600	13,700
Deduct: Non-refundable tax credits:			
Basic personal tax credit (married)			(3,300)
Employee tax credits (× 2)			(3,300)
Tax liability			**7,100**

continued overleaf

(b) Separate Assessment

Patrick – Income Tax Computation 2021	€
Income: Schedule E	10,500
Tax payable:	
€10,500 @ 20%	2,100
Deduct: Non-refundable tax credits:	
Basic personal tax credit	(1,650)
Employee tax credit	(1,650)
Excess tax credits transferred to wife	**(1,200)**

Helen – Income Tax Computation 2021	€	€
Income: Schedule E		50,000
Schedule E – BIK		2,100
Total income		**52,100**
Less: Permanent Health Insurance		(950)
Taxable income		51,150
Tax payable:		
€44,300 @ 20% (standard rate band of €26,300	8,860	
not fully utilised by Patrick)		
€6,850 @ 40%	2,740	11,600
€51,150		
Deduct: Non-refundable tax credits:		
Basic personal tax credit		(1,650)
Employee tax credit		(1,650)
Tax credits transferred from husband		(1,200)
Tax liability		**7,100**

Check:	Patrick	Helen	Total
Liability under separate assessment	0	7,100	7,100
Liability per joint assessment			7,100

(c) Single Assessment

Patrick Income Tax Computation 2021	€	€
Income: Schedule E		10,500
Tax payable:		
€10,500 @ 20%		2,100

continued overleaf

Deduct: Non-refundable tax credits:

Basic personal tax credit	(1,650)	
Employee tax credit	(1,650)	
	(3,300)	
Tax credits limited to tax liability		(2,100)
Net tax liability		**NIL**

Helen Income Tax Computation 2021	€	€
Income: Schedule E	50,000	
Schedule E – BIK	2,100	
Total income	52,100	
Less: Permanent Health Insurance	(950)	
Taxable income		**51,150**
Tax payable:		
€35,300 @ 20%	7,060	
€15,850 @ 40%	6,340	
€51,150		13,400
Deduct: Non-refundable tax credits:		
Basic personal tax credit		(1,650)
Employee tax credit		(1,650)
Tax liability		**10,100**

Under single assessment Helen pays an additional €3,000 in tax as she is unable to utilise Patrick's surplus tax credits and 20% tax band.

Question 9.2

(a) (i) No change to Deed of Separation

Mrs Thorne Income Tax Computation 2021	€	€
Income:		
Schedule E	35,000	
Schedule D, Case IV (€200 × 12)(Note)	2,400	
Total income		37,400
Tax payable: (single parent)		
€37,400 @ 20%		7,480
Deduct: Non-refundable tax credits:		
Basic personal tax credit	(1,650)	
Single person child carer credit	(1,650)	
Employee tax credit	(1,650)	(4,950)
Tax liability		**2,530**

Note: maintenance payments specifically for children are ignored (i.e. €800 − €600).

continued overleaf

(ii) Deed of Separation changed

Mrs Thorne Income Tax Computation 2021	€	€
Income:		
Schedule E	35,000	
Schedule D, Case IV (€900 × 12)	10,800	
Total income		45,800
Tax payable: (single parent)		
€39,300 @ 20%	7,860	
€6,500 @ 40%	2,600	
€45,800		10,460
Deduct: Non-refundable tax credits:		
Basic personal tax credit	(1,650)	
Single person child carer credit	(1,650)	
Employee tax credit	(1,650)	(4,950)
Tax liability		**5,510**

(b) Comparison

If the deed is not reviewed, Mrs Thorne's financial position is as follows:

	€
Maintenance payments (€800 × 12)	9,600
Salary	35,000
	44,600
Less: tax payable	(2,530)
Net income after tax	**42,070**

If the deed is reviewed, Mrs Thorne's financial position is as follows:

Maintenance payments (€1,000 × 12)	12,000
Salary	35,000
	47,000
Less: tax payable	(5,510)
Net income after tax	**41,490**

Mrs Thorne is worse off financially by €580 (€42,070 – €41,490) if the deed is reviewed.

Question 9.3

(a) Claim for joint assessment

As Mrs Lynch has income other than the maintenance payments, the separate assessment rules are used.

Mrs Lynch Income Tax Computation 2021	€	€
Income: Schedule E		15,000
Tax payable:		
€15,000 @ 20%	3,000	
€0 @ 40%	0	
€15,000		3,000
Deduct: Non-refundable tax credits:		
Basic personal tax credit	(1,650)	
Employee tax credit	(1,650)	(3,300)
Excess tax credits transferred to Mr Lynch		**(300)**
Tax liability		0

Mr Lynch Income Tax Computation 2021	€	€
Income:		
Schedule E		48,000
Tax payable: (married)		
€44,300 @ 20%	8,860	
€3,700 @ 40%	1,480	
€48,000		10,340
Deduct: Non-refundable tax credits:		
Basic personal tax credit	(1,650)	
Employee tax credit	(1,650)	
Excess tax credits transferred from Mrs Lynch	(300)	(3,600)
Tax liability		**6,740**
Combined tax liability		**6,740**

(b) No claim made for joint assessment

Mrs Lynch Income Tax Computation 2021	€	€
Income: Schedule E	15,000	
Schedule D, Case IV (€600 × 12)	7,200	
Total income		22,200

continued overleaf

Tax payable: (single)

€22,200 @ 20%	4,440	
€0 @ 40%	0	
€22,200		4,440

Deduct: Non-refundable tax credits:

Basic personal tax credit	(1,650)	
Single Person Child Carer credit	(1,650)	
Employee tax credit	(1,650)	
	(4,950)	
Tax credits restricted to amount needed to reduce tax liability to NIL		(4,440)
Tax liability		**0**

Mr Lynch Income Tax Computation 2021	€	€
Income: Schedule E – self		48,000
Less: maintenance payments (€600 × 12)		(7,200)
Net income		40,800

Tax payable: (single)

€35,300 @ 20%	7,060	
€5,500 @ 40%	2,200	
€40,800		9,260

Deduct: Non-refundable tax credits:

Basic personal tax credit	(1,650)	
Employee tax credit	(1,650)	(3,300)
Tax liability		**5,960**
Combined tax liability		**5,960**

Chapter 10

Question 10.1

USC calculation for 2021	Peter	€	Andrew	€
Schedule E salary		39,000		39,000
USC Calculation:				
€12,012 @ 0.5%		60.06	€12,012 @ 0.5%	60.06
€8,675 @ 2.0%		173.50	€ 8,675 @ 2.0%	173.50
€18,313 @ 4.5%		824.09	€18,313 @ 2.0%	366.26
€39,000		1,057.65	€39,000	599.82

Peter pays €457.83 more in USC as he does not have a medical card.

Question 10.2

Anne USC calculation for 2021	€	€
Gross income for USC:		
Schedule E salary		32,000
Case I Schedule D (50%)		<u>115,500</u>
Total income		**147,500**
USC Calculation:		
€ 12,012 @ 0.5%	60.06	
€ 8,675 @ 2.0%	173.50	
€ 49,357 @ 4.5%	2,221.07	
€ 61,956 @ 8.0%	4,956.48	
<u>€ 15,500</u> @ 11.0% (trading income > €100,000)	<u>1,705.00</u>	
€147,500	9,116.11	
Deduct: USC paid on salary	<u>(742.65)</u>	
Net USC payable	**8,373.46**	

Question 10.3

Gerry & Mary Brickley Income Tax Computation 2021		€	€
Income:			
Schedule D, Case I – Gerry			72,500
Schedule D, Case IV – Gerry	(€825/0.67)		1,231
Schedule D, Case IV – Mary	(€321/0.67)		479
Schedule E – Mary			23,000
Schedule F – Gerry	(€1,125/0.75)		<u>1,500</u>
Taxable income			**98,710**
Tax Calculation:			
€67,300 @ 20%	(€44,300 + €23,000)	13,460	
€1,710 @ 33%		564	
<u>€29,700</u> @ 40%		<u>11,880</u>	
€98,710			25,904
Deduct: Non-refundable tax credits			
Basic personal tax credit (married)		3,300	
Employee tax credit (Mary)		1,650	
Earned income tax credit (Gerry)		1,650	
DIRT paid		<u>564</u>	<u>(7,164)</u>
			18,740

continued overleaf

Deduct: Refundable tax credits		
Tax deducted under PAYE (Mary)	1,300	
DWT (Gerry)	375	(1,675)
Net tax liability		**17,065**

Universal Social Charge (Note)

Gerry:

Schedule D, Case I	72,500	
Add: Pension contribution	7,000	
Adjusted Case 1 income	79,500	
Schedule F	1,500	
Income subject to USC	81,000	

USC Calculation:

€12,012 @ 0.5%	60	
€8,675 @ 2.0%	173	
€49,357 @ 4.5%	2,221	
€10,956 @ 8.0%	877	
€81,000		3,331

Mary:

Schedule E	23,000	

USC Calculation:

€12,012 @ 0.5%	60	
€8,675 @ 2.0%	173	
€2,313 @ 4.5%	104	
€23,000	337	
Deduct: USC paid through payroll	(337)	
USC due		NIL

Total USC due		**3,331**

Note: although Gerry and Mary are jointly assessed, each individual is separately assessed to USC and unused rate bands cannot be shared.

PRSI

Gerry:

Schedule D, Case I	72,500	
Add: Pension contribution	7,000	
Adjusted Case I income	79,500	
Schedule D, Case IV	1,231	
Schedule F	1,500	
Income subject to PRSI	82,231	

continued overleaf

PRSI Calculation:

€82,231 @ 4%		3,289

Mary:

Schedule E	23,000	
Schedule D, Case IV	<u>479</u>	
Income subject to PRSI	<u>23,479</u>	

PRSI Calculation:

€ 23,479 @ 4%	939	
Deduct: PRSI paid through payroll	(920)	
PRSI due		<u>19</u>
Total PRSI due		**<u>3,308</u>**
Income tax, USC and PRSI payable		**<u>23,704</u>**

Chapter 11

Question 11.1

Net pay receivable by Mary – August 2021		€	€	€
Gross salary – this employment			2,200	
Gross salary per P45			<u>16,310</u>	
Cumulative gross pay to date				<u>18,510</u>
Cumulative SRCOP to date	€2,941.67 × 8			<u>23,533</u>
Tax @ 20%	€18,510 @ 20%			3,702
Cumulative tax credits to date	€275 × 8			<u>(2,200)</u>
Cumulative tax due to date				1,502
Less: tax paid per RPN				<u>(1,337)</u>
Tax due for August 2021				<u>165</u>
Net Salary for August 2021:				
Gross salary August 2021				2,200
Less:				
Tax				(165)
PRSI	€2,200 @ 4%			(88)
USC: cut-off point 1	€1,001 × 8 @ 0.5%	8,008	40	
cut-off point 2	€723 × 8 @ 2.0%	5,784	116	
Balance	€18,510 − (€8,008 + €5,784) @ 4.5%	<u>4,718</u>	212	
Cumulative pay to date		<u>18,510</u>	368	
Less: USC paid per RPN			<u>327</u>	<u>(41)</u>
Net pay for August 2021				**<u>1,906</u>**

Question 11.2

Total Gross Taxable Pay for Andrew – June 2021	€
Benefit in Kind Calculation:	
Original market value of car	28,000
% applicable for annual business travel (km): 51,200 – 8,000 = 43,200 km = 12%	
Cash equivalent €28,000 @ 12%	3,360
Less: annual amount paid to employer	(1,500)
Annual benefit in kind assessable	1,860
Gross taxable pay June 2021:	
June 2021 salary	4,167
BIK (monthly)	155
Gross taxable pay June 2021	**4,322**

Question 11.3

(a) Value of BIK on Van		€
	OMV of van	17,500
	Cash equivalent 5% of €17,500	875
	Less: refunded by Sean	(120)
	Annual BIK on van	755
	Taxable BIK 2021 (6/12ths)	378
(b) (i) With PPSN (Emergency Basis)		
	Gross wages – this employment	500.00
	SRCOP	678.85
	Tax @ 20% (€500 @ 20%)	100.00
	Tax credits (emergency)	NIL
	Tax due for first week	100.00
	PRSI: €500 @ 4%	20.00
	USC €500 @ 8% (emergency)	40.00
	Gross salary for August 2021	500.00
	Tax	(100.00)
	PRSI	(20.00)
	USC	(40.00)
	Net pay for August 2021	340.00
(ii) Without PPSN (Emergency Basis)		
	Gross wages – this employment	500.00
	SRCOP	0.00
	Tax @ 40% (€500 @ 40%)	200.00

continued overleaf

Tax credits (€nil/52)		(0.00)
Tax due for first week		200.00
PRSI: €500 @ 4%		20.00
USC €500 @ 8% (emergency)		40.00
Gross salary for August 2021		500.00
Tax		(200.00)
PRSI		(20.00)
USC		(40.00)
Net pay for August 2021		240.00

Question 11.4

(a) Net pay receivable by Paul for w/e 17 October 2021 (Week 46)

Week 1/Month 1 basis			€	€
Gross salary – this employment	$(39 \times €21) + (11 \times €21 \times 1.5)$		1,165.50	
Gross salary per RPN – not used			0	
Gross pay to date				1,165.50
SRCOP to date	€851.92	× 1		851.92
Tax @ 20%	€851.92	@ 20%		170.38
Tax @ 40%	€313.58	@ 40%		125.43
	€1,165.50			295.82
Tax credits this period	€95.19	× 1		(95.19)
Tax due for week 46				200.62

Net pay for Week 46:

Gross pay for week 46				1,165.50
Less:				
Tax				(200.62)
PRSI:	€1,165.50 @ 4%			(46.62)
USC:	€231 @ 0.5%	€231.00	1.16	
(Week 1 basis)	€166.83 @ 2.0%	€166.83	3.34	
	Balance @ 4.5%	€767.67	34.55	(39.04)
		€1,165.50		
Net pay for Week 46				**879.22**

continued overleaf

(b) Net pay receivable by Paul for w/e 17 October 2021 (Week 46)

Cumulative Basis		€	€
Gross salary – this employment	$(39 \times €21) + (11 \times €21 \times 1.5)$	1,165.50	
Gross salary per RPN		43,540.00	
Cumulative gross pay to date			44,705.50
Cumulative SRCOP to date	€851.92 × 46		39,188.46
Tax @ 20%	€39,188.46 @ 20%		7,837.69
Tax @ 40%	€5,517.04 @ 40%		2,206.82
	€44,705.50		10,044.51
Cumulative tax credits to date	€95.19 × 46		(4,378.85)
Cumulative tax due to date			5,665.66
Tax paid per RPN			(5,465.04)
Tax due for week 46			200.62
Net pay for Week 46:			
Gross pay for week 46			1,165.50
Less:			
Tax			(200.62)
PRSI:	€1,165.50 @ 4%		(46.62)
USC: cut-off point 1	€231 × 46 @ 0.5%	10,626	53.13
cut-off point 2	€166.83 × 46 @ 2.0%	7,674	153.48
Balance	€44,705 − (€10,626 + €7,674) @ 4.5%	26,405	1,188.25
Cumulative pay to date		44,705	1,394.86
Less: USC paid per RPN			(1,355.82) (39.04)
Net pay for Week 46			**879.22**

Question 11.5

Net pay receivable by Charlotte for w/e 6 July 2021 (Week 27)		€	€
Gross wages this week		1,050.00	
Gross wages to 30 June 2021		27,300.00	
Cumulative gross pay to date			28,350.00
Cumulative SRCOP to date	€678.85 × 27		18,328.85
Tax @ 20%	€18,328.85 @ 20%	3,665.77	
Tax @ 40%	€10,021.15 @ 40%	4,008.46	
	€28,350.00		7,674.23
Cumulative tax credits to date	€63.46 × 27		(1,713.46)

continued overleaf

Cumulative tax due to date			5,960.77
Less: tax paid to date			(5,740.00)
Tax due this week			220.77

Net pay for Week 27:

Gross pay w/e 6 July 2021			1,050.00
Less:			
Tax			(220.77)
PRSI:	€1,050 @ 4%		(42.00)

USC: Cut-off point 1	€231.00 × 27 @ 0.5%	6,237.00	31.19	
Cut-off point 2	€166.83 × 27 @ 2.0%	4,504.33	90.09	
Balance	€28,350 − (€6,237 + €4,504.33) @ 4.5%	17,608.67	792.39	
Cumulative pay to date		28,350.00	913.66	
Less: USC paid to 30 June 2021			(879.82)	(33.84)
LPT deducted				(10.00)
Net pay for Week 27				**743.39**

Net pay receivable by Charlotte for w/e 13 July 2021 (Week 28)		€	€
Gross wages this week		1,050.00	
Gross wages to 6 July 2021		28,350.00	
Cumulative gross pay to date			29,400.00
Cumulative SRCOP to date	€678.85 × 28		19,007.69
Tax @ 20%	€19,007.69 @ 20%	3,801.54	
Tax @ 40%	€10,392.31 @ 40%	4,156.92	
	€29,400.00		7,958.46
Cumulative tax credits to date	€63.46 × 28		(1,776.92)
Cumulative tax due to date			6,181.54
Less: tax paid to date			(5,960.77)
Tax due this week			220.77
Net pay for Week 28:			
Gross pay w/e 13 July 2021			1,050.00
Less:			
Tax			(220.77)
PRSI:	€1,050 @ 4%		(42.00)
USC: Cut-off point 1	€231.00 × 28 @ 0.5%	6,468.00	32.34

continued overleaf

Cut-off point 2	€166.83 × 28 @ 2.0%	4,671.15	93.42
Balance	€29,400 − (€6,468 +		
	€4,671.15) @ 4.5%	<u>18,260.85</u>	<u>821.74</u>
Cumulative pay to date		<u>29,400.00</u>	947.50
Less: USC paid to 6 July 2021			<u>(913.66)</u>	(33.84)

LPT deducted	<u>(10.00)</u>
Net pay for week number 28	**<u>743.39</u>**

Question 11.6

John Wages: Week 32		€	€
Tax Calculation:			
Gross wages week 32	(€16 × 20)	320.00	
Gross wages to week 31		<u>19,840.00</u>	
Cumulative gross pay to date			**<u>20,160.00</u>**
Cumulative SRCOP to date	(€851.92 × 32)		<u>27,261.54</u>
Tax payable:			
€20,160 @ 20%		4,032.00	
Less: cumulative tax credits to date	(€95.19 × 32)	<u>(3,046.15)</u>	
Cumulative tax due to date		985.85	
Less: tax paid to week 31		<u>(1,017.04)</u>	
Tax refund for week 32			**<u>(31.19)</u>**
PRSI Calculation:			
Wages €320 – Class A0 – EE PRSI @ NIL%			<u>0.00</u>
ER PRSI @ 8.8%			<u>28.16</u>
USC Calculation:			
Cumulative Gross Pay to date for USC		<u>20,160.00</u>	
USC cut-off point 1	(€231 × 32)	€7,392 @ 0.5%	36.96	
USC cut-off point 2	(€166.83 × 32)	€5,338 @ 2.0%	106.77	
USC cut-off point 3	(balance)	<u>€7,430</u> @ 4.5%	<u>334.33</u>	
Cumulative pay to date		<u>€20,160</u>	478.06	
Less: USC paid to week 31			<u>(477.07)</u>	
USC due for week 32				**<u>0.99</u>**
Net wages week 32:				
Gross				320.00

continued overleaf

Less:

Tax refunded		31.19	
PRSI		0.00	
USC		(0.99)	30.20
Net wages week 32			**350.20**

John Wages: Week 33		€	€
Tax Calculation:			
Gross wages week 33	(€16 × 25)	400.00	
Gross wages to week 32		20,160.00	
Cumulative gross pay to date			**20,560.00**
Cumulative SRCOP to date	(€851.92 × 33)		28,113.46
Tax payable:			
€20,560 @ 20%		4,112.00	
Less: cumulative tax credits to date	(€95.19 × 33)	(3,141.35)	
Cumulative tax due to date		970.65	
Less: tax paid to week 32		(985.85)	
Tax refund for week 33			**(15.19)**
PRSI Calculation			
Wages €400 – Class AL			
EE PRSI @ 4%		16.00	
PRSI credit calculation:			
Maximum credit	€12.00		
Less: 1/6th × (€400 − €352.01)	(€8.00)		
Deduct PRSI credit		(4.00)	
EE PRSI			12.00
ER PRSI @ 11.05%			44.20

USC Calculation:			
Cumulative gross pay to date for USC			20,560.00
USC cut-off point 1	(€231 × 33)	€7,623 @ 0.5%	38.12
USC cut-off point 2	(€166.83 × 33)	€5,505 @ 2.0%	110.11
USC cut-off point 3	(balance)	€7,432 @ 4.5%	334.42
Cumulative pay to date		€20,560	482.65
Less: USC paid to week 32			(478.06)
USC due for week 33			**4.59**
Net wages week 33:			
Gross			400.00

continued overleaf

Less:

Tax refunded		15.19	
PRSI		(12.00)	
USC		(4.59)	(1.40)
Net wages week 33			**398.60**

John Wages: Week 34		€	€
Tax Calculation:			
Gross wages week 34	(€16 × 23)	368.00	
Gross wages to week 33		20,560.00	
Cumulative gross pay to date			**20,928.00**
Cumulative SRCOP to date	(€851.92 × 34)		28,965.38
Tax payable:			
€20,928 @ 20%		4,185.60	
Less: cumulative tax credits to date	(€95.19 × 34)	(3,236.54)	
Cumulative tax due to date		949.06	
Less: tax paid to week 33		(970.65)	
Tax refund for week 34			**(21.59)**
PRSI Calculation:			
Wages €368 – Class AX			
EE PRSI @ 4%		14.72	
PRSI credit calculation:			
Maximum credit	€12.00		
Less: 1/6th × (€368 – €352.01)	(€2.67)		
Deduct PRSI credit		(9.33)	
EE PRSI			**5.39**
ER PRSI @ 8.8%			**32.38**
USC Calculation:			
Cumulative gross pay to date for USC		20,928.00	

USC cut-off point 1	(€231 × 34)	€7,854 @ 0.5%	39.27	
USC cut-off point 2	(€166.83 × 34)	€5,672 @ 2.0%	113.44	
USC cut-off point 3	(balance)	€7,402 @ 4.5%	333.09	
Cumulative pay to date		€20,928	485.80	
Less: USC paid to week 33			(482.65)	
USC due for week 34				**3.15**
Net wages week 34:				
Gross				368.00

continued overleaf

Less:

Tax refunded	21.59	
PRSI	(5.39)	
USC	(3.15)	13.05
Net wages week 34		**381.05**

Chapter 12

Question 12.1

ABC

Accountants

Dear Mr Murphy,

I refer to your letter requesting some information regarding the system of self-assessment.

Income Tax Returns and Surcharges

A self-assessed taxpayer must submit a tax return, regardless of whether or not they have been requested by Revenue to do so. The return must be submitted before 31 October in the year following the tax year; otherwise a surcharge of up to 10% on the tax ultimately due (subject to a maximum of €63,485) is imposed.

The taxpayer must enter details of income and capital gains from all sources, and claim allowances and reliefs, for the tax year. The return will also request details of all capital assets acquired. An individual within the self-assessment system must submit their return on or before 31 October in the year after the tax year to which the return refers. Accordingly, a tax return for 2021 would normally have to be submitted on or before 31 October 2022.

However, as you have only commenced to trade in 2021, you have until 31 October 2023, the due date for the filing of your 2022 tax return, to file your 2021 tax return without incurring any penalties.

Note that individuals who enter the self-assessment system because they have commenced to trade have until the return filing date for the second year to submit tax returns for both the first and second year of trading. However, this does not extend to tax payments, preliminary tax for 2021 must be paid by 31 October 2021 and the balance of the 2021 tax due is payable in full by 31 October 2022, even though your 2021 return is not due for filing until 2023.

Preliminary Tax

All taxpayers within the self-assessment system are required to pay preliminary tax by 31 October in the tax year. Accordingly, preliminary tax for 2021 must be paid on or before 31 October 2021.

If interest charges are to be avoided, preliminary tax must amount to:

(1) 90% of the final liability for the tax year; or

(2) 100% of the final liability for the preceding tax year.

Failure to pay preliminary tax by 31 October will result in interest accruing on the full liability from 31 October to the date the tax is paid. If a preliminary tax payment is made in time but proves to be less than 90% of the tax ultimately due (or 100% of the preceding year's liability, as adjusted for USC, whichever is lower), interest will run on the full underpayment at the rate of 0.0219% per day. Also, insufficient payment of preliminary tax will mean that the balance of tax for the year (the full income tax liability) will become due from 31 October for the year concerned. For example, the 2021 income tax liability would be due in full by 31 October 2021.

An individual may opt to pay preliminary tax by direct debit. If one chooses to do this, instead of paying 90% of the current year's liability or 100% of the previous year's adjusted liability, there is the option of paying instead 105% of the pre-preceding year's liability.

The direct debit payments are made on the 9th day of each month. For the first year in which a taxpayer opts to pay preliminary tax by direct debit, they can opt to pay the liability in a minimum of three equal instalments in that year. In subsequent years, the taxpayer must pay their liability in at least eight equal instalments. If these conditions are satisfied, the person is deemed to have paid their preliminary tax on time. The Collector-General can agree to vary the number of instalments to be made, or agree to increase or decrease the instalments, after one or more instalments have been made.

Balance of Income Tax

After the payment of preliminary tax, an individual must pay the balance of the income tax due on the due date for the filing of their income tax return. Accordingly, the balance of income tax due for 2021 must be paid on or before 31 October 2022, assuming sufficient preliminary tax was paid the previous year.

For the tax year 2021, as this will be your first year to pay tax and file your return under the self-assessment system, you will not be required to make a preliminary tax payment on 31 October 2021. This is because you had no liability under the self-assessment system for the tax year 2020, so 100% of your prior year's liability is nil. Your total liability for 2021 is therefore due on 31 October 2022. You must pay your entire liability on or before this date if you wish to avoid interest, even though your return for 2021 is not due until 31 October 2023.

Mandatory Requirement to File Tax Returns Electronically

Self-employed individuals are required to submit their tax returns and payments of tax due using the Revenue Online Service (ROS). Specifically, self-employed taxpayers subject to the high-earners restriction and/or claiming numerous reliefs and exemptions (e.g. EII relief, and property-based reliefs, etc.) are required to pay and file electronically. As you will be registering for income tax self-assessment for the first time in 2021 you will be subject to mandatory e-filing. The advantage is that the taxpayer receives an extension to the filing date, which in 2021 is 17 November 2021, as opposed to 31 October 2021 (assuming that the taxpayer pays and files using ROS and that a sufficient amount of preliminary tax has been paid by the relevant due date).

If you require any further information please do not hesitate to contact me.

Yours faithfully,

ABC Accountants

Question 12.2

Income Tax Calculation for 2021 Paul and Sandra Joist	€	€
Income:		
Schedule D, Case I	112,000	104,000
Less: capital allowances	(8,000)	
Schedule D, Case IV		1,275
Schedule E – Paul		6,000
Taxable income Paul		111,275
Schedule E – Sandra		62,000
Taxable income		173,275
Tax payable:		
€70,600 @ 20%	14,120	
€1,275 @ 33%	421	
€101,400 @ 40%	40,560	
€173,275		55,101
Deduct: Non-refundable tax credits		
Basic personal tax credit (married)	3,300	
Earned income tax credit – Paul	1,650	
Employee tax credit – Paul (Note 1)	0	
Employee tax credit – Sandra	1,650	
DIRT paid (€1,275 @ 33%)	421	(7,021)
Income tax liability		48,080
Deduct: Refundable tax credits		
Tax paid under PAYE – Sandra		(12,640)
Tax due		**35,440**
PRSI due: (Note 2)		
Paul's income €111,275 @ Class S1 (4%)	4,451	
Less: PRSI paid under Schedule E	(240)	4,211
USC due – Paul: (Note 2)	60	
€ 12,012 @ 0.5%	174	
€ 8,675 @ 2.0%	2,221	
€ 49,357 @ 4.5%	2,876	
€ 35,956 @ 8.0%	440	5,771
€ 4,000 @ 11.0% (Note 3)		
€ 110,000		
Net tax liability 2021		45,422

continued overleaf

Notes:
1. The sum of Paul's earned income tax credit and employee tax credit cannot exceed €1,650.
2. Sandra is understood to have paid her liabilities to PRSI and USC through the PAYE system.
3. USC at 11% is payable on non-PAYE income greater than €100,000.

Preliminary tax due for 2021:

Lower of:	Year 2020 @ 100%	=	€38,100	**or**
	Year 2021 €45,422 @ 90%	=	€40,880	

Preliminary tax payment for 2021 will be €38,100 and is payable **online** by 17 November 2021. Balance of €7,322 is payable by 31 October 2022.

If Paul pays his preliminary tax by way of direct debit, his preliminary tax for 2021 will be as follows:

Lower of:	Year 2019 @ 105%	=	€37,590	**or**
	Year 2020 @ 100%	=	€38,100	**or**
	Year 2021 @ 90%	=	€40,880	

Preliminary tax payment for 2021 will be €37,590 and is payable **online** by 17 November 2021. Balance due of €7,832 is payable by 31 October 2022.

Question 12.3

As Una's assessable income for 2021 is greater than €5,000, Jane and Una, as a jointly assessed couple, are "chargeable persons" under self-assessment. They will have to prepare a return of income for 2021, pay over any tax, PRSI and USC due for 2021 by 31 October 2022 and estimate and pay any preliminary tax due for 2022 by the same date.

Jane and Una: Income Tax Computation 2021	€	€
Income – Jane:		
Schedule D, Case IV	(€592/0.67)	884
Schedule E		131,500
Schedule F	(€2,125/0.75)	2,833
Total income: Jane		135,217
Income – Una:		
Schedule D, Case I	(€8,300 – €800)	7,500
Schedule D, Case IV	(€635/0.67)	948
Total income: Una		8,448
Total taxable income		**143,665**
Tax Calculation:		
€51,800 @ 20% (€44,300 + €7,500)	10,360	
€1,832 @ 33%	605	
€90,033 @ 40%	36,013	
€143,665		46,978

continued overleaf

Deduct: Non-refundable tax credits

Basic personal tax credit (married)	3,300	
Incapacitated child tax credit	3,300	
Employee tax credit (Jane)	1,650	
Earned income tax credit (Una) (max. €7,500 @ 20%)	1,500	
Medical expenses (€780 @ 20%)	156	
DIRT paid	<u>605</u>	(10,511)
		36,467

Deduct: Refundable tax credits

Tax paid under PAYE (Jane)	35,490	
DWT (Jane)	<u>708</u>	(36,198)
Net tax liability		**269**

USC:

Jane:

Schedule E	131,500	
Schedule F	<u>2,833</u>	
Income subject to USC	<u>134,333</u>	

USC Calculation:

€12,012 @ 0.5%	60	
€8,675 @ 2.0%	174	
€49,357 @ 4.5%	2,221	
<u>€64,289</u> @ 8.0%	<u>5,143</u>	
€134,333	7,598	
Less: USC deducted under PAYE	<u>(7,371)</u>	227

Una:

Schedule D, Case I	<u>7,500</u>	
USC due (income less than €13,000)		NIL

PRSI:

Jane:

Total income	<u>135,217</u>	
PRSI @ 4%	5,409	
Less: PRSI deducted under PAYE	<u>(5,260)</u>	149

continued overleaf

Una:

Total income	8,448	
PRSI @ 4%	338	
Minimum PRSI payable		500
Income tax, USC and PRSI payable 2021		**1,145**

While over 96% of the tax, PRSI and USC for 2021 has already been paid by Jane through the PAYE system, if the return of income is late, the surcharge is calculated at either 5% or 10% of the total liability and not of the amount outstanding.

Jane and Una: Preliminary Tax Computation 2022	€	€
Estimated income – Una:		
Schedule D, Case I	8,500	
Schedule D, Case IV (gross)	1,000	
Total	9,500	
Tax @ 20% (Case I only)	1,700	
Less: earned income tax credit	(1,650)	
Tax due		50
USC (income less than €13,000)		NIL
PRSI @ 4%	380	
Minimum PRSI payable		500
Jane – estimated non-PAYE income:		
Schedule D, Case IV (gross)	900	
Schedule F (gross)	2,850	
Total	3,750	
Tax @ 40% (Schedule F only)	1,140	
Less: DWT @ 25%	(712)	
Tax due		428
USC €2,850 @ 8%		228
PRSI €3,750 @ 4%		150
Estimated liability for 2022		**1,356**
Preliminary tax payable 31 October 2022 – 90% of estimated 2022 liability		**1,220** OR
100% of 2021 final tax liability		**1,145**

Chapter 13

Question 13.1

(a) Calculation of LPT

House valuation	€560,000
Valuation Band 6	€525,001 – €612,500
Mid-value Band 6	€568,751

LPT for 2022:

€568,751 @ 0.1029%   €585

(b) Deferral

Full Deferral

To qualify for a full deferral, Bill and Frida's gross income must not exceed €30,000 plus 80% of their gross mortgage interest payments:

Gross income threshold: €30,000 + (€6,000 × 80%)	€354,800
Bill and Frida's gross income	€42,000

As Bill and Frida's gross income is greater than the full deferral adjusted income threshold, they do not qualify for a full deferral.

Partial Deferral

To qualify for a partial deferral, Bill and Frida's gross income must not exceed €42,000 plus 80% of their gross mortgage interest payments:

Gross income threshold: €42,000 + (€6,000 × 80%)	€46,800
Bill and Frida's gross income	€42,000

As Bill and Frida's gross income is less than the partial deferral adjusted income threshold, they do qualify for a partial deferral (50%).

LPT partial deferral for 2022: €585 @ 50%   €293

If they wish to opt for partial deferral, they should enter "Deferral Condition Number 4" at Option 6 of the LPT1 return form and select one of the payment options for the balance (€293) of the LPT due. A charge for the deferred amount, including interest at 3%, will be placed on the property.

Question 13.2

1. Deferral based on income

Calculation of adjusted income threshold:

Full deferral €30,000 + (€16,000 × 80%)	€42,800
Partial deferral €42,000 + (€16,000 × 80%)	€54,800

continued overleaf

Theo and Emer gross income:

Gross Case I income	€35,000
Schedule E income	€13,500
Child Benefit	N/A
DEASP Illness Benefit	€10,491
Gross income	€58,991

As their combined gross income is greater than both adjusted income thresholds, Theo and Emer do not qualify for a full or partial deferral of LPT for 2022 on income threshold grounds.

2. Deferral based on hardship

Theo and Emer's gross income	€58,991
Less: unexpected medical expenses	€19,000
Adjusted gross income 2021	€39,991

As the unexpected significant expense is more than **20%** of their gross income **and** it reduces their gross income to below the full deferral income threshold of €42,800, Revenue may consider an application for a deferral where appropriate documentary evidence is provided by Theo and Emer in support of their claim that, as a result of payment of the un-reimbursed medical expenses, payment of the LPT would cause excessive hardship.

Question 13.3

Kevin Ryan: Market value (1 November 2021)		€1,400,000
Valuation Band 15	€1,312,501 – €1,400,000	
Mid-value Band 15	€1,356,251	

LPT for 2022:

€1,050,000 @ 0.1029%	€1,080
€306,251 @ 0.25%	€766
LPT 2022	**€1,846**

Chapter 14

Question 14.1

ABC Accountants
Main Street
Dublin 2

Dear Mr Bricks,

Re: Relevant Contractors Tax (RCT) – Subcontractors

Under the electronic RCT system you were automatically credited for the deducted tax on the days the payments were notified to Revenue by OMG Ltd. These deductions are available as a down payment against any liability to income tax in the period the tax was deducted. Therefore all the deductions to 30 September 2021 are available against your tax liability for 2021. The deduction on 12 October 2021 is not available until the tax year 2022 as it was deducted in your accounts year 30 September 2022.

Repayments of RCT will not be made until your income tax return has been filed. However, the deducted RCT is available for offset against any liability to VAT and PAYE as it arises and this may assist you in managing your cash flow.

At 30 September 2021 this situation is as follows:

RCT deducted (to 30/09/2021)	€10,400
Estimated tax liability 2021	€5,500
RCT refundable	€4,900

As you have liabilities of €6,450 for VAT and PAYE, it would be in your interest to offset the RCT deducted as this would use up the deduction immediately instead of waiting until the submission of your return for a RCT refund.

If you require any further information, please do not hesitate to contact me.

Yours sincerely,

ABC Accountants

Chapter 15

Question 15.1

(a) Corporation tax liabilities

Lemmon DAC

	12 months ended 31/12/2021		2 months ended 28/02/2022
	€		€
Case I (time-apportioned*)	264,000		44,000
Case III (actual)	3,000		2,000
Total income	267,000		46,000
Chargeable gain	5,156		0
Total profits	272,156		46,000

Corporation tax:			
Case I: €264,000 @ 12.5%	33,000	Case I: €44,000 @ 12.5%	5,500
Chargeable gain: €5,156 @ 12.5%	644		
Case III: €3,000 @ 25%	750	Case III: €2,000 @ 25%	500
	34,394		6,000

* Case I time-apportioned: for the 12 months ended 31 December 2021 is 12/14ths; for the two months ended 28 February 2022 is 2/14ths.

Rentco Ltd

Year ended 31/12/2021	
€	
Case V	50,000
Corporation tax @ 25%	12,500

Yann DAC

8 months ended 31/03/2022	
€	
Case I	20,000
Corporation tax @ 25%	2,500

(b) Payment of corporation tax liabilities and filing returns

	Lemmon DAC		Rentco Ltd	Yann DAC
	Year ended 31/12/2021	2 months ended 28/02/2022	Year ended 31/12/2021	8 months ended 31/03/2022
Preliminary tax due	€30,955	€5,400	€11,250	€2,250
Date preliminary tax due	23/11/2021	23/01/2022	23/11/2021	23/02/2022
Final CT balance	€3,439	€600	€1,250	€250
Date final CT balance due AND return filing date	23/09/2022	23/11/2022	23/09/2022	23/12/2022

Chapter 16

Question 16.1

Telstar DAC
Corporation Tax Computation
for 12-month Accounting Period ended 31 December 2021

	€	€
Profit before tax per accounts		116,000
Add: Depreciation	15,149	
Motor leasing (Note 1)	240	
Entertainment (Note 2)	1,050	
Finance lease charges (Note 3)	1,300	
Legal fees (Note 4)	2,400	20,139
		136,139
Less: Grant for extension of premises (Note 5)	10,000	
Employment grant (Note 6)	1,000	
Patent royalty (Note 7)	1,600	
Dividends from Irish quoted shares (Note 8)	1,300	
Profit on sale of van (Note 9)	1,000	
Profit on sale of shares (Note 10)	2,000	
Bank deposit interest (Note 11)	600	
Finance lease payments (Note 3)	9,400	
Capital allowances	7,272	(34,172)
Case I Schedule D		101,967
Case III Schedule D – bank interest (gross)		600
Case IV Schedule D – royalty $\left(\text{gross} = \dfrac{1,600}{80} \times 100\right)$		2,000
Total income		104,567
Chargeable gain (Note 12)		3,759
Total profits		108,326

Corporation tax:

Case I:	€	101,967 @ 12.5%	12,746	
Chargeable gain:	€	3,759 @ 12.5%	470	
Cases III and IV:	€	2,600 @ 25%	650	13,866
Less: income tax suffered on royalty €2,000 @ 20%				(400)
Corporation tax payable				**13,466**

As this is a small company, i.e. corporation tax payable in 2020 did not exceed €200,000, preliminary tax of €80,000 (100% of preceding period) or 90% of this period (i.e. 90% of €13,466 = €12,119) must be paid on/before 23 November 2021 and the balance of €1,347 must be paid on/before 23 September 2022.

Notes:

1. The lease payments are in respect of a Category B vehicle leased when its retail price was €25,000. Therefore, the amount disallowed is:

$$€6,000 \times \frac{€25,000 - €24,000}{€25,000} = €240$$

2. Entertainment costs disallowed:

	€
Christmas gifts for suppliers	150
Entertainment costs incurred by MD	350
General customer entertainment	550
	1,050

Costs incurred for the benefit of staff, i.e. Christmas party and prizes, are deductible.
3. Finance lease charges (i.e. interest) are disallowed and gross payments made are deductible.
4. Legal fees are of a capital nature and are disallowed.
5. Grant for extension of premises is a capital receipt and not liable to corporation tax.
6. Employment grant is not taxable.
7. Patent royalty – as this is not trading income it is not taxable under Case I. The gross amount is taxable under Case IV of Schedule D. However, the income tax suffered can be set off against the corporation tax chargeable. As only the net amount (i.e. the amount after deduction of standard rate income tax) has been credited in the income statement, then this is the correct amount to deduct.
8. Dividends from Irish quoted shares – is franked investment income (FII) and is not liable to corporation tax.
9. Profit on sale of van is a capital profit and not a trading receipt and so is not taxable under Case I (see Note 12).
10. Profit on sale of shares is a capital profit and not a trading receipt and so is not taxable under Case I (see Note 12).
11. Bank deposit interest – this is taxable under Case III as it was not subject to DIRT.
12. Chargeable gain:
    (a) Sale of van – although a loss arose on the sale of the van, this is not an allowable loss. Relief for this loss will be given through capital allowances.
    (b) Sale of shares.

	€	€
Proceeds		6,000
Cost	4,000	
Indexed cost (2000/01: €4,000 @ 1.1444)		(4,576)
Gain		1,424
Chargeable gain: €1,424 @ 33/12.5		**3,759**

Question 16.2

Zaco Ltd
Corporation Tax Computation Year Ended 30 September 2021

	€	€
Profit per accounts		378,100
Add: Repairs	5,200	
Professional fees	300	
Political donations	750	

continued overleaf

Entertainment	600	
Depreciation	13,000	19,850
		397,950
Less: Dividends	3,000	
Profit on sale of investments	5,200	
Interest on tax overpaid	1,200	
Profit on sale of fixtures and fittings	3,100	(12,500)
		385,450
Less: Capital allowances		(9,846)
Case I Schedule D		375,604
Add: Chargeable gains (Note 1)		Nil
		375,604

Corporation tax:

Case I: €375,604 @ 12.5%	46,950

Notes:

1. Chargeable gains

	€	€
Sale of investments:		
(a) Sale of Irish Treasury bonds		Exempt
(b) Quoted investment company shares		
Proceeds		5,548
Cost	1,000	
Indexation factor: 1.232		
Indexed cost		(1,232)
Total gains		4,316
Less: capital loss forward		(10,000)
Capital loss forward to 2022		(5,684)

2. Dividends not subject to tax as franked investment income.

Question 16.3

Overseas Limited

Corporation Tax Computation Year Ended 31 December 2021

	€	€
Case I: Branch trading profits		600,000
Case III: Branch interest income		20,000
		620,000
Gain on branch assets: €32,000 @ 33/12.5		84,480
		704,480

continued overleaf

Corporation tax:

€684,480 @ 12.5%	85,560	
€20,000 @ 25%	5,000	
€704,480		**90,560**

Question 16.4

Enya Ltd Corporation Tax Computation		
	€	€
Year ended 31/03/2018:		
Case I		60,000
Case III		10,000
Case V 2017	5,000	
Less: loss re. 2019	(4,000)	1,000
Taxable income		71,000
Corporation tax:		
€60,000 @ 12.5%	7,500	
€11,000 @ 25%	2,750	
Corporation tax payable		**10,250**
Year ended 31/03/2019:		
Case I	70,000	
Less: trading loss from 2020	(70,000)	Nil
Case III		5,000
Case V		Nil
Taxable Income		5,000
Corporation tax:		
€5,000 @ 25%	1,250	
Less: relief on a value basis (loss memo)	(1,250)	
Corporation tax payable		**Nil**
Year ended 31/03/2020:		
Case I		Nil
Case III		10,000
Case V		6,000
Taxable income		16,000
Corporation tax:		
€16,000 @ 25%	4,000	
Less: relief on a value basis (loss memo)	(4,000)	
Corporation tax payable		**Nil**

continued overleaf

Year ended 31/03/2021:

	€	€
Case I	10,000	
Less: trading loss from 2020	(10,000)	Nil
Case III		3,500
Case V		8,000
Taxable income		11,500
Corporation tax:		
€11,500 @ 25%		2,875
Corporation tax payable		**2,875**

Loss Memo:	€
Relevant trading loss for y/e 31/03/2020	130,000
Utilised by way of section 396A(3) against y/e 31/03/2019	(70,000)
Utilised by way of section 396B(3) against y/e 31/03/2020 (€32,000 @ 12.5% = €4,000)	(32,000)
Utilised by way of section 396B(3) against y/e 31/03/2019 (€10,000 @ 12.5% = €1,250)	(10,000)
Utilised by way of section 396(1) forward against y/e 31/03/2021	(10,000)
Loss forward to 2022	8,000

Question 16.5

Hells Bells Ltd
Corporation Tax Computation

	€	€
Year ended 31 March 2021:		
Case I	167,000	
Section 396A(3) loss back (Note 1)	(125,250)	41,750
Case III		10,000
Case V	4,000	
Less: loss (Note 2)	(3,000)	1,000
Total income		52,750
Chargeable gain		–
Total profits		52,750
Corporation tax:		
€11,000 @ 25%	2,750	
€41,750 @ 12.5%	5,218	
Tax payable		7,968
Less: relief on a value basis (Note 4)		(3,094)
Corporation tax payable		**4,874**

continued overleaf

Nine months ended 31 December 2021:

Case I	–
Case III	20,000
Case V	=
Total income	20,000
Chargeable gains (Note 3)	=
Taxable profits	20,000
Corporation tax:	
€20,000 @ 25%	5,000
Less: relief on a value basis (Loss Memo)	(5,000)
Corporation tax payable	**Nil**

Notes:

1. Loss available for carry back — €190,000

   Trading profit of corresponding period – €167,000 × 9/12ths — €125,250

   Offset total — €125,250

2. A Case V loss can be carried back to a previous accounting period of the same length. A loss for nine months can be carried back against income for nine months, i.e. €4,000 × 9/12ths = €3,000.

3. Chargeable gain:

	€
Gain	10,000
Less: capital loss forward	(19,000)
Capital loss forward	(9,000)

4. The maximum tax that can be saved is 9/12ths of the corporation tax, i.e. €7,968 × 9/12ths = €5,976. However, the losses still available are only €24,750. Therefore, the value of the losses is €24,750 × 12.5% = €3,094. This is the maximum reduction in corporation tax.

Loss Memo	€
Relevant trading loss for p/e 31/12/2021	190,000
(i) Utilised by way of section 396A(3) against y/e 31/03/2021	(125,250)
(ii) Utilised by way of section 396B(3) against p/e 31/12/2021	
€40,000 @ 12.5% = €5,000	(40,000)
(iii) Utilised by way of section 396B(3) against y/e 31/03/2021	
€24,750 @ 12.5% = €3,094	(24,750)
Loss forward to 2022	Nil

Note: (i) to (iii) shows sequence of claims.

Question 16.6

<table>
<tr><td colspan="3" align="center">**Monk Ltd**
Corporation Tax Computation</td></tr>
<tr><td></td><td align="center">€</td><td align="center">€</td></tr>
<tr><td>**Year ended 31 December 2021:**</td><td></td><td></td></tr>
<tr><td>Case I</td><td></td><td>–</td></tr>
<tr><td>Case III</td><td></td><td>30,000</td></tr>
<tr><td>Case V</td><td></td><td>20,000</td></tr>
<tr><td>Total income</td><td></td><td>50,000</td></tr>
<tr><td>Chargeable gain</td><td></td><td>26,000</td></tr>
<tr><td>Taxable profits</td><td></td><td>76,000</td></tr>
<tr><td>*Corporation tax:*</td><td></td><td></td></tr>
<tr><td>€50,000 @ 25%</td><td>12,500</td><td></td></tr>
<tr><td>€26,000 @ 12.5%</td><td>3,250</td><td>15,750</td></tr>
<tr><td>*Less:* relief on a value basis (Loss Memo)</td><td></td><td>(10,000)</td></tr>
<tr><td>**Corporation tax payable**</td><td></td><td>5,750</td></tr>
</table>

The gain on development land cannot be sheltered as it is liable to CGT, i.e. €100,000 × 33% = €33,000.

<table>
<tr><td>**Year ended 31 December 2020:**</td><td></td><td></td></tr>
<tr><td>Case I</td><td>340,000</td><td></td></tr>
<tr><td>*Less:* Case I loss forward section 396(1)</td><td>(20,000)</td><td></td></tr>
<tr><td>Case I</td><td>320,000</td><td></td></tr>
<tr><td>*Less*: section 396A(3)</td><td>(320,000)</td><td></td></tr>
<tr><td>Case I</td><td></td><td>–</td></tr>
<tr><td>Case III</td><td></td><td>5,000</td></tr>
<tr><td>Case V</td><td></td><td>15,000</td></tr>
<tr><td>Total income</td><td></td><td>20,000</td></tr>
<tr><td>Chargeable gain</td><td></td><td>12,000</td></tr>
<tr><td>Taxable profits</td><td></td><td>32,000</td></tr>
<tr><td>*Corporation tax:*</td><td></td><td></td></tr>
<tr><td>€20,000 @ 25%</td><td>5,000</td><td></td></tr>
<tr><td>€12,000 @ 12.5%</td><td>1,500</td><td></td></tr>
<tr><td>**Corporation tax payable**</td><td></td><td>6,500</td></tr>
</table>

<table>
<tr><td>*Loss Memo*</td><td align="center">€</td></tr>
<tr><td>Relevant trading loss for y/e 31/12/2021</td><td>400,000</td></tr>
<tr><td>Utilised by way of section 396A(3) against y/e 31/12/2020</td><td>(320,000)</td></tr>
<tr><td>Utilised by way of section 396B(3) against y/e 31/12/2021</td><td></td></tr>
<tr><td> €80,000 @ 12.5% = €10,000</td><td>(80,000)</td></tr>
<tr><td>Loss forward to 2022</td><td>Nil</td></tr>
</table>

Must claim under section 396A(3) first, as required by law, and then on a value basis in the current period.

Question 16.7

	Monaghan Ltd		
Corporation Tax Computation year ended 30 June			
	2019	**2020**	**2021**
	€	€	€
Assessable Case I profit	180,000	Nil	140,000
Section 396(1) loss relief	(20,000)		(140,000)
Section 396A loss relief	(160,000)	–	–
Case I	Nil	Nil	Nil
Case III – interest on Government stocks	5,000	30,000	10,000
Case V – rental income	10,500	20,000	20,000
Capital gains – as adjusted	10,200	40,000	50,000
Total profits	25,700	90,000	80,000
Less: non-trade charges	–	–	(50,000)
Taxable profits	25,700	90,000	30,000
Corporation tax:			
Corporation tax @ 12.5% (Note 1)	1,275	5,000	3,750
Corporation tax @ 25%	3,875	12,500	–
	5,150	17,500	3,750
Less: Section 243B relief (Note 2)	(1,250)	(1,250)	(750)
Section 396B(3) relief (Note 3)	(3,900)	(16,250)	–
Corporation tax payable	**Nil**	**Nil**	**3,000**

Notes:

1. Non-trade charges paid in y/e 30/06/2021 are offset against income liable at 25% first.
2. Excess trade charges in y/e 30/06/2019 and 30/06/2020 = €10,000
   Relief on a value basis in y/e 30/06/2019: €10,000 @ 12.5% = €1,250
   Relief on a value basis in y/e 30/06/2020: €10,000 @ 12.5% = €1,250
   Excess trade charges y/e 30/06/2021: €6,000 @ 12.5% = €750. Relief for €4,000 charges paid in July 2021 will be given in y/e 30/06/2022.
3. Losses for y/e 30/06/2020 available to carry forward and offset against profits arising in the year ended 30/06/2021 and subsequent years.

	€
Case I adjusted loss	530,000
Utilised by way of section 396A relief y/e 30/06/2019	(160,000)
Utilised by way of section 396B relief:	
y/e 30/06/2020 €130,000 @ 12.5% = €16,250	(130,000)
y/e 30/06/2019 €31,200 @ 12.5% = €3,900	(31,200)
Losses available to carry forward to y/e 30/06/2021	208,800
Utilised against y/e 30/06/2021	(140,000)
Losses available to carry forward to y/e 30/06/2022	68,800

Chapter 17

Question 17.1

<table>
<tr><td colspan="3" align="center">**Nifty Investments Ltd**
Accounts year ended 31 March 2021</td></tr>
<tr><td></td><td align="right">€</td><td align="right">€</td></tr>
<tr><td>Profit per accounts</td><td></td><td align="right">90,000</td></tr>
<tr><td>Add: Depreciation</td><td align="right">10,000</td><td></td></tr>
<tr><td>Interest</td><td align="right">9,000</td><td></td></tr>
<tr><td>Patent royalties</td><td align="right">8,000</td><td align="right">27,000</td></tr>
<tr><td></td><td></td><td align="right">117,000</td></tr>
<tr><td>*Less:* Interest received:</td><td></td><td></td></tr>
<tr><td>Loan interest</td><td align="right">6,000</td><td></td></tr>
<tr><td>Bank interest</td><td align="right">1,000</td><td align="right">(7,000)</td></tr>
<tr><td></td><td></td><td align="right">110,000</td></tr>
<tr><td>*Deduct*: Case I charge (Note 2)</td><td></td><td align="right">(10,000)</td></tr>
<tr><td>Case I</td><td></td><td align="right">100,000</td></tr>
<tr><td>Case III</td><td></td><td align="right">1,000</td></tr>
<tr><td>Case IV (Note 1)</td><td></td><td align="right">6,000</td></tr>
<tr><td>Income</td><td></td><td align="right">107,000</td></tr>
<tr><td>Add: Chargeable gain (Note 3)</td><td></td><td align="right">26,400</td></tr>
<tr><td>Profits</td><td></td><td align="right">133,400</td></tr>
<tr><td>*Deduct*: non-trade charge (Note 4)</td><td></td><td align="right">(9,000)</td></tr>
<tr><td>**Taxable profits**</td><td></td><td align="right">**124,400**</td></tr>
<tr><td>Corporation tax due on profits (Note 5)</td><td></td><td align="right">15,550</td></tr>
<tr><td>Add: Income tax withheld on patent royalties</td><td></td><td align="right">2,000</td></tr>
<tr><td>*Deduct*: Income tax deducted from Case IV receipts</td><td></td><td align="right">(1,200)</td></tr>
<tr><td>**Total tax liability**</td><td></td><td align="right">16,350</td></tr>
</table>

Notes:

1. Case IV:

	Net received	**Tax deducted**	**Taxable Case IV**
Loan interest	€4,800	€1,200	€6,000

2. Case I charge:

	Net paid	**Tax withheld**	**Deductible as a charge**
Patent royalties	€8,000	€2,000	€10,000

continued overleaf

3. As the tax rate for year ended 31 March 2021 is 12.5% and the CGT rate at the time of disposal is 33%, the gain is grossed up as follows: €10,000 × 33/12.5 = €26,400.
4. As the interest is paid to an Irish bank, there is no requirement to withhold income tax and as it qualifies as a non-trade charge, it is deductible against total profits. When calculating corporation tax, it will be offset against any profits taxable at 25%.
5. Corporation tax liability on €124,400:

Income liable @ 25%:	€
Case III	1,000
Case IV	6,000
Less: non-trade charge	(9,000)
Available for offset against trading income	(2,000)

Income liable @ 12.5%:	€
Case I	100,000
Less: non-trade charge available for offset	(2,000)
	98,000
Add: Chargeable gain	26,400
Taxable @ 12.5%	124,400
Corporation tax	**15,550**

Question 17.2

Alpha Ltd

Corporation Tax Computation year ended 31 December 2021

		€	€
Case I	Profit per accounts		424,605
	Add: Rent and rates (re sub-let)	1,000	
	Repairs (capital)	15,000	
	Insurance (re sub-let)	350	
	Loss on sale of investments	600	
	Legal expenses (re capital)	2,000	
	Depreciation	13,260	
	Subscriptions (Note 1)	1,835	
	Other interest – not trade (Note 4)	7,000	
	Motor expenses (Note 2)	845	
	Sundry (Note 3)	2,201	
	Entertainment	1,191	
	Finance lease charges	1,700	46,982
			471,587

continued overleaf

Less: Irish dividends received	4,500	
Interest on Irish Treasury bonds	2,500	
Gain on sale of Irish shares	1,000	
Enterprise Ireland employment grant – exempt	240	
Interest on tax overpaid	475	
Rents received	6,000	
Deposit interest	1,500	
Finance lease payments	12,200	(28,415)
		443,172
Less: Capital allowances		(26,006)
Net Case I		417,166
Case III Interest on Irish Treasury bonds	2,500	
Deposit interest	1,500	4,000
Case V Gross rents re sublet	6,000	
Less: Rent and rates paid	(1,000)	
Insurance	(350)	4,650
Chargeable gains (Note 5) €400 @ 33%/12.5%		1,056
Total profits		426,872
Less: Charge (protected interest)		(7,000)
Profits liable to corporation tax		**419,872**

Corporation tax (Note 6):		€
Case I:	€417,166 @ 12.5%	52,146
Chargeable Gain:	€1,056 @ 12.5%	132
Case III/V:	€1,650 @ 25%	412
	€419,872	**52,690**

Notes:

1. Subscriptions:

	€
Football club	20
Political	1,815
	1,835

2. Motor expenses – leasing charges: 845

$$€21{,}126 \times \frac{€150{,}000 - €144{,}000\,^{*}}{€150{,}000} = €845$$

*€24,000 × 6 cars = €144,000.

3. Sundry:

	€
Interest on late payment of VAT	1,630
Parking fines	30
Gifts to customers	541
	2,201

4. Protected interest: non-trade charges are deductible against total profits. The conditions to be satisfied for a payment to be deductible as a non-trade charge are satisfied, i.e. use loan to acquire shares in a trading company, have a material interest (>5%), common director and no recovery of capital. €7,000 was paid, so that is the amount deductible.

5. Chargeable gains:

	€
Gain on Irish quoted shares	1,000
Loss on UK shares	(600)
Net chargeable gain	400

6. Corporation tax: non-trade charges are offset against total profits. The taxpayer can choose which source of income/gain against which to offset the non-trade charge. It is most tax efficient to offset the €7,000 against income taxable at 25%.

	€
Case III	4,000
Case V	4,650
	8,650
Less: non-trade charge	(7,000)
Net Case III/V	1,650

Chapter 18

Question 18.1

(a) **DWT Payable**

	Lance Investments Ltd	
	Gross Dividend	**DWT**
	€	€
Mr C (Note 1)	60,000	15,000
National Investments Ltd (Note 2)	360,000	Nil
Irish registered charity	20,000	–
Local Investments Ltd (Note 2)	60,000	Nil
	500,000	15,000

The total DWT payable by Lance Investments Ltd is €15,000.

continued overleaf

Notes:

1. Irish resident individual not exempt from DWT.
2. Irish resident company dividend is treated as franked investment income and so is not within the charge to corporation tax and is also exempt from DWT.

(b) The DWT must be paid before 14 December 2021.

(c) Local Investments Ltd must make a declaration to Lance Investments Ltd to the effect that the company, being the company beneficially entitled to the dividend, is a company resident in the State. National Investments Ltd is not required to make any declaration to Lance Investments Ltd in order to be exempt from DWT as it qualifies as a "parent" company, i.e. it owns more than 50%.

Chapter 19

Question 19.1

1. Maurice – CGT Computation 2021

	€	€
Sale proceeds		80,000
Less: legal costs on disposal		(750)
Net sale proceeds		79,250
Deduct: Allowable cost:		
House cost	20,000	
Legal costs	600	
	20,600	
Indexed @ 1.819		(37,471)
Gain		41,779
Deduct: Annual exemption		(1,270)
Taxable gain		40,509
CGT @ 33%		**13,368**

2. Vincent – CGT Computation 2021

	€	€
Sale proceeds		9,300
Deduct: Allowable cost	1,200	
Indexed @ 1.406		(1,687)
Gain		7,613
Less: Annual exemption		(1,270)
Taxable gain		6,343
CGT @ 33%		**2,093**

3(a) John – Capital Asset Sold

	€
Cost June 2001	7,600
Sale December 2021	7,800
Actual profit	200

Computation of capital gains 2021:

	€
Sale proceeds	7,800
Cost June 2001: €7,600 indexed @ 1.087	(8,261)
"Loss"	(461)

Therefore, no gain/no loss.

Note: indexation cannot create a loss where there is an actual monetary gain.

3(b) Philip – Capital Asset Sold

	€
Cost July 1980	3,000
Sale proceeds December 2020	2,700
Actual loss – maximum allowable	(300)

Computation of capital gains 2021:

	€
Sale proceeds	2,700
Cost: €3,000 indexed @ 3.240	(9,720)
"Loss"	(7,020)
Restricted to maximum allowable loss	(300)

Note: indexation cannot create an allowable loss greater than the actual monetary loss.

3(c) Paul – Capital Asset Sold

	€
Cost June 1973	5,700
Sale proceeds December 2021	5,500
Actual loss	(200)

Computation of capital gains 2021:

	€
Sale proceeds	5,500
Market value April 1974: €5,800 indexed @ 7.528	(43,662)
"Loss"	(38,162)
Restricted to maximum allowable loss	(200)

3(d) Oliver – Capital Asset Sold

	€
Cost July 1980	15,000
Sale proceeds	18,000
Actual gain	3,000
Computation of capital gains 2021:	
Sale proceeds	18,000
Cost €15,000 indexed @ 3.240	(48,600)
"Loss"	(30,600)

Therefore, no gain/no loss.

Note: indexation cannot operate so as to turn an actual monetary gain into an allowable loss.

Question 19.2

1.   James – CGT Computation 2021

	€
Sale proceeds	650,000
Deduct: Allowable costs:	
Acquisition cost €260,000 – €10,000 = €250,000 indexed @ 1.356	(339,000)
Enhancement expenditure:	
August 2001 – not capital expenditure	0
May 2004	(90,000)
Chargeable gain	221,000
Less: Annual exemption	(1,270)
	219,730
CGT due @ 33%	**72,511**

2. Declan – CGT Computation 2021

	€	€
Sale proceeds		400,000
Deduct: Allowable costs		
6 April 1998 €85,000 @ 1.212	103,020	
Expenditure August 2001 €20,000 @ 1.087	21,740	
Expenditure February 2003 €39,250 @ 1.000	39,250	(164,010)
"Gain"		235,990
Less: annual exemption		(1,270)
		234,720
CGT due @ 33%		**77,458**

Question 19.3

	€
Courtaulds Plc shares: proceeds	1,162
Deduct: Market value 06/11/1974: €888 @ 7.528	(6,685)
Indexed loss	(5,523)
Monetary gain (€1,162 – €888)	274

Therefore, no gain/no loss.

	€
Box Plc shares: proceeds	1,662
Deduct: Cost €1,732 @ 2.678	(4,638)
Indexed loss	(2,976)
Restrict to monetary loss	(70)
Cox Plc shares: proceeds	16,000
Deduct: Cost €1,693 @ 1.331	(2,253)
Chargeable gain	13,747
Nox Plc shares: proceeds	1,305
Deduct: Cost	(623)
Chargeable gain	682
Summary	
Chargeable gain	13,747
Chargeable gain	682
Allowable loss	(70)
	14,359
Less: Annual exemption	(1,270)
	13,089
CGT due @ 33%	**4,319**

Question 19.4

	€	€
1. 12 Jan 2021 Sold – market value		50,000
31 Jan 2000 Value at date of inheritance	8,000	
Indexed @ 1.193		(9,544)
Gain		40,456
2. 05 Feb 2021 Sale of Florida home		320,000
30 Oct 1999 Cost	110,000	
Indexed @ 1.193		(131,230)
Gain		188,770

continued overleaf

3. 05 May 2021 Sale of shares in Plc		30,000
30 Apr 2002 Cost price	50,000	
Indexed @ 1.049		(52,450)
Loss		(22,450)
Limited to monetary loss (€50,000 – €30,000)		(20,000)
4. 10 Dec 2021 Sale of house		2,000,000
31 Dec 1992 Purchase price	300,000	
Less: cost used (see *Note*)	(100,000)	
	200,000	
Indexed @ 1.356		(271,200)
Gain		1,728,800

Note: cost attributable to 2001 disposal is:

$$€300,000 \times \frac{€500,000}{€500,000 + €1,000,000} = €100,000$$

5. 21 Dec 2021 Deemed sale price of chair		3,500
03 Dec 2001 Cost	2,600	
Indexed @ 1.087		(2,826)
Gain		674

Summary

	€
Tax payable on 15 December 2021:	
1. Sale of shares	40,456
2. Sale of holiday home	188,770
3. Sale of shares	(20,000)
	209,226
Less: exemption	(1,270)
Taxable	207,956
CGT @ 33%	**68,625**

Tax payable on 31 January 2022:	
1. Sale of shares	40,456
2. Sale of holiday home	188,770
3. Sale of shares	(20,000)
4. Sale of house	1,728,800
5. Sale of chair	674
	1,938,700
Less: exemption	(1,270)
Taxable	1,937,430
CGT @ 33%	**639,352**

continued overleaf

Total liability for year	639,352		
Less: paid 15 December 2021	(68,625)		
Due 31 January 2022	570,727		

Chapter 20

Question 20.1

<table>
<tr><td colspan="5" align="center">Philip Even
Capital Gains Tax Computation 2021</td></tr>
<tr><td></td><td></td><td>Gain @
33%</td><td>Gain Dev.
Land @
33%</td><td></td></tr>
<tr><td></td><td>€</td><td>€</td><td>€</td><td>€</td></tr>
<tr><td>1. Gift to wife – exempt</td><td>Nil</td><td></td><td></td><td></td></tr>
<tr><td>2. Gift to John</td><td></td><td></td><td></td><td></td></tr>
<tr><td>Market value (connected persons) at 01/09/2021</td><td>200,000</td><td></td><td></td><td></td></tr>
<tr><td>Deduct: CUV €3,000 @ 2.253</td><td>(6,759)</td><td></td><td></td><td></td></tr>
<tr><td>Development premium €2,000 @ 1.000</td><td>(2,000)</td><td></td><td></td><td></td></tr>
<tr><td>Gain</td><td></td><td></td><td>191,241</td><td></td></tr>
<tr><td>3. Sale of farm</td><td></td><td></td><td></td><td></td></tr>
<tr><td>Sale proceeds</td><td>260,000</td><td></td><td></td><td></td></tr>
<tr><td>Less: €32,000 indexed @ 1.442</td><td>(46,144)</td><td></td><td></td><td></td></tr>
<tr><td>Gain</td><td></td><td>213,856</td><td></td><td></td></tr>
<tr><td>4. Sale of National Loan Stock – exempt (Note 1)</td><td>Nil</td><td></td><td></td><td></td></tr>
<tr><td>5. Sale of antique necklace – exempt (Note 2)</td><td>Nil</td><td></td><td></td><td></td></tr>
<tr><td>6. Sale of painting – no loss relief available (Note 3)</td><td>Nil</td><td></td><td></td><td></td></tr>
<tr><td>7. Gift of commercial property</td><td></td><td></td><td></td><td></td></tr>
<tr><td>Market value on disposal</td><td>875,000</td><td></td><td></td><td></td></tr>
<tr><td>Less: allowable costs</td><td></td><td></td><td></td><td></td></tr>
<tr><td>Jan 1983 – €50,000 indexed @ 2.253</td><td>(112,650)</td><td></td><td></td><td></td></tr>
<tr><td>Jun 1989 – €60,000 indexed @ 1.503</td><td>(90,180)</td><td></td><td></td><td></td></tr>
<tr><td>Mar 2007 – €50,000 indexed @ 1</td><td>(50,000)</td><td></td><td></td><td></td></tr>
<tr><td>Gain</td><td></td><td>622,170</td><td></td><td></td></tr>
</table>

continued overleaf

8. Sale of development land

Sale proceeds	18,000	
Less: allowable cost		
No indexation – acquired after 01/01/03	(10,000)	
Gain		8,000

9. Sale of vase – exempt (Note 2)   Nil

Total gains	836,026	199,241
Deduct: Losses unrelated to dev. land	(6,000)	
	830,026	830,026
Deduct: Development land losses*		(1,500)
Net gain		1,027,767
Less: Annual exemption		(1,270)
Taxable		1,026,497
CGT @ 33%		**338,744**

*Development land losses may be set-off against all gains.

Notes:

1. Exempt – government security.

2. Exempt – non-wasting tangible movable property sold for less than €2,540.

3. No loss relief available – loss arose on the disposal of tangible movable property for less than €2,540; consideration deemed to be €2,540 and no loss deemed to arise.

Question 20.2

Mrs O'Sullivan
Capital Gains Tax Computation 2021

(a) Chargeable gain on sale of property

	€	€
Proceeds		1,585,000
Less: Selling costs		
Legal costs	12,500	
Agent's commissions	7,000	(19,500)
		1,565,500
Deemed cost of property €60,000 @ 7.528	451,680	
Enhancement in 1994/95 €162,000 @ 1.309	212,058	(663,738)
Chargeable gain		901,762

continued overleaf

(b) Tax on sale of development land

Proceeds		1,800,000
Deduct: Deemed cost: current use value of property		
€12,500 @ 7.528	94,100	
Deemed cost: development value of property		
(€25,000 – €12,500) = €12,500 × 1	12,500	(106,600)
Gain		1,693,400
CGT @ 33%		**558,822**

Question 20.3

Bill O'Rourke
Capital Gains Computation 2021

	€	€
Proceeds		1,680,000
Costs of disposal		(18,000)
		1,662,000
Less: allowable costs		
Purchase cost 06/04/1986 – €75,000 (all current use value)		
indexed @ 1.637	122,775	
Incidental costs: €4,251 (all attributable to current use)		
indexed @ 1.637	6,959	(129,734)
Gross gain		1,532,266

Exempt portion of gain – private residence

Current use value at date of disposal	800,000
Costs of disposal attributable to private residence:	
$\dfrac{€800,000}{€1,680,000} \times €18,000$	(8,571)
	791,429
Indexed cost of acquisition – as above	(129,734)
Exempt gain	661,695
Chargeable gain = gross gain – exempt gain	
= €1,532,266 – €661,695	870,571

Alternative Calculation

Excess of proceeds over current use value	
Development premium: €1,680,000 – €800,000	880,000
Costs attributable to development premium:	
€880,000/€1,680,000 × €18,000	(9,429)
Taxable gain	870,571

Question 20.4

Mr. Smart
Capital Gains Tax Computation 2021

	€
Shop premises	
Sale proceeds	695,000
Cost of disposal	(7,000)
	688,000
Value at 06/04/1974 as indexed: €10,000 @ 7.528	(75,280)
Enhancement expenditure 1991/92 as indexed: €12,000 @ 1.406	(16,872)
	595,848
Personal exemption	(1,270)
Capital gain	594,578
CGT @ 33%	**196,211**
Holiday cottage	
Sale proceeds (deemed to be market value) (Note 1)	20,000
Cost	(25,000)
Loss (Note 2)	(5,000)

Notes:

1. In this situation market value is substituted for the sale proceeds.
2. This loss can only be set against future gains made on transactions with his nephew as this is a disposal to a connected person.

Question 20.5

Christine Martin
Capital Gains Tax Computation 2021

	€
1. Disposal of shop	
Proceeds	224,000
Less: related costs	(3,100)
Cost 1991/92 €63,000 @ 1.406	(88,578)
Chargeable gain	132,322
2. Disposal of painting	
Proceeds	2,600
Cost	(1,900)
Gain	700
Potential CGT due: €700 @ 33%	231
Max. CGT: €2,600 – €2,540 @ 50%	30

continued overleaf

Summary:

Chargeable gains – disposal of shop	132,322
Less: Annual exemption	(1,270)
Taxable	131,052
CGT @ 33%	43,725
Plus CGT on disposal of painting	30
Total CGT liability	**43,277**

Chapter 21

Question 21.1

(a)   Obligation to register

A person is required to register for VAT if his turnover from the supply of taxable goods or services exceeds, or is likely to exceed, in any continuous period of 12 months whichever of the following limits is appropriate:

(i)   €37,500 in the case of persons supplying services;

(ii)   €37,500 in the case of persons supplying goods liable at the 9%/13.5% or 21%/23% rates which they have manufactured or produced from zero-rated materials;

(iii)   €35,000 in the case of persons making mail-order or distance sales into the State;

(iv)   €41,000 in the case of persons making intra-Community acquisitions;

(v)   €75,000 in the case of persons supplying both goods and services where 90% or more of the turnover is derived from supplies of goods (other than goods referred to at (ii) above);

(vi)   a non-established person supplying goods or services in the State is obliged to register and account for VAT regardless of the level of his turnover;

(vii)   a person receiving services from abroad for business purposes in the State must register irrespective of the level of turnover; and

(viii) EU and non-EU businesses will have to register and account for VAT in every Member State in which they supply telecommunications, broadcasting and e-services (including gaming) to consumers.

In determining whether or not the relevant turnover threshold has been exceeded, actual turnover may be reduced by VAT on stock purchased for resale.

For example, in a 12-month period a trader purchases stock for €61,767 (including VAT of €11,550) and sells it on for €78,000. For the purpose of determining if the €75,000 threshold has been exceeded, the trader's turnover of €78,000 is reduced by VAT on purchases of stock of €11,550. Accordingly, the trader's turnover is deemed to be €66,450. As this is less than the €75,000 threshold, the trader is not obliged to register.

No threshold applies in the case of taxable intra-Community services received from abroad and in the case of cultural, artistic, sporting, scientific, educational or entertainment services received from a person not established in the State. All such services are liable to VAT.

Suppliers of goods and services that are exempt from VAT, and non-taxable entities such as State bodies, charities, etc., are obliged to register for VAT where it is likely that they will acquire more than €41,000 of intra-Community acquisitions in any 12-month period.

(b) Records and information

A taxable person must keep full and true records of all business transactions that affect, or may affect, their liability to VAT. The records must be kept up to date and must be sufficiently detailed to enable the trader to accurately calculate their liability or repayment, and for Revenue to check if necessary.

The record of purchases should distinguish between purchases of goods for resale and goods and services not intended for resale. The records should show the date of the purchase invoice, the name of the supplier, the cost exclusive of VAT and the VAT. Purchases at each date should be separated and similar records kept for imports.

The record of sales must record the amount charged in respect of every sale to a registered person and a daily total of the amounts charged in respect of sales to unregistered persons. Transactions liable at different rates must be distinguished, as must exempt transactions.

All entries must be cross-referenced to the relevant invoices, cash register tally rolls, etc. and must be retained.

The bi-monthly, monthly, quarterly or annual VAT return to the Collector-General must show the VAT charged on supplies (output tax), the VAT suffered on supplies, self-supplies, and imports used in the business (input tax), and adjustments to previous returns, and the net amount payable or repayable. The return should be on form VAT 3 and should be sent online to the Collector-General within 23 days of the end of each tax period.

Input and output tax figures must be supported by the original or copy tax invoices. Records, including a VAT account, must be maintained for six years. A taxable person must keep a record of all taxable goods and services received or supplied, including any self-supplies and exempt supplies. It is not necessary to submit the supporting documentation with the return, but it must be made available for inspection if required by Revenue.

Question 21.2

(a) Unless a taxable person has been specifically authorised by Revenue to account for tax on the basis of monies received (cash receipts basis), liability for VAT arises at the time when taxable goods or services are supplied. This general rule is, however, subject to a number of qualifications:

(i) in dealings between taxable persons, tax becomes due on the date of issue of the tax invoice, or the date on which the invoice should have been issued if issue has been delayed;

(ii) where payment in whole, or in part, in respect of a transaction was received before the date on which the VAT would normally be due, the VAT was due on the amount received on the date of receipt.

(b) Goods supplied on a sale or return basis are treated as supplied on the earlier of acquisition by the customer or when they are invoiced or paid for.

(c) If the services are supplied under a contract over a period during which periodic payments are made, each payment will have its own tax point as, under the general rule, the actual tax point for each payment will be the earlier of the date of the payment received or the issue of the tax invoice.

(d) Tax in respect of 'self-supplies' becomes due in all cases when the goods are appropriated or withdrawn from business stock or when the services are performed.

Question 21.3

(a) Records A taxable person must keep full and true records of all business transactions which affect or may affect his liability to VAT. The records must be kept up to date and must be sufficiently detailed to enable the trader to accurately calculate their liability or repayment and for the Inspector of Taxes to check if necessary.

The record of purchases should distinguish between purchases of goods for resale and goods and services not intended for resale. The records should show the date of the purchase invoice, the name of the supplier, the cost exclusive of VAT and the VAT. Purchases at each rate should be separated and similar records kept for imports.

The record of sales must record the amount charged in respect of every sale to a registered person and a daily total of the amounts charged in respect of sales to unregistered persons. Transactions liable at different rates must be distinguished, as must exempt transactions.

All entries must be cross-referenced to the relevant invoices, cash register tally rolls, etc. which must be retained.

(b) VAT Returns and Payment   If filing bi-monthly returns, the return and payment must be submitted electronically (via ROS) by the 23rd of the month following the end of the bi-monthly taxable period, i.e. 23 March; 23 May; 23 July; 23 September; 23 November and 23 January. The following taxable periods may be authorised by the Collector-General:

- Monthly – if you are in a constant repayment position.
- Annual – if you are making equal instalments by direct debit.
- Four-monthly – if your annual VAT liability is between €3,001 and €14,400.
- Six-monthly – if your annual liability is €3,000 or less.

If VAT is not paid within the proper time limit, interest will be charged at the rate of 0.0274% for each day or part of a day by which payment is late.

Question 21.4

John Hardiman VAT September–October 2021	€
Sales: cash receipts €30,250 × 23/123	5,656
Less: purchases (Note)	(1,192)
VAT due	4,464

Note:

Total VAT on purchases:	
(€6,150 × 23/123) + (€2,270 × 13.5/113.5)	1,420
Not allowable:	
Item 4 (i) €160 × 13.5% × 25%	(5)
Item 4 (ii) €300 × 23% × 80%	(55)
Item 4 (iii) €123 × 23/123	(23)
Item 4 (v) €64 × 23/123	(12)
	1,325
Less: 10% exempt	(133)
VAT on purchases	1,192

Question 21.5

The VAT liability of Mr Byte for the period July–August 2021 is:

	VAT-exclusive Amount €	VAT €	VAT Rate
Sales	<u>75,000</u>	<u>17,250</u>	23%
Purchases:			
Purchases for resale	40,000	9,200	23%
Stationery	6,000	1,380	23%
Wages	20,000	–	(Note 1)
Electricity	2,000	270	13.5%
Hotel bills	1,000	–	(Note 2)
Rent	2,400	<u>–</u>	(Note 3)
VAT deductible		<u>10,850</u>	
VAT payable		6,400	

* VAT, if applied for and authorised by Revenue, is payable on the cash receipts basis, as sales are less than €2 million.

Notes:

1. Services provided by employees are specifically exempt from VAT.
2. While VAT is payable at the rate of 13.5% on hotel accommodation, it is specifically not recoverable, except on "qualifying accommodation" in connection with the attendance at a "qualifying conference".
3. Rents in most cases are exempt from VAT. While a landlord may waive his exemption, it is assumed that he has not done so in this case.

Question 21.6

Since Joe supplies goods at the zero rate of VAT, he will be in a permanent VAT repayment position. This means that he is entitled to submit monthly VAT returns on the 23rd day of each month in respect of the previous month's purchases and sales.

	VAT-exclusive Amount €	VAT €	Rate €
May 2021			
Sales	10,000	–	(0%)
Purchases:			
Ingredients	5,000	–	
Petrol	1,000	–	(Note 1)
Lease rentals – vans	2,000	460	(23%) (Note 2)
Bank interest	400	<u>0</u>	

continued overleaf

VAT recoverable		460	
June 2021			
Sales	8,000	–	(0%)
Purchases:			
Ingredients	2,000	–	(0%)
Petrol	1,000	–	(Note 1)
Fixed assets	6,000	1,380	(23%)
Lease rental – vans	2,000	460	(23%)
Bank interest	400	–	
		1,840	
VAT recoverable May–June 2021		2,300	

Notes:

1. VAT arises at the rate of 23% on purchases of petrol but is specifically not recoverable.
2. VAT on the lease of vans is recoverable. VAT on the lease of passenger motor vehicles is restricted to 20% of the VAT if the vehicle is a "qualifying vehicle", otherwise it is not recoverable.

Question 21.7

The following persons are not obliged to register for VAT unless they otherwise formally make an election to register:

(a) Persons whose turnover does not exceed €75,000 per annum, provided that 90% of their total receipts arise from the supply of taxable goods. The €75,000 registration limit is reduced to €37,500 for persons producing goods liable at the 9%/13.5% or 21%/23% rates from zero-rated raw materials.
(b) Farmers.
(c) Persons whose supplies of taxable goods/services consist **exclusively** of the following:
   (i) supplies of unprocessed fish caught in the course of a sea-fishing business;
   (ii) supplies of machinery, plant, etc. which have been used by that person in the course of his sea-fishing business.
(d) Persons whose supplies of services do not exceed €37,500 per annum.

A person might choose to apply for voluntary registration if:

(a) they supply goods or services to VAT-registered persons. If the person registers for VAT, they will receive an input credit for any purchases. Although the sales would then be liable to VAT, VAT-registered purchasers would be entitled to an input credit;
(b) they export goods or deal in zero-rated goods, such as food. VAT would not be payable on sales, but a credit or repayment of any VAT invoiced on business purchases can be claimed.

Another category of person who might voluntarily register for VAT is a person who has not actually commenced supplying taxable goods or services but will soon become a taxable person. This will enable the trader to obtain credit for VAT on purchases made before trading commences.

Question 21.8

(a) The place of supply of goods is deemed to be:
   (i) In a case where it is a condition of supply that they are transported, it is the place where such transportation starts.

(ii) In all other cases, it is where they are located at the time of supply (i.e. when ownership is transferred). Services are generally deemed to be supplied where the business making the supply is located.

(b) There is a self-supply of goods when a VAT-registered person diverts to private or exempt-use goods which they have imported, purchased, manufactured or otherwise acquired and in respect of which they are entitled to a tax deduction.

Where this occurs, the VAT-registered person is liable to VAT at the appropriate rate on the cost of the goods in question.

Valuation rules for the self-supply of services

(i) Where the supply consists of the private use of business assets, VAT is due on the cost to the taxable person of providing the service.

(ii) Where the supply is a non-deductible business service, then VAT is due on the market value of the service.

Question 21.9

Andrew March–April 2021 VAT Return

		VAT
		€
Sales:		
(1)	Sales @ 23% (€1,815 × 23/123)	339.40
(2)	Sales @ 9% (€2,837.50 × 9.0/109.0)	234.29
		573.69
Purchases:		
(1)	Stock for resale (€605 × 23/123)	113.10
(2)	Stock for resale (€334 @ 0%)	Nil
(3)	Tables and chairs (€440 @ 23%)	101.20
(4)	Rent (no invoice/exempt letting)	N/A
(5)	Cash register (€665.50 × 23/123)	124.45
(6)	Tiling (€200 @ 13.5%)	27.00
(7)	Shop fitting lease for two months:	
	30 March and 30 April (€700 × 2 @ 23%)	322.00
(8)	Legal fees (€1,452 × 23/123)	271.50
(9)	Van (€9,840 × 23/123)	1,840.00
(10)	Petrol (non-deductible item)	N/A
		2,799.25
Net VAT refund due		2,225.56

Index

THANKS FOR JOINING US

We hope that you are finding your course of study with Chartered Accountants Ireland a rewarding experience. We know you've got the will to succeed and are willing to put in the extra effort. You may well know like-minded people in your network who are interested in a career in business, finance or accountancy and are currently assessing their study options. As a current student, your endorsement matters greatly in helping them decide on a career in Chartered Accountancy.

HOW CAN YOU HELP?

If you have an opportunity to explain to a friend or colleague why you chose Chartered Accountancy as your professional qualification, please do so.

Anyone interested in the profession can visit www.charteredaccountants.ie/prospective-students where they'll find lots of information and advice on starting out.

Like us on Facebook, follow us on Twitter.

Email us at info@charteredaccountants.ie

We can all help in promoting Chartered Accountancy, and the next generation to secure their success, and in doing so strengthen our qualification and community. We really appreciate your support.